3701905898

KT-521-461

A Practical Guide to Knowledge Acquisition

A. Carlisle Scott
Jan E. Clayton
Elizabeth L. Gibson

ADDISON-WESLEY PUBLISHING COMPANY
Reading, Massachusetts • Menlo Park, California • New York
Don Mills, Ontario • Wokingham, England • Amsterdam • Bonn • Sydney
Singapore • Tokyo • Madrid • San Juan • Milan • Paris

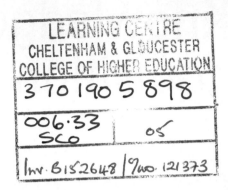
Many of the designations used by manufacturers and sellers to distinguish their products are claimed as trademarks. Where these designations appear in this book, and Addison-Wesley was aware of a trademark claim, the designations have been printed in initial caps or all caps.

The programs and applications presented in this book have been included for their instructional value. They have been tested with care, but are not guaranteed for any particular purpose. The publisher does not offer any warranties or representations, nor does it accept any liabilities with respect to the programs or applications.

Library of Congress Cataloging-in-Publication Data

Scott, A. Carlisle.
  A practical guide to knowledge acquisition / A. Carlisle Scott,
Jan E. Clayton, Elizabeth L. Gibson.
      p.   cm.
  Includes bibliographical references (p.   ) and index.
  ISBN 0-201-14597-9
  1. Knowledge acquisition (Expert systems)   I. Clayton, Jan E.
II. Gibson, Elizabeth L.   III. Title.
QA76.76.E95S39   1991
006.3′3—dc20   90–1223
                                                          CIP

1 2 3 4 5 6 7 8 9 10–MA–9594939291

To Denny

Preface

Knowledge acquisition—leading other people to describe how they do what they do—is one of the greatest challenges in building expert systems. If you raise the topic of knowledge acquisition with a group of seasoned knowledge engineers, they will respond immediately with stories about the trying experiences they have had. You might expect to hear tales like:

> We asked one simple question, and the expert talked nonstop for an hour. We scribbled frantically to keep up with him, because it all sounded important. But when we reviewed our notes after the interview, we found that he never answered our question! We couldn't use anything he told us.

> Our expert would go off on tangents all the time. No matter what we asked, she had a story to tell. The stories were great—we cracked up laughing—but they sure didn't help us build the system!

> You wouldn't believe the expert on my last project. He just refused to work with us. Whenever we asked him to explain how he did something, he'd say, "I analyze the problem and decide on the best approach. This is very complicated. It's just not something you can expect a computer to do." It's a wonder we finally managed to build a system!

Stories like these are fairly common. Do the stories mean that experts are generally uncooperative? Not really, the stories are more indicative of the knowledge engineers' inexperience at the time. In the early days of knowledge engineering, knowledge acquisition was a haphazard process. Meetings between knowledge engineers and experts were sometimes productive, sometimes futile. Knowledge engineers and experts alike might have come away from an interview session enthusiastic at having such intelligent and articulate colleagues; alternatively, they might have left frustrated at having to work with such uncooperative and uncommunicative people. Through trial and error, however, the determined knowledge engineers managed to understand their experts well enough to develop successful expert systems.

Luckily for today's practitioner, knowledge-engineering methodology has come a long way. We have learned from our mistakes and our successes. Although it is fun to join the veterans' circle and to tell our own war stories about knowledge acquisition, the experiences on which the stories are based were no fun at all. In retrospect, it is often embarrassing to realize how our own mistakes caused the very difficulties we attributed to the experts. The purpose of this book is to save today's knowledge engineer from repeating these mistakes. Knowledge-acquisition skills are best developed through experience. This book makes heavy use of examples that share the authors' knowledge-acquisition experiences with first-time knowledge engineers. The examples are simplified illustrations of the kinds of interaction that occur during knowledge acquisition. We include examples of what to do and what to avoid doing.

A Practical Guide to Knowledge Acquisition was written for the new developer of expert systems; it discusses knowledge acquisition as an integral part of the development process. The book presents knowledge-acquisition techniques that have proven successful. It describes problems that knowledge engineers are likely to encounter, how to avoid these problems, and how to correct them when they do occur. The neophyte will find practical guidelines for conducting knowledge-acquisition interviews. These guidelines explain not only how to ask questions but also what questions to ask. We expect the reader to have a basic understanding of what expert systems are and of how such systems are built. An introductory book, seminar, or workshop should provide the necessary background. Experience developing an expert system is not required; this book will be particularly useful to those people who are just starting to build their first expert systems. Much of the material in this book will also provide a review for more experienced practitioners.

This book presents general techniques relevant to all applications. Our descriptions of these techniques are pragmatic; we do not discuss the theoretical basis for the techniques that would interest readers with a background in either artificial intelligence or cognitive psychology. We divide the techniques into activities of two kinds. *Knowledge-engineering* activities enable knowledge engineers to build an expert system. *Interviewing* activities enable knowledge engineers to obtain information from an expert through interviews.

- Part 1 presents knowledge-engineering activities. This part describes the kinds of information that should be obtained to build an expert system and the activities by which this information can be obtained.

- Part 2 presents interviewing activities. This part describes techniques that knowledge engineers can use to ensure a productive interaction with the expert who supplies knowledge for an expert system.

Of course, every knowledge-acquisition session includes both knowledge-engineering activities and interviewing activities. As a result, Parts 1 and 2 present two parallel views of the knowledge-acquisition process.

The development of an expert system encompasses many knowledge-engineering activities in addition to knowledge acquisition.

- Assessment of the suitability of knowledge-engineering technology for a prospective application

- Planning and management of an expert-system project

- Design of appropriate representation formalisms for the knowledge that is acquired

- Design of the inference and control mechanisms to use the knowledge

- Implementation or selection of a suitable expert-system shell

- Design and implementation of the knowledge base

- Integration of the expert system with its operating environment

- Evaluation of the expert system

In this book, we restrict our attention to knowledge acquisition. We discuss additional activities only to the extent that knowledge-acquisition techniques relate to these activities. At the back of the book, we suggest references for readers who would like to pursue topics the book does not discuss in detail.

We should also note that several topics of particular interest to experienced knowledge engineers are beyond the scope of this book. For example, we do not describe automated knowledge acquisition or the use of tools that automate parts of the knowledge-acquisition process. We do not discuss how knowledge acquisition differs with different application types (diagnosis, configuration, planning, monitoring, and so on) or with different kinds of expert reasoning (for example, spatial or temporal).

A reader who would like an indepth introduction to knowledge acquisition should read the entire book from beginning to end. Each chapter ends with a section entitled *Points to Remember* that reiterates the key lessons of the chapter. A reader who would like a quick review of the highlights can read these summary sections and then scan through the remainder of the book.

Acknowledgments

We would like to thank our friends and colleagues who shared their ideas and their knowledge-acquisition experiences with us and who provided valuable comments on early drafts of the book: Beverly Barron, Miriam Bischoff, Richard Brooks, Denny Brown, Andrea Fella, Tom Rindfleisch, David Smith, and Mike Wilber. We are indebted to the editors and reviewers engaged by Addison-Wesley. Lyn Dupré edited an early draft and reviewed our writing style. Philip Klahr, Marianne LaFrance, and Jean Stanford reviewed the content and technical accuracy of a more complete manuscript. Judith Gimple edited the final manuscript in preparation for printing. All these individuals provided comments and suggestions that helped us improve the book. Finally we are grateful to numerous friends and relatives whose enthusiasm and support encouraged us to undertake this project and helped us to complete it.

Some of the example dialogs are adapted from material in the *Knowledge Acquisition Workshop* that was developed at Teknowledge, Inc., in 1987. We are grateful to our colleagues who assisted in the development of that workshop, and we thank Cimflex Teknowledge Corporation for allowing us to use this material.

Much of the knowledge[1] of toaster repair used in examples throughout this book comes from Toastmaster Form No. 051084, "Two-Slice Toaster Repair Procedures," from Toastmaster, Inc., and from Tech Bulletin #86-20 from WearEver Proctor-Silex, Inc.

---

1. Additional "knowledge" of toaster repair was fabricated by the authors. We ask that readers do *not* attempt to repair toasters on the basis of the information in this book.

Contents

Part 1

Knowledge-Engineering Activities

Knowledge acquisition is the process of gathering the information that is needed to build an expert system. We start our exploration of knowledge acquisition by looking at this process from the perspective of knowledge engineering. In Part 1, we describe basic knowledge-acquisition activities that are useful in all applications. We explain *what* information must be obtained to build an expert system, and we describe activities through which this information can be acquired.

- Chapter 1 presents knowledge acquisition within the context of building an expert system. The overview of knowledge engineering in this chapter introduces terms and concepts that will be used throughout the book. This chapter also introduces the two stages of knowledge acquisition. In the *initial inquiry stage*, the knowledge engineers gather the general knowledge they will need as they prepare for the development of the expert system. In the *detailed investigation stage*, the knowledge engineers obtain the specific knowledge that will enable the expert system to perform its task.

1

The next three chapters focus on the initial inquiry stage of knowledge acquisition.

- Chapter 2 describes the activities that initiate an expert-system project. It explains what information must be obtained and which people must be involved in defining what the expert system will do.

- Chapter 3 introduces activities for obtaining a general understanding of the task that the expert system will perform.

- Chapter 4 describes activities that lead to an understanding of how the total functionality of the expert system can be subdivided for incremental development.

The remaining chapters in this part address the detailed investigation stage of knowledge acquisition.

- Chapter 5 describes activities for identifying the steps the expert takes in performing the task in different situations.

- Chapter 6 explains how to understand the process by which the expert reasons from the input data to the final results of performing the task.

- Chapter 7 tells how to identify those characteristics of a situation that are relevant to the task.

To do a thorough job of knowledge acquisition, knowledge engineers must understand how the knowledge will be used. Whereas Chapters 2 through 7 explain how to *obtain* information, Chapters 8 through 11 explain *what to do* with the knowledge that is acquired. These chapters describe the organization, analysis, and review activities through which knowledge engineers can verify that they have understood the expert correctly and that they have acquired all the information they need for system development.

- Chapter 8 describes how to organize the knowledge into project documents to facilitate further knowledge-acquisition and design activities.

- Chapter 9 presents techniques for creating a conceptual model of the expert system by analyzing the information collected during knowledge-acquisition interviews.

- Chapter 10 discusses how knowledge engineers use the conceptual model to review their current understanding of the expert's knowledge with the expert, to guide further knowledge acquisition, to analyze requirements for implementation of the expert system, and to guide the implementation of the knowledge base.

- Chapter 11 describes how knowledge engineers can review the expert system with the expert to ensure that it performs its task correctly.

In Part 1, we introduce the participants in a fictitious project to develop an expert system in the field of toaster repair. Throughout the chapters in this part, we shall examine the various knowledge-acquisition activities that come into play as this project progresses. As you read the dialog examples in this part, concentrate on the *content* of the discussions. Pay attention to *the particular information* that the knowledge engineers seek to learn in each dialog and to *the methods* by which they lead the expert to articulate this information.

Chapter 1

Knowledge Acquisition and Knowledge Engineering

Frank Fixit knows just about everything there is to know about repairing toasters. He will tell you what is wrong with a toaster and will have it working again before most people in the service department can even locate the malfunction. When other members of the service staff are stumped by difficult problems, Frank is the person they ask for help. Frank has been repairing toasters for 40 years; he will retire in a few years. The next most senior member of the repair staff, Barbara Burnt, has 10 years of experience. She is very good at repairing toasters, but even she needs Frank's help occasionally. When Frank leaves the company, his expertise will leave with him. Without Frank's help, the repair staff will have to rely on trial and error to repair difficult toaster problems.

The head of the service department, Margaret Major, has been looking for ways to improve the productivity of her department. Frank alone does not have time to help with all the problems that arise; Margaret could use another expert just like Frank. Instead, she faces having no expert at all when Frank retires. Margaret is concerned that productivity will drop prohibitively after Frank's retirement; she raises this issue in the weekly meeting of department heads. Charles Cypher, head of the computation department, suggests a possible solution: an expert system.

The scenario is typical. Frank Fixit's years of experience allow him to perform far better than the average repair person. His understanding of toasters and their defects is not codified, even in his own mind. When presented with a broken toaster, he can repair it. He cannot write a checklist for the repair staff, however, that would permit them to fix toasters as quickly and as unerringly as he does.

According to Charles Cypher, Frank Fixit's expertise need not be lost when he retires; it could be captured in a computer system that advises the service staff on repairing toaster problems. Before such a system can be built, however, someone must come to understand what goes through Frank's mind when he fixes a faulty toaster. This is the goal of **knowledge acquisition:** to understand how another person carries out some activity so that the activity can be automated.

Frank Fixit is considered an **expert** at toaster repair because his training and years of experience allow him to outperform most other people. The computer system that embodies Frank's knowledge will be an **expert system**—that is, a computer program that can perform a particular task significantly better than can the average person. The **task** in this example, is to identify problems with toasters and to suggest how they can be repaired.

The expert system will provide advice on repairing many different toasters, just as Frank Fixit does. Each situation in which an expert system performs its task is called a **case;** the complete set of input data that describe the situation will define the case. For example, in one case Frank may repair a Toasts-Best model TB0601 toaster that burns toast. In another case, he may repair a General Appliance model GA00952 toaster in which the toast does not pop up.

Expert systems are built through a process known as **knowledge engineering.** This process consists of a number of activities including knowledge acquisition. Expert systems enable the electronic distribution of expert-level knowledge and problem-solving capabilities. They can make the assistance of expert consultants readily accessible at times when, and in locations where, human experts are not available. Where human experts are available, expert systems can handle the more routine problems, freeing the experts to deal with more challenging cases.

As the name implies, expert systems typically perform tasks that require human expertise. Some examples are:

- Trouble-shooting problems in mechanical devices, electronic circuits, or manufacturing processes

- Configuring complex systems, such as telecommunications equipment or networks of computers, to satisfy customer requirements

- Checking orders for computer systems to ensure that the specified components are compatible and that the components collectively constitute a complete system

- Reviewing applications for life insurance to determine whether they should be accepted or rejected

You may also have heard the term **knowledge system,** which refers to a computer program that is similar to an expert system except that it is based on knowledge that is accessible to the average professional in a given field in forms such as manuals or catalogs. In the remainder of this book, we shall ignore this subtle distinction between the two terms and shall use *expert system* exclusively to include both expert systems and knowledge systems.

Expert systems can range from advisory programs that assist nonexpert users to job aids for the experts themselves. Some expert systems interact directly with human users. Others serve as intelligent components of larger software systems and interact only with other programs. Two key features of expert systems distinguish them from other software: the architecture of the computer programs themselves and the process by which these programs are developed. Another distinguishing characteristic of most expert systems is that they are built as a collaborative effort between **experts** who are able to perform some task, and **knowledge engineers** who know how to acquire knowledge and encode it into a computer program. We describe these distinguishing characteristics of expert systems in the next three sections.

1.1 Architecture of Expert Systems

The architecture of an expert system has two components that enable it to perform its task:

1. A **knowledge base,** which contains knowledge relevant to a particular task

2. An **inference engine,** which provides the control and inference mechanisms for applying this knowledge

When the inference engine applies the knowledge in the associated knowledge base, the expert system performs its task. The separation of knowledge from the program that interprets and applies this knowledge is important; it facilitates the development, extension, and maintenance of computer programs that embody complicated logic. When more traditional program architectures are used, the development of such systems is difficult; the update, extension, and maintenance of these systems can be almost impossible. The separation of knowledge base from inference engine also facilitates the development of systems that can explain their behavior.

An **expert-system shell** is a software system that provides a framework on which expert systems can be developed. A shell contains an inference engine and supports representation formalisms in which knowledge can be encoded. Several expert-system shells are available commercially; others are only used internally by software houses that develop expert systems. To build an expert system with an existing shell, the knowledge engineer must develop only the knowledge base; the shell supplies the program that interprets and applies the knowledge. Some knowledge engineers build expert systems without using an existing shell. Instead they design and implement the inference engine and representation formalisms in conjunction with developing the knowledge base. In this book, when we use the term expert-system shell or simply shell, we mean the inference engine and representation formalisms that are used in building an expert system. We do not make a distinction between expert systems that are built with existing shells and those whose shells are constructed as part of the system's development.

Different expert systems require different interfaces, depending on their input–output needs. Figure 1.1 illustrates the components of an expert system, and the interfaces that may exist between a system and its operating environment. The development of interfaces, and the integration of the system with its operating environment are not unique to expert systems. As a consequence, interface development and integration are considered to be software-engineering, rather than knowledge-engineering, activities; this book does not address software-engineering activities.

1.2 Development of Expert Systems

Charles Cypher has chosen Patricia Programmer to lead a project to build an expert system to assist with toaster repair. Patricia is a knowledge engineer who has participated in the development of several expert systems. Howard Hacker will work with Patricia. Howard is a software engineer who wants to learn how to develop expert systems; this will be his first expert-system project.

When it has been completed, the toaster-repair advisor will incorporate Frank Fixit's expertise. It will assist less experienced members of the repair staff much as Frank helps them now. Instead of finding Frank and waiting until he has time to help them, the repair personnel will be able to interact with the expert system.

We can look at an expert system project from two perspectives. Focusing on the *knowledge-engineering* process, we identify the steps the team must take to create the working computer program (Figure 1.2). Focusing on the *knowledge-acquisition* process, we look at the steps by which Patricia Programmer and Howard Hacker will come to understand how Frank Fixit repairs toasters. This section presents overviews of the knowledge-engineering (Section 1.2.1) and knowledge-acquisition (Section 1.2.2) perspectives followed by more detailed descriptions of the steps in the development of an expert system (Section 1.2.3).

Figure 1.1 Expert-system architecture and interfaces. An expert system consists of a *knowledge base* and an *inference engine*. The knowledge base uses *representation* formalisms to encode knowledge. The inference engine consists of inference and control mechanisms that apply knowledge. The *inference* mechanisms enable the system to reason from its input data to its output results. The *control* mechanisms govern the order in which the system performs reasoning steps, accepts inputs, and produces outputs. Expert systems do not operate in isolation. An expert system may be called from another program and may in turn call additional programs. Many expert systems are interactive; their user interfaces provide the means for communicating with human users. Some expert systems obtain information from databases or other on-line files or from sensors. Expert systems may update databases, write files, print reports, or direct instruments and device controllers.

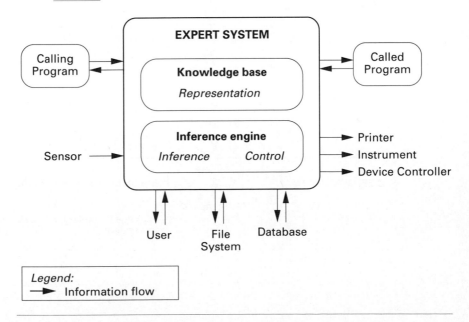

Figure 1.2 Steps in the development of an expert system. The steps in the development of an expert system are grouped into four phases. In the **analysis phase,** interested parties explore the possibility of developing an expert system. In the **specification phase,** the developers initiate the project and lay the groundwork for the development of an expert system. In the **development phase,** the developers design and implement the expert system, and in the **deployment** phase, they make the system available for routine use.

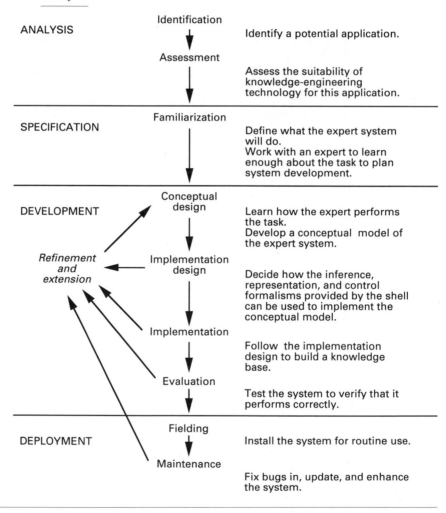

ANALYSIS

Identification

Identify a potential application.

Assessment

Assess the suitability of knowledge-engineering technology for this application.

SPECIFICATION

Familiarization

Define what the expert system will do.
Work with an expert to learn enough about the task to plan system development.

DEVELOPMENT

Conceptual design

Learn how the expert performs the task.
Develop a conceptual model of the expert system.

Refinement and extension

Implementation design

Decide how the inference, representation, and control formalisms provided by the shell can be used to implement the conceptual model.

Implementation

Follow the implementation design to build a knowledge base.

Evaluation

Test the system to verify that it performs correctly.

DEPLOYMENT

Fielding

Install the system for routine use.

Maintenance

Fix bugs in, update, and enhance the system.

1.2.1 Iterative Development

The first point of interest in Figure 1.2 is that the development of an expert system is an iterative process.[1] After the analysis and specification phases are completed, the steps of conceptual design through evaluation usually are repeated several times. A cycle can be terminated after any step, in which case the developers return to conceptual design without completing the remaining steps. We refer to the process of starting another cycle of development as **refinement and extension.** A new cycle of development can focus on the *refinement* of the existing knowledge base by making that knowledge more accurate. Alternatively, a cycle may focus on the *extension* of the existing knowledge base to broaden the scope of the expert system.

The **scope** of an expert system defines that system's coverage—that is, the *extent of the task* that the system can perform and the *range of situations* in which it can perform the task. The first complete iteration through the development cycle produces an initial prototype that is limited in scope. Each additional cycle of development extends the scope of the system. The cyclic nature of development, therefore, reflects a gradual increase in the capabilities of the expert system. In its initial implementation, a typical expert system will not be able to perform its task as thoroughly as can the human expert.

- The system might not perform the entire task. For example, the initial version of the toaster-repair advisor might be able to identify the cause of a problem but might not be able to suggest the appropriate repair.

- The system might not be able to handle a wide range of cases. For example, the toaster-repair advisor initially might be limited to helping with wiring problems in one model of toaster. Then, it could be extended to handle all of the most common problems that occur with that model. Ultimately, it would handle all common problems for a range of models.

The cyclic development of an expert system allows knowledge engineers to produce a *working prototype* of the expert system early in the development stage.[2] The initial prototype can be a catalyst of

---

1. Individual knowledge engineers have individual preferences on how to order design, implementation, and testing activities during the development phase. In this book, we recommend a development methodology that has been applied productively in a large number of expert-system projects. Other knowledge engineers have been equally successful using different approaches.

2. A software-development methodology that produces a working prototype early in the development process is often called *rapid prototyping*.

knowledge acquisition, because it provides the expert's first concrete illustration of the project goal. In many projects, the first demonstration of the prototype stimulates the expert to become a more active participant in the project.

For some expert systems, the deployment phase begins as soon as the system's coverage is broad enough to be useful. For others, deployment begins only after the system has been extended to its full scope. Deployment begins when the system is *fielded*—when it is installed and made available for routine use. Once fielded, the system will need to be maintained. Bugs must be fixed, and users' requests for modifications must be considered. Maintenance includes fixing errors, making minor modifications, and installing new releases of the expert system. Development itself can continue after a system has been fielded as indicated by the arrow from maintenance to refinement and enhancement in Figure 1.2.

- Some systems are put into regular use when they are limited in scope. Additional cycles of development are needed to complete the system's coverage.

- In some applications, even after the system has reached its full scope, the knowledge base must be kept up to date. For example, the toaster-repair advisor will have to be updated periodically to allow the system to handle new toaster models as they are introduced.

- Sometimes fixing a bug that occurs in a fielded system requires a major modification. In such cases, the people responsible for maintaining the system must repeat the steps in the development cycle. Consequently, we consider large modifications to be part of the development phase.

1.2.2 Role of Knowledge Acquisition

The second point to notice in Figure 1.2 is that no step is labeled "knowledge acquisition." Knowledge acquisition encompasses obtaining *all* information that the knowledge engineers need to build an expert system. This gathering of information does not occur as a single isolated step in the system's development; rather, it plays a role in *each* step. Figure 1.3 illustrates the proportion of the time that is spent in knowledge acquisition in each step of building an expert system. The graph is for a prototypical project, and the proportions will vary; however, the shape of the graph is important.

Knowledge acquisition is an ever-changing process. As a project progresses from initial inquiry to detailed investigation, knowledge engineers engage in different activities and employ different techniques.

- **Initial inquiry** is the preparatory stage. Information obtained in this stage yields a broad and shallow overview of what the expert system does, how it will be used, and how it will be developed.

- **Detailed investigation** is the discovery stage, characterized by narrow and deep focus, with emphasis on details. The information obtained in this stage gives the knowledge engineers a comprehensive understanding of how the expert performs the task so that they can duplicate this same process in the expert system.

The purpose of knowledge *engineering* is to build an expert system. The purpose of knowledge *acquisition* is to obtain the knowledge that is needed to build the system. Figure 1.4 shows the correspondence between the steps in building an expert system, and the stages of obtaining the necessary knowledge.

Figure 1.3 Percentage of time spent in knowledge acquisition. The percentage of effort that is devoted to knowledge acquisition increases through the analysis and specification phases, decreases through the development phase, and becomes negligible during deployment. Knowledge acquisition is most intense during the familiarization and conceptual-design steps.

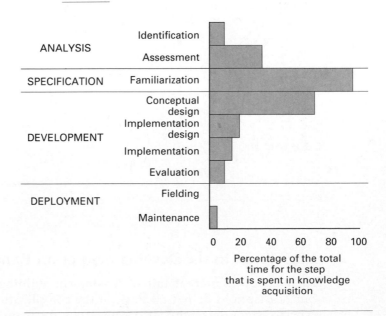

Figure 1.4 Stages of knowledge acquisition. During the analysis and specification phases of expert-system development, knowledge acquisition is characterized as *initial inquiry*. In this stage, the knowledge engineers obtain enough information to prepare themselves to develop the expert system. While the expert system is developed, refined, and extended, knowledge acquisition is characterized as *detailed investigation*. In this stage, knowledge engineers obtain the specific knowledge that the expert system will need to perform its task.

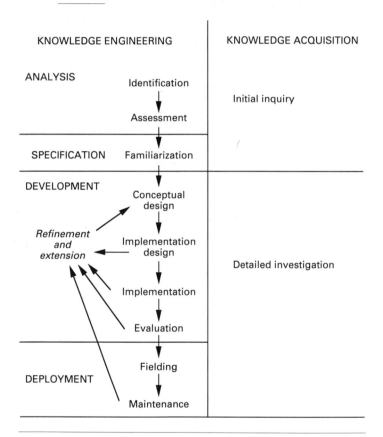

1.2.3 Steps in the Development of an Expert System

We look now in more detail at the steps in building an expert system. Our descriptions do not address all the complexities that can arise in expert-system development; rather, they focus on the general objectives of each step. The objectives of a step influence the knowledge-acquisition activities that occur during that step.

Identification

In our example, Margaret Major identified a problem, and Charles Cypher recognized that an expert system might provide the solution. This was the first step in the knowledge-engineering process: identifying a potential application. Identification requires becoming sufficiently familiar with current operations to see how an expert system could be helpful. Any task for which performance improves significantly with experience is a good candidate. If few people are experts at the task, the task is a better possibility because the expert system would make scarce expertise more accessible. If an important expert is about to retire, transfer to a different location, or change jobs, the potential is even greater because the system could prevent the loss of critical expertise.

A task that requires frequent reference to poorly organized documents or manuals of policies, procedures, and requirements is a good candidate for an expert system. The expert system could apply the knowledge in straightforward circumstances and make the knowledge more readily available to humans in more complex circumstances. A task is a suitable application if the humans who perform the task frequently make errors because they forget important details. The expert system could serve as an assistant to ensure that the human remembers all the necessary guidelines.

Assessment

Once an application has been identified, the next step is to assess whether it is a good candidate for a knowledge-based computer solution. This is where Patricia Programmer's job starts. She must obtain a more detailed understanding of the task and of the organization that will use the system—namely, the service department. Her assessment should consider three aspects of feasibility: technical, economic, and practical.

- Is it technically feasible to build an expert system to perform this task?

- Do the benefits of developing the system outweigh the costs? The benefits could include not only economic return but also increased consistency, staff training, and so on. The costs could include not only the development of the system but also the disruption to normal operations when procedures change as the system is introduced and the cost of maintenance throughout the lifetime of the system.

- Will the system be used? Is there a real need for the system? Is there a perceived need? If the system is interactive, how do the intended users feel about the system? Will using the system replace or simplify one of their current activities, or will using the system be an additional chore for them?

The assessment of a potential application should also consider the organizational, social, and legal implications of the introduction of the system. The definition of what the expert system does may need to be modified to address these issues.

Although Patricia Programmer plays an important part in obtaining and analyzing the pertinent information, the decision to proceed with the project is made at a higher level. Gary General, who is in charge of operations for the entire company, must decide whether to authorize the project. Patricia's assessment finds that the toaster-repair advisor is definitely worth pursuing. Gary reviews the results of the assessment and agrees to finance the project from his operating budget.

Familiarization

If an application passes the assessment, work on the system begins with familiarization. In this step, Patricia Programmer must obtain a clear definition of what the system will do. She must gain a general overview of how Frank Fixit performs the task, and must learn how the full functionality of the expert system can be divided for incremental development.

Conceptual Design

Conceptual design starts the development phase. The first cycle through this step focuses on the initial scope that was defined during familiarization. Each subsequent cycle focuses on a different extension to the system's coverage.

In this step, Patricia Programmer will achieve a coherent understanding of the process by which Frank Fixit repairs toasters (within the selected scope). She will learn what input data are needed and how different data guide Frank's decisions, hypotheses, and actions in repairing toasters. At the end of this step, Patricia will have a conceptual model of how the system will perform the task. A **conceptual model** specifies the sequence of steps the expert system will take in order to accomplish its task, the inference it will perform, and the information it will use.

At the end of the conceptual design step in the first cycle of development, Patricia will assess the inference, representation, and control requirements of Frank's knowledge and will select an expert-system shell in which to implement the toaster-repair advisor. In other projects, the knowledge engineers will design an expert-system shell, which they will develop and use to implement the expert system. Still other projects will be limited in their choice of expert-system shell. For example, the knowledge engineers might work for a small company that has bought one shell and does not have the resources to invest in others. In such projects, the knowledge engineers must review the requirements of their application against the capabilities of the shells available to them. They might need to limit the functionality of the expert system because of limitations in the available shells.

Implementation Design

Next, Patricia Programmer will develop an implementation design by selecting appropriate representations for the knowledge that she has gathered. Her conceptual model specifies *what* the system must do. The implementation design will specify *how* this task can be accomplished with the expert-system shell she is using. During this step, Patricia may discover that she needs to refine her understanding of Frank Fixit's problem-solving process by gathering additional details.

In many projects, the implementation design step brings together the knowledge-engineering activities that have produced a conceptual model with the software-engineering activities that have specified integration requirements. The implementation design for the expert system must merge the requirements of the conceptual design with the constraints of the operating environment.

Implementation

Patricia Programmer will create a working expert system by implementing a knowledge base according to her implementation design. Implementation may uncover incomplete or inconsistent knowledge; if so, Patricia will gather the necessary information to resolve these problems. In the advanced cycles of development, the implementation stage may require integration of the expert system into its operating environment.

Evaluation

After implementation, the knowledge engineers test the expert system to evaluate how well it performs its task.

- In an early cycle of development, the evaluation step may be a simple "unit test" of the functionality that was added to the system in the preceding design and implementation steps. The results of such an evaluation indicate whether the knowledge engineers have understood the expert correctly. If testing uncovers incorrect or undesirable behavior, the knowledge engineers will work with the expert to learn how they should modify the knowledge base to correct these problems.

- In a cycle that precedes deployment, on the other hand, the evaluation may be a more formal validation that the system performs correctly. An evaluation step may be a decision point. The results of the evaluation indicate whether the system is ready to be fielded, or whether it should be refined further in another cycle of development.

In each evaluation step, Patricia Programmer and Frank Fixit will test the toaster-repair advisor on a representative collection of cases to determine whether the system performs its task correctly. Because this system is interactive, some of their evaluations will examine how well the system serves its users' needs. Before deployment, Patricia and Frank will present the results of their recent evaluation to Margaret Major, who will decide whether the system is ready to be put into regular use. As director of the service department, Margaret is in the best position to judge when the benefits of having the system justify the slowdown in production as service personnel are trained in the system's use. Margaret can also schedule the system's introduction at a time when the demand on the service department is relatively low.

Fielding

The issues involved in fielding an expert system are similar to those that arise in fielding any software system. Fielding may include final integration with other software systems such as corporate databases or equipment that provides input from sensors. If the expert system is interactive, users may require training. The hardware on which the system will run may need to be installed and may need to be integrated with an existing computer network.

After the toaster-repair advisor has been extended in scope to the point at which it will be useful and has passed its evaluation, it will be put into day-to-day use. Frank Fixit, Patricia Programmer, and her colleague, Howard Hacker, will meet with members of the service staff to demonstrate how to use the system. For the first month of operation, Howard and Frank will be on hand to help users, to answer their questions, and to record their suggestions.

Maintenance

The goal of maintenance is to keep the expert system usable and used. Maintenance includes starting additional cycles of development when necessary and installing new versions of the system. As with any software system, the success of an expert system can be increased by responsiveness of maintenance personnel to users' problems.

After the toaster-repair advisor has been introduced, its users will be given a maintenance "hot-line" telephone number. If they encounter problems, they will be able to reach Howard Hacker, or to leave a message for him, at this number. When Frank Fixit retires, Barbara Burnt will be the most senior member of the repair staff. Margaret Major has asked Barbara to inform Howard whenever new models of toasters are released. Howard and Barbara will work together to extend the knowledge base to cover these additional models.

1.2.4 Goals of Knowledge Acquisition

Now that we understand the steps in building an expert system, we can summarize the goals of the two stages of knowledge acquisition.

Initial Inquiry

During initial inquiry, information must be obtained not only from the person who is expert at performing the task but also from the managers of the operations that will be affected by the system and from representatives of the system's intended users. Anyone who directly uses the results or outputs produced by the expert system is called a **user** of the system. For an interactive system, users include the people who interact with the system.

The first, and most important, goal of initial inquiry is to define what the system will do. The developers of the system must reach agreement with the affected managers on:

- What the introduction of the expert system will accomplish
- What specific task the expert system will perform
- Who will use the system
- How the system will fit into the current work environment
- Who will supply the knowledge and the expertise

Chapter 2 describes the process of defining what an expert system will do.

After the task is defined, the knowledge engineers can start to understand how the expert performs the task. They should learn, in general terms, the steps the expert takes in performing the task, the kinds of information the expert uses in performing the task, and the results of, or outputs from, performing the task. The knowledge engineers should obtain a *broad* view of the task: they should become acquainted with *all aspects of the task*, and with *the full range of situations in which the task can be performed*. This broad view will enable the knowledge engineers to develop a sound design for the expert system that will accommodate extensions to the system throughout the development phase. Chapter 3 explains how to obtain a general understanding of the task.

The knowledge engineers' overview of the task provides the background for discussions of ways in which the full functionality of the system can be partitioned for cyclic development. Common alternatives for dividing the coverage of an expert system are to limit the steps in the task it performs, to confine the range of inputs to which it can respond, or to restrict the possible conclusions it can reach. Chapter 4 describes how to identify ways to divide the coverage of an expert system.

Before development can begin, an initial scope must be selected for the first cycle of development, and increments for future cycles must be identified. If the expert system will be fielded before its full coverage has been reached, management representatives will generally need to participate in selecting the initial scope and deciding the order in which different increments to the system's coverage are added.

Detailed Investigation

In the detailed investigation stage of knowledge acquisition, knowledge engineers interact primarily with the expert; they need to consult members of management and potential users of the system only occasionally. During this stage, the knowledge engineers obtain a detailed understanding of the problem-solving techniques and the reasoning process that enable the expert to perform the task. To obtain a thorough comprehension of the expert's process, a knowledge engineer must gain detailed answers to three questions.

1. *What steps does the expert take in performing the task?* The expert's **strategic knowledge** indicates the *process* by which the task is performed. Any task can be viewed as a sequence of steps. The expert may perform a fixed series of steps or may select different steps in different cases. Some tasks can be accomplished if the necessary steps are performed in any order. For other tasks, knowledge of the correct ordering of the steps is precisely what allows the expert to outperform others.

2. *How does the expert reason from the input data to the output results?* The expert's **judgmental knowledge** specifies how the expert uses information that is currently known about a case to infer additional information about that case. The expert uses judgmental knowledge

to reason from the input through intermediate conclusions to reach the output results of performing the task. The **input** consists of all data that are entered interactively by a user, data read from databases and other on-line files, readings from sensors, values returned from called programs, and so on. The **output** from an expert system includes results that are displayed for the user of an interactive system, reports that are printed or written to files, signals that are sent to devices, and information that is written into databases or returned to the calling program. **Intermediate conclusions** are any facts or hypotheses that the expert deduces based on input data (and on other intermediate conclusions), and uses to deduce the output results.

3. *What characteristics of the case does the expert use in performing the task?* The definitions of the relevant characteristics of the case constitutes the expert's **factual knowledge.** The characteristics themselves include all the facts and hypotheses about the case that the expert uses and deduces: the input data, the intermediate conclusions, and the output results.

Answers to these three questions provide the information that knowledge engineers need to start implementation of an expert system. As we saw in Figure 1.4, detailed investigation coincides with the cyclic development phase of an expert-system project. During detailed investigation, knowledge acquisition is intimately coupled with the other knowledge-engineering activities necessary for the development of an expert system (Figure 1.5). Although these other activities are beyond the scope of this book, we shall touch on them in enough detail to provide a complete view of knowledge acquisition.

In each cycle of development, the knowledge engineers add some particular capabilities to the expert system. As a result, the knowledge engineers will focus knowledge acquisition on the topics that are relevant for the new functionality. As a cycle progresses, the knowledge-acquisition activities change.

- At the beginning of the cycle, the knowledge engineers *learn how the expert performs the task*, within the scope of the current cycle (Chapters 5, 6, and 7).

- This investigation of the expert's problem-solving process generally requires several interviews. As a consequence, the knowledge engineers must organize their written records of the knowledge into a form that will be easy to use when they design the expert system (Chapter 8). The organization process allows the knowledge engineers to uncover apparent inconsistencies in the information about

Figure 1.5 Detailed investigation: knowledge acquisition and system development. Knowledge acquisition is an integral part of the development of an expert system. The *collection* of knowledge cannot be separated completely from the *use* of that knowledge. It is through the organization, analysis, and review activities that knowledge engineers can verify that they have understood the expert correctly and that they have acquired all the information they need for system development.

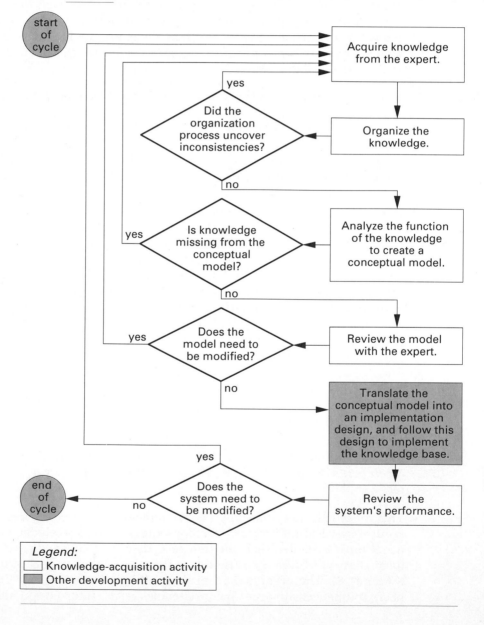

a topic that they obtained in different interviews. The knowledge engineers then review their understanding of the topic with the expert. In these reviews, they *find out what they misunderstood, or what information they missed* when they originally discussed the topic.

- The knowledge engineers next analyze the function of each piece of knowledge. This analysis allows them to develop a conceptual model that shows how the expert system can use the knowledge to perform its task (Chapter 9).

- The conceptual model guides further knowledge acquisition in two ways (Chapter 10). First, the analysis may indicate that knowledge is missing. If so, the partial conceptual model provides the focus as the knowledge engineers *obtain missing knowledge.* Second, when the knowledge engineers think their conceptual model is complete, they review the model with the expert. If the expert finds problems with the model, the knowledge engineers must *resolve the misunderstandings that led to the errors in their conceptual model.*

- The knowledge engineers later use the conceptual model to guide the development of the expert system. First they translate the model into an implementation design; then they implement (or extend) the knowledge base according to this design. When the portion of the knowledge base that implements the new functionality has been added to the expert system, the knowledge engineers ask the expert to review the system's performance (Chapter 11). If the expert finds problems with the system, the knowledge engineers focus on correcting these problems. In subsequent knowledge-acquisition interviews, they seek to *learn how the system's knowledge base is incorrect or incomplete.*

1.3 Developers of an Expert System

The diverse activities that contribute to building an expert system require a variety of skills. We complete our overview of knowledge engineering by focusing on the people who participate in the development of an expert system: who they are and what skills they need.

Expert systems are usually developed through collaboration between knowledge engineers who understand how to select and use an expert-system shell and human experts who are able to perform the chosen task. We refer to the knowledge engineers and experts together as the **project team.** In the simplest example, a single person plays the roles of both expert and knowledge engineer. Because this book focuses on knowledge acquisition, we ignore this situation altogether. A knowledge engineer who also serves as expert, however, may be interested in the techniques for organizing knowledge, for creating and using a conceptual model, and for testing the expert system.[3]

Project teams vary greatly in size, depending on the complexity of the application and the resources available for the development of the expert system. In this book, we use examples of medium-sized projects with two to four team members. The techniques and activities we describe, however, are equally appropriate for small and large projects. For simplicity, most of the discussions in this book are phrased as though the project team includes a single expert. Chapters 2, 13, and 17 discuss issues that arise in projects with more than one expert and techniques that are appropriate in projects with multiple experts.

In general, some members of a project team will start working together in the analysis phase; other members may not join the team until the start of the development phase. The complete team will work together through the development phase to build the expert system. Some of the team members will be involved in the system's deployment, but this phase will not necessarily involve the entire team. As we have seen, the analysis and deployment phases will include managers and users in addition to the members of the project team itself.

1.3.1 Knowledge Engineers

What skills should a knowledge engineer have? Rather than discuss the skills of an individual, we describe the skills that must be represented within the team. The knowledge engineers on a project team together must possess strong software- and knowledge-engineering skills and interpersonal skills. Although any individual who will be the sole knowledge engineer on a project team should have *all* the necessary skills, a knowledge engineer with strengths in a single area can be a productive contributor to larger teams.

Software-Engineering Skills

An expert system is, after all, a computer program. The team's programming skills should include an understanding of fundamental algorithms and data structures, as well as the ability to assess the relative efficiency of alternative algorithms and data representations. Good software-design skills are important for developing a well-designed knowledge base that can be understood and extended by its maintainers.

Depending on the expert system's operating environment, the team may need to include user-interface design skills and software-integration skills. If the expert system will interact with other software pack-

---

3. These topics are discussed in Chapters 8 through 11.

ages, familiarity with those packages, with operating systems, with network communications protocols, and so on may be needed. Fielding and maintaining the system requires an understanding of techniques for releasing software, including version control, and distribution of new software releases and updates to user documentation.

Knowledge-Engineering Skills

Knowledge engineers have to translate the expert's knowledge into a knowledge base. To perform this translation, they must be familiar with the expert-system shell that is used to build the system. They must understand the built-in inference and control mechanisms provided by the inference engine. They must know what representation formalisms the shell supports and how the inference engine uses each representational form. With many shells, the knowledge engineers will need to be able to evaluate the tradeoffs between alternative ways of representing the same knowledge.

If the project will develop its own underlying shell rather than using an existing one, a strong background in artificial intelligence is needed. At the minimum, someone on the team should be familiar with various representation, inference, and control paradigms.

Interpersonal Skills

Knowledge acquisition relies heavily on the knowledge engineers' interpersonal skills—primarily on their ability to communicate effectively and to work well with others.

- To lead experts in diverse fields to articulate their problem-solving and reasoning strategies, knowledge engineers must express themselves precisely and clearly. They must be adept at learning to understand and use new technical vocabularies.

- The collaborative nature of the development of expert systems requires that knowledge engineers be good team players. They must be able to work cooperatively with other members of the project team, being sensitive to both the talents and the needs of their teammates.

1.3.2 Experts

Our primary requirement for experts is that they be able to perform their particular tasks better than the average person can. "Better" can mean more accurately, more quickly, more economically, or more consistently. Experts generally have years of experience at what they do. Ideally, they should have *current* experience: They should perform their tasks on a routine basis. They are often individuals without whom their organizations could not function. Less experienced people often seek out their help, instruction, or advice. Experts do not necessarily have advanced degrees, or hold high positions within their company hierarchies. Experts need not be world authorities or the absolute *best* at performing their tasks. The more the expert system's task relies on *knowledge* of the field rather than *expertise* at performing the task, the less experience is required on the part of the expert. In any project, however, the expert should be a competent professional who is recognized as able to perform the task very well and to judge whether other people have performed the task correctly.

In addition to ability, a practical requirement for experts is *availability*. An expert must be able to commit time to the expert-system project. The expert's manager often must be convinced that the benefits provided by expert systems will justify freeing some of the expert's time. Some projects involve multiple experts precisely because the most experienced individual is also the least available to the participants in the project. The expert who devotes the most time to the project may be a skilled professional with less experience but more available time.

It is a rare luxury to be able to select a project expert from among a number of equally qualified people. If this circumstance does arise, the choice of expert should be made with consideration for qualities that will facilitate knowledge acquisition. The ideal expert is articulate and introspective and has experience teaching less experienced people to perform the task. As is true of knowledge engineers, the ability to work well with other people is an important trait. Finally, an expert who is already enthusiastic about the prospect of building an expert system is of great benefit to the project team.

1.4 Points to Remember

Knowledge acquisition is the process of obtaining all the information that a developer needs to build an expert system. This information-gathering activity takes place throughout the development of the system. As the project progresses from laying the initial groundwork to developing the system, knowledge acquisition switches from initial inquiry to detailed investigation.

Initial inquiry prepares for system development. The goals of this stage are:

- To define what the expert system will do

- To gain a general understanding of how the expert performs the task

- To learn how the full functionality of the system can be divided for incremental development

   Detailed investigation produces a coherent understanding of how the expert performs the task. The goals of this stage are:

- To distinguish the individual steps an expert takes in performing the task and to recognize the order in which the steps are performed and the conditions under which each step is performed
- To understand how the expert reasons from input data to reach the final conclusions on which the results are based
- To identify the information the expert uses in performing the task

Expert systems are built by project teams composed of knowledge engineers and experts. Both are equally important members of the team; their individual skills are essential for development of the system.

Chapter 2

Defining the Expert System

The participants in the toaster-repair advisor project have been identified (Figure 2.1). Before any other work can begin, the project must achieve the first goal of initial inquiry: The participants must define what the expert system will do.

Patricia Programmer and Howard Hacker will implement the system; they must understand what they need to accomplish. Their boss, Charles Cypher, must know what is expected of Patricia and Howard in order to judge how much of their time to authorize for the project.

Frank Fixit will provide most of the expertise; Barbara Burnt will assist him. Frank and Barbara must know what the system will do so that they can examine their own procedures for performing the selected task. Margaret Major, their boss, must understand the role that the system will play so that she can assess its benefits. This will allow her to decide how much time Frank and Barbara should dedicate to the project.

Margaret is also the supervisor of the other members of the repair staff—the people who will *use* the system. She must be sure that the system will address the needs of its users.

Charles and Margaret both report to Gary General, who is in charge of operations for the entire company. Gary has agreed to finance the toaster-repair advisor from his operating budget. He must know what the system will do and how it will benefit the company in order to justify the project's budget.

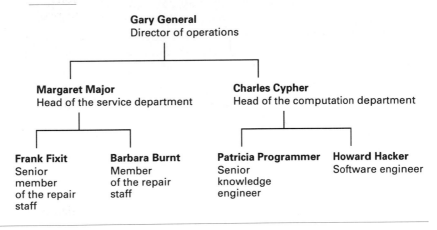

Figure 2.1 Participants in the toaster-repair advisor project. Patricia Programmer and Howard Hacker will implement the toaster-repair advisor, using expertise provided by Frank Fixit and Barbara Burnt. Their managers, Charles Cypher and Margaret Major will participate in planning and in setting the goals for the project. Gary General, who will provide funding for the project, will decide how the expert system can best serve the needs of his organization.

For an expert-system project to be successful, all concerned parties must agree on a clear and complete definition of what the system will do. The concerned parties comprise four constituent groups:

1. The **knowledge engineers** who implement the system

2. The **experts** who provide the know-how

3. The system's intended **users**

4. The **funders,** the group that supplies funding for the project

The first knowledge-acquisition activity in an expert-system project is both crucial and challenging: the knowledge engineers must gather information from all four constituent groups.[1] A very real danger in an expert-system project is that each group (or worse, each individual) will form a different model of what the system should do. To prevent

---

1. This chapter discusses activities that occur during the assessment step of an expert-system project. Although we describe knowledge-acquisition activities relevant to this step, we do not describe the process of assessing a potential expert-system application. For more information on this subject, refer to the Additional Reading section.

any group from developing unrealistic expectations, the four groups should reach agreement at the beginning of the project. Misunderstanding among the groups can jeopardize the entire project.

The knowledge engineers' first challenge is to *obtain the necessary information*. At the initiation of a project, most participants will have only vague ideas of what they would like an expert system to do. Some individuals may find it difficult to articulate their ideas concerning the expert system. Others may say what they think the knowledge engineers want to hear instead of trying to formulate their own ideas.

The second challenge for knowledge engineers is to *lead the participants to reach consensus*. The personal agenda of different individuals may be in conflict; the objectives of the different groups may compete. Political interactions across the participating organizations may impede cooperation among the groups. This chapter describes how to develop the definition of an expert system; it illustrates how the members of the toaster-repair advisor project reached agreement on the definition of that system.

The definition of an expert system consists of five facets:

1. The **objectives** that the system's introduction should accomplish

2. The **task** that the system will perform

3. The **users** of the system

4. The data-processing **environment** in which the system will operate

5. The **experts** who will provide the necessary expertise

These five facets are interrelated, so the activities that collect information about one facet must be interleaved with the activities related to the other facets.

Although the information-gathering activities related to the different facets of the definition occur in parallel, we will focus on each facet sequentially. Section 2.1 discusses how to establish the context in which the expert system's definition can be discussed. Sections 2.2 through 2.6 address the five facets in the definition of an expert system. Section 2.7 describes how to document the definition of the expert system. Section 2.8 presents knowledge-acquisition activities that are useful in defining an expert system.

2.1 Understanding the Context

The funders, experts, and users of a proposed expert system generally have different perspectives on the need for the system. The implementers often are not aware of any of these perspectives when the project is first suggested. On the other hand, the implementers understand what expert systems are and what they can do. In most projects, the majority of the experts, users, and funders have little or no understanding of expert systems. Before discussions about the definition of the expert system can begin, the four constituent groups need to share an understanding of the potential benefits of an expert system and of the current situation that the expert system will address. This aim can be accomplished by a group meeting that establishes the context for discussions about the expert system.

The meeting to launch an expert system project should start with introductions of the various participants and an explanation of the purpose of the meeting. Often the manager of the funding group will open the initial project meeting. Following introductions, a representative of the implementers should present a brief *overview of knowledge engineering* that explains:

- What an expert system is

- How expert systems are built

- What role experts play in the development of expert systems

Some knowledge engineers like to end their overviews with a demonstration of an expert system in a related field.

The main item of business in the meeting is an **introductory overview** that describes the situation or problem that the expert system will address. The introductory overview can be presented by an expert, a member of the funding group, or a member of the organization that will use the expert system. For projects that span a number of functions within an organization, it may be necessary for the users, the funders, and the experts each to present an overview that presents a different perspective.

The speaker who presents an introductory overview has the flexibility to introduce the information that he or she feels is important. After the presentation, the knowledge engineers can lead a discussion by asking the speaker or the group to expand on topics that were covered in the overview and to address topics that were not covered. Table 2.1 summarizes the information that the knowledge engineers should learn from the introductory overview(s) and subsequent discussions. Following the overview presentation and discussion, the group should make plans to collect the information necessary to define the system.

We join the participants in our example project shortly after the toaster-repair application has been suggested.

> At a weekly meeting of the department heads, Gary General, Margaret Major, and Charles Cypher schedule a time for the kickoff meeting of

Table 2.1 Introductory Overview to an Expert System

Type of Information	Questions to Be Answered
General background information	What do I need to know to understand the expert system's role? (This might include the definition of important terms.)
Organizational problems	Is expertise scarce? Is it difficult or time consuming to get access to expertise? Is personnel turnover high? Does management want to improve some aspect of current performance?
Current operations	What is the normal sequence of activities? What is the expert's role?
Importance of expertise	Why does this task require an expert? How long does it take to become proficient at the task? How skilled are the intended users of the system? How important is expert-level mastery of the task?

the toaster-repair advisor project. Charles invites Patricia Programmer and Howard Hacker to the meeting. He asks Patricia to meet with Margaret to explain what information should be presented in an introductory overview. He also asks Patricia to take responsibility for directing the discussion at the meeting to ensure that the necessary topics are covered.

Patricia meets briefly with Margaret and explains that a user or expert should present an introductory overview, about 30 to 60 minutes in length. The overview should describe the normal operations of the service department and Frank Fixit's role helping the repair staff. Margaret invites Frank Fixit and Barbara Burnt to the meeting. She asks Frank to prepare the introductory overview.

At the meeting, Gary General introduces the participants to each other. He then explains that the purpose of the meeting is to present background material for a series of discussions on how an expert system can improve the current operations in the service department. After Gary's opening remarks, Charles Cypher presents a brief description of expert systems. Then, Frank Fixit presents his introductory overview (Figure 2.2). After Frank's overview, Patricia Programmer asks whether Margaret or Gary have anything to add. Both add minor elaborations to Frank's points. Charles Cypher ends the inaugural project meeting by explaining that he and Patricia will work with Gary to organize a number of meetings in which the various members of the group can meet to discuss the role an expert system could play within the service department.

In some projects, no one will be prepared to present an overview. In that case, it is up to the knowledge engineers to lead an **overview discussion** that establishes the context for the expert system. For example, if Frank Fixit had not prepared an overview, Patricia Programmer could have led the discussion by asking Frank the questions in Figure 2.3. After Frank had answered each question, Patricia could have asked the other participants whether they had additional comments or different perspectives on the topic.

2.2 Defining the Objectives

Once the context for the expert system has been presented, discussions can turn to the objectives of the expert system—what will its introduction accomplish? Often the users, experts, and funders will have different ideas of what is most important. Each individual who hears

Figure 2.2 Outline for an introductory overview. Frank Fixit presents an overview of toaster repair. As this outline of Frank's talk indicates, he describes the normal operations of the service department, the problems with current operations, and the procedure for repairing toasters.

OVERVIEW OF TOASTER REPAIR

1. Service department operation
   a. Three people per shift; day shift only
   b. Hourly wages; union employees
   c. Repair prices associated with type of toaster, cost of parts, type of repair, NOT labor hours
   d. Maximum repair charge of $40
2. Problems with operations
   a. Repair labor cost greater than charge to customer
   b. Repair staff work too slowly
   c. Repair staff do not test thoroughly
   d. Repair staff do not always fix real problem
   e. Difficult to keep inventory of parts well stocked; need parts for 75 toaster models from 6 manufacturers
3. Handling repairs
   a. Repair order is received from customer
   b. Repair is assigned to a staff member
   c. Toaster is tested and repaired
   d. Billing form is filled out and delivered to the billing clerk
   e. Parts-used form is filled out and sent to inventory clerk (this is usually skipped)
   f. Toaster is returned to customer

Figure 2.3 Questions for an overview discussion. Patricia Programmer prepared this list of questions before the meeting. She was ready to use these questions to lead a discussion if Frank Fixit had not presented an introductory overview or if Frank's overview did not provide the necessary information.

OVERVIEW QUESTIONS

How is the service department organized?

Would you please describe the normal operation of the service department?

Can you tell us how you assist the repair staff?

What problems do you see with current operations?

What improvements would you like to see?

about the proposed expert system will develop a vision of what the system should do; each individual's vision represents one perspective on the relevant organizational issues.

The objectives of the system should be defined through discussions among representatives of the four constituent groups. It is the job of the knowledge engineers:

- To lead representatives of the other three groups to articulate their objectives

- To ensure that the objectives are defined clearly

- To lead discussions about the relative priorities of the objectives

- To identify conflicts among different objectives

- To recognize objectives that appear unrealistic

The knowledge engineer who leads discussions about the objectives for an expert system should encourage the participants to consider *all* the purposes the expert system might serve. Table 2.2 lists common objectives for expert systems. The objectives identified through these discussions will be used to determine the functionality of the expert system as described in Section 2.3. This information is also useful for managers who need to build a business case of the development of an expert system, but this latter topic is beyond the scope of this book.

Gary General represents the funders in defining the objectives of the toaster-repair advisor. Margaret Major represents the users; Frank Fixit, the experts; and Charles Cypher, the implementers. These four individuals define the system's objective through a series of discussions. Margaret and Frank present their views on the immediate needs within the service department. Gary General takes a more global view of the needs of the company as a whole. Charles provides information on the technical feasibility and the cost of different alternatives.

When Gary General, Margaret Major, Frank Fixit, and Charles Cypher first meet to discuss the system, they quickly agree that the toaster-repair advisor should improve both the speed and the accuracy with which the repair staff find and repair problems with toasters. After that, the four participants turn their attention to some additional functions that the system might serve.

Frank Fixit feels that the system should also provide instruction to the less experienced repair staff. When he helps the more junior staff members, he is careful to explain what he is doing so they will be able to recognize and repair similar problems in the future. The expert system is supposed to reduce the amount of time Frank spends helping the service staff. To do this, it must serve as a *training aid* as well as a repair assistant.

Table 2.2 Common Objectives for Expert Systems

Factor	Objective
Customer satisfaction	Improve quality of goods or services
	Shorten time to provide services
	Reduce cost of goods or services
Staff utilization	Free expert's time for more important activities
	Reduce time to train new staff members
	Permit less experienced staff to take on more responsibility
	Allow a decision maker to explore and evaluate more alternatives in a limited period of time before selecting an alternative to pursue
	Capture scarce expertise and distribute it to all practitioners
	Reduce the effort needed to keep a software system up to date with changing information
Product uniformity	Improve consistency of performance
	Increase adherence to policy
	Reduce number of products that do not meet manufacturing specifications
Revenues	Generate additional income by selling the expert system (or the results produced by the system)
	Reduce production costs of goods or services
	Reduce time to produce goods and services
	Increase quantity of goods and services that can be delivered to customers

Margaret Major says that the members of the repair staff[2] want a system to help them fill out billing forms. This is a straightforward but tedious task. The repair staff members feel that they would be able to repair more toasters if they did not have to spend so much time looking up rates and writing bills.

Margaret herself thinks that the system should assist with the management of the inventory of spare parts. The service department has a database of information on all the removable parts for all toaster models that the department repairs. The repair staff can use the toaster-part database to look up a part's price or its technical specifications. They can also look up a particular toaster model to find out which parts can be used in that model. The toaster-part database also contains fields for inventory management. After fixing a toaster, the repair person should fill out a parts-used form that lists all replacement parts used in the repair. At the end of the day, all repair personnel submit the parts-used forms to the department's inventory clerk. This use of parts-used forms is part of the "standard" operating procedure within the service department. Unfortunately, very few members of the repair staff actually follow this procedure.

Each morning, the inventory clerk uses the parts-used forms from the previous day to update the inventory fields of the toaster-part database. Because these forms do not provide an accurate summary of the parts that were used the previous day, the database does not contain accurate inventory information. The inventory information in the database generally shows *more* parts than are actually in stock. This discrepancy is the source of a major problem in the service department. The inventory clerk orders new parts when the toaster-part database indicates that the supply is low. The staff habitually runs out of parts because the clerk's information is inaccurate. When a repair requires a part that is not in stock, the repair is delayed unnecessarily. Margaret would like the expert system to update the inventory fields of the toaster-part database whenever a repair person uses a replacement part.

On the subject of inventory management, Gary General suggests that it would be interesting for the expert system to keep statistics on the frequency of various toaster problems. This might help the department predict how often different spare parts will be needed. The statistics might allow the department to manage inventory more carefully. Gary's main concern, however, is productivity. He wants to focus on functions that will help the repair staff fix more toasters more accurately and more quickly.

Charles Cypher summarizes the discussion by listing the objectives that have been proposed (Table 2.3). As his summary illustrates, the users and their management (Margaret) have slightly different views on what objectives are important. The group's next task, he explains, is to decide which of these objectives the expert system should address. Charles asks the group to review this list to see whether he has captured the important points of the discussion.

After the group has reviewed Charles' list of objectives, Gary General says that he does not view reducing the repair staff's paperwork as an objective in itself. The real objective, he says, is to reduce the time customers have to wait before their toasters are returned.

---

2. Conversations with the repair staff are described in Section 2.4. Remember that the activities discussed in this chapter are interleaved, *not* conducted sequentially.

Table 2.3 Objectives Proposed for the Toaster-Repair Advisor

Objective	Group(s) Who Endorse the Objective
Shorten the time to repair a toaster	Experts, users, funders
Improve the accuracy of toaster repair	Experts, users, funders
Reduce the time Frank Fixit spends assisting the repair staff	Experts
Educate the less experienced members of the repair staff	Experts
Reduce the repair staff's paperwork	Users
Improve inventory control	Users' management

Margaret Major says that improvement in the accuracy of repair is equivalent to reduction of "repeat problems"—toasters that are repaired and returned to the customer then brought back to the service department with the same malfunction. Improvement of inventory control can be expressed as a reduction in the number of times a repair person needs a part that is not in stock (because inventory information in the toaster-part database was not kept up to date).

Charles Cypher corrects his list of objectives. He then asks the group to assign a priority to each objective and to try to specify what tangible change they would like to see after the expert system is in use. When the group discusses priorities,[3] they agree that some objectives are equally important. They decide to rate the objectives as *essential* to the system, *important* for inclusion, or *optional*. They then try to quantify the improvement they would like to see after the expert system is introduced. Charles Cypher explains that this exercise should be brief. If possible, the group should propose rough estimates of the improvements they would like to see. The numbers do not need to be precise because the knowledge engineers will not be able to predict how much improvement they can achieve. The knowledge engineers, however, may be able to identify desired improvements that seem infeasible. As the project progresses, the knowledge engineers can use the desired improvements as performance goals; if they discover that any goal is unattainable, they can inform management immediately and discuss consequences for the project. Charles creates a new table (Table 2.4) with the results of the discussions.

2.3 Defining the Task

Once the objectives of the expert system have been defined, the focus of discussions can shift to the task—what must the system do in order

---

3. Section 2.8.2 contains more details about how the group agreed on the priorities of the different objectives.

Table 2.4 Objectives of the Toaster-Repair Advisor

Objective	Priority	Current situation	Desired situation
Accuracy of repair: Reduce the occurrence of repeat problems	Essential	15 per month	2 to 5 per month
Speed of repair: Shorten the time to repair a toaster	Essential	2 to 3 hours	1 hour
Expert productivity: Reduce the amount of time Frank Fixit spends assisting the repair staff	Important	20 hours per week	4 to 8 hours per week
Inventory control: Reduce the number of times a repair person needs a part that is not in inventory	Important	15 per month	3 to 5 per month
Customer service: Shorten the time to return a repaired toaster to the customer	Important	1 week	1 to 2 days
Staff training: Educate the less experienced members of the repair staff	Optional	Not quantified	Not quantified

to accomplish the objectives? As we discussed in Chapter 1, the exact functionality of an expert system will be refined during the course of the project. The definition at this stage will describe the task in general terms. The definition should *specify the important functions of the expert system and the objective that each function addresses.* Discussions about the task should consider the extent to which each of the objectives can be achieved.

After agreeing on the objectives of the toaster-repair advisor, Gary General, Margaret Major, Frank Fixit, and Charles Cypher meet again to describe the task the system should perform. They decide that the system's primary task will be to advise the repair staff on identifying and repairing toaster problems. This should reduce the time Frank needs to spend helping the repair staff; it should also improve the accuracy of the repairs. In addition, the system should generate bills for the customers. These measures will reduce the time needed to repair toasters. Finally, the system should update the inventory information in the toaster-part database whenever parts in a toaster are replaced.

Charles Cypher warns the group that the desired improvement in inventory control (shown in Table 2.4) is unrealistic, at least initially. The expert system will be able to update the toaster-part database when it is consulted about repairing a toaster. Initially, the system will be limited in scope so it will not be used for all repairs. Furthermore, the expert system will need to rely on its user to verify that a recommended replacement part was actually used in repairing the toaster. Instead of the desired 3 to 5 not-in-inventory problems per month, there might be 10 to 12 such problems per month when the system is first introduced. Table 2.5 summarizes how the various functions in the toaster-repair advisor's task will address the system's objectives.

The task of the toaster-repair advisor, as summarized in Table 2.5, addresses the objectives of the expert system and the needs of the experts. As we shall see in Section 2.4, the definition of the task will be modified in response to the needs of the users.

2.4 Identifying the Users

Understanding exactly who will use an expert system is an integral part of defining what the system will do. Remember that the users are not limited to those people[4] who interact directly with the system. The users include *everyone* who will use the results or outputs produced by the expert system. In practice, the definition of an expert system's task cannot be separated from the identity of the system's users. When a potential application is identified, the tentative definition of the expert system's task will suggest the identity of the system's users. Additional information should be gathered from and about these potential users. A clear understanding of the needs of the expert system's intended users can help to ensure that the system will be used. The

---

Table 2.5 Task of the Toaster-Repair Advisor

Function	Objectives Addressed by the Function
Advise the service staff on repairing toasters	Accuracy of repair Speed of repair Expert productivity
Generate bills for the customers	Customer service
Update the toaster-part database	Inventory control Customer service

---

4. The expert system may also obtain input from, and direct output to, programs, files, and devices. These input sources and output destinations are not considered users; they are considered components of the expert system's operating environment.

project team may find it necessary to modify the original idea of the system's task and its environment in order to make the system acceptable to its users. As the task is modified, the identity of the users may be altered. If this situation occurs, more information will need to be obtained from the new users, and this information may affect the definition of the task.

The lead knowledge engineer on an expert-system project should provide guidance about *what* information to obtain concerning the users. Table 2.6 summarizes the questions that should be answered. The project knowledge engineers might participate in collecting this information, or they might leave the collection to someone who is more familiar with the users. For example, the manager of the user group might survey individuals within the group. Alternatively, a "typical" user might be chosen to participate in the project. This person could speak for the user community or collect the consensus of the potential users.

The answers to the questions in Table 2.6 can be obtained through discussions *about* the intended users of the expert system (Section 2.4.1), and *with* the users (Section 2.4.2). The answers to these questions may have implications for user acceptance of the expert system (Section 2.4.3).

Table 2.6 Understanding the Users of an Expert System

Purpose	**Questions to Be Answered**
Identify the intended users of the expert system	Who will use the results of the expert system?
	Who will provide input to the system?
Assess the users' requirements	What kind of assistance do the users need from the expert system?
	What kind of assistance do the users *think* they need?
	What kind of assistance do the users *want?*
	What is the users' level of skill or knowledge relative to the level of the expert?
Consider how the expert system will be used	What is the users' normal routine?
	How will the expert system fit into this routine?
	Are the users comfortable working with computers?
	Are the users open to having computers introduced into their jobs?
	Are the users open to using results or recommendations produced by a computer?

2.4.1 Discussions about the Users

Discussions about the users of an expert system address the first four questions in Table 2.6.

1. Who will use the results of the system?

2. Who will provide input to the system?

3. What kind of assistance do the users need from the expert system (as perceived by their management and by the experts)?

4. What is the user's level of skill or knowledge relative to the level of the expert?

The first two questions identify the users of the expert system. The third question reviews the definition of the task, given the identity of the users. The fourth question specifies what kind of information the expert system will need to provide the users. If the system is aimed at novices, it may need to provide detailed explanations that tell the users what information to enter and how to interpret the system's results. On the other hand, if the system is a job aid for an expert (or a near expert), extensive explanations would be unnecessary and annoying. Instead, the system might need to provide justifications for its recommendations that enable its users to judge for themselves whether to accept the system's advice. If the system is intended for users with varying levels of skill, it will need to reach a balance that makes it acceptable to all users or to provide alternative modes of interaction for experts and novices.

> The members of the service staff were initially identified as the users of the toaster-repair advisor. Margaret Major, the head of the service department; Frank Fixit, senior member of the repair staff; and Patricia Programmer, the lead knowledge engineer, meet to discuss the users of the system.
>
> Frank Fixit and Margaret Major both believe that the many members of the repair staff need help repairing toasters. Staff members sometimes have trouble identifying the cause of a problem; sometimes they are unsure how to repair a problem. Frank, Margaret, and Patricia decide that members of the repair staff should interact directly with personal computers to run the toaster-repair advisor. They should enter information about a toaster through the computer's keyboard and see the system's recommendations displayed on the computer's screen.
>
> Patricia asks if the system will be used by *all* members of the repair staff or just the novices. Patricia suggests that novices may need more extensive explanations of how to perform test and repair procedures. Frank confirms that the new staff members would not be able to follow the system's advice without such explanations. He adds that the experienced staff members would be insulted by wordy explanations.

> After discussing this issue, Margaret and Frank decide that the system should be used by all members of the repair staff.

2.4.2 Discussions with the Users

Discussions with the intended users of an expert system address the remaining questions in Table 2.6.

- What kind of assistance do the users *think* they need?
- What kind of assistance do the users *want?*
- What is the users' normal routine?
- How will the expert system fit into this routine?
- Are the users comfortable working with computers?
- Are the users open to having computers introduced into their jobs?
- Are the users open to using the results or recommendations produced by a computer?

> In the toaster-repair advisor project, Patricia Programmer and Margaret Major decided to obtain answers to these questions in teams, each team containing one member of the service department and one knowledge engineer. Patricia and Frank Fixit form one team; Margaret and Howard Hacker, the other. Each team meets individually with various members of the repair staff. In these meetings, the teams explain the idea behind the toaster-repair advisor. They answer questions about the proposed system and ask for opinions, suggestions, and concerns.
>
> During meetings with members of the repair staff, both teams find resistance to the idea of asking a computer for help. Some of the staff members do not believe that they need assistance in repairing toasters. Most of the staff members mention unhappy experiences with the existing computer system in the service department, the toaster-part database. This is accessible to the repair staff, but few of them use it. If they need to know which parts can be used in a particular model toaster, they look up the information in their catalogs instead of checking the database. They admit that searching the catalogs takes more time than querying the database; the catalogs, however, are more convenient. To use the database, they must go to the single personal computer that is installed in the reception area of the service department. The catalogs, on the other hand, are on bookshelves in the service bays where the toasters are repaired.
>
> Several staff members provide another reason for not using the toaster-part database: they are reluctant to touch the keyboard. One staff member said that she cannot type, and does not feel comfortable using the keyboard. Another staff member said that he was afraid that he would hit a wrong key accidentally and cause serious problems.
>
> Most members of the repair staff say that what they *really* needed is help writing bills for the customers. They currently need to look up the rates for various repairs, and the price for replacement parts. They need

to itemize these charges on the billing forms, add the charges, compute sales tax on the parts, total the bill, and take the finished form to the billing clerk in the reception area. The repair personnel universally feel that this should not be a part of *their* job.

2.4.3 Discussions about User Acceptance

Representatives of the users, the experts, and the implementers should discuss how the task and the operating environment of the expert system can be defined to ensure that the system will be used. Participants in these discussions should answer the following questions, taking into account all the information they obtained from and about the potential users.

- Are the users inclined to use the expert system?

- What modifications to the task would provide incentives for using the system?

- What restrictions do the users' needs put on the operating environment of the expert system?

- What modifications to the users' responsibilities are required to make using the system feasible?

If the users do not perceive any benefit from the expert system, they may be unwilling to use it. In many applications, it is necessary to extend the task of the expert system to include a function that the *users* want in order to encourage use of the system. Interaction with an expert system should not be an *additional* activity in anyone's job; it should replace or remove current job obligations. If an expert system does not automate a current task, management intervention may be needed to redefine the users' jobs so that they have time to use the system. In some applications, a new job will need to be created for the people who will operate the expert system.

The expert system should be easy to use and to learn to use. The system should be accessible; terminals for interactive systems should be placed in convenient locations. All outputs of the system should be easily available to the persons who will use those outputs. The system's interfaces should be designed to facilitate its use.

> After the meetings with members of the repair staff, Patricia Programmer, Margaret Major, Howard Hacker, and Frank Fixit reconvene to discuss the implications of what they have learned. The following description summarizes their conversations regarding modifications to the task of the toaster-repair advisor; Section 2.5 contains their discussions about the system's operating environment.
>
> Patricia Programmer opens the discussion by raising the issue of the

varying skill levels within the repair staff. In the discussions about the users, the group decided that the expert system should appeal to all members of the staff. Some users will need more instruction than others. Patricia suggests that the system could allow the user to *request* explanations of unfamiliar procedures. That way novices could get the help they need, but the more experienced staff members would not be bothered by unnecessary explanations.

Next Patricia proposes that the system could look up the cost of replacement parts in the part database and fill out billing forms. Mar-

---

Figure 2.4 Task of the toaster-repair advisor. The toaster-repair advisor will perform five distinct functions. The system will have three entry points. If the user requests assistance with the repair of a toaster, the system will identify the cause of the malfunction and recommend an appropriate repair. It will update the toaster-part database and print a customer bill. If the user requests the bill for a specific repair, the system will update the toaster-part database and print the bill. If the user requests the explanation of a procedure, the system will display a description of that procedure.

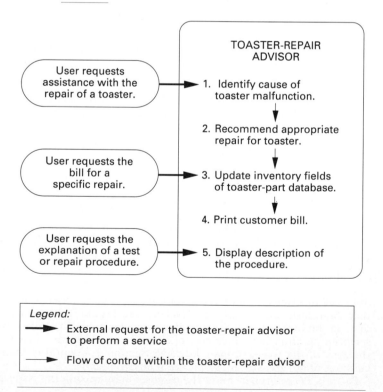

garet says that the system might not be able to complete the billing forms. The charges for the different kinds of repairs are *not* currently available online; these figures are also needed in computing a bill. Patricia explains that repair charges could be added to the database or included in the system's knowledge base. Filling out the billing forms would be a small and simple addition to the expert system; adding this functionality might make the difference between the system's success and its failure. If the system serves a need that the *users* perceive, they will be much more likely to use it.

Margaret raises the issue of the more experienced staff members who did not think they needed help. Should she require them to use the system? Patricia answers that people who do not currently go to Frank Fixit for help are not likely to go to the expert system for help.

She asks Frank whether having the system produce a bill would be sufficient incentive for using the system. Frank says that even *he* would like to have the system fill out bills, but that it would not be worth his time to ask for advice. For himself and for some of the other senior people it would be nice to be able to enter the repair and have the system produce a bill. Patricia says that this option would be an easy addition.

Patricia points out that, if the system produces bills, the billing clerk should be considered a "user" of the system. His opinions should also be considered. The following day Patricia talks to the billing clerk. He is enthusiastic about having the bills filled out correctly; he routinely has to rectify errors in the bills. His only concern is whether the bills will be delivered to him when he needs them. Certain members of the repair staff accumulate about a week's worth of bills before bringing them to him. The billing clerk explains that the completed billing forms are his only indication that a toaster has been fixed. When a customer comes to pick up a toaster, he checks through the billing forms to see if the toaster is ready. The billing clerk sometimes incorrectly tells a customer that a toaster is not ready because the repair person has neglected to bring him the bill.

Figure 2.4 illustrates the final definition of the task that the toaster-repair advisor will perform.

2.5 Specifying the Operating Environment

A complete definition of an expert system includes a clear description of how the system will fit into the users' work environment. Regardless of the value of the system's results if the expert system does not integrate smoothly into the work environment, it will never be used. In many projects, the existing data-processing environment within the company specifies one of the objectives of the expert system project: to develop an expert system that will integrate with the current computing environment. In other projects, the primary restriction on the operating environment is that it be cost effective.

To assess the environment for an expert system, consider all the inputs it will need and all the outputs it will produce. Try to specify an environment that makes all interfaces as smooth as possible.

Frank Fixit, Margaret Major, Howard Hacker, and Patricia Programmer meet to discuss the environment for the toaster-repair advisor. They consider two sources of input to the system and three output destinations as illustrated in Figure 2.5.

Frank Fixit starts the discussion by saying that the system would have to be available in the service bays. Experience with the toaster-part database has shown that the repair staff will not leave the service bays to use a computer. The bays themselves have plenty of extra room. A personal computer in the service bay would not get in the repair person's way.

Howard Hacker notes that the expert system would need a user-interface that allows the repair personnel to enter information with a minimum of typing; the interface should present menus of options whenever possible. Howard suggests that the project team should work with some of the repair staff to see whether they would prefer to use a keyboard or a mouse to select menu items.

Frank reminds Patricia Programmer that she suggested that the system could allow novice users to request descriptions of repair procedures. He says that these explanations will need to include diagrams, tables, and schematics. Patricia responds that the user interface can include graphic capabilities.

Howard explains that the personal computers in the service bays will need to be connected by network to the computer that contains the

---

Figure 2.5 Operating environment for the toaster-repair advisor. The toaster-repair advisor will receive input from the repair person who uses the system and from the toaster-part database. It will provide output results to the repair person, the toaster-part database, and the billing clerk.

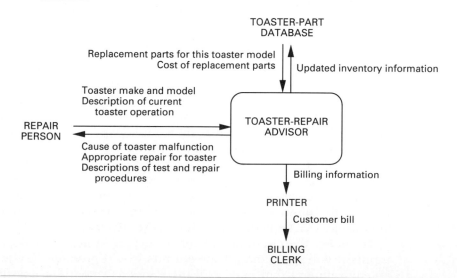

toaster-part database. It would be simple to extend the network to include a printer in the reception area of the service department. The expert system could send the customers' bills to that printer, and the billing clerk could collect the bills directly from the printer instead of relying on the service staff to bring him the bills.

As the foregoing example illustrates, the discussion of the expert system's operating environment identifies initial requirements for the system's user interface; interfaces to other software packages; and interfaces to devices, networks, and other hardware. If the interface requirements for an application are extensive, a software-engineering effort should be started parallel to the knowledge-engineering effort. While the knowledge-engineering effort focuses on developing the expert system, the software-engineering effort can focus on integrating the system with its operating environment.

2.6 Identifying the Source of Expertise

The final facet in the definition of an expert system is the source of expertise. Knowledge engineers cannot begin work on the project until they identify individuals who have both the time and the knowledge to supply the necessary expertise for the system. In some applications, at least one expert is identified shortly after a potential expert-system application is suggested. For example, a key objective of the expert system project may be to capture the expertise of a particular individual who is about to retire. In these projects, the expert participates in defining what the expert system will do. In other projects, managers of various work groups participate in the defining the expert system. These managers must identify the individuals who have the requisite skills to act as project experts. They must decide how these individuals can devote time to an expert system project without interrupting smooth operations within their organizations.[5] Once the task has been defined, the knowledge engineers and the representatives of the expert group should examine the task definition and discuss the following issues:

- *Written materials* (Section 2.6.1): What manuals, catalogs, or other written documents contain knowledge that is relevant to the application? How much help will the knowledge engineers need in interpreting these documents? Who would be able to provide this assistance?

---

5. Once an expert is selected, an additional challenge may remain: The expert may be reluctant to participate in the project. In Part 2 we shall address how to win the support and the collaboration of a reluctant expert.

- *Human experts* (Section 2.6.2): What different areas of expertise are relevant to the task? Who are the experts for each specialty?
- *Inclusion of experts in the project team* (Section 2.6.3): How much time can each expert devote to the project? If the project requires more than one expert, how will the different experts work with the knowledge engineers?
- *Final authority* (Section 2.6.4): Who will judge whether the expert system's behavior is correct? If experts disagree, who will settle the disputes?

In many applications, more than one expert will participate in these discussions; the experts' manager(s) will generally participate in the discussion of project organization.

2.6.1 Identifying Written Material

Often, at least some of the relevant knowledge is available in manuals, catalogs, or other written form. The knowledge engineers should ask the expert to identify any such documents that might be of use to the project team. The knowledge engineers can then review the materials with the expert to ascertain what information each document contains and whether the knowledge engineers will be able to use the documents without assistance. In general, knowledge engineers will need help in using written documents; they must rely on a human expert:

- To explain the terminology used and the concepts discussed in the documents
- To supply details omitted from the documents but crucial to a thorough understanding of the task
- To point out where current practice differs from documented procedures
- To point the knowledge engineer to a small quantity of relevant material within a voluminous collection of manuals
- To explain hand-written annotations in working documents

When knowledge engineers are able to obtain information from written documents, with or without help from an expert, the total knowledge-acquisition time for the project can be reduced. A review of the documents will help the knowledge engineers to estimate how much time the documents will save them. They can take this factor into account when they plan the project development.

Patricia Programmer meets with Frank Fixit in his service bay to find out what written materials Frank uses when he repairs toasters. Frank first shows Patricia his eight service manuals, which describe the various models of toasters in detail. Frank explains that some of the information in the manuals can also be found in the toaster-part database; other material appears only in the manuals. As Patricia and Frank flip through the manuals, Patricia finds many sections that she thinks will be needed by the toaster-repair advisor; she remarks that she would never be able to find this material without Frank's help. Patricia also discovers several tables that she suspects she can use almost verbatim in the expert system; unfortunately, each of these tables has footnotes that Frank will have to explain to her.

Next, Frank shows Patricia a few recent service bulletins. Frank explains that these bulletins contain the manufacturers' latest policies on repair procedures and replacement parts for various toasters. Frank says that he receives a few new service bulletins each month. Patricia reviews the bulletins and finds that she can understand them without too much difficulty. She suspects that, when she has learned more about toaster repair from Frank, she will be able to obtain information from the bulletins without assistance. Patricia notes that the service bulletins will be crucial to the ongoing maintenance of the toaster-repair advisor. As the service department receives new bulletins, the system's knowledge base will need to be updated accordingly.

2.6.2 Identifying the Experts

In the simplest projects, a single expert has both the knowledge and the available time to provide all the requisite knowledge. This person becomes a member of the project team and works closely with the knowledge engineers. This expert also has the authority to judge whether the expert system's behavior is correct. In other projects, more than one expert will be needed. For complex applications, no single person will be knowledgeable about all aspects of the task. For many applications, no single expert will be able to commit sufficient time to the project.

The project experts can be selected in meetings that include the knowledge engineers, the people who have been identified as possible experts for the project, and the managers of these individual experts. The knowledge engineers and the experts should discuss the proposed task to decide who can provide the necessary expertise for each component of the task. The knowledge engineers should provide rough estimates of the amount of time that will be needed from the different experts. The experts and their managers should discuss each expert's current responsibilities, and how much time each can devote to the project.

Patricia Programmer, Frank Fixit, Barbara Burnt, and Margaret Major meet to discuss this issue. Patricia starts the discussion by asking Frank and Barbara to describe situations in which they have difficulty repairing toasters. Barbara says that she needs Frank's help for certain toaster problems that occur very rarely. She simply does not have enough experience to recognize these unusual problems. She also needs help occasionally with some of the older models of toaster.

Frank adds that he deals almost exclusively with traditional electric toasters. When he sees a problem with a newer model toaster that has electronic controls and integrated circuits, he usually discusses it with Barbara. These toasters were already on the market when Barbara went through her training program, and she has much more experience working with them. Frank feels comfortable with some of the simpler problems with electronic toasters; for complicated problems, he asks Barbara for help.

Patricia realizes that Frank Fixit cannot be the sole expert for the toaster-repair advisor. The system will need to incorporate Barbara Burnt's expertise as well. Patricia schedules a meeting with Margaret Major to discuss how they should organize the project to work with the two experts. Margaret must decide how she can manage the service department with both Frank and Barbara taking time away from their normal repair responsibilities to work on the expert system.

2.6.3 Inclusion of Experts in the Project Team

Once experts have been identified, the knowledge engineers, the experts, and the involved managers must decide how to include experts in the project team (Figure 2.6). If a project obtains information from a single expert, that expert will become a member of the project team as illustrated by option 1a in Figure 2.6. If the project includes more than one expert, the group must decide whether the *project team* should include one expert or more than one. Knowledge acquisition is more streamlined in a team with a single expert because the knowledge engineers can obtain the majority of information from a single source. Some project teams, however, require multiple experts. In those projects, the knowledge engineers will need to integrate information from more than one source (Section 2.8). The remainder of this section describes the different ways to include experts into the project team and the circumstances in which each of the options in Figure 2.6 is appropriate.

Designating One Project Expert

In the simplest organization of a project with multiple experts, a single expert is designated to be the *project expert* (Figure 2.6, option 1b). This expert becomes a part of the project team that develops the expert system. The knowledge engineers work directly with the single project expert; other participating experts provide information *through* the project expert. When the team needs knowledge outside the project expert's area of specialization, the project expert obtains the necessary knowledge through discussions with colleagues and relays this knowledge to the project knowledge engineers. Sometimes, the project expert may ask another expert to attend a knowledge-acquisition session as a "guest lecturer" so that the second expert communicates directly with the knowledge engineers while the project expert is on hand to clarify points that the knowledge engineers may not understand.

This project organization is appropriate when the experts share the general area of expertise but have different specialties. For example, Frank Fixit and Barbara Burnt are both experts in toaster repair. Frank specializes in unusual problems and problems with older models. Barbara specializes in problems with electronic toasters. Frank Fixit is chosen as the project expert for the toaster-repair advisor project. When the project team begins to discuss electronic toasters, Frank will ask Barbara Burnt to present an overview of the function of an electronic toaster and how it varies from a standard toaster. Later in the project, when the team needs additional details about particular problems in electronic toasters, Frank will confer with Barbara and present Barbara's knowledge to Patricia Programmer and Howard Hacker.

This organization is usually the easiest for the knowledge engineers. As described in Part 2, knowledge engineers must build a good working

Figure 2.6 Alternative ways to include experts in a project team. In many applications, the project team includes a single expert although the project may use the expertise of more than one expert (options 1b and 1c). Other project teams require more than one expert.

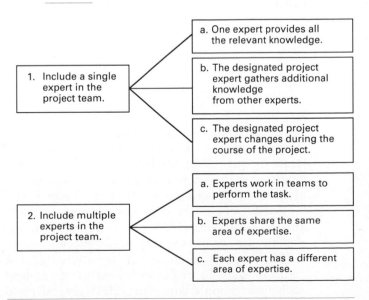

relationship with the project experts; they must learn to communicate with the project experts and make the experts comfortable with the knowledge-acquisition process. It is simpler to build a relationship with *one* expert than it is to do so with many participating experts. Similarly, it is easier to learn to communicate with a single expert. The project expert can communicate efficiently with the other participating experts because they all share the same general area of expertise and the same technical vocabulary.

The experts' management also may prefer to designate a single project expert. Only one expert will need to make a major time commitment to the project. Only the project expert will need to be enthusiastic about the expert system. The other experts can view their participation as occasional assistance with their colleague's pet project.

Changing Project Experts

In some applications, no single expert will be available for the duration of the expert-system project; the project team will need to include two or more experts in succession (Figure 2.6, option 1c). One person will act as designated project expert for a period of time; then the expert will leave the project and be replaced by a new project expert. Such changes in project personnel cannot always be predicted. The initial expert may leave the project for a variety of personal or professional reasons. Other changes can be anticipated. For example, the expert might be a visiting scientist who is spending a short time with the organization that is developing the expert system. Alternatively, the expert might be scheduled to retire before the completion of the project.

Whenever a change in project expert can be predicted, the knowledge engineers should make sure that the organization funding the project is aware that the change will interrupt progress. The knowledge engineers will need to learn to work with the new expert; the new expert will need to learn what to expect from knowledge acquisition. Initially, therefore, knowledge acquisition with the new expert will be less productive than it was with the first expert. More serious delays can occur when two experts have significantly different approaches to performing the task. The second expert may find it difficult to understand the process or the framework the first expert established. In the worst case, the knowledge engineers may need to redesign and reimplement large sections of the knowledge base. In the best case, the knowledge engineers may need to explain the first expert's approach and the rationale behind it and to make minor adjustments to accommodate the second expert's preferences.

If a change in project expert is anticipated, the knowledge engineers can take steps to make the transition as smooth as possible. Ideally, each expert should work on a relatively independent aspect of the task.

(In many applications, of course, it will not be possible to separate the task to avoid interaction among the experts.) As soon as a new project expert is identified, the knowledge engineers should start introducing the new expert to the project. The new expert should receive copies of project memoranda, summaries of knowledge-acquisition sessions and other project meetings, project progress reports, and other documents. If possible, the new expert should attend knowledge-acquisition sessions to learn about the project and about the knowledge-acquisition process itself. The knowledge engineers should encourage the current project expert to consult with the new expert so that the new expert will be aware of the current expert's assumptions and decisions. This consultation will also encourage the new expert to identify with the project even before becoming the project expert.

Using a Team of Project Experts

In some applications, the experts normally perform the task in teams of two or more members (Figure 2.6, option 2a). This situation can occur whether the experts share the same area of expertise or specialize in different areas. The important characteristic of these applications is that the experts are accustomed to performing the task through a collaborative effort with other people, not individually. In applications such as these, the knowledge engineers should arrange to work with a team of project experts. An expert who is accustomed to team problem solving may be hesitant to discuss the task without the other team members being present. In addition, a single member of a problem-solving team may not present an accurate account of the process of performing the task.

When an expert-system project includes a team of experts, the knowledge engineers will need to establish a good working relationship with each expert on the team. They will only need to learn a single technical vocabulary, however—the vocabulary in which the experts converse with one another when they collaborate to perform the task.

Using Project Experts with the Same Area of Expertise

Occasionally, an expert-system project team will need to include a number of experts who share an area of expertise and who are used to performing the task individually (Figure 2.6, option 2b). In some applications, the client who funds the development of the system will dictate that two or more experts should participate. In other applications, no single expert will have enough time to be the sole project expert. The knowledge engineers in such projects can make the most efficient use of the experts' time by giving each expert primary responsibility for supplying the knowledge for a particular aspect of the task. If the project team contains enough knowledge engineers who are skilled interviewers, a different knowledge engineer can work with each expert.

The knowledge engineers should encourage the experts to discuss the different aspects of the task with each other. The knowledge engineers should inform each expert of any design decisions that may affect the aspects of the task for which that expert is responsible. One knowledge engineer should be accountable for understanding how the different aspects of the task interact and for ensuring that portions of the knowledge base that are developed independently will fit together.

Using Project Experts with Different Areas of Expertise

If the task of an expert system encompasses different areas of expertise, the project team will need to include an expert for each speciality (Figure 2.6, option 2c). For example, in an application to schedule the production activities within a factory, an expert who is familiar with the manufacturing equipment can explain how procedures can be modified in response to equipment failure. A different expert can describe how to alter production with variations in the supply of raw materials. A third expert can specify how to adjust production according to changes in projections of customer demands for different products. Note that these experts are not accustomed to working together as a team to perform a task; instead each of them performs one aspect of the task individually.

A project that spans several areas of expertise requires more initial effort for the knowledge engineers. They will need to establish good working relationships with each expert and to learn the technical vocabulary of each area of expertise. If the experts are not already accustomed to collaborating with each other, the knowledge engineers may need to mediate disputes that arise among the experts.

2.6.4 Agreeing on a Final Authority

At various times during the course of an expert system project, the project team may need to ask some outside party to make a judgment or a decision.

- Someone must assess the results of an evaluation of the expert system and decide whether the system is ready to be fielded.

- If project experts are unable to reach agreement on an issue critical to implementation of the system, someone must provide the knowledge engineers with direction.

The definition of the expert system should specify what person or group of people will make these decisions.

Evaluation

Knowledge engineers need to know who will judge whether the expert system's behavior is correct. This individual (or group) will decide whether the expert system passes its evaluation and will specify when the system is ready to be fielded. When the evaluators have been identified, the knowledge engineers can meet with them to define the success criteria for the evaluation, and to plan the evaluation.

> Margaret Major says that she will take responsibility for assessing the outcome of an evaluation of the toaster-repair advisor. During the evaluation, she will rely on Frank Fixit to judge whether the system recommends the appropriate repairs for standard electric toasters and on Barbara Burnt to evaluate whether the system recommends the appropriate repairs for electronic toasters.

Expert Disagreement

In any project with multiple experts, the potential exists that the experts may occasionally disagree. Individual experts may have different opinions or may use different strategies. In some fields, such as medicine, research continually changes the body of available knowledge. Research, however, does not always produce exact results. One study may provide good evidence for one theory whereas a second study may provide equally convincing evidence for an opposing theory. Some experts will give credence to the first study; others, to the second. In such fields, recognized world authorities do not always agree with each other; disagreements among project experts are to be expected.

The knowledge engineers who implement the expert system must know what they should do in the case of a disagreement. Before the project begins, the knowledge engineers, the experts, and the funders must agree on a final arbiter. All participating experts must be willing to abide by the decisions of the final arbiter *even when they disagree* with a decision.

The final arbiter may be a single expert or a member of management. When different experts share the area of expertise, the final arbiter may be the most senior expert. If the experts have the same seniority, their superior may be called upon to arbitrate disagreements. If the participating experts have different areas of expertise or specialization, a different expert may be chosen as the final authority for each different area of coverage. For example, in the toaster-repair advisor project, Frank is chosen as the arbiter for all matters that do not involve electronic toasters. He agrees to defer to Barbara's decisions on issues that concern electronic toasters. The important point is that all involved parties should discuss the potential of disagreements among experts and decide how to handle such disagreements *before disagreements have a chance to arise.*

2.7 Recording the Definition

After participants in the project have reached a final decision on each facet of the expert system's definition, the lead knowledge engineer should prepare a document that makes the definition explicit. The preparation of this document serves two purposes. First, it gives the knowledge engineer an opportunity to review the entire definition. The knowledge engineer should verify that all necessary questions have been answered and that all facets of the definition are consistent with one another. Second, the document itself will inform all participants

---

Figure 2.7 Recording the definition of an expert system. Patricia Programmer follows this outline to create a document that records the definition of the toaster-repair advisor. Patricia's document incorporates tables and diagrams that the group developed during their discussions.

OBJECTIVES OF THE TOASTER-REPAIR ADVISOR
   Rating of objectives
      Essential:
      • Reduce the occurrence of repeat problems
      • Shorten the time to repair a toaster
      Important:
      • Reduce the amount of time that Frank Fixit spends assisting the repair staff
      • Improve the management of the spare-parts inventory
      • Reduce the time that customers have to wait for their toasters to be repaired
      Optional:
      • Educate the less experienced staff members
   Desired consequences of system introduction
      Table 2.4

TASK THE SYSTEM WILL PERFORM
   Description of the task
      • Identify the cause of a toaster malfunction
      • Recommend an appropriate repair for the toaster
      • Update the inventory fields of the toaster-part database
      • Generate a customer bill
      • Describe a test procedure or a repair procedure
      Figure 2.4
   How the task addresses the objectives
      Table 2.5

Figure 2.7 (continued)
USERS OF THE SYSTEM

- Members of the repair staff will be the primary users; they will interact directly with the system
- The billing clerk will receive the customer bill

OPERATING ENVIRONMENT

- The system will run on personal computers in service bays
- These computers will be connected by network to the toaster-part database
- The network will also link the computers to a printer in the service department reception area
   Figure 2.5

SOURCES OF EXPERTISE
Written materials

- Service manuals with detailed descriptions of toasters
- Service bulletins with latest policies and procedures

Experts

- Frank Fixit for standard toasters
- Barbara Burnt for electronic toasters

Project team organization

- Frank Fixit will be a member of the project team
- Frank will consult with Barbara Burnt as necessary on topics that relate to electronic toasters

Final authorities

- Margaret Major will be responsible to judge whether the system performs its task correctly
- Frank Fixit will make all decisions that relate to standard toasters
- Barbara Burnt will make decisions that relate to electronic toasters

---

what decisions were made; the document can minimize misunderstandings about the outcome of the various discussions.

After preparing the document, the knowledge engineer should distribute copies to all concerned parties. When everyone has had a chance to review the document, a final meeting should be held to ensure that everyone understands and accepts the definition. After the discussions at the meeting, the knowledge engineer may need to modify the document. The end result should be a common view of the expert system, which all participants share.

> Patricia Programmer prepares a document to summarize the definition of the toaster-repair advisor (Figure 2.7) and distributes copies to Gary General, Margaret Major, Charles Cypher, Frank Fixit, Barbara Burnt, and Howard Hacker. Patricia schedules a meeting for the following week to discuss the definition. At the meeting, Patricia briefly discusses each facet of the definition: the objectives, the task, the users, the environment, and the expert. For each facet, she makes sure that everyone understands what the definition specifies and that everyone accepts

the decisions. The participants in the toaster-repair project agree with the the the definition of the system in Patricia's document. They are ready to proceed with the development of the system.

2.8 Integrating Information from Multiple Sources

We have seen that the definition of an expert system is based on information supplied by a variety of people:

- Experts

- Potential users

- Knowledge engineers

- Managers of the experts, of the users, and of the knowledge engineers

- Managers who provide the funding for the project

An important characteristic of knowledge acquisition at the beginning of an expert-system project is that the knowledge engineers must integrate information obtained from diverse sources. This section presents knowledge-acquisition activities that are useful for integrating information from multiple sources. These activities are important at the beginning of most expert-system projects; the activities may also be useful throughout a project that includes more than one expert.

As we mentioned at the beginning of this chapter, defining an expert system presents two challenges: knowledge engineers must *obtain information* from the relevant individuals, and they must *achieve consensus* among all participants. Knowledge engineers can meet these challenges with a combination of two methods: they can *lead group discussions*, and they can *consult participants individually*.

Group discussions are often the most productive means of collecting the information because they permit all participants to hear what each individual has to say. The participants can debate the pros and cons of different options and can work together to consolidate different viewpoints. The knowledge engineer plays three roles in a group discussion (Table 2.7).

Try to arrange group discussions whenever it is feasible to do so. Participants at different locations can sometimes overcome geographical differences by using the telephone. For example, a remote participant could join a group discussion over a speaker telephone. Similarly, a number of participants in different locations could conduct a group discussion by means of a conference call.

Group discussions are not always practical. In some applications, it will be impossible to get all participants together in the same location at the same time. For example, in Section 2.4.2 we saw that the potential users of the toaster-repair advisor were consulted individually. Margaret Major decided that the service department could not afford to interrupt operations by holding a discussion that included the entire repair staff. Individual consultations are often the most efficient means of collecting information from potential users of an expert system. Even if the users could all meet for a group discussion at one time, their number might be too large to permit a productive discussion.

Unfortunately group discussions may be impractical for another reason—the participants may be unwilling or unable or work together productively. Individual conflicts or organizational differences may prevent cooperation. In some applications, insurmountable conflicts can be anticipated. In other projects, the knowledge engineers may try to conduct group discussions but may be unable to keep the participants from arguing among themselves. In either circumstance, the knowledge engineers will need to gather information by interviewing the participants individually or by leading discussions among homogeneous subgroups. (Interviewing techniques are described in detail in Part 2.)

We now turn our attention to the two purposes that the knowledge engineers must accomplish. Section 2.8.1 discusses methods for obtaining the information from groups of people. Section 2.8.2 describes methods for achieving consensus.

Table 2.7 Leading a Group Discussion

Role	Actions
Facilitator	Facilitate a productive conversation.
	Stimulate the exchange of ideas.
	Prevent any individual from monopolizing the conversation.
	Make sure that each individual has an opportunity to voice opinions.
	Ensure that participants understand one another.
	Keep the discussion focused on the issue at hand.
Moderator	Moderate any disagreements that may arise.
	Defuse hostilities between participants.
	Rephrase inflammatory statements in productive terms.
Documentor	Document the decisions that are reached.
	Write a summary of the decisions and distribute it to all participants.

2.8.1 Obtaining the Information

The knowledge engineers' first challenge in defining an expert system is to obtain information from all concerned parties. In many projects, this undertaking will be straightforward. Participants will have a clear idea of what they want the expert system to do, they will have no difficulty answering the knowledge engineers' questions, and they will volunteer their ideas and opinions willingly. Problems arise when participants have *only vague ideas* and are *not able to articulate their thoughts* easily. In some applications, certain individuals feel inhibited from volunteering their ideas and opinions. The knowledge engineers need to obtained information from *all* relevant sources; they cannot afford to ignore the ideas of timid participants.

In group discussions, **brainstorming** is a useful technique for encouraging participants to express their ideas. This technique can be particularly useful in discussions about the objectives of the expert system. Brainstorming can be a productive way for a group to formulate ideas; it can serve as a means for ensuring that the group considers all topics that any individual finds important.

> As we saw in Sections 2.2 through 2.6, the participants in discussions about the toaster-repair advisor had fairly clear ideas of the benefits that they hoped to accrue through the introduction of an expert system. Their discussions were productive, and no participant was hesitant to volunteer ideas, to express opinions, or to state reservations. If the participants had encountered more difficulties in expressing their preferences, Patricia Programmer would have lead brainstorming sessions.

The primary ground rules in a brainstorming session are:

- Anyone may *volunteer* an idea. The ideas must be related to the topic currently under discussion.

- No one may *respond to* an idea that has been suggested. For example, a participant should not express disagreement with the idea of another participant, criticize the idea, or comment on the importance of the idea. It is acceptable, of course, for a participant to expand on the idea with additional details or related ideas.

Start a brainstorming session by introducing the topic to be discussed or the question to be answered. Then explain the ground rules. Let the participants volunteer ideas as the ideas occur, and continue as long as anyone has an idea to suggest. Record each idea that is proposed in a location where all participants can see them (on a flip chart or whiteboard, for example). If possible, have at least two people take turns writing the suggestions; most brainstorming sessions produce suggestions more rapidly than a single reporter can write them.

Pay attention to the participants. Notice whether one person appears to be dominating the session. Look for individuals who seem to have something to say but who are too hesitant or too timid to speak up. If the participants are not contributing uniformly, you may need to impose more order on the proceeding. Stop the discussion, and explain that you want to be sure to collect ideas from everyone. Ask the participants to take turns making suggestions. Select one person to start; ask that person to volunteer an idea or to pass the turn to the next person. Continue around the room in this manner until all participants have had a turn; then begin again with the first person. Repeat the process until the participants run out of suggestions.

After you have collected ideas, lead the group in a discussion to try to organize the ideas. Remove duplicate items, combine closely related points, and group similar ideas that should be considered together.

2.8.2 Building Consensus

After you have collected information (through discussions, brainstorming sessions, individual interviews, or some combination of these methods), you may need to ask the participants to select among competing alternatives or to assign relative priorities to various options. For example, if a group proposes more objectives for the expert system than can be met with the available resources, the group will need to decide which of the objectives should be omitted or deferred. If the achievement of one objective will preclude the achievement of a second objective, the group must choose between the two objectives. The participants who provided the information will need to evaluate the candidates objectives, compare these candidates against one another, and assign them relative priorities.

To start the discussion of a number of competing options, list the options where all participants can see them. Ask each participant in turn to answer two questions:

1. What options do you think are most important? (You may want to limit the number of options each participant can select.)

2. Why did you choose the options you selected?

In many discussions, the answers to the first question will indicate fairly close agreement, and the group will be able to reach consensus after this exercise.

> As we saw in Section 2.2, Charles Cypher lead a discussion to evaluate the six objectives of the toaster-repair advisor against one another.[6]

---

6. The six objectives and the result of evaluating these objectives against one another are shown in Table 2.4.

Charles asked Gary General, Margaret Major, and Frank Fixit each to select the four most important objectives. Table 2.8 shows which options each participant favored.

After Gary, Margaret, and Frank had voted for their favorite objectives, they discussed the importance of each objective. They quickly agreed that the objectives with three votes were essential for the expert system and that the objectives with two votes were important and should be addressed by the expert system if possible. They decided that the remaining objective with no votes (staff training) was optional.

In more complicated situations, the participants' answers to the first question will not reflect such close agreement. In those discussions, you can use the participants' answers to the second question to identify a number of dimensions along which to evaluate the alternatives. Try to lead the group to consensus by asking each participant to rate the options along the different dimensions. When the participants take all dimensions into consideration, they might agree that the best alternative is one that balances these dimensions rather than one that optimizes a single dimension. If the participants do not agree about the importance of the dimensions themselves, ask them to rate the relative importance of the dimensions. The relative weights of the dimensions will allow the group to compare two options that are strong in different dimensions. Figure 2.8 illustrates this technique.

Discussions can get bogged down when the participants have to consider a large number of options. To avoid this problem, you should ask the participants to narrow their discussion to a few of the most promising candidates. To select the most important options, you might ask each candidate to vote for a small number of alternatives (Figure 2.9a) or to indicate varying degrees of support for the different alternatives (Figure 2.9b). Use a simple numerical scheme for accumulating votes. Some people are uncomfortable using numbers to rate alternatives. If you notice a hesitation to assign numerical weights, ask the participants to rate the alternatives with a small number of descriptive

Table 2.8 Rating the Objectives of the Toaster-Repair Advisor

Objective	Gary	Margaret	Frank
Accuracy of repair	✓	✓	✓
Speed of repair	✓	✓	✓
Expert productivity		✓	✓
Inventory control	✓	✓	
Customer service	✓		✓
Staff training			

Figure 2.8 Building consensus. The participants in a discussion could not agree which of four options to choose (a). The representative of the funding group favored the approach that would be the least expensive to implement. The expert favored the approach that would produce the most accurate results. The representative of the users preferred the approach that would produces a result in the shortest time. The knowledge engineer in the discussion used *reasons* for the participants' choices to identify three dimensions for comparison: the cost of implementation, the quality of the results, and the time to produce a solution. The participants next rated each option according to the three dimensions (b). When the participants took all three factors into consideration (c), their votes showed much closer agreement. Finally, the participants rated the relative importance of the three dimensions (d). The funder, who initially preferred option A for its low cost, agreed to follow option C because accuracy was the most important consideration and because the available budget would cover the cost of option C.

Participant	Preferred Option	Reason
Funder	A	Low cost
Expert	D	Accurate results
User	B	Quick solution

(a)

Option	Cost of Implementation	Accuracy of Results	Time to Produce a Solution
A	Very low	Moderate	Moderate
B	Low	Low	Low
C	Moderate	High	Moderate
D	High	Very high	High

(b)

Option	Funder	Expert	User
A	First choice	Second choice	Second choice
B			
C	Second choice	First choice	First choice
D			

(c)

Dimension	Importance
Cost	2
Accuracy	1
Speed	3

(d)

Figure 2.9 Narrowing the list of alternatives. The participants in a discussion need to focus on a few alternatives from a set of 20 options. In (a), the knowledge engineer asks each participant to vote for the five most important options. The group selects the options that get the most votes. In (b), the knowledge engineer asks each participants to give three points to the most important options, two points to options of moderate importance, one point to options of some importance, and zero points to options that are not important. The group totals the points for each option and selects the options with the highest totals.

Option	Funder	Expert	User	Selected	Option	Funder	Expert	User	Total	Selected
A	✓				A	2	1		3	
B			✓		B			3	3	
C	✓	✓		✓	C	2	3		5	✓
D					D				0	
E		✓	✓	✓	E	1	2	2	5	✓
F					F			1	1	
G	✓	✓		✓	G	3	2	1	6	✓
H					H				0	
I					I	1	1		2	
J					J				0	
K		✓	✓	✓	K	1	2	2	5	✓
L					L	1			1	
M					M				0	
N	✓				N	2	1		3	
O					O			1	1	
P					P				0	
Q	✓	✓	✓	✓	Q	3	2	3	8	✓
R					R			1	1	
S			✓		S	1		2	3	
T					T	1	1	1	3	

| (a) | (b) |

terms (for example, good, moderate, or bad *or* very high, high, moderate, low, or very low). The most important guideline is to be flexible; work with the participants to develop a voting scheme that is most comfortable to the majority of the group.

Participants in some discussions will not be able to reach consensus. If a discussion does not lead to agreement, close the meeting by presenting a summary of the analysis. State what decisions were made;

identify the opposing points of view. Make sure that all participants agree that their opinions are fairly represented by your summary. If a group fails to reach agreement, the decision will need to be made by an individual in a position of authority, for example the manager of the funding organization. Depending on the issue under discussion, the appropriate person to make the decision might be the senior expert or the manager of the users. In some applications, corporate decision makers will chose among competing alternatives. If the final decision maker did not attend the group discussion, meet with this individual afterward to present your summary of the discussion. Once a decision has been made, be sure that the decision (and the rationale behind it) are communicated to the participants in the group discussion.

2.9 Points to Remember

The first goal of initial inquiry is to define what the expert system will do. The success of an expert-system project depends on having a clear definition of the expert system *before* development begins. The definition of an expert system should be shared by four constituent groups:

1. The knowledge engineers who will implement the system

2. The experts who will provide the knowledge

3. The system's intended users

4. The managers who will fund the project

The first activity in an expert-system project should be a meeting to establish the context for discussions about system's definition. The agenda for this meeting should include:

- An introduction of the participants

- An explanation of the goals of the meeting

- A brief description of expert-system technology

- An overview of the situation that the expert system should address

- Plans for the subsequent meetings to define the expert system

Through a series of group discussions or individual interviews, representatives of the four constituent groups should reach consensus on five facets of the definition of the expert system:

1. The objectives the system's introduction should accomplish

2. The task the system will perform

3. The identity of the users of the system and how each class of user will use the system

4. The computing environment in which the system will operate

5. The identity of the experts who will provide the necessary expertise and how the experts will work with the knowledge engineers

Table 2.9 lists the questions that should be answered about each facet of the definition. The table also indicates which groups *must* be represented in discussions about the various facets. The other groups may participate in any discussion if this is convenient and desirable. All groups must agree with the final decisions.

After decisions have been made on all facets of the definition, the lead knowledge engineer on the project should summarize the defi-

---

Table 2.9 Defining an Expert System

Facet of the Definition	Knowledge Engineers	Experts	Users	Funders	Questions to Be Answered
	Participants				
Objectives of the system	√	√	√	√	What current problems are perceived by managers, experts, and users? What situations need improvement according to managers, experts, and users? Is it feasible to correct these problems or to improve these situations with an expert system? If it would be too costly to address *all* problems, which should be given the highest priority?
Task the system will perform	√	√	√		What must the system do to achieve each objective? What must the system do to be acceptable to its intended users ?
System's intended users	√	√	√		Given the definition of the task, who will need to supply input? Who should receive the results, recommen-dations, or other output of the expert system?

Table 2.9 (continued)

Facet of the Definition	Participants				Questions to Be Answered
	Knowledge Engineers	Experts	Users	Funders	
System's operating environment	✓		✓		Given the definition of the task, what programs, devices, or on-line storage media will need to supply input to the expert system? What programs, devices, or on-line storage media should receive the output results of the system? For each source of input, what interface is most direct? What would be most convenient to the person (if any) who supplies the input? For each output destination, what interface is most direct? What would be most convenient for the person (if any) who receives the output?
Source of expertise	✓	✓			What different areas of expertise are relevant to the performance of the task? For each area, who has the necessary knowledge and is available to participate in the project? Which experts will need to interact directly with the knowledge engineers? If experts disagree about what behavior is correct for the system, who will have the final say about what the system should do?

nition of the expert system in a written document. When all four groups approve the written definition, work on the expert-system project can proceed. In some applications, the project will include two parallel activities:

1. A knowledge-engineering effort to develop the expert system

2. A software-engineering effort to develop the necessary interfaces and to integrate the expert system into its operating environment

To define an expert system, knowledge engineers must integrate information that they obtain from a variety of sources. They must obtain information from a variety of individuals, and they must lead these individuals to reach consensus.

Defining an expert system presents a number of knowledge-acquisition challenges. Table 2.10 contains a summary of these challenges and the activities that can help to overcome them.

Table 2.10 Challenges of Defining an Expert System

Challenge	Relevant Activities
Participants start with vague ideas of what they want the expert system to do. They may have difficulty putting their ideas into words.	Lead group discussions to help the participants formulate their ideas. Try brainstorming to help lead a group to express their ideas and to make these ideas more concrete.
It may be difficult to obtain reliable information. Some participants may tell the knowledge engineers what they *think* the knowledge engineers want to hear.	Try to obtain information from a variety of individuals. If some participants are inhibited by group discussions, conduct individual interviews. If you think you (as a knowledge engineer) cannot obtain reliable information from some participants, try to enlist the aid of a person with whom these participants would be more comfortable. Try to avoid injecting bias. (Follow the interviewing guidelines in Part 2.)
The participants may envision functionality for the expert system that is not consistent with the objectives they want the system to accomplish.	Agree on the objectives for the system *before* starting to discuss the task. When a participant suggests functionality for the expert system, ask what objective the functionality will address.
Different individuals may have conflicting personal agenda. Objectives of the different groups may compete.	Make each person's preferences explicit in group discussions. Ask participants to give the *reasons* why they consider various options important. Use these reasons to identify dimensions for evaluating alternatives. Ask the participants to rate alternatives along *all* dimensions.

Table 2.10 (continued)

Challenge	Relevant Activities
Political interactions across organizations may impede cooperation among the four groups.	Act as mediator if disputes arise. If necessary, meet with different groups individually, then present a summary of your findings to representatives of all groups. If consensus cannot be reached, rely on an individual in authority (for example the manager of the funding organization) to make a final decision.

Chapter 3

Obtaining a General Understanding of the Task

The participants in the toaster-repair advisor project have achieved the first goal of the initial inquiry stage of knowledge acquisition: They have defined what the expert system will do. The focus of knowledge acquisition can shift from building consensus among all concerned parties to learning about the task from the expert.

The time has arrived for Patricia Programmer and Howard Hacker to meet with Frank Fixit for their first knowledge-acquisition interview. Howard is very anxious about the approaching meeting. In one conversation with a co-worker, he said, "What do I know about toasters? Boy, am I going to be lost! How can I possibly get through the first meeting without Frank thinking that I am a complete idiot?"

Frank Fixit is also apprehensive about the meeting. When Charles Cypher presented an overview of expert systems at the initial project meeting, Frank got the impression that *he* was to be the center of attention in the project interviews. He is not sure what he can contribute. As he told his colleague, Barbara Burnt, "I know what I can talk about for the first couple of hours, but what can I say of any interest after that?"

We have defined knowledge acquisition to encompass the collection of *all* information needed for an expert system, from *all* relevant sources. The major focus of knowledge acquisition, however, is the collection of *knowledge* from the project *expert*. This process begins during the initial inquiry stage when the knowledge engineers interview the expert to acquire a general understanding of how the expert performs the task. The first several knowledge-acquisition interviews are often the most difficult for both the knowledge engineers and the expert. Neither party can anticipate how the interviews will proceed or what the eventual outcome will be. The expert is likely to be skeptical and apprehensive about the project. Frank Fixit, for example, does not know what to expect from the interviews. It seems impossible to him that a computer program can duplicate his skills.

The knowledge engineers' apprehension over the initial interviews is frequently just as acute as the expert's. Very often, the knowledge engineers know nothing about the application subject area (for example, toaster repair or insurance underwriting) before the project begins. They may not have strong backgrounds in the fields of study (such as physics, mathematics, biology, or accounting) relevant to the application. They may fear that they do not know enough to understand the concepts the expert uses or to follow the steps in the expert's reasoning process.

The key to a successful first interview is to control the anxiety of the entire project team while collecting the necessary information. To control anxiety, knowledge engineers should have a clear understanding of their goals and of the activities that will help them to achieve these goals. The initial interviews with the expert should give the knowledge engineers a general understanding of the task. This chapter describes two activities that can help knowledge engineers achieve this goal: the **task overview,** and the **case discussion.**

In the task overview (Section 3.1), the expert presents an overview of the task. For some applications, the experts' actions in performing a task are guided by a well-understood model and a clearly defined set of operating principles. When the knowledge engineers learn the model and the operating principles, they will know most of what there is to learn about performing the task. In such applications, a task overview can include a fairly thorough description of the process of performing the task. In other applications, the principles that guide the experts' actions are less obvious. The experts themselves may never have thought about how they decide what to do in performing the tasks. In these applications, a task overview will generally supply a superficial description of how to perform the task.

With either kind of application, the knowledge engineers can learn how the expert performs the task through a series of case discussions. In each of these discussions, the expert explains how to perform the task in some particular situation or case. Case discussion are less important in applications that have a clear underlying model; they are crucial to applications that lack such a model.

3.1 Task Overview

A task overview is the ideal way to start the first knowledge-acquisition interview. This activity is the knowledge engineers' opportunity to hear the *expert's perspective* on the task the expert system will perform.

Before your first interview, ask the expert what background information you will need to know before you can understand how to perform the task. For example, you may need to learn:

- Definitions of technical terms for the concepts, objects, and procedures relevant to the task

- The structure of objects central to the task

- Details of important procedures

Find out whether you can learn this information from available training materials before the interview. For example, you may be able to read manuals, to watch videotapes, or to attend training seminars.

Ask the expert to plan to speak for 15 to 30 minutes at the first interview. The talk should require minimum preparation and should present:

- Background information you will not be able to learn from available training materials

- The process by which the expert performs the task

- Aspects of the task that are especially important

- Aspects of the task that are especially difficult

In the interview, follow the expert's overview with a brief discussion to make sure that you have obtained the information you need and that you understand the important issues. If the expert is hesitant to present an overview without more direction, lead a discussion by prompting the expert for the relevant information. As you discuss the expert's overview, remember that the initial inquiry stage of knowledge acquisition should serve to prepare you for the development of the expert system. In this stage, it is not important to delve into the hows and whys of every action the expert takes in the performance of the task. You should learn enough to develop a framework for future knowledge-acquisition and system-design sessions. In the detailed investigation stage of knowledge acquisition, you will fill the framework with specific details.

> Before the first knowledge-acquisition interview in the toaster-repair advisor project, Patricia Programmer and Howard Hacker read a training pamphlet that identifies the major parts of a standard two-slice

toaster and explains how this kind of toaster works. At the interview, Frank Fixit begins his overview of toaster repair with a brief description of the different styles of toaster. Frank explains that the two-slice toaster is the simplest toaster design. The one minor variant is the two-slice toaster with a bakery switch; the three major variants are the four-slice toaster, the toaster oven, and the under-cabinet toaster.

Frank then describes how he repairs a toaster. He tells Patricia and Howard that the first step in the repair process is to see what is wrong with the toaster. Very often the customer's description of the problem is vague ("the toaster doesn't work") or inaccurate ("I think the element is weak"). So, Frank first tests the toaster to see what *really* happens. From there, he can track down the cause of the problem and try to fix it. The final step is to retest the toaster to make sure that it operates correctly. The initial and final tests are important, but less experienced staff members frequently omit one or the other.

3.2 Case Discussion

A case discussion illustrates how the expert would perform the task in some particular situation. Each case is defined by a set of input data to the problem-solving process; these data describe the situation in which the task is performed. In the toaster-repair advisor, each malfunctioning toaster represents a different situation or case; information about a particular toaster defines a case. In other applications, the definition of a case is less clear. For example, an expert system that monitors sensors in a processing plant does not perform its task for discrete situations. Rather it performs its task continuously; no particular *incident* defines a case so there is no natural boundary between the end of one case and the beginning of the next one. In such applications, the project team can define a case by the data that arrive within a meaningful unit of time. In one application, each case might cover a 24-hour period; in another application, a 5-minute interval.

Case discussions can take three different forms: current, historical, or hypothetical (see Table 3.1). For example, Patricia Programmer might go to the service department and observe while Frank Fixit repairs the *current* toaster that needs to be fixed. For a current case, Patricia would ask Frank to talk aloud while he is working on the toaster so that she will know what he is doing and thinking. Alternatively, Patricia might ask Frank to recall the *history* of a toaster he repaired recently. She would ask Frank to describe, as clearly as he can remember, what was wrong with the toaster and what he did to repair it. Finally, Patricia might ask Frank to think up an *hypothetical* example. If Frank has never actually encountered a certain malfunction in a particular model of toaster, he could explain how he would go about repairing the problem if it occurred.

Many project teams use all three forms of case discussion. In some applications, however, it is impractical to observe the expert's per-

Table 3.1 Types of Case Discussion

Type	Description	Advantages	Disadvantages
Current	The knowledge engineers watch while the expert performs the task for the case.	Knowledge engineers can observe actions that the expert might forget to mention. It enables knowledge engineers to visualize the process by which the expert performs the task.	The available cases may not illustrate a wide variety of situations. The available cases may not illustrate the most important situations.
Historical	The expert discusses a case for which the task was performed in the past (by this expert or by someone else).	The expert often remembers important cases and cases that are out of the ordinary. In many applications, a case can be described more quickly than the task can be performed.	Complete data may not be available for the cases. The expert may not correctly remember all details of the case.
Hypothetical	The expert describes how the task should be performed in an hypothetical situation.	It provides a way to talk about situations for which historical data do not exist.	The expert may not anticipate complications that might arise in the case.

formance of the task so discussions are limited to descriptions of past experience and of hypothetical examples. Initially, some applications may need to rely entirely on hypothetical examples. For example, if an expert system is intended to diagnose problems in a piece of equipment under development, no one will have experience in the repair of problems with that equipment. The expert will need to describe hypothetical situations that might arise. Once the piece of equipment is manufactured and put into operation, actual examples of equipment failure can be accumulated. These cases can be discussed in future passes through the expert system's development cycle. The system's knowledge base can be updated and enhanced on the basis of these examples.

A case discussion during initial inquiry should focus on *what* the expert does. In the detailed investigation stage of knowledge acquisition, you will discuss cases in much more detail. At that stage, you will need to understand *why* the expert takes each action and makes each decision. Chapter 5 describes case discussions during detailed investigation. This section gives guidelines for case discussions during the initial inquiry stage only.

3.2.1 Select a Variety of Cases for Discussion

To obtain a general understanding of the task, you should discuss a small number of cases with the expert; five to ten cases will be sufficient in most applications. You will need to ask the expert to supply the example cases for discussion. The cases should illustrate a variety of different situations so that you can get a good idea of the range of situations that the expert system will need to handle. It is usually beneficial to start by discussing a case the expert considers simple. Then discuss increasingly more difficult cases. During initial inquiry, you should discuss at least one case the expert considers difficult or complicated and at least one case the expert considers out of the ordinary.

If it is practical to do so, you should observe the expert performing the task at least once. If possible, schedule this demonstration close to the beginning of the initial inquiry stage. Once you have watched the expert go through the entire process, you will find it easier to understand future case discussions. For the majority of applications, however, it will be most efficient to use historical or hypothetical cases to ensure that you discuss a wide range of situations. Discuss cases that occurred and were documented whenever possible. Fall back on hypothetical cases (or hypothetical details of actual cases) only where historical data are not available.

3.2.2 Arrange to Discuss a Case

The first step in a case discussion is to make arrangements with the expert. You will need to ask the expert to specify a time when you can observe task performance for a current case. When you plan to discuss historical or hypothetical cases, you should give the expert time to select and think about the cases and to collect materials that describe the cases.

Ask the expert to prepare a written description of each historic or hypothetical case to be discussed (Table 3.2). The case description does not need to include the rationale for the expert's conclusions and ac-

Table 3.2 Contents of a Case Description

Information	Description
Data	Data about the situation the expert used while performing the task
Actions	Steps the expert took in performing the task
Conclusions	Major decisions the expert remembers having made Results of performing the task
Time sequence	The order in which the expert obtained data, performed actions, and made conclusions

tions. You will be able to get those details when you discuss the case with the expert. If the case is hypothetical, the expert should develop a *consistent example* and should specify all the information listed in Table 3.2.

3.2.3 Ask the Expert to Step Through the Case

Once the expert has prepared a case description, begin the case discussion by asking the expert to describe the process of performing the task, step by step, for that particular case.[1] In general, you will need to lead the expert through the case discussion, using the interviewing techniques that are described in Part 2. As the expert steps through the case, *focus on the process*. Try to learn how the expert starts and what happens at each step. Notice what information the expert uses at each step and what decisions the expert appears to make.

If you do not understand the expert's description, ask for a clarification. After the expert clears up the source of confusion, return to the case description by reminding the expert where you interrupted the case discussion. Make notes to yourself about the issues you need to pursue when the expert has finished describing the process. Make notes of topics that should be discussed later but that are not necessary for understanding how the expert performed the task in this case. *Do not ask questions that will divert the expert's attention from the process of performing the task.*

Dialog 3.1 illustrates how Patricia Programmer leads Frank Fixit through his first case discussion.

---

1. Many knowledge engineers find it useful to make tape recordings of case discussions (and other interviews). We shall discuss the use of recording equipment in Chapter 15.

Dialog 3.1 Discussing a Case during Initial Inquiry

Setting

This dialog takes place in the first knowledge-acquisition interview. Before this interview, Patricia Programmer asked Frank Fixit to prepare a description of a recent situation in which he repaired a toaster. We join the interview after Frank has completed his task overview. The team members have taken a short break; they are now ready to proceed with their first case discussion.

Patricia Programmer, Frank Fixit, and Howard Hacker are all seated at a table. Patricia and Howard both have notebooks and a few papers on the table in front of them. Frank has a partly disassembled toaster and a few papers in front of him.

Dialog

Patricia: Frank, the next thing I would like you to do is to take us through the example you prepared for us.

I'd like you to give us a step-by-step description of how you repaired the toaster. Howard and I can refer to the descriptions of this case you sent us.

Patricia, Howard, and Frank each retrieve a copy of Frank's case description from the papers on the table in front of them.

Frank: Should I begin now?

Patricia nods.

OK. This is a burnt-toast problem that came in a couple of days ago. We see a lot of problems like this. Dick took the toaster, but he asked for my help—he's new with the department. Anyway, the toaster was a Toasts-Best, model TB80601, model year 1985. This is a two-slice toaster. I'd say this is the most basic model that Toasts-Best sells.

The complaint on the repair slip was "toast too dark."

Patricia: So what did you do first?

Frank: Well, as we do for all color problems, I performed a color test. It should duplicate the customer's problem.

Patricia: Frank, before you go on, would you please tell me what you mean by "color problems?"

Frank: Oh, sure. Any time the complaint has to do with the toast coming out the wrong color, we call it a "color problem." The color can be either too light or too dark.

Patricia: Thanks for making that clear, Frank. You said that you performed a "color test." What is that?

Frank: A color test checks whether the thermostat is functioning properly. It is quite simple. You put the color selector on a medium setting, and then you toast a slice of white bread. When the toast pops up, it should be a nice golden-brown color.

Patricia writes in her notebook:

Color problems seem to imply a malfunctioning thermostat. Pursue this
  relationship:
  Are color problems always *caused by the thermostat?*

Topics for future discussion:
  What are other possible results of the color test?
  What would the different results mean?

Patricia: Thanks. So back to the toaster: What were the results of the color test?

Frank: The toast popped up completely black—I knew there was a severe problem with the thermostat.

Patricia: Let me see if I understand the process so far. You saw a color problem so you suspected a thermostat malfunction. You did a color test to check whether there *was* a thermostat problem, and the test confirmed a fairly serious problem with the thermostat.

Frank: Exactly.

Patricia: Good. What did you do next?

Frank: Well, I tried to adjust the thermostat to see if that would fix the problem. But it didn't.

Patricia writes in her notebook:

Topic for future discussion: How do you adjust the thermostat?

Patricia: And then?

Frank: There was nothing left to do but replace the thermostat.

Patricia: Did that fix the problem?

Frank: Yes. I tested it to make sure. I had to make some minor adjustments after the new thermostat was installed, but that was definitely the problem.

Patricia writes in her notebook:

Topics for future discussion:
  Find out how to replace the thermostat and how to adjust a new ther-
    mostat.
  Is it always *necessary to adjust a thermostat after installing it?*

Patricia: When you fix a problem, do you always need to test the toaster?

Frank: Well, sure. That's how you know that you've really fixed the problem. Every time I try something, I have to test to see if the problem is fixed.
  In this case, I first tried to adjust the thermostat. Then I repeated the color test, but the toast still burned so I knew that I hadn't fixed the problem. After I replaced the thermostat, I did the color test again. The toast didn't burn, but it was a little bit light. This told me that the new thermostat was slightly out of adjustment. I made small adjustments and tried the color test again. This time the toast was done just right.

Patricia: Did you do anything else when you verified that you had fixed the problem?

Frank: Yes, the standard dumb stuff. I had to fill out a repair form with the part number of the replacement thermostat I used. And I had to fill out the billing form.

Patricia: This was a great example, Frank. I've got a much better feel for what you do.

Howard: Me too. That was very interesting.

Patricia: Frank, before we move on, I have one question about your general approach to problems like this.

Frank: Shoot.

Patricia: In this particular example, you saw a color problem, and you suspected the thermostat. Do you *always* suspect the thermostat when the toast is the wrong color?

Frank: Well, let me think. I guess that the thermostat is to blame for almost all color problems. Of course in this example, the toast *popped up* burnt. If I the toast had burned *without* popping up, I would have thought that some mechanical problem prevented the toast from popping up. The thermostat might have cut off at the right time, but the elements take a while to cool down. If the bread is stuck down *inside* the toaster while the elements are cooling, it will get more and more toasted until it burns.

Patricia: I see. And would you consider that a color problem, too?

Frank: Well, not really. I guess I have to *see* the toast before I say that I've got a color problem. If I could smell the toast burning, but it was stuck inside, I guess I'd know that the toast was black. But I don't think I would call it a color problem.

Patricia: So to sum up, if the toast pops up the wrong color, you classify that situation as a "color problem." And when you see a color problem, you immediately suspect the thermostat as the source of the problem.

Frank: Yes. That's right.

Patricia: Thanks. Why don't we take a ten-minute break now?

Discussion

This dialog illustrates the questions that Patricia Programmer uses to prompt Frank Fixit to describe how he repaired the toaster. It is equally important to notice what questions Patricia *does not ask*. Note that she does not interrupt Frank's discussion of the case to ask how the case might have been different. She wonders about other possible results for the color test, but she keeps her attention, and Frank's, focused on *this* particular case.

Frank mentions two procedures he performed: adjusting and replacing the thermostat. At some point in the development of the toaster-repair advisor, Patricia will probably need to understand how Frank performs these procedures. For the depth of understanding she needs during initial inquiry, however, she does not need to learn about the procedures.

Patricia may also have wondered what was wrong with the original thermostat and what problems can cause a thermostat to fail. Although these questions might appeal to her intellectual curiosity, she represses them because they are not relevant to *understanding how Frank performed the task.*

3.2.4 Develop a Standard Form for Case Descriptions

The expert's first case descriptions may not contain all the information you need. The lack of critical information in a case description will become apparent when the expert explains how to perform the task. The expert may get stuck because a particular decision depends on unavailable data. If this situation occurs, ask the expert to propose a plausible value for the missing data, then to proceed with the task as though that value had been recorded. The process of discussing a case will make it clear to the expert what information should be included in a case description.

After your first case discussion, take a little time to talk about the expert's written description of the case. If you found it helpful, let the expert know you did. If it was everything that you wanted, be sure to express your appreciation and to encourage the expert to provide similar details in future case descriptions. If the expert's written case description did not include all the details that you needed, revise the description to include additional information that the expert provided during the interview. Similarly, if the expert did not prepare a written case description, prepare one yourself after the interview. Give the expert your revised case description to use as a guide in the future.

After you have discussed a number of cases, you and the expert will both learn what information is needed in a complete case description. At that point, you should develop a standard form or outline the expert can use for case descriptions:

1. Refer to Table 3.2 to be sure you include all important information.

2. Identify the specific data, actions, and conclusions common to case descriptions in your application.

3. Create a form that lists these data, actions, and conclusions in an order that reflects the sequence of events during performance of the task.

Make the form as specific as possible but general enough to cover a variety of cases. In some applications, it will be possible to specify the exact data gathered in each case and the exact sequence of actions to be performed. In other applications, the expert will use different data in different cases and will perform different actions and make different conclusions based on these data. A case description in such an application might list the data common to all cases and leave space for additional data needed in a particular case. The form might include space in which the expert can describe the sequence of actions. Figure 3.1 illustrates the form that Patricia Programmer developed after several case discussions with Frank Fixit.

Once you have developed a standard form for case descriptions, you can ask other experts or intended users of the expert system to supply you with descriptions of additional cases. For example, Patricia Programmer or Frank Fixit could ask other members of the repair staff to fill out a case-description form whenever they encounter an unusual or difficult case.

3.3 Preparation for the First Interview

We have discussed the knowledge-acquisition activities that should be included in the first interview with the project expert. Now we turn our attention to preparation for this interview. Careful preparation can improve the productivity of the interview and can reduce the anxiety of both knowledge engineers and expert.

Because the first interview is likely to be stressful, try to keep the meeting short. For example, plan the following interview activities:

- Brief introduction of the goals of the meeting
- Expert's overview of the task
- Short break
- Case discussion
- Short break
- Brief summary of the meeting
- Brief discussion of plans for the next interview

Before the interview itself, make sure that the expert knows what to expect and that the knowledge engineers are prepared for the interview.

3.3.1 Prepare the Expert

A successful expert-system project requires active participation by the project expert. Encourage active participation by explaining the expert's role in the project, in the knowledge-acquisition process, and in the interview being planned. Table 3.3 summarizes the steps that you should take to prepare your project expert.

If the project schedule permits, start preparing the expert for the

Figure 3.1 Case description form. Patricia Programmer created this form for Frank Fixit to use when he writes descriptions of toaster-repair cases. After several case discussions, Patricia learned that Frank may perform several repair procedures for a given toaster. After each repair, Frank tests the toaster; the test results indicate whether the repair fixed the test. Different toasters require different numbers of repair procedures. Patricia's form provides room for Frank to record details about four repair procedures.

Case prepared by: Date:

Notes:

Data
  Type of toaster:
  Customer complaint:

Action
  Test procedure:

Conclusion
  Toaster problem:

Action
  Repair procedure:
  Test procedure:

Data
  Result of test:

Action
  Repair procedure:
  Test procedure:

Data
  Result of test:

Action
  Repair procedure:
  Test procedure:

Data
  Result of test:

Action
  Repair procedure:
  Test procedure:

Data
  Result of test:

Table 3.3 Preparing an Expert for the First Interview

Objective	Activities
Orient the expert to the project.	If you have not already met the expert in earlier project meetings, introduce yourself to the expert. Tell the expert a little bit about yourself and your role in the project. If other knowledge engineers will participate in the project, introduce them by name.
	If the expert did not participate in defining the expert system, explain briefly the aims of the project. Give the expert a copy of the document* that describes the expert system definition. Ask the expert to read this before the meeting, and offer to answer any questions the document may raise.
Introduce the knowledge-acquisition process.	Explain that you will be scheduling a series of interviews with the expert.
	Let the expert know what you want to accomplish. Tell the expert that your initial goal will be to obtain a very general understanding to prepare you to develop the expert system. After that, you will try to learn the details of what the expert does.
	Reassure the expert that, although the process may seem unfamiliar at first, there is no need for apprehension. You will do all you can to make interaction easy. After the first few interviews, the expert will know what to expect and will feel more comfortable with the process.
	Let the expert know that he or she is an important part of the development team, and that you look forward to having the opportunity to work together.
Prepare the expert to participate in the first interview.	Give the expert a copy of the agenda for the first interview.
	Explain each of the activities you have planned.
	Make sure the expert understands what role he or she is to play. If possible, provide examples that will make clear what the expert needs to do.

*The document of an expert system's definition is described in Section 2.7.

first interview a minimum of two weeks before the meeting itself. We have found a four-step process to be most effective in ensuring that the expert is adequately prepared for the first interview.

1. In your *initial conversation* with the expert, make sure that the expert is familiar with the project. Tell the expert what to expect from the first interview and how to prepare for it.

2. Next, *collect or create examples* that illustrate how the expert can prepare for the meeting.

3. A few days after the initial conversation, send a *follow-up letter* (or memo) as a written reminder. Along with the letter, send a copy of the agenda for the meeting and the examples collected in step 2.

4. Finally, about a week after sending the follow-up letter, make a *confirmation telephone call* to verify that the expert received and understood the material you sent. In this conversation, you can provide final details about the meeting.

The proximity of the expert's workplace to your own will affect the formality of your communication with the expert. If you both work in the same building, you might walk to the expert's office for the initial conversation and send a follow-up memo through interoffice mail or deliver it in person. On the other hand, if the expert works in a different state, you will need to conduct your initial conversation over the telephone and send a follow-up letter by mail.

Initial Conversation

Refer to Table 3.3 to be sure you cover all the necessary topics in your initial conversation. The amount of information you need to provide will depend on the extent to which you and the expert were involved in earlier project meetings.

Dialog 3.2 illustrates Patricia Programmer's initial conversation with Frank Fixit. Because they both participated in defining the expert system, Patricia concentrated on plans for the interview itself.

Dialog 3.2 Preparing the Expert for the First Interview

Setting

Patricia Programmer last saw Frank Fixit at the meeting in which the definition of the toaster-repair advisor was finalized.[2] At the end of that meeting, Patricia scheduled her first interview with Frank. At that time, Patricia told Frank that she would call him later with more information about the meeting.

Dialog

The telephone rings. Frank answers it.

Frank: Service department. Frank Fixit speaking.

---

2. The meeting to finalize the definition of the toaster-repair advisor is described in Section 2.7.

Patricia: Hello Frank, this is Patricia Programmer. I'd like to tell you a little about the meeting on the fifteenth.

Frank: Good. I guess it's not going to be like the group discussions we've had so far?

Patricia: You're right. This meeting, and the ones that follow, will be different. Howard Hacker and I will be at these meetings with you. Do you remember Howard?

Frank: Sure.

Patricia: Good. Howard and I are going to try to learn enough about how you repair toasters so that we can capture your expertise in the computer system. Before the meeting on the fifteenth, Howard and I would like to learn some of the basic terminology and concepts that will enable us to understand your descriptions. Can you recommend any manuals or training materials that would help us?

Frank: Well, I don't know. There really isn't much. The department has a training pamphlet that all new staff members are supposed to read. It describes the basics of how a toaster works, and it might get you familiar with the structure of toasters. It really doesn't help much with repairing toasters; I never use it.

Patricia: That sounds like a good place for Howard and me to start. Could you send me a copy through interoffice mail?

Frank: Sure thing.

Patricia: Thanks. Does the service department have any introductory videotapes, or training classes for new members of the repair staff?

Frank: No. Most of our people have had some training before they start to work here.

Patricia: OK. Howard and I will rely on the pamphlet for our training. In the meeting on the fifteenth, we would like to learn a little about what you do as a consultant to the repair staff.

Frank: Well, I'm not sure how much there is to tell you about that.

Patricia: We'd like you to describe, in general terms, how you help the staff repair toasters. We're particularly interested in learning what you think are the most difficult and the most important parts of the repair process. We'd also like your opinions about why the repair staff needs your help.

Frank: I guess I can prepare something for you.

Patricia: Great. We don't expect a formal presentation—unless you've already given a talk on these topics and have presentation material prepared. Just plan to give us a quick overview; it should only take you 15 to 30 minutes.

Frank: OK, that should be easy.

Patricia: You can assume that all Howard and I will know about toasters is what we'll learn by reading the training pamphlet. If you think there's additional background material that we'll need to know, you should plan to start your talk with that material.

Frank: I'll try to think of everything I need to tell you.

Patricia: Thanks. But don't spend much time planning what to tell us. If we find that we don't know enough to follow you, we'll let you know and ask you to explain whatever we need to know.

Frank: Thanks, I was a little worried that I might forget something.

Patricia: After your overview, we would like you to tell us about an actual situation in which you had to help repair a toaster in the recent past. That will give us a concrete example of the process that you go through.

Frank: Fine. I had to help Dick with a problem last week. I could tell you about that. What are you going to need to know?

Patricia: Well, it would be nice to know the entire story. What did Dick say when he brought you the toaster? Where did you start? How did you figure out what was wrong? How did you know how to fix the problem? We'd like you to give us a step-by-step description of what you did and what you thought while you were helping Dick repair the toaster.

Frank: OK. I guess I can do that.

Patricia: It would help us if you could write a description of this problem for us to review before the meeting. At the meeting, we can use the description to follow along while you tell us about the problem. If you like, I would be happy to send you an example that shows how another expert described one of his experiences.

Frank: That would be nice. I have some notes on several recent problems, but I don't think anyone else could understand them. It would be good to see what sort of things you want me to put in the description.

Patricia: I'll send you an example. Also, I'd like you to bring anything to the meeting that will make it easier for you to explain how you repair toasters and to describe the toaster you helped Dick repair. Can you think of manuals or charts you might like to show us?

Frank: Yes. I can bring some toaster schematics and some service bulletins. I guess the easiest thing would be to have a toaster so I can *show* you.

Patricia: Can you bring a toaster to the meeting with you and whatever tools you will need to show us what you did?

Frank: Sure. I've got some old models we use when we train new people. I'll bring one of those.

Patricia: Great. And please bring the schematics and service bulletins if you think you'd like to refer to them.

Frank: Will do.

Patricia: Frank, I want to thank you very much for being willing to help us with this project. Howard and I are excited about the project, and we look forward to being able to work with you. If you have any questions between now and the fifteenth, please feel free to call me.

Frank: OK. Thanks for all the information. Bye.

Patricia: Goodbye, Frank.

Examples for the Expert

After your initial conversation, gather examples to illustrate how the expert can prepare for the interview.

- In your initial conversation, you should have described the content you expected in a task overview. As a reminder, prepare an outline of the topics the expert should include in the overview.

- Provide an example of a case description. This will guide the expert on what to include in the description of the case you will discuss at the meeting. If possible, select an example case from a similar application. For instance, the toaster-repair advisor will diagnose problems in an electrical appliance and recommend an appropriate repair. Patricia Programmer selected an example from a similar application: an expert system to diagnose and repair problems in television sets. Figure 3.2 shows the case description that Patricia sent to Frank Fixit. The case in this example is very simple; however, it shows the kind of information that Frank should include in a case description.

Follow-up Letter

Send the expert a short letter (or memo) that reviews the initial conversation; this letter can help to ensure that the expert prepares for the meeting. The letter acts as a reminder of items the expert should send you or bring to the meeting. The letter need not be a formal reminder; instead it can be a cover letter for your agenda and examples. Figure 3.3 shows Patricia Programmer's follow-up memo to Frank Fixit.

Confirmation Telephone Call

After you send your follow-up letter, allow about a week for the expert to receive and read the letter. Then telephone to confirm that the expert has received the letter. Ask whether the expert has any questions on the materials you sent. Make sure the expert knows the time and place for the meeting.

If you have received materials from the expert to help prepare yourself for the meeting, express your thanks. Ask any simple questions you may have on these materials. Limit your questions to clarifications that will allow you to understand the materials; save more detailed questions for the interview. If you have not yet received materials you expected, ask whether the expert has encountered difficulty in securing them.

3.3.2 Prepare the Knowledge Engineers

In addition to preparing the expert for the first interview, you should prepare yourself and your fellow knowledge engineers. Before the first

Figure 3.2 Example of a case description. Patricia Programmer sends Frank Fixit this case description to illustrate how he should describe cases. Notice that the case description includes the data the expert used, the actions the expert performed, and the conclusions the expert made. The description also indicates the chronological sequence in which events occurred.

GRIMBLE TV—BROUGHT IN MARCH 23

Notes:
This case is an easy one that shows how simple it is to identify problems that occur with the oscillator tubes. For other cases, we have to gather much more data. In more difficult cases, replacement of a tube might not fix the problem.

Customer Complaint:
No picture.

Action Taken:
Turn on TV to observe screen and listen to sound

Data Collected:
Audio is fine
Picture is reduced to a horizontal line

Conclusions:
Power supply is functional
Audio circuitry and audio tubes are OK
Problem is probably in the vertical oscillator

Actions Taken:
Replace vertical oscillator tube
Turn on TV to observe screen

Data Collected:
Picture is normal now
Audio is still fine

Conclusions:
Replacing the vertical oscillator tube fixed the problem; the vertical oscillator tube must have been bad.

---

interview, all knowledge engineers on the project should be familiar with:

- The plans for the project
- The standard terminology of the application subject area
- The agenda for the interview
- Basic knowledge-engineering methodology
- The roles they will play in the interview

Project Plans

Before the first interview, make sure that all knowledge engineers have read the document that presents the definition of the expert system.[3] If additional proposals or reports about the project exist, try to obtain

---

Figure 3.3 Follow-up memo to prepare the expert for the first interview. Patricia Programmer sent this memo to Frank Fixit to review their initial telephone conversation and to remind him what preparations he should make for the interview.

To: Frank Fixit
From: Patricia Programmer
Date: June 1, 1990
Subject: Plans for our meeting on June 15, 1990

Attached is the agenda for our meeting on June 15. The first item on the agenda is your overview of toaster repair. As we discussed on the telephone, your overview should cover:

- How you help the repair staff repair toasters
- What aspects of toaster repair you consider most difficult
- What aspects you consider most important
- Why the repair staff needs your help

Please bring a toaster to the meeting and any schematics and service bulletins that would be helpful for your overview.

    The second item on the agenda is for you to describe how you repaired a toaster recently. I have enclosed an example of a case description to show how another expert presented a specific problem he had solved. This example is from an expert who repairs television sets; it explains how he repaired a problem in an old-fashioned vacuum-tube television set. Notice that the description includes:

- The information the expert used to solve the problem
- The actions he took during the process
- The conclusions he made along the way
- The time sequence in which events occurred

    If you could prepare a similar description of a toaster problem for our meeting on the fifteenth, we would greatly appreciate it. We urge you not to spend more than an hour

---

3. The document of an expert system's definition is described in Section 2.7.

Figure 3.3 (continued)

preparing the description. If you complete your description before the meeting, please send it to me through interoffice mail. I can get copies for Howard and myself before the meeting. If you are not able to complete the description before the meeting, just bring it with you to the meeting.

   If you have any questions about the content of your overview talk or about the enclosed example, please call me at extension 7153.

   Howard and I are preparing for the meeting. We are both looking forward to reading the pamphlet about toasters that you will send us. Thank you for helping us to prepare. I look forward to seeing you on the fifteenth.

---

copies of these reports, and also have the knowledge engineers review these reports.

   If you were not involved in meetings to define the expert system,[4] speak to the knowledge engineers or managers who did participate in those meetings. They may be able to tell you about the politics within the organization that will use the expert system. Try to understand the nature of the relationships among the experts, the intended users of the system, and the funding organization. Try to learn whether any areas of sensitivity, or any organizational problems, became apparent during the early project meetings. If you are aware of the political issues surrounding the project, you can avoid asking the expert embarrassing questions during interviews.

Terminology of the Application Area

Try to obtain and read introductory textbooks or training manuals that define the basic terms used in the application subject area. Ask the project expert to suggest documents you can read. Find out whether any video tapes exist that provide an overview of the application area. If so, arrange to watch the tapes before the first interview.

   As you read the preparatory materials, look for definitions of the terminology and the concepts that your expert is likely to use. Your objective is to *prepare yourself to understand the expert.* Try to avoid reading too much about how to perform the task; you will learn about the task from the expert during the interviews. If you go into the interviews with a strong model of how the task should be performed, this model may bias your interpretation of what the expert has to tell you. Instead of listening to learn how *the expert* performs the task, you

---

4.   The meetings to define an expert system are described in Chapter 2.

may be inclined to listen for confirmation that *your* model is the correct approach to the task.

Interview Agenda

Ask all interview participants to review the planned agenda before the meeting. If the expert has prepared a description of a case to be discussed in the interview, ask all the knowledge engineers to review the case description before the interview.

If the agenda includes a task overview, be prepared to lead a discussion if the expert does not feel comfortable giving an overview. Make a list of the questions you want to have answered either by the expert's overview or by a discussion of the task. If you are new at leading interviews, review the guidelines for asking questions that are presented in Chapter 16.

Knowledge-Engineering Methodology

If your project contains any first-time knowledge engineers, make sure they understand what an expert system is and how expert systems are built. They should be familiar with the material presented in Chapters 1, 2, and 3 of this book.

Roles in the Interview

All knowledge engineers who attend the interview should understand the roles they will play in the interview and the importance of building and maintaining a good working relationship with the project expert (Chapters 12 through 15). The knowledge engineer who will lead the interview should also be familiar with the techniques for conducting a productive interview (Chapters 16 and 17).

3.4 Common Problems

The first few interviews for an expert-system project often provide a knowledge engineer's initial exposure to the application subject area. During the first few interviews, a huge amount of new information pours forth from the expert. The knowledge engineers do not know enough about the area to judge what is important and what is not. Two problems are common in early interviews. First, the knowledge engineers may become overwhelmed by the quantity of information the expert provides. Second, the knowledge engineers may focus their attention on details that are not relevant to the performance of the task.

3.4.1 Information Overload

One of the most common feelings that knowledge engineers experience in their initial interviews with an expert is information overload: They feel overwhelmed by the quantity of information they need to learn. They feel deluged by the new terms, concepts, and processes that arrive more quickly than the knowledge engineers can fully assimilate. As you conduct your first few interviews, be on the lookout for this feeling in yourself and in your fellow knowledge engineers. When you feel overwhelmed, you probably will have difficulty absorbing what the expert tells you. Rather than waste the expert's time, you should take a break or end the interview.

Try to control the rate at which you encounter new concepts by keeping the expert's explanations focused at a fairly general level. At this stage of knowledge acquisition, you do not need to know minute details. You are unlikely to understand these details, and you are liable to be overwhelmed by them. If the expert's description of a process or a piece of equipment is too complex for you to follow, ask the expert to give a high-level overview, to create an outline, or to draw a diagram that will show you the big picture. With the expert's help, identify the major pieces of the process or equipment. Then ask the expert to describe the pieces one at a time.

Above all, when you feel overwhelmed, recognize this feeling as *normal and expected*. Do not let this feeling make you doubt your ability to complete the project. Do not worry that the material is too complicated for you to understand. If you control the pace of the interviews, the information you hear will all make sense eventually. After you have participated in a number of expert-systems projects, you will probably become tired by early interviews rather than overwhelmed; your experience will have taught you to dismiss the feelings of anxiety you felt in your first project. When you reach this stage, be sensitive to your less experienced team mates. Reassure new knowledge engineers on your project when you notice that they have experienced information overload.

3.4.2 Focus on Irrelevant Details

Inexperienced knowledge engineers have a tendency to focus on details at a level so low that they are not relevant to the expert's performance of the task. Most experts do not need to take the time to reason from first principles. Instead, they recognize familiar patterns in the data and relate these patterns to solutions they have learned through experience. For example, Frank Fixit knows a great deal about electricity and the physical properties of metals. When he first learned to repair toasters, he studied the physical principles that govern toaster operation. When Frank fixes a toaster, however, he does not think about the principles of electricity or the mechanics by which the toaster functions. Frank's experience has taught him to recognize toaster problems and to associate these problems directly with known solutions. When Patricia Programmer interviews Frank Fixit, she will ask questions that allow her to understand how Frank repairs toasters. She will not waste Frank's valuable time by asking him to tutor her in the underlying principles he learned years ago.

As you first start to learn about the expert's subject area, be aware of the tendency to delve into unnecessary details. Be particularly careful when your reaction to an explanation is, "Hmm, that's interesting. I wonder why. . . ." If you would like to learn more details, stop and ask yourself whether you *need* the details in order to understand how the expert performs the task or whether you are simply curious. *Only ask questions that will help your understanding of how the expert performs the task.* You should also pay attention to the level of detail the expert volunteers. Sometimes an expert who is uncertain of what you want to know will describe everything in great depth. Give your expert direction. State clearly what you want to learn, and keep the expert focused on information that will help you to develop the expert system.[5]

3.5 Points to Remember

The first few interviews can be very trying for both the expert and the knowledge engineers. Careful preparation can help to control the anxiety of the entire project team. Follow these steps to prepare for your first interview.

- Make sure that all participants understand the goals of the project, the goals of the interview, and the agenda for the interview.

- Try to learn the basic terminology of the application area to improve your understanding of the expert's descriptions.

- Provide the expert with advice about, and examples of, the materials that he or she should prepare for the interview.

- Anticipate the possibility that the expert may not prepare the necessary materials. Make a list of question to ask during a discussion to obtain an overview of the task. Be prepared to prompt the expert to recall a recent example of performing the task, or to propose an hypothetical example.

---

5. In Chapter 17, we shall discuss techniques that will help you keep the expert focused on topics that are of interest to you.

Table 3.4 Guidelines for Case Discussions during Initial Inquiry

Do	Don't
Focus on the process of performing the task.	Delve into unnecessary details.
Try to identify the steps the expert took, the reasoning the expert performed in each step, and the information the expert used in each step.	Ask what else *might have* happened in a step.
	Ask questions that indulge your curiosity but are not relevant to the current case.
Keep yourself and the expert focused on the case under discussion.	Ask questions that might disrupt the expert's train of thought.
Ask only questions that are relevant to understanding how the expert performs the task.	Proceed to the development phase until you understand the range of situations the expert system will need to handle.
Ask for clarification if you cannot follow the expert's description.	
Record ideas to pursue in this interview after the expert has finished discussing the case. These ideas should be pertinent to the case under discussion and to the goals of initial inquiry.	
Record additional topics to discuss later in the project.	
Discuss five to ten cases that illustrate a variety of situations, ranging from simple to difficult and from commonplace to out of the ordinary.	

Two activities can help you to obtain a general understanding of the expert system's task:

1. A task overview in which the expert presents a summary of the process by which the task is performed and identifies the important and the difficult aspects of this process

2. Case discussions (Table 3.4), which illustrate how the expert would perform the task in particular situations

Two problems are common among knowledge engineers who are trying to obtain a general understanding of a task. First, the knowledge engineers may become overwhelmed at the amount of information the task involves. Second, the knowledge engineers may lose their focus on the task and delve into unnecessary details. Table 3.5 provides guidelines for avoiding these problems, and for dealing with them when they occur.

Table 3.5 Common Problems in Obtaining a General Understanding of a Task

Problem	Solution
Information overload	Do not continue an interview when you feel overwhelmed or when you are too tired to absorb new information. Take breaks when you need them.
	Recognize that it is normal to feel overwhelmed by a new area. Do not let this feeling scare or discourage you.
	Keep discussions at a fairly general level so that you do not become submerged in unnecessary detail.
	Understand the overall structure of a process or piece of equipment before discussing it in any detail.
Focus on irrelevant details	Focus on the task the expert performs.
	Do not ask questions out of curiosity.
	Make sure the expert understands what information you need to obtain.

Chapter 4

Dividing the Functionality of the Expert System

Patricia Programmer and Howard Hacker have obtained a general overview of the task of toaster repair. Howard is overwhelmed at the amount he has learned. He tells Patricia, "There are so many different toasters and so many different problems that, whenever I think about how I would implement the system, I get lost in all the variations we will have to consider. I'd like to begin, but I can't tell where we should start." As Patricia explains, their overview has just provided the background that will enable them to accomplish the final goal of initial inquiry: to divide the system's coverage for incremental development.

In order for the detailed investigation stage of knowledge acquisition to be productive, the project team must be able to focus on a reasonably circumscribed problem. Both the knowledge engineers and the expert are likely to become bogged down in details and overwhelmed by the complexity of a task that is too large. The final goal of initial inquiry, therefore, is to understand how the full scope of the expert system can be divided. When the knowledge engineers have accomplished this goal, they will be ready to enter the development phase of the project. The division of scope for incremental development is a necessary step in planning the expert system project. Project planning itself lies outside the extent of this book; in this chapter we focus on the knowledge-acquisition activities that are an integral part of the planning process.

Dividing the functionality of an expert system is a three-step process; each of these steps presents a particular knowledge-acquisition challenge. First, knowledge engineers must *identify possible classifications* of functionality that are meaningful to the expert (Section 4.1). Most experts do not consciously categorize problems or subdivide the task they perform; most experts, however, do subconsciously structure or organize the problem space in some manner. The challenge for the knowledge engineer is to obtain an unbiased understanding of the expert's organization of the relevant knowledge. A knowledge engineer who imposes a classification that is incongruent with the expert's own organization is almost certain to run into difficulties throughout the detailed investigation stage of knowledge acquisition.

The knowledge engineers' second step is to *assess the relative size, difficulty, and importance of the categories within each functional classification* (Section 4.2). The knowledge engineers' challenges are to understand how to measure the vague quantities of size, difficulty, and importance and to lead the expert to articulate relevant measures for these quantities.

In the final step, members of the project team review the different classifications they identified and *decide which of these classifications they will use to divide the functionality of the expert system*. The chosen classifications will partition the system's functionality into increments that can be added in separate cycles of development. The knowledge engineers plan the incremental development of the system by ordering and scheduling the addition of each increment of functionality (Section 4.3). The challenge at this step is for the knowledge engineers to create a plan from the inexact information they obtained in the two previous steps.

4.1 Identifying Possible Classification

The first step toward dividing the scope of an expert system is to identify different ways in which the total functionality of the expert system could be divided.[1] To identify possible classifications, consider limiting:

---

1. As we discussed in Chapter 2, many expert-system projects include both a *knowledge-engineering* component, and a *software-engineering* component. In this chapter, we discuss only the knowledge-engineering component of the project. Many project teams also plan for the incremental development of the system's user interface and for incremental integration of the system with its operating environment.

- The *functions* the system will be able to perform (Section 4.1.1)
- The *inputs* to which the system will be able to respond (Section 4.1.2)
- The *results* the system will be able to produce (Section 4.1.3)

As you examine each of these three dimensions, first try to learn how the expert system's coverage *might be* divided. Then identify the classifications that seem the *most natural* to the expert.

4.1.1 Identifying Subtasks

You may be able to divide the expert system's task into a number of steps, or *subtasks,* and implement the different subtasks in different cycles of development. First, *identify the major functions that the system will perform.* Often the definition of a task will specify distinct functions. For example, the diagram in Figure 2.4 lists five functions for the toaster-repair advisor. If your task definition did not explicitly identify discrete functions, try to partition the major outputs of the expert system. Define the system's complete task as the process of generating all of the outputs the system will produce. This definition will allow you to view the generation of each different output as a *single subtask.* For example, the toaster-repair advisor will produce the following outputs:[2]

- The cause of the toaster malfunction
- The appropriate repair for the toaster
- Updated inventory information for the toaster-part database
- Billing information used in printing customer bills
- Descriptions of test procedures and repair procedures

Note that these outputs correspond to the five functions shown in Figure 2.4.

When you have identified the functions your system will perform, review these functions with the expert. *Decide which functions are essential for initial deployment* and which are optional. Each optional function may be a single independent step. *Look for interdependence between the functions.* If one function cannot be performed without another, the two functions may not represent separate subtasks.

---

2.   Figure 2.5 illustrates outputs that the toaster-repair advisor will produce.

Patricia Programmer and Frank Fixit meet to discuss the functions of the toaster-repair advisor. Frank explains that he does not consider finding the cause of a toaster malfunction and deciding the appropriate repair to be two independent steps. The minimum functionality for the expert system would be to determine *both* cause and repair. Frank adds that the remaining functions can be viewed as extras. Patricia and Frank identify four distinct subtasks for the toaster-repair advisor.

1. Find and repair a toaster malfunction.

2. Update the inventory fields of the toaster-part database.

3. Generate a bill for the customer.

4. Describe a test procedure or a repair procedure.

The first subtask is the main focus of the toaster-repair advisor; the other tasks are auxiliary (although crucial to the ultimate success of the system).

4.1.2 Classifying Cases by Inputs

A case or situation in which a task is performed is defined by the input data to the task. If you can classify cases into *input categories*, you can limit the kinds of case for which the expert system could perform its task—that is, you can limit the inputs to which the system can respond. With each cycle of development, you can add the ability to respond to additional input categories.

After you have identified subtasks, try to understand how the expert classifies different situations in which each subtask can be performed. Although many experts do not consciously think in terms of classifying situations, they often subconsciously compare a new situation against their past experience and look for familiar patterns (input categories). They map a vast number of potential situations to a relatively small number of common patterns. The patterns dictate how the expert will perform the task. The expert's ability to relate a new situation to a known pattern and to select a general problem-solving strategy on the basis of the pattern is often what allows the expert to outperform novices.

To identify input categories, see how the expert would classify different combinations of input data. First, list the major inputs to each subtask. For example, Table 4.1 illustrates the inputs for each subtask of the toaster-repair advisor. Consider each subtask in turn. *Try to learn which combination of inputs to the subtask represent different patterns to the expert.*

Patricia Programmer needs to learn whether different toaster makes and models suggest different problem-solving categories to Frank Fixit. Patricia and Frank meet to discuss how they might classify toaster-repair situations. They focus on the main subtask. In other words, Patricia tries to learn whether it would be possible to limit the range of

Table 4.1 Inputs for the Toaster-Repair Advisor

Subtask	Inputs
Find and repair the toaster malfunction.	Toaster make and model Description of current toaster operation
Update inventory fields for the toaster-part database.	Description of repair (generated by expert system or entered by user)
Produce a customer bill.	Description of repair (generated by expert system or entered by user)
Describe test or repair procedure.	Test or repair procedure for which user requested a description

toaster makes and models that the expert system would "know" how to repair. She tries to find out whether she could limit the kinds of toaster operation for which the system would be able to give advice. In more complex applications, it is necessary to classify situations in which each subtask can be performed. In the toaster-repair advisor, however, the inputs to the auxiliary subtasks can be divided naturally on the basis of limitations to the main task. For example, when the system is able to repair only two toaster models, it could be limited to providing descriptions of only the test procedures and repair procedures that are relevant to the repair of those two models. Similarly, the system could include the capability of updating the toaster-part database and of generating bills for only those repairs that are relevant to the two toaster models.

To learn how the expert classifies inputs to the expert system, *ask the expert to group descriptions of the cases* you have discussed in earlier interview sessions. Write a brief description of the input data for each case on a separate index card (Figure 4.1).

Ask the expert to sort the index cards into groups of similar situations. Do not influence the expert's choice of grouping—the purpose of the exercise is to *learn whether the expert categorizes the cases* in a specific way and if so what characteristics of the case determine the categories. If the expert has difficulty with this exercise, try to specify what you would like to accomplish without biasing the expert's choice of categories. Dialog 4.1 illustrates how Patricia Programmer asked Frank Fixit to sort the cards shown in Figure 4.1.

Dialog 4.1 Learning How the Expert Classifies Cases

Setting

Patricia Programmer, Howard Hacker, and Frank Fixit are seated at a table. Patricia holds the stack of index cards that contain descriptions

Figure 4.1 Index cards with case descriptions. Patricia Programmer fills in an index card for each case that Frank Fixit described in earlier knowledge-acquisition sessions. Patricia assigns each case a unique reference number. Each index card contains the identifying number of a case and a brief description of the input data for that case.

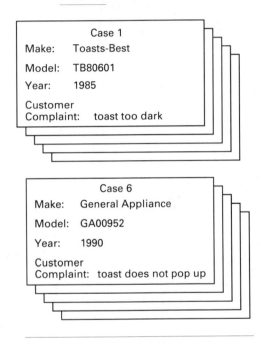

of case inputs. Patricia has explained that she and Howard will use an incremental approach to the development of the toaster-repair advisor and that she would like Frank to help her understand how they might subdivide the full coverage of the system.

Dialog

Patricia puts the stack of cards on the table in front of Frank.

Patricia: Today we're going to try something a little different. These cards contain descriptions of the cases we have discussed in the last couple of weeks. I'd like you to read through these cards and then sort them into groups of cases you consider similar.

Frank (*sounding a little unsure of himself*): OK.

> *Frank flips through the cards, reading each one. Then he lays all the cards face up on the table in front of him. He studies the cards for a while, then looks up at Patricia.*

I'm sorry, but I don't really know what I'm supposed to do next.

Patricia: Don't worry; most people find this exercise a bit puzzling at first. I'm trying to understand whether you view some of these cases as similar to one another other, but different from the other cases. It may turn out that the cases simply *can't* be sorted into groups that are meaningful to you. They all may be too much alike. Or they may be so different that each one is in a class by itself. If we *can* identify groups that are meaningful to you, however, we might be able to organize the development of the expert system around those groups.

Think of Howard as your new apprentice. You want to teach him to repair all these particular toasters. Would you organize the toasters in any way as you showed Howard how to repair them?

Frank: I think I see what you're getting at. Let me think.

> *Frank studies the cards on the table. Slowly and hesitantly, he starts moving the cards around. After a while, he rearranges the cards more confidently. When he has finished, the cards are in two groups.*

There!

Patricia: Great! Now, can you tell us what makes the two groups different?

Frank (*pointing to the first group of cards*): These are two-slice toasters. I want Howard to start with these toasters because they are the simplest. The others are four-slice toasters. We'll get to those after Howard learns about the simple toasters.

Howard: Give me a screwdriver—I'm ready to begin!

> *Patricia, Howard, and Frank all laugh.*

Patricia: I have one quick question. The cards don't say whether the toasters are two- or four-slice varieties. Did you know the style from the model numbers?

Frank (*chuckling*): Yes, but I cheated, too! These are all toasters that we talked about recently so I remembered them—I *knew* which were two-slice toasters. I do recognize the most common model numbers, but for a lot of the models, I would have to look up the model number to find out what the style is.

Patricia: But in general, if you know the model number, you can find out whether it is a two- or four-slice toaster.

> *Frank nods.*

And this division of cases according to two-slice versus four-slice seems natural to you?

Frank: Yes. I never really thought about it before, but that's probably the first thing I notice when I look at a toaster.

Patricia: Thanks.

Patricia picks up the cards for the four-slice toasters. She stacks them and puts them to one side. She leaves the other cards on the table in front of Frank.

You did so well that I'd like you to do the same thing again. I've left you with the two-slice toasters. Can you group those for me?

Frank looks at the cards for a short time then starts to rearrange them. As he does so, he begins to speak.

Frank: Now that I know what I'm doing, it's a lot easier. OK. I'm done.

Patricia examines the groups of cards.

Patricia: It looks as though you have grouped the cards by customer complaint, but some groups contain more than one complaint. Can you explain why you've organized the cards as you have?

Frank: You're right that I was thinking about the customer's complaint. When I put more than one complaint together, it's because I go about fixing those toasters in the same way. For example, I put *toast always burns* in with *toast too light*. Those are both color problems, and I'd repair them in same way.

Patricia: This is interesting. It seems that each group represents a *category* of customer complaint.

Frank: Sure. You could call it a category.

Patricia: Does this grouping seem natural?

Frank: Yes. The customer's complaint tells me where to begin. So if I were teaching Howard, I might first show him how to fix the toasters that burn the toast. By the time we'd gone through those toasters, I would bet Howard could also fix a toaster that toasts too light. Then we could move on to the toasters where the toast won't pop up—I call those "no-trip" problems. Then we could talk about toasters where the bread won't stay down—"no-latch" problems, and so on.

Patricia: Good. Can you do this again? Pick the group with the most toasters and sort those cards?

Frank studies the cards

Frank: Well, I suppose I could group them by make. There are a lot of minor differences between the toasters, depending on the make.

Patricia: I'm not sure I know what you mean by *the make.*

Frank: The manufacturer.

Patricia: Thanks. You sounded a bit hesitant about this grouping. Do you think the division by *toaster make* would be useful?

Frank: I don't really think in those terms. When I get down to the detailed procedure for fixing a line switch, say, I need to know whether I'm working on a General Appliance toaster or a CrustMaster. But the differences are very small.

Patricia: All right. It sounds to me as though it would be artificial for us to divide toasters by *make* or to try to subdivide the groups of cards any further.

Frank nods.

So we're finished with this exercise. Thanks, Frank. You've helped us a lot.

Frank: You're welcome. I can't wait to tell Barbara and Margaret that you had me playing card games today!

Discussion

In this dialog, Patricia Programmer learns that Frank Fixit classifies toaster-repair cases by the *toaster style* and the *complaint category;* she identifies several input categories within each of these two classification (Figure 4.2).

Notice that the interactions between Frank and the knowledge engineers is a little less formal than the interactions that we saw in earlier dialogs. After several interviews, the team members now feel comfortable joking with one another.

If your expert is not able to group the index cards, try to group them yourself, then ask the expert to comment on your grouping. Sort the cards according the the input datum that appeared most important when you discussed the cases. As you investigate the expert's reaction to your grouping, you may discover how the expert categorizes cases.

Dialog 4.2 is an alternative to Dialog 4.1; this time, Frank Fixit is not able to group the cards. Patricia Programmer groups the cards herself and asks for Frank's opinion of her organization.

Dialog 4.2 Proposing Possible Categories for Cases

Setting

Patricia Programmer has asked Frank Fixit to group the index cards with descriptions of case inputs. Although she has tried several ways of explaining what she would like Frank to do, he is at a loss. He has not been able to group the cards.

Patricia Programmer, Howard Hacker, and Frank Fixit are all seated at a table. The index cards are spread face up on the table in front of Frank.

Dialog

Patricia: Let me try a different approach. I'll group the cards, and you can tell me what you think of the grouping.

Frank *(relieved):* OK.

Patricia reaches for the cards and rearranges them into groups. Each group has the same customer complaint.

Figure 4.2 Input categories for the toaster-repair advisor. Patricia Programmer learned that Frank Fixit classifies toaster-repair situations by *toaster style* and *complaint category*. She identifies input categories within each of these two classifications.

Input			Input Category	
Toaster Make	Toaster Model	Customer Complaint	Toaster Style	Complaint Category
Toasts-Best	TB80601	Toast always burns	Simple two-slice	Color problem
General Appliance	GA01313	Operating lever will not stay down	Simple two-slice	No-latch problem
General Appliance	GA70098	Toast too light	Two-slice with bakery switch	Color problem
Crust Master	CM99071	Operating lever will not go down	Four-slice	No-latch problem
Crust Master	CM81114	Toasts on one side only	Simple two-slice	Heating-element problem
General Appliance	GA00952	Toast does not pop up	Four-slice	No-trip problem
Toasts-Best	TB71222	Toast too dark	Under-cabinet	Color problem
Toasts-Best	TB54545	Toast does not pop up	Four-slice	No-trip problem

Patricia: Now, Frank, would you please look at these groups and let me know if the cases in each group seems similar to you.

Frank: I can see what you've done. All the *toast always burns* cases are together, and all the *toast does not pop up* cases are together.

Patricia: How does this grouping seem to you?

Frank: Well, it's not bad. I'm thinking about the cases we talked about. Some of your groups are exactly right, but others just don't feel right.

Patricia: Pick a group that doesn't feel right.

Frank points to the group of cards with the complaint "toasts on one side only."

What don't you like about this group?

Frank: The problem is that you've lumped two- and four-slice toasters together.

Patricia: I see. Does the model number tell you whether the toaster is a two- or four-slice variety?

Frank: Yes. I remember these toasters so I knew which was which. In general, I'd have to look up the model number.

Patricia: It seems to me that you might group cases by two different factors: the customer's complaint and the style of the toaster—two-slice versus four-slice.

Frank *(tentatively):* That might be right.

Patricia: Which of these two factors is more important to you?

Frank: Well, they are both important. Now that I think about it, I guess the first thing I notice when I look at a toaster is the style.

Patricia: Would you sort the cards according to style?

Frank quickly rearranges the cards into two groups. He points to the first group.

Frank: These are the two-slice toasters, and the rest are four-slice models.

Patricia: Are you more comfortable with this grouping than you are with my grouping?

Frank: Yes. That's funny. I can't really say why, but I *do* like this arrangement better.

Patricia: Good.

Patricia picks up the cards for the four-slice toasters. She stacks the cards and puts them to one side. She leaves the other cards on the table in front of Frank.

Now. Can you subdivide the two-slice toasters into groups?

Frank studies the cards for a while, then starts to rearrange them. As he does so, he begins to speak.

Frank: I'd do just what you did. I'm putting *toast always burns* in one pile, *toast does not pop up* in another pile, and so on. Here's a toaster that toasts too light. I'll put that in with the burnt toast, because they are both color problems.

Patricia *(when Frank has finished sorting the cards):* You mentioned that you put *toast always burns* and *toast too light* together because they are both color problems. I see that you've grouped a few other complaints. Can you tell me what made you put cards into these groups?

Frank: I divided the cards by customer complaint. I put different complains together if I would go about fixing them in the same way. That's how I think about the complaint: by the way I would fix the problem.

Patricia: Thanks. It seems that each group represents a *category* of customer complaint.

Frank: Sure. You could call it a category.

Patricia: Does this grouping seem natural?

Frank: Yes. The customer's complaint tells me where to begin.

If you were not able to identify meaningful classifications of case input through sorting the cases yourself, try to discern whether this failure is because the cases are *too different* or *too similar*. If the cases are too different, each may represent a meaningful subdivision of the data. If they are too similar, your application may be sufficiently circumscribed that there is no need to subdivide coverage on the basis of input data.

4.1.3 Classifying Cases by Results

The final dimension that you should consider is defined by the results the expert system produces. You may be able to divide the possible results the system can reach into groups that are meaningful to the expert. If so, you can initially limit the system to producing results in a single category. With each cycle of development, you can add the ability to produce results in additional categories. The procedure for identifying result categories is analogous to the procedure for identifying input categories, which we discussed in Section 4.1.2.

Consider each subtask you identified (as described in Section 4.1.1). For each subtask, identify the major results that the expert system should produce. Your discussion of cases in earlier knowledge-acquisition sessions should allow you to identify the important results.

> When Patricia Programmer reviews the subtasks of the toaster-repair advisor, she finds that the system will make conclusions only in its major subtask: Find and repair a toaster malfunction. Patricia reviews the cases that Frank Fixit presented and decides that the major result in these cases was the *problem* causing the malfunction and the appropriate *repair* procedure.

Once you have identified the major results, fill in an index card for each case with the results concluded for that case. Ask the expert to sort these cards into meaningful groups. If that exercise fails, try to sort them yourself, and ask the expert to comment on your organization of the cards. If you are still unable to identify categories, find out whether the cases all belong in a single category or whether each represents its own category.

Patricia Programmer prepares index cards, each containing the appropriate repair for a different case that Frank Fixit described in earlier knowledge-acquisition sessions. When she asks Frank to group these cards, he quickly arranges them into two groups. He explains that toasters in the first group had mechanical problems while those in the second group had electrical problems. Frank then subdivides each of those two groups into groups with identical repairs. He is unable to subdivide the groups further (Figure 4.3).

4.2 Comparing Categories

Once you have identified possible classifications along the three dimensions (function, input, results), you should investigate the relative *size*, *difficulty*, and *importance* of the different categories within each classification. The purpose of this exercise is to gather and organize information on which to base planning decisions. The more precise the information you obtain, the more accurately you can plan the project. In expert-systems projects, however, precise measures of relative size and difficulty are seldom available. Do not expect or demand exact numbers. You will need to compare the categories you identified within each classification of the coverage of your expert system.

Figure 4.3 Result categories for the toaster-repair advisor. Patricia Programmer learns that Frank Fixit classifies the results of a toaster repair by *problem type* and *repair procedure*. She identifies result categories within each of these two classifications. Note that Frank considers each different repair (such as *replace vertical shaft*) to define a separate category of repair procedure.

Result		Result Category	
Problem	**Repair**	**Problem Type**	**Repair Procedure**
Rusted vertical shaft	Replace vertical shaft	Mechanical	Replace vertical shaft
Defective carriage-latch spring	Replace carriage-latch spring	Mechanical	Replace carriage-latch spring
Thermostat out of adjustment	Adjust thermostat	Mechanical	Adjust thermostat
Loose busbar weld	Weld busbar to element terminal	Electrical	Weld busbar to element terminal
Defective heating element	Replace heating element	Electrical	Replace heating element

Patricia Programmer and Frank Fixit classified the functions of the toaster-repair advisor into *subtasks*. They classified the input by *toaster style* and *complaint category* and the results by *problem type* and *repair procedure*. Patricia needs to compare the categories within each row of Table 4.2. For each classification of the system, Patricia will try to evaluate the relative size of the categories (Section 4.2.1), their relative difficulty (Section 4.2.2), and their relative importance (Section 4.2.3).

4.2.1 Relative Size

The **size** of an expert-system application is an indication of the *amount of information that the knowledge engineers will need to acquire* before they can implement that application. During initial inquiry, knowl-

Table 4.2 Categories of Functionality for the Toaster-Repair Advisor

Classification	Categories
Subtask (function)	Find and repair malfunction Update toaster-part database Generate customer bill Describe procedures
Toaster style (input)	Two-slice toaster Four-slice toaster Two-slice toaster with bakery switch Under-cabinet toaster Toaster oven
Complaint category (input)	Color problem No-trip problem No-latch problem Heating-element problem . . .
Problem type (result)	Electrical Mechanical
Repair procedure (result)	Adjust thermostat Replace thermostat Replace carriage-latch spring Replace vertical shaft Weld busbar to element terminal . . .

edge engineers try to obtain at least a rough evaluation of the size of the application and of the size of each category of functionality so that they can estimate how long it will take them to develop the system.

No absolute measures exist for specifying the size of an application. After an expert system has been developed, its size can be measured by the number of entries in its knowledge base or by the number of lines in a listing of its knowledge base. Even these measures are inexact, however, because different knowledge engineers would encode the same knowledge in different ways. In addition, some expert-system shells use fairly concise syntax while the languages of other shells are relatively verbose. The same expert system implemented in two different shells would yield different measures of size. Nonetheless, knowledge engineers need to estimate the size of their applications. They generally make estimates by comparing the current project to other projects in which they have participated. For example, a typical comment is, "It took us 15 months to complete the auto-loan advisor. This project feels a little smaller. I would guess that we can do it in about 12 months."

Because the measurement of system size is so inexact, it can be challenging to lead the expert to specify the relative size of different functional categories of the application. In Dialog 4.3, Patricia Programmer demonstrates that the knowledge engineer must be flexible and must try different ways to obtain the necessary information.

Dialog 4.3 Obtaining Numerical Measures of the Relative Size of Task Categories

Setting

Patricia Programmer has written a summary of the different functionality categories of the toaster-repair advisor on the whiteboard. Her summary contains the information that is shown in Table 4.2. Patricia has explained to Frank Fixit that she wants to understand how much work each category represents in terms of the amount of information she and Howard will need to learn for each category.

Dialog

Patricia: Let's start with the toaster style. Can you estimate how many models of each style we will need to discuss?

Frank: In our department, we service 41 models of simple two-slice toasters and 6 additional two-slice models that include a bakery switch. We service 19 models of four-slice toasters, 5 toaster ovens, and 4 under-cabinet toasters.

Patricia: That was easy! Now, let's consider the problem type. Can you give me numbers like that for electrical and mechanical problems?

Frank: That's a lot harder. There are definitely more electrical problems. The mechanical parts are generally very reliable.

Patricia: Do you have any idea how many different electrical problems can occur in a toaster?

Frank: I really can't give you a number, Patricia. It depends on the toaster model. Some are quite simple; others are fairly complex. For Toasts-Bests simple two-slice toasters, I've probably seen a couple dozen electrical problems. In their new top-of-the-line model, however, I'd say a hundred or so things could go wrong.

Patricia: What about mechanical problems?

Frank: That's a little easier. There are about a dozen mechanical parts that can fail on a simple toaster, and this number doesn't increase much for the more complex toasters.

Patricia: OK. Now, think about *all* problems with all kinds of toaster. You said that there were more electrical problems. What percentage of all problems would you say are electrical?

Frank: Well, I don't know if I can give you the right percentage.

Patricia: The number doesn't need to be exactly right. I am just trying understand the relative number of problems of each type. Would you say that 60 percent of all problems are electrical?

Frank: No. More than that, maybe 75 percent.

Patricia: Thanks. In the cases we have discussed so far, we saw four different electrical problems. What percentage of all electrical problems do you think these cases represent?

Frank: I don't know. There are lots more.

Patricia: We've talked about less than half of the electrical problems?

Frank: Yes, definitely.

Patricia: Less than a quarter?

Frank: I don't think so. I'm not really sure, but I'd say it's closer to a third. I could be wrong.

Patricia: That's good enough. We don't need exact numbers if you don't have them. Now, lets go on to the complaint category.

Patricia walks to the whiteboard and draws a two-column table. In the left column she fills in the different complaint categories Frank identified in an earlier session. She points to the right column.

Frank, I'd like you to try to give me some numbers to put in this column. Let's start with color problems. Can you tell me how many customer complaints you would classify as color problems?

Frank: Well, at least *toast always burns* and *toast too light*, but it's really hard to say. We see all kinds of crazy complaints. I don't feel comfortable guessing what number to put there.

Patricia: Then, let's try for a percentage. Approximately what percentage of customer complaints are color problems.

Frank: Gee, I don't know.

Patricia: Do you think it's 25 percent?

Frank: I really couldn't say.

> *Patricia fills the number 10 into the right column next to the category "color problems."*

Patricia: Let's try something different.

Frank *(interrupting):* Is that 10 customer complaints or 10 percent?

Patricia: It's neither. It's just 10. We don't know what the units are. Let's say that Howard was able to look at all possible customer complaints, and somehow he measured the color problems. He gave us the measure ten. We don't know how Howard got this number or what it means.

Howard *(chuckling):* I have my methods.

Patricia: Howard rated color problems *10* on some scale. All we know about the scale is that a category with about the same number of complaints as color problems would also be rated *10*. A category with more complaints would be rated *more than 10*, and so on. Frank, if you know that color problems measure 10 on this scale, how would you measure no-trip problems on that same scale?

Frank: I'm not sure about this scale.

Patricia: Suppose I give no-trip problems a 10 also. Does that seem right?

Frank: No, I think I'd give no-trip problems less than color problems. Let's give it a 6 for now. Can I change my mind later?

Patricia: Of course! If color problems are *10* and no-trip problems are *6*, how would you rate no-latch problems.

Frank: About 3 or 4—say 4.

Discussion

In this dialog, Patricia Programmer uses three different approaches to lead Frank Fixit to rate the size of different categories. First, Patricia asks Frank to specify numbers in some unit related to the size of the different categories. She is successful with this approach when she and Frank discuss toaster style. Frank is able to state the exact number of models in each category. This statement gives Patricia a measure of the size of the application and of the size of the five categories in terms of the unit "toaster model." Patricia can now try to estimate, on the basis of case discussions in earlier interviews, how much information is needed to understand one toaster model. The full application will contain about 75 times as much information. Assuming that the five toaster-style categories are of the same complexity, and the information about one category is irrelevant to the other categories, Patricia would schedule about twice as much time to implement coverage of two-slice toasters as to implement coverage of four-slice toasters.[3]

---

3. The discussion of numbers of toaster models is included in this dialog to illustrate a knowledge-acquisition technique: This discussion shows how a knowledge engineer

When Patricia's first approach fails, she tries a second one: She asks Frank to specify percentages that will tell her the *relative* (but not the *absolute*) *size* of the categories. This approach succeeds when Patricia asks Frank about problem types. Patricia is able to prompt Frank to judge that 75 percent of all problems are electrical. Patricia then pursues this topic further to try to estimate absolute sizes for the categories. Patricia and Frank have discussed four cases with electrical problems. From the case discussions, Patricia can make a rough estimate of the amount of information relevant to those four cases. Patricia tries to get Frank to relate the electrical problems in those cases to the total number of electrical problems. When Frank is able to estimate that those cases illustrate about one third of all electrical problems, Patricia has enough information to determine the approximate amount of information relevant to all problems.

When her first two approaches fail, Patricia's third approach is to assign a number to one category and to ask Frank to use that number as a basis for selecting numbers for the other categories. When Frank has filled in the entire table with numbers, Patricia will have relative measures of all the categories of customer complaint. She can try to estimate the absolute size of the categories by asking Frank to relate the cases they discussed in each category to the entire size of the category.

Some experts are uncomfortable using numerical measures when they do not know exact numbers or percentages. If your expert is not at ease using numbers to rate the categories, try to assess the relative size using descriptive terms. Dialog 4.4 is and an alternative to Dialog 4.3. This time, Frank Fixit is uncomfortable with Patricia's attempt to rate the sizes of the customer-complaint categories.

Dialog 4.4 Obtaining Nonnumerical Measures of the Relative Size of Task Categories

Setting

Patricia Programmer is trying to assess the relative size of the customer-complaint categories. She has drawn a two-column table on the whiteboard, with the complaint categories in the left column. Frank Fixit has been unable to specify absolute numbers or percentages to fill in the right column of the table. Patricia has just written the number 10 in the right column next to the category *color problems* and has explained how to use the relative scale.

might ask for and receive *an exact number that is related to the size of a category.* In fact, the number of toaster models of each style is *not* a good estimate of the size of the toaster-style category. Many models differ only slightly; Frank Fixit's method for repairing one model might be identical to his method for repairing a different model. A better measure of the size of the toaster-style category would be the number of problems that occur with toasters of each style; however, Frank would not have been able to give Patricia exact numbers of problems that occur for the different toaster styles.

Dialog

Frank: I'm not sure about this scale.

Patricia: Suppose I give no-trip problems a ten also. Does that seem right?

Frank: I can't say.

> *Patricia fills the right column next to "no-trip problems" with the number 5.*

Patricia: Is that any better?

> *Frank shakes his head. He looks perplexed.*

This means that more complaints go into the *color problems* category than into the *no-trip* category. If I put a *ten* next to *no-trip problems,* that would mean that about the same number of complaints are in the two categories.

Frank: I'm sorry, Patricia, but I just don't know what those numbers mean.

Patricia: That's OK. This was just an experiment, and I guess it didn't work.

> *Patricia writes on the whiteboard:*
> very few   few   average number   many   very many
> *She erases the numbers from the table, and writes "average number" in the right column next to "color problems."*

We'll try a new scale. If I say there are an *average* number of color problems, how would you rate no-trip problems?

Frank: Actually, I wouldn't rate color problems *average*. Can I change that?

> *Patricia erases "average number."*

Patricia: Of course! Just tell me what to write.

Frank: I'd put *many* for color problems and *average* for no-trip problems.

> *Patricia updates the table with Frank's ratings.*

Patricia: Good. This seems to work better than the scale I tried before. How would you rate no-latch problems?

Frank: Few.

4.2.2 Relative Difficulty

The **difficulty** of an expert-system application is an indication of *the complexity of the reasoning process and of the strategies the expert employs* in performing the task. *Difficulty* and *size* are similar in several ways. First, both are vague and approximate measures. Knowledge engineers use both measures to estimate the amount of time they will need to implement the expert system. Knowledge engineers typically judge both the size and difficulty of an application with reference to other applications they have developed.

Although experts are often able to specify which of two categories is *more difficult,* they generally have trouble *quantifying* the difficulty. It is usually necessary to infer difficulty on the basis of some other measure. For example, you may be able to estimate the difficulty from the amount of time the expert needs to perform the task in different situations or from the number of possible alternatives the expert needs to consider.

The four techniques illustrated in Section 4.2.1 are appropriate for leading the expert to rate the relative difficulty of different categories within a classification.

1. Ask the expert for a number that measures difficulty. For example, ask for the amount of time it would take to perform the task in each situation, the number of steps the expert would take in each situation, or the number of alternatives the expert would consider in each situation.

2. If the expert is unable to specify an absolute measure, try to determine a percentage. This method is generally not appropriate for comparing the relative difficulty of different situations in which a task can be performed; it can be useful, however, in comparing the difficulty of subtasks. For example if a task has been broken into four independent steps, find out what percentage of the time to perform the task the expert spends on each step.

3. Assign a number to one category (without specifying a unit), and ask the expert to rate other categories with respect to that number.

4. If a numerical rating scheme fails, label one alternative "average difficulty" and ask the expert to rate others relative to that alternative. (The expert may prefer to move the "average" label to another category and give your starting category a different rating.)

As you assess the relative difficulty of different categories, pay particular attention to any category the expert considers significantly more difficult than other categories within the same classification. An unusually high difficulty rating might indicate that the problem-solving process for that category is not well understood. If the expert rates a category as exceptionally difficult, try to verify that the expert *does have a method* for performing the task in the situations represented by this category. Patricia Programmer does not encounter this complication when she asks Frank Fixit to rate the difficulty of the functionality categories of the toaster-repair advisor. Dialog 4.5 illustrates how another knowledge engineer dealt with this situation.

Dialog 4.5 Checking the Feasibility of an Unusually Difficult Task Category

Setting

Denny is an expert at trouble-shooting problems with a fairly new piece of equipment. Melanie is a knowledge engineer who is working with Denny to develop an expert system. In a recent interview, Denny and Melanie were able to identify a number of ways to divide the coverage of the expert system. Melanie is currently trying to learn how Denny rates the relative difficulty of various categories of problem. Melanie drew a two-column table on the whiteboard and wrote names of problem categories in the left column. She then filled in 10 as the difficulty rating for the first problem category and asked Denny to rate the other categories, using the first category as a reference point.

Denny has just completed filling in the table. He gave the category "interlocking rings" a rating of 100. He gave all other problem categories ratings between 5 and 15.

Dialog

Melanie: You gave interlocking rings a very high rating.

Denny: Yes. That's definitely the most difficult type of problem.

Melanie: Judging from your ratings, it's quite a bit more difficult than the others. You gave interlocking rings a difficulty of 100, but no other category got higher than 15. Does this large a gap seem consistent with the difference in difficulty?

Denny: Yes. Interlocking rings can be a nightmare.

Melanie: When you see an interlocking-ring problem, do you feel confident about your ability to solve it?

Denny: Well, I do the best that I can. I've really only had to deal with a few of these problems. The first one came up just two months ago. I guess I'm *not* as confident about interlocking rings as I am about the other problems.

Melanie: Is there anyone else who has more experience with these problems who could help?

Denny: No there isn't. Actually, I'd like to be able to go to this expert system you're going to build and ask it what I should do.

Melanie: The problem with that idea is that the expert system can't tell you what to do until *we* tell the system how to handle these problem. I need to learn from you, or from someone else, what to do about interlocking-ring problems.

Denny: That's too bad. There isn't all that much that we can tell you.

Melanie: Are you or other engineers able to solve interlocking-ring problems most of the time?

Denny *(hesitantly):* Well, the problems are not impossible. We have had *some* success. But we usually have to guess. We use a lot of trial and error.

I don't really want you to think I'm an *expert* when it comes to these problems.

Melanie: It sounds as though no one really understands much about inter-locking-ring problems.

Denny: That's right.

Melanie: We may decide to leave this problem out of the expert system for now. We could add it in the future if your organization learns more about the problem. I think I should discuss this issue with management and find out how we should proceed.

Denny: That sounds like a good idea.

Discussion

Denny's rating of 100 for interlocking-ring problems is a red flag for Melanie. She tries to learn why Denny's difficulty rating for this problem was so much higher than his other ratings. Melanie considers two possibilities. First, Denny might be confident about his ability to solve these problems but might consider them significantly more difficult than other problems. That would tell Melanie to schedule proportionally more time for the implementation of the portion of the knowledge base that deals with interlocking-ring problems. Second, Denny might not be sure how to solve problems of this type. That would indicate that these problems may lie outside the scope of the expert system.

Melanie learns that neither Denny nor anyone else in his organization knows very much about interlocking-ring problems. This means that this problem category is not a good candidate for an expert-system solution. After the interview, she raises this issue with the manager who is funding the expert system project. They discuss the matter and decide to omit interlocking rings from the expert system, at least until someone reaches a better understanding of the problems.

4.2.3 Relative Importance

The final comparison among the categories of functionality should assess the relative importance of each subtask and of each category of situation for which the task can be performed. The **importance** of a category of functionality is a rough measure of how significant that category is to the objectives of the project, taking into account relative priorities of the objectives.[4] Importance should be judged by weighing and combining several factors. For example:

- *Frequency:* The more frequently a problem occurs, the more important the problem.

---

4. Section 2.4 describes how the objectives of an expert system are defined and how their priorities are determined.

- *Need for help:* The more help the expert system's users need with a problem, the more important the problem.

- *Consequence:* The larger the benefit of including the functionality, the more important the functionality. The larger the detriment of *not* including the functionality, the more important the functionality.

The assessment of importance should reflect the views of all four groups who have an interest in the expert system: the experts, the knowledge engineers, the users, and the funders. In some projects, representatives of the users and the funders will join the knowledge engineers and expert in discussions about the importance of the various categories. In other projects, the knowledge engineers and expert will judge the importance by themselves. In these projects, the knowledge engineers and expert should consider all the issues raised during the process of defining the expert system.

> Margaret Major and Gary General ask Patricia Programmer and Frank Fixit to assess importance by themselves. Because both Patricia and Frank participated in the definition of the expert system and because the four constituent groups in this project did not have strong disagreements, Margaret and Gary are confident that Frank and Patricia will address the concerns of all parties. Before they meet to discuss the importance of the categories, Frank and Patricia both review the document of the system definition to refresh their memories on all the issues raised during the meetings to define the expert system.[5]

You will follow the same steps whether you assess relative importance in an interview with the project expert or in a discussion with a larger group. If you conduct a group meeting, follow the guidelines presented in Section 2.8. For an individual interview with the expert, use the techniques illustrated in Section 4.2.1.

1. Before the meeting, write the project objectives, ordered by priority, where all participants can see them (on a whiteboard, for example). Encourage the participants to refer to this list as they consider importance ratings.

2. Ask the participants to evaluate the frequency, need, and consequence of each category of the system's functionality. If other dimensions of importance are appropriate for your project, ask participants to rate the categories along those dimensions as well. Use either numerical or descriptive scales, according to the pref-

---

5. The document of an expert system's definition is described in Section 2.7. Chapter 2 describes the meetings to define an expert system.

erence of the participants. Create a table with the possible categories of the system's functionality down the left side and the dimensions of importance along the top (Figure 4.4). Fill in the table as the participants decide on ratings.

3. Ask the participants to judge the relative weight of each dimension of importance and to take these weights into account in judging the overall importance of each category.

4. Ask the participants to rank order the overall importance of the categories based on the ratings in the table.

5. Ask the participants to identify gaps in importance. For example, ask whether the most important category is only slightly more important or very much more important than the second one.

4.3 Planning for Development

The two previous sections explain how to obtain the information on which you can base a project plan. This section describes how you will use the information to create a project plan. Planning the development of an expert-system project consists of three steps, all of which include knowledge-acquisition activities.[6]

1. Identify **development increments,** segments of functionality each of which will be added to the expert system in a single cycle of development.

2. Order the development increments.

3. Estimate the development time for adding each increment to the knowledge system.

In many projects, the planning decisions will be made by managers rather than by the expert-system development team. In the toaster-repair advisor project, for example, Patricia Programmer and Frank Fixit held discussions with Gary General and Margaret Major; Gary and Margaret made the final decisions about the project plans.

4.3.1 Identifying Development Increments

If you succeeded in classifying the functionality of the expert system along more than one dimension (function, input, or results), you will

---

6. For more information about project planning, refer to the Additional Reading section.

Figure 4.4 Relative importance of categories. Patricia Programmer and Frank Fixit rated the relative importance of the subtasks that the toaster-repair advisor will perform and the different situations in which the system will perform its task. They judged importance based on the *frequency* with which the functionality will be exercised, the repair staff's *need* for the functionality, and the *consequence* of including the functionality in the expert system. They used a three-point scale (high, medium, or low) to rate the importance along each of the three dimensions. Patricia and Frank combined the three ratings for each category into a rank order of its importance within its classification. They used the number 1 to indicate the most important category.

	Frequency	Need for help	Consequence	Importance
Subtask				
Find and repair malfunction	High	High	High	1
Update database	High	Low	High	2
Generate customer bill	High	Low	Medium	3
Describe procedure	Medium	Medium	Low	4
Toaster style				
Two-slice	High	Medium	High	1
Four-slice	Medium	High	Medium	2
.	.	.	.	.
.	.	.	.	.
.	.	.	.	.
Complaint category				
Color problem	High	High	Medium	1
No-trip problem	Medium	High	Medium	2
.	.	.	.	.
.	.	.	.	.
.	.	.	.	.
Problem type				
Electrical	High	High	High	1
Mechanical	Medium	Low	Low	2
Repair procedure				
Adjust thermostat	High	High	High	1
Replace thermostat	Medium	Medium	Medium	3
Replace carriage-latch spring	Medium	Medium	High	2
.	.	.	.	.
.	.	.	.	.
.	.	.	.	.

need to decide which of these classifications to use as a basis for dividing the scope of the expert system. If you use more than one classification, you will need to decide how these classifications interact to define the increments for development of the system. As you assess the merits of each classification, you should favor classifications that will allow the project to meet early development goals. For example, if one project goal is to show management the feasibility of expert-system technology, choose a classification that will permit an early demonstration of a useful (but possibly limited) system. If a goal is to field the system before it achieves full functionality, choose a classification that allows you to develop a system that benefits users even when its functionality is limited.

> Patricia Programmer and Frank Fixit meet with Margaret Major to discuss the pros and cons of defining development increments in terms of the five classifications: *subtask, toaster style, complaint category, problem type*, and *repair procedure* (see Table 4.2). Patricia recommends using the *subtask* classification. This classification would permit Patricia and Howard Hacker to focus initially on the expert system *in isolation*. Patricia suggests that she and Howard should implement a stand-alone expert system to find and repair toaster malfunctions. When Frank Fixit is satisfied with the system's performance, Patricia and Howard can turn their attention to the subtasks that are necessary for the integrated operation of the system. Namely, they can add the ability to update the toaster-part database, to generate customer bills, and to describe procedures for inexperienced repair people. Frank and Margaret Major agree with Patricia's suggestion.
>
> Next, the discussion turns to *toaster style*. Frank says he would prefer to concentrate on a single toaster style at a time. After he has discussed how to repair two-slice toasters, for example, he could explain what additional steps are necessary for four-slice toasters. Patricia asks Frank how he would like to divide the problems for a two-slice toaster. Should they concentrate on one complaint category at a time, for example, color problems? Or would it be better to concentrate on a particular problem type, for example, electrical problems? Frank answers that it would be easier for him to discuss different electrical problems together rather than to combine electrical and mechanical problems. If they focus on customer complaints, they will have to mix electrical problems with mechanical problems—some complaints can be caused by either an electrical or a mechanical problem.
>
> Margaret Major raises an objection when Frank proposes organization of development by *problem type*. Margaret would like to install the toaster-repair advisor, at least on a trial basis, as soon as possible. If the initial version of the system can only handle electrical problems, how will members of the repair staff know whether the system can help them with a particular toaster? An inexperienced repair person may not be able to judge whether the customer's complaint is caused by an electrical problem or a mechanical one. Frank agrees that his suggestion might not be the best approach; from the user's point of view, it probably would be best to focus on *complaint category*. If Frank announces that the expert system can help with color problems in two-slice toast-

ers, the repair staff will be able to judge when to use the expert system and when to come to Frank for help. Margaret, Frank, and Patricia end their discussion with a decision to divide the coverage of the toaster-repair advisor on the basis of three classifications: the subtask, the toaster style, and the complaint category (Figure 4.5).

After you have chosen the classifications that will divide your expert system's functionality, identify the increments for development. Each category of functionality defined by your classifications may be a separate development increment. For example, each cell in Figure 4.5(c) might correspond to a separate cycle of development. On the other hand, the different cells in Figure 4.5(c) might represent significantly different amounts of work. If so, a group of cells in which each represents a small amount of work could be combined into a single development increment. To decide whether to consolidate some categories of functionality, refer to their measures of relative size and difficulty. If a number of categories are fairly small and simple, you may choose to combined them into a single development increment.

> Patricia Programmer and Frank Fixit review their earlier assessment of the size and difficulty of the subtasks, toaster styles, and complaint categories. Patricia and Frank rated the main subtask (find and repair toaster malfunction) *moderately difficult* and *large* in size. In contrast, they rated all auxiliary subtasks (update toaster-part database, generate a customer bill, and describe a test or repair procedure) either *easy* or *very easy* and either *small* or *very small* in size. On the basis of these ratings, Patricia and Frank decide that the auxiliary subtasks do not need to be subdivided by toaster style or customer complaint. When one of these subtasks is added to the system, it should cover *all* the customer complaints and toaster styles that are currently covered within the main subtask. If additional toaster styles and customer complaints are later added to the system, the coverage of these new toaster styles and customer complaints should be added to the auxiliary subtasks as well as to the main subtask.
>
> Patricia and Frank assigned relative, not absolute, size and difficulty ratings to the different toaster styles. The two-slice category was rated the largest and the second most difficult; the four-slice category was rated the most difficult and the second largest. Patricia and Frank decide that those two categories should be subdivided by customer complaint. In comparison with those two categories, the categories two-slice toaster with bakery switch and under-cabinet toaster were rated considerably smaller and less difficult. Patricia and Frank decide those two categories do not need to be subdivided by customer complaint. As Figure 4.6 shows, Patricia and Frank identify 11 development increments from the 48 functionality cells of Figure 4.5(c).

4.3.2 Ordering Development Increments

After you have identified the development increments, select one to be the initial scope of the expert system—that is, the focus for the first

Figure 4.5 Dividing the functionality of the toaster-repair advisor. Patricia Programmer, Margaret Major, and Frank Fixit decided to divide the functionality of the toaster-repair advisor along three dimensions. First, they divide the task into subtasks (a). Then they divide the situations in which each subtask can be performed (b) based on toaster-style and complaint category. (For simplicity, we illustrate a limited number of toaster styles and complaint categories.) The total functionality can be viewed as a two-dimensional grid of cells (c) in which each cell represents particular functionality. For example, the shaded cell represents the ability to find and repair color problems in two-slice toasters.

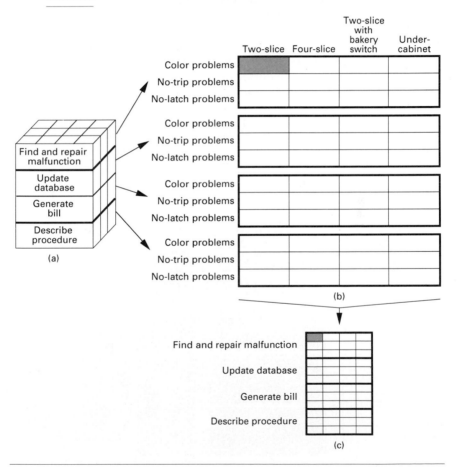

Figure 4.6 Development increments for the toaster-repair advisor. From
the 48 units of functionality, Patricia Programmer and Frank Fixit identified eleven development increments for the toaster-repair advisor.

A. Find and repair color problems in two-slice toasters.
B. Find and repair color problems in four-slice toasters.
C. Find and repair no-trip problems in two-slice toasters.
D. Find and repair no-trip problems in four-slice toasters.
E. Find and repair no-latch problems in two-slice toasters.
F. Find and repair no-latch problems in four-slice toasters.
G. Perform the system's task for two-slice toasters with bakery switches.
H. Perform the system's task for under-cabinet toasters.
I. Update the toaster-part database.
J. Generate a customer bill.
K. Describe a test procedure or a repair procedure.

Notice that a development increment specifies a *focus for one cycle of
development*, but does not necessarily specify which units of functionality will be added during that cycle. For example, some of the 48 units
of functionality that appear in increments G or H also appear in I, J,
or K. Obviously, each functional unit needs to be added to the toaster-
repair advisor only once. The order in which the project adds the development increments G, H, I, J, and K will determine when the individual units of functionality are added; Patricia's next task is to decide
the order in which the increments should be added.

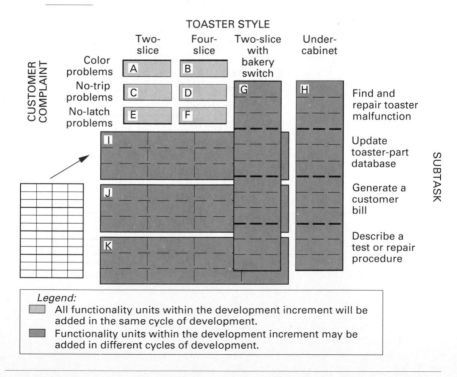

Legend:
All functionality units within the development increment will be
added in the same cycle of development.
Functionality units within the development increment may be
added in different cycles of development.

cycle of development. In many projects, the development team will order *all* increments; they will create a project plan that covers the full system development. In other projects, the team will plan only the first cycle of development. At the end of each development cycle, the project team will select the increment to add in the next cycle.

In most projects, managers of the funding organization, the experts, and the users all participate in deciding how to order development increments. Decisions are generally based on the measures of importance, difficulty, and size of the increments. The decision criteria will vary from project to project. If a goal of the project is to field a useful system as soon as possible, for example, the project team might start with a development increment of high importance and of small or moderate size and difficulty. On the other hand, if a project goal is to demonstrate the feasibility of expert-system technology to management in order to ensure funding for the complete project, the team may start with a small and simple increment of only moderate importance.

As you consider how to order development increments, check for those with a relatively low *importance* measure and a relatively high *size* or *difficulty* measure. In some applications, it is best to eliminate such increments from the system scope altogether. For example, in many diagnostic applications, five to ten percent of the possible malfunctions occur so infrequently that it is not worth the effort to implement the ability to handle these malfunctions.

> Patricia Programer prepares a summary of the estimates of relative size, difficulty, and importance that she and Frank Fixit assigned to the different development increments. Then, Patricia and Frank present this summary to Margaret Major in a meeting to select the order for the development increments of the toaster-repair advisor. After she reviews Patricia's summary, Margaret decides that importance is the only measure of interest to her. Margaret says her primary goal is to make the toaster-repair advisor available to the repair staff as soon as possible. She says that the system must perform three subtasks before it will be useful: It must find and repair some malfunctions, update the toaster-part database, and generate customer bills. Frank suggests that the initial release of the system should be limited to color problems. Margaret agrees and adds that the system should cover both two- and four-slice toasters. Margaret believes that the remaining customer complaints should be added to the system in order of importance, first for two-slice then for four-slice toasters. When the system is able to handle all customer complaints, Patricia and Howard Hacker can add the ability to describe procedures for inexperienced repair personnel. In the short term, those users will have to rely on their manuals for descriptions of the procedures. Margaret suggests that the remaining toaster styles can be added to the system's coverage after all subtasks have been implemented for two- and four-slice toasters. Figure 4.7 shows the order in which development increments will be added to the toaster-repair advisor.

Figure 4.7 Incremental development of the toaster-repair advisor. Development increments will be added to the toaster-repair advisor in the order shown. The shading indicates how fully the system covers its the total intended scope after each cycle of development. (The functionality grid is explained in Figure 4.5.) Notice that when the focus is a new *subtask* (cycles 3, 4, and 9), this functionality is added for *only the customer complaints and toaster styles that have already been added* to the system. When the focus is a new *customer complaint* (cycles 5, and 7) or a new *toaster style* (cycles 2, 6, 8, 10, and 11), the functionality is added *for all subtasks that have already been added*.

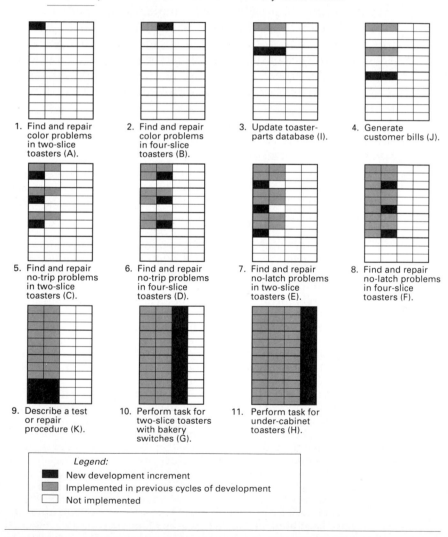

1. Find and repair color problems in two-slice toasters (A).

2. Find and repair color problems in four-slice toasters (B).

3. Update toaster-parts database (I).

4. Generate customer bills (J).

5. Find and repair no-trip problems in two-slice toasters (C).

6. Find and repair no-trip problems in four-slice toasters (D).

7. Find and repair no-latch problems in two-slice toasters (E).

8. Find and repair no-latch problems in four-slice toasters (F).

9. Describe a test or repair procedure (K).

10. Perform task for two-slice toasters with bakery switches (G).

11. Perform task for under-cabinet toasters (H).

Legend:

■ New development increment
▨ Implemented in previous cycles of development
□ Not implemented

Figures 4.5 through 4.7 illustrate how knowledge engineers identified and ordered development increments in one expert-system project. It should be clear from these figures that the 48 individual functional units could have been grouped in many different ways to form development increments and that the development increments could have been ordered in a variety of ways. The toaster-repair advisor is an example of *one way* of planning incremental development; other projects will define and order development increments differently.

For example, the toaster-repair project had a management goal to deploy the system as soon as it could be useful. This goal led the knowledge engineers to chose a depth-first plan in which they developed each of the 48 functional units *in its entirety* in some cycle of development. Other projects may prefer a breadth-first development plan in which some development on each unit of functionality occurs in each cycle of development (Figure 4.8). Other projects may combine depth-first and breadth-first approaches.

The following are important points to remember when you identify and order development increments for an expert-system project.

Figure 4.8 Breadth-first development plan. This illustrates an alternative to the development approach illustrated in Figure 4.7. In this project, each development increment *spans all 48 functional units*. In the first cycle of development, the knowledge engineers implement minimal functionality throughout the entire task and the full range of situations in which the system should perform its task. In each subsequent cycle of development, the expert system is enhanced until it covers its full intended scope at the necessary level of performance.

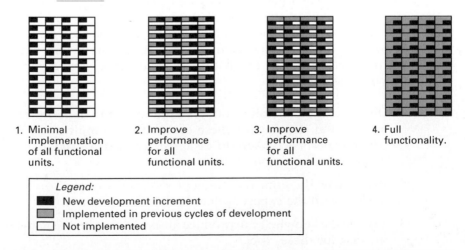

1. Minimal implementation of all functional units.

2. Improve performance for all functional units.

3. Improve performance for all functional units.

4. Full functionality.

Legend:
- ■ New development increment
- ▨ Implemented in previous cycles of development
- ☐ Not implemented

- Plan development so that you will be able to show the expert a meaningful demonstration *as early in the project as possible.* (The demonstration does not necessarily have to come at the *end* of a cycle of development.)

- Allow for iterative refinement of your system to accommodate the improvements and modifications that the expert will suggest after seeing demonstrations.

- Define the development increments as precisely as you can; the more precise your definitions are, the more accurately you will be able to estimate the time required for each increment.

- Define the development increments to be small enough that the development team will be able to focus on the relevant areas without becoming overwhelmed by their extent and complexity.

4.3.3 Estimating Development Time

The final planning step is to estimate the time you will need for each cycle of development. Making time estimates for an expert-system project is very much like making time estimates for any software-development project—this activity is more an art than it is a science. The accuracy of time estimates is strongly correlated with the novelty of the application relative to the experience of the developers and their prior projects: the more novel the application, the less accurate the estimates will be.

To estimate the time for a development increment, review your measures of *size* and *difficulty* of each increment. The development time will be increase as the combined *size* and *difficulty* measures increase. For each development increment, study your notes of case discussions within the scope of the increment. You will need to extrapolate from the information you learned in the case discussions to the development time for the increment. Based on the information you learned, estimate how much time it would take you to perform the following activities.

1. Obtain a more detailed understanding of the expert's reasoning process and strategy for these cases. If your application is one in which experts are likely to disagree, add extra time for resolving differences of opinion.

2. Decide how the same reasoning process and strategy can be accomplished with the expert system tool.

3. Encode the knowledge to produce an expert system that can perform the task for these cases.

4. Test the system to verify that it performs correctly on these cases; implement necessary corrections. (In early cycles of development, corrections may require a certain amount of redesign.)

5. After you have made a time estimate based on the cases you have discussed, use the measures of size and difficulty to scale your estimate into a time estimate for the entire increment.

6. Add some time to your estimates to cover unexpected difficulties or delays.

7. Review and discuss the plan with the expert. When the expert sees how you have used the measures of size and difficulty to estimate development time, he or she may be able to identify discrepancies— development increments that have been allotted too much or too little time relative to the other increments.

Time estimates are subject to error because they must be forecast from a very superficial understanding of the knowledge to be encoded. To make matters worse, this knowledge is only quantified in terms of rough measures of vague dimensions (*size* and *difficulty*). The ideal way to plan an expert-system project is to do so incrementally. First, plan the entire project on the basis of your measures of size and difficulty. Then, after the first cycle of development, review both your plan and your measures of size and difficulty for the development increment. With your improved understanding of the task and the expert's improved understanding of the knowledge-acquisition process, you may both be able to estimate size, difficulty, and time more accurately. Try to obtain approval from your project management to plan for a revision of the project schedule after each cycle of development. If you obtain approval, include replanning activities in your project plan.

> Patricia Programmer estimates time for the 11 development increments of the toaster-repair advisor. She uses these estimates to create a project plan and she meets with Gary General, Margaret Major, Charles Cypher, and Frank Fixit to discuss this plan. Patricia presents her project schedule to the group and explains briefly why the group chose the development increments they did and why they ordered the increments as they did. She briefly explains how she estimated the times for the different increments. After she answers a few questions about the plan, Patricia explains the advantages of revising the plan periodically throughout the development phase of the project. Gary General agrees that the project team should schedule a replanning step after each cycle of development. Gary asks Patricia to notify him immediately if any revised time estimate indicates that the project cannot be completed within the allotted time. If this situation ever arises, Gary will need to review the project status. He will have to decide whether to authorize more funds and human resources for a longer development period or to scale back the scope of the project.

If you are able to review your plan after each cycle of development, ask the expert to judge the amount of work that is needed for the remaining increments on the basis of experience with past increments. Dialog 4.6 illustrates how Patricia Programmer and Frank Fixit revised their estimates.

Dialog 4.6 Revising Time Estimates on the Basis of Early Project Experience

Setting

The first cycle of development has just ended. Patricia Programmer and Frank Fixit meet to revise their time estimates for the remaining development increments. Before the meeting, Patricia creates the outline of a table on the whiteboard. The table has four columns, labeled *development increment, size, difficulty,* and *development time;* the table has eleven rows, one for each development increment.

Dialog

Patricia: Frank, do you remember that at the beginning of the project we estimated the size and difficulty of the various parts of the toaster-repair task?

Frank: Yes.

Patricia: We used these measures to estimated development time. I'd like us to review our estimates on the basis of our experience with color problems in two-slice toasters. We may be able to come up with more accurate measures.

Frank *(a little hesitant):* OK.

Patricia: As you recall, *size* was our measure of the amount of knowledge I would need to learn for each increment. *Difficulty* was our measure of the complexity of the reasoning you use for the increment.

Frank nods. He is scowling slightly.

We have just finished with color problems in two-slice toasters. It took us three weeks to complete development. During that time, we discussed 10 different cases in about 20 hours of interviews. You said that these cases cover all the major color problems with two-slice toasters.

Frank nods again, still scowling.

I'd like to you to try to relate your experience in these last three weeks to the remaining increments. Let's try to estimate the *size* by the number of different cases we need to discuss. Let's estimate the *difficulty* by the amount of time it takes us to discuss the necessary material.

Patricia goes to the whiteboard. She adds the units number of cases, interview hours, *and* weeks *to the column headings for* size, difficulty, *and* development time, *then she fills in the first row of the table (Figure 4.9a). Frank nods again. His scowl starts to fade.*

Based on our experience with two-slice toasters, how many cases do you think we'll have to discuss before Howard and I understand color problems in four-slice toasters at the same depth that we understand these problems in two-slice toasters?

Figure 4.9 Revising time estimates. Patricia Programmer applies experience from the first cycle of development to revise time estimates for the remaining cycles. She uses the number of cases discussed in the first cycle to measure the *size* of the first development increment and the number of interview hours to measure the *difficulty* (a). Then she asks Frank Fixit to estimate the number of cases and interview hours that would be required for other increments that also relate to the task of finding and repairing a toaster malfunction (b). Patricia uses Frank's numbers in the *size* and *difficulty* columns to estimate development time; her experience during the first cycle of development allows her to judge the amount of work required for every case and every hour of interview.

Development increment	Size (number of cases)	Difficulty (interview hours)	Development time (weeks)
Color problems in two-slice toasters (A)	10	20	3
Color problems in four-slice toasters (B)			
Update toaster-part database (I)			
Generate customer bills (J)			
No-trip problems in two-slice toasters (C)			
No-trip problems in four-slice toasters (D)			
No-latch problems in two-slice toasters (E)			
No-latch problems in four-slice toasters (F)			
Describe a test or repair procedure (K)			
Two-slice toasters with bakery switches (G)			
Under-cabinet toasters (H)			

(a)

Figure 4.9 (continued)

Development increment	Size (number of cases)	Difficulty (interview hours)	Development time (weeks)
Color problems in two-slice toasters (A)	10	20	3
Color problems in four-slice toasters (B)	15	10	1
Update toaster-part database (I)	—	—	—
Generate customer bills (J)	—	—	—
No-trip problems in two-slice toasters (C)	25	20	2
No-trip problems in four-slice toasters (D)	20	15	2
No-latch problems in two-slice toasters (E)	10	10	1
No-latch problems in four-slice toasters (F)	10	10	1
Describe a test or repair procedure (K)	—	—	—
Two-slice toasters with bakery switches (G)	20	20	2
Under-cabinet toasters (H)	10	15	2

(b)

Frank *(smiling):* You know, Patricia, this question is *much* easier than the questions that you asked about size before!

Patricia: Good! I was hoping you'd find this question easy.

Frank: There are a few additional problems we have to think about with four-slice toasters. I guess 15 cases should do it.

Patricia: Thanks. And how much time do you think we should plan for these discussions ?

Frank: A lot of what we've already discussed also holds true for four-slice toasters. We only have to talk about the things that are different, right?

Patricia: Right. Of course, you also need to tell us what information in the knowledge base will also apply to four-slice toasters.

Frank: Sure. That won't take long.

Frank scratches his head and looks intently at the whiteboard. He turns to Patricia as he starts to speak.

I would say that we only need about 10 hours of interviews.

Patricia: Great! Now, do you think we'll have time to cover all 15 cases in just 10 hours of interviews?

Frank: Yes, because we only need to discuss things that are new to you.

Patricia goes to the whiteboard and fills in the second row of the table.

Patricia: What about no-trip problems in two-slice toasters.

Frank: Let's see. I would say about 25 cases in 20 hours.

Discussion

During the first cycle of development on the toaster-repair project, Frank Fixit has learned what to expect during knowledge acquisition. He understands the kinds of information he will need to tell Patricia Programmer and Howard Hacker about finding and repairing additional toaster problems. The experience during the first cycle has given the team some tangible measurements of *size* and *difficulty*. Based on his experience to date, Frank is able to estimate the *size* of other increments in number of cases and the *difficulty* in interview hours.

Notice that Patricia skips over increments that correspond to new subtasks *(update toaster-part database, generate customer bill*, and *describe a test or repair procedure)*. Patricia and Howard may be able to revise their estimates for these increments on the basis of their experience. However, Frank's experience during knowledge acquisition has not taught him what information Patricia and Howard will need to know when they address these subtasks. Patricia and Howard will not be able to estimate the time for these subtask from interview hours and number of cases because all the tasks involve software-engineering activities (integration) as well as knowledge-engineering activities.

After the meeting, Patricia makes new time estimates based on Frank's more accurate measures of *size* and *difficulty* and on her own improved ability to judge the amount of work involved per case and per hour of interview (Figure 4.9b). Patricia makes minor adjustments to her project plan and distributes copies to Gary General, Margaret Major, Charles Cypher, Frank Fixit, and Howard Hacker.

4.4 Points to Remember

Before the development phase of an expert-system project can begin, the project team must achieve the final goal of initial inquiry: to divide the full functionality of the system for incremental development. This goal consists of three steps.

1. Identify possible classifications of the total functionality of the expert system. In this step, it is particularly important to learn how *the expert* divides the task and classifies the situations in which the task can be performed rather than to suggest *your own* classifications. To identify classifications, look for ways to divide the *func-*

tions the expert system will perform, the *inputs* to which the system will respond, and the *results* the system will produce (Table 4.3).

2. Compare the categories within each classification for relative size (amount of knowledge to be acquired), difficulty (complexity of the expert's reasoning and strategy), and importance relative to the project objectives (Table 4.4).

Table 4.3 Identifying Possible Classifications of System Functionality

Technique	Description
Divide the task into subtasks.	1. Propose one subtask for each major function the system will perform.
	2. Ask the expert whether the subtasks can be performed independently.
	3. Combine dependent subtasks until you are left with a set of subtasks the expert considers modular.
Classify the situations in which the task can be performed (by *input* or by *results*).	1. Put case descriptions on index cards (describe either major input data or major results).
	2. Divide the cards into groups of similar cases.
	a. Ask the expert to arrange the cards into groups of similar cases.
	b. If the expert is unable to group the cards, group them yourself according to some characteristic that seemed important during case discussions. Ask the expert to comment on your classification and to rearrange the cards if the grouping does not seem reasonable.
	c. If all attempts to group cards fail, try to find out whether the cases are too similar (and belong in a single category) or are too different (and each represents its own category).
	3. Ask the expert what characteristics of the cases in each group distinguish the different categories.
	4. Repeat the exercise, asking the expert to subdivide groups of cards as many times as he or she is able to make meaningful distinctions among the cases.

3. Plan for the incremental development of the system. First decide how to divide the system's coverage into development increments—segments of functionality that you will add to the system in separate cycles of development. You may use some or all of the classifications you identified. Next decide on the order in which you will add the increments to the system. Finally estimate the time that you will need for each development increment (Table 4.5).

The final goal of initial inquiry is particularly challenging because knowledge acquisition must address vague concepts such as *categories of functionality* and *size, difficulty,* and *importance* of the categories.

Table 4.4 Comparing Categories within a Classification

Technique	Description
Estimate absolute size or difficulty.	1. Select some unit related to size or difficulty (for example, number of problems that can occur or time to perform the task). 2. Ask the expert to measure each category in the selected unit.
Estimate size or difficulty as percentages.	1. Select some unit related to size or difficulty (for example, number of problems that can occur or time to perform the task). 2. Using this unit, ask the expert to express the size or difficulty of each category as a percentage of the total system functionality (for example, what percentage of problems fall into this category or what percentage of time is spent in this subtask?).
Estimate relative size or difficulty with a numeric scale.	1. Assign a number to one category. 2. Ask the expert to assign numbers to other categories relative to the first. Instruct the expert to use the same number for a category of the same size (or difficulty), a larger number for a category that is larger (or more difficult), and so on.
Estimate relative size or difficulty with a nonnumerical scale.	1. Propose a descriptive scale whose middle rating is average (size or difficulty). 2. Assign the rating "average" to one of the categories. 3. Ask the expert to modify your rating if necessary and to rate the other categories using the same scale.

Table 4.4 (continued)

Technique	Description
Estimate absolute size based on cases you have discussed.	1. Ask the expert to estimate what percentage of the category is represented in the cases you have discussed. 2. If the expert is unable to suggest a percentage, ask whether the cases represent more or less than 50 percent. If less, find out whether they represent more or less than 25 percent and so on. Do not try to obtain a very exact percentage; stop when the expert is unable to answer your questions.
Estimate importance relative to project objectives.	1. Select a few dimensions for measuring importance such as the frequency with which the functionality will be exercised, the need for the functionality, and the consequence of including the functionality in the expert system. 2. For each dimension, ask the expert (and possibly representatives of the users and the funders) to evaluate the importance of the categories. Use either numerical or descriptive scales. 3. Ask the expert (and other evaluators, if any) to rank order the overall importance of the different categories, taking into account the relative weights of the dimensions along which they evaluated importance. 4. Ask the expert (and other evaluators, if any) to identify gaps in the rank ordering where one category is significantly more important than the next.

Tables 4.3 through 4.5 provide summaries of the techniques that can help you to meet the challenges of this goal. An overriding guideline when you apply any of these techniques is *do not continue with a technique that makes the expert uncomfortable.* If one technique fails, move quickly to an alternative.

Table 4.5 Estimating Development Time

Technique	Description
Estimate time from size and difficulty.	1. Review the cases you discussed that are within the scope of a given development increment. Estimate how much time you would need to complete a development cycle with only those cases. 2. Use measures of size and difficulty for the development increment to scale your estimate up to the time that you would need for the entire increment. 3. Add time to your estimate to cover unexpected difficulties and delays.
Reestimate time after the first cycle of development.	1. Total the interview time you spent in the first development cycle and the number of cases you discussed. 2. Ask the expert to compare the remaining development increments with the first increment. Judging by the project team's experience with the first increment, ask the expert to estimate the number of hours of interviews and the number of cases that will be needed for the remaining development increments. 3. Use your experience in the first cycle of development to estimate how to convert interview time and number of cases into development time.

Chapter 5

Learning the Steps in the Task

Patricia Programmer, Howard Hacker, and Frank Fixit have completed the specification phase of the toaster-repair advisor project. They have a clear definition of what the system will do. Patricia and Howard have a general understanding of the task of toaster repair. The team has decided how to divide the full functionality of the system for incremental development; they are now ready to move into the development phase. Their focus for the first cycle of development will be two-slice toasters with color problems.

Howard tells Patricia, "I'm sure Frank knows a lot more about toasters than he has told us, but he seems to have explained how he *repairs* toasters. I know what the expert system should do, but I still don't think I know enough to start implementation."

Howard Hacker has identified the knowledge-acquisition challenges of detailed investigation. The knowledge engineers cannot possibly learn everything the expert knows about the application subject area. Furthermore, a great deal of the expert's knowledge is not relevant to the expert system's task. The knowledge engineers must acquire just the knowledge relevant to the task; their understanding of this knowledge must be at a level of detail sufficient to permit them to implement an expert system. This chapter describes techniques that enable knowledge engineers to meet these challenges.

Patricia Programmer and Howard Hacker must achieve the three goals of detailed investigation:

1. They must learn the exact steps Frank takes in performing the task.

2. They must understand precisely how Frank reasons from input data about a case to reach the final results.

3. They must identify the specific facts and hypotheses Frank uses in his reasoning process.

Although Patricia and Howard will gather information relevant to all three goals in parallel, they will concentrate on each goal in turn. This chapter describes the first goal; Chapters 6 and 7 describe the second and third goals respectively.

Most experts follow tried-and-true procedures when they perform their tasks. It is of utmost importance for the knowledge engineers to learn *the expert's* strategy or procedure for performing the task. In many applications, the process by which the expert approaches the task is based on years of experience; this process typically differs from textbook procedures and allows the expert to outperform the average practitioner.

By the time knowledge engineers reach the detailed investigation stage of knowledge acquisition, they should have a high-level understanding of the process by which the expert performs the task. Some experts find it easy to articulate their procedures in general terms. For example, when Frank Fixit presented his task overview,[1] he described his general procedure for fixing toasters.

1. First Frank looks at the customer complaint and tests the toaster to see what is really wrong.

2. Then he tracks down the problem.

3. Once he has identified the problem, he fixes it.

4. Finally he retests the toaster to make sure it operates correctly.

Other experts find it difficult to describe their strategies, and the knowledge engineers obtain a high-level understanding of the expert's procedure through case discussions during initial inquiry.[2]

---

1. The task overview is described in Section 3.1.
2. Case discussions during initial inquiry are discussed in Section 3.2.

A high-level description of the expert's strategy serves as a starting point for a detailed investigation of the procedure. For example, Patricia Programmer must obtain a step-by-step description of the methods by which Frank Fixit tests a toaster to find out what is wrong. She must learn what steps Frank takes to track down a problem and to fix it. She must understand how he retests the toaster. Patricia must learn which steps are particular to specific situations and which ones are general. She must learn the conditions under which different steps are applicable.

Many experts who have instructed novices can describe their strategies at a detailed level. Experts in some applications are guided by well-understood scientific principles. For example, experts who trouble shoot problems in electrical circuits follow procedures based on the physical laws of electromagnetism.

Experts in such applications often are able to articulate their procedures exactly and in full detail. By the time you have finished initial inquiry, you should be able to judge whether the expert will be able to provide an indepth description of the steps that constitute the task. If so, ask your expert to describe the general procedure in detail. In most applications, however, the knowledge engineers will need to construct the specific procedure with the expert. The project team can construct the detailed definition of the expert's procedure through **case discussions.** The knowledge engineers can observe while the expert performs the task, and the project team can discuss how the expert would perform the task in a variety of situations. In Chapter 3, we introduced case discussions as a means for obtaining an overview of the task. During detailed investigation, however, knowledge engineers must probe for details that were unimportant during initial inquiry. Each case provides the focus for a series of knowledge-acquisition activities.

- The project team first discusses the case to elucidate the process by which the expert performs the task (Section 5.1).

- The knowledge engineers then review the case discussion to see whether it changes their understanding of the expert's procedure for performing the task (Section 5.2).

- The team discusses slight variations to the case to identify conditions under which the general procedure may vary (Section 5.3).

When the knowledge engineers understand the expert's procedure for performing the task, they define how the *expert system* should perform the task (Section 5.4).

5.1 Learning the Expert's Strategy

Case discussions are an effective tool for identifying the expert's strategy. For most projects, case discussions provide the means by which the project team can transform the high-level description of the expert's procedure into a detailed description. In such a project, the team will need to discuss many cases to develop a complete definition of the procedure. On the other hand, a project team whose expert is able to articulate a detailed description of the process for performing the task will need to discuss fewer cases.

Whether the initial detailed definition of the expert's procedure comes from case discussions or from the expert's description, case discussions serve as a means for *refining* the detailed definition. Through case discussions, the knowledge engineers can identify:

- Steps that occur infrequently

- Steps that are performed so quickly or so automatically that the expert forgets to mention them

- Circumstances under which different steps and approaches are appropriate

For a task that requires physical (in addition to mental) activity, the expert many find it easier to *demonstrate* the procedure than to describe it. (Consider, for example, how you would explain how to tie a shoelace. You would probably find it much easier to explain the process while you demonstrate with a real shoe.) If your application involves physical activities that are difficult for the expert to describe, try to arrange to observe while the expert performs these activities.

Dialog 5.1 illustrates how Patricia Programmer learns more details about Frank Fixit's procedure for repairing toasters.

Dialog 5.1 Discussing a Case to Learn the Steps in the Task

Setting

Patricia Programmer explained to Frank Fixit that she and Howard Hacker needed to learn the exact procedures by which Frank tests a toaster and tracks down its problem. Frank said it would be easier for him to show them the procedures than to try to explain what he does. Frank checked with other members of the repair staff until he found a two-slice toaster with a color problem. Frank arranged to repair this toaster himself, and he invited Patricia and Howard to watch.

This interview takes place in the service department in Frank's service bay. Frank is sitting in front of his work table. The toaster is on the table in front of him. On the left rear corner of the table is a loaf of white bread. Patricia and Howard arrive at the service bay; Patricia is carrying a tape recorder and a few cassettes. Patricia and Howard exchange greetings with Frank before they begin the dialog.

Dialog

Patricia: If you have no objection, Frank, I'd like to record this session. Today, I want you to go through the complete process of repairing the toaster without interruptions. Later I will want to ask you to explain what you are thinking at each step. The recording will provide an easy way for me to get the information I need without making you lose track of what you're doing. Is it OK to record the discussion?

Frank: Sure! No problem.

Patricia sets up the recorder. She labels a cassette with the date and the topic of the meeting; then she inserts the cassette into the recorder. She switches the recorder on and speaks into the microphone.

Patricia: It's July 30, 1990. Patricia, Howard, and Frank are meeting to observe how Frank repairs a two-slice toaster with a color problem.

(to Frank)

Frank, I'd like you to repair the toaster as if we weren't here. As you work, try to think aloud so that Howard and I will know what you are doing.

Frank: OK. I first look at the repair slip that is taped to the toaster.

Frank removes the repair slip and reads it; then he shows it to Patricia and Howard.

They only checked one complaint, "toast always burns." I'm going to test the toaster to see what the real problem is.

Frank proceeds to test the toaster; as he does so, he describes his actions.

I plug the toaster in, OK. Now I put in a slice of bread. I turn the color knob down to the lightest setting, push down the operating lever, and wait to see what happens.

Patricia, Howard, and Frank chat about the current events while they wait for the results of the test. After about five minutes they notice a burning smell.

Well, it seems to be burning all right.

The toast starts to emerge from the toaster. It is smoking and burnt to a crisp.

There it comes! Well, not much question about it—there is a serious problem.

Patricia: What would you do next?

Frank: Well, I think the thermostat is way out of whack. My guess is that I'll have to replace it. But first I'm going to see if it's just out of adjustment. Customers sometimes monkey with the toaster and get everything messed up before they bring it in. Of course they never *tell you* that they touched it! Anyway, it doesn't take me long to adjust the thermostat. If that fixes the problem, it will be much less expensive for the customer.

Should I just go ahead and do the adjustment, or do you want to know what I'm doing?

Patricia: Please tell us what you're doing as you make the adjustment.

Frank: OK. I'm turning the toaster on its side. You see the head of the adjusting screw sticking out of this hole in the crumb tray?

Frank points to the adjusting screw. Patricia and Howard nod.

I turn the adjustment screw two full turns counterclockwise—like so. Now, let's try to toast some more bread.

Patricia: What do you hope to accomplish?

Frank: Well, two full turns is a *very* large adjustment. If the thermostat is working, the toast should come out much lighter than before. Let's see what happens.

Patricia, Howard, and Frank make small talk while they wait for the toast. Once again the toast is burnt.

OK, we're not going to be able to adjust this thermostat. We'll have to replace it; that should fix the problem.

Patricia: Is your next step to replace the thermostat?

Frank: Yep. I'm going to the supply room to get a new one. Why don't you two wait here? I'll be right back.

Frank leaves to go to the supply room. He comes back empty handed.

Out of stock again! And even worse I checked the toaster-part database, and it says we have three in stock. I had to ask Jeff to run to the nearest appliance-supply store to get a couple of those thermostats. I can't finish the repair now. When Jeff comes back, what I'll do is remove the old thermostat and put in the new one.

Patricia: If it won't take too much time, could you show us how to remove the thermostat?

Frank: Sure! I open the crumb tray on the bottom of the toaster—like this. I undo the color-adjustment spring—OK. Then I pull out the clip that holds the thermostat, and I remove the old thermostat—there.

Frank shows the thermostat to Patricia and Howard.

Patricia: Thanks. Now, could you pretend that the old thermostat is really the new one and show us how you would put it in?

Frank: OK. That's easy. I just slip in the new thermostat and secure it with the clip. Then I replace the color-adjustment spring and close the crumb tray—done.

Patricia: Thanks, Frank. I'm sorry to make you do extra work, but it helps us to see the complete process.

Frank: No problem. As you saw, it doesn't take very long.

Patricia: What would you do after you replaced the thermostat?

Frank: Well, I'd calibrate it. I'd have to measure how long the toaster takes to pop up with the color control set on medium. If the length of time is OK, given the room temperature, the thermostat is calibrated correctly. If not, I'd go through the adjustment procedure I showed you. After I finished the calibration, I'd toast a slice of bread to see if the new thermostat really fixed the problem.

Patricia: Thanks, Frank.

Patricia switches off the tape recorder.

This is as far as we can go with this toaster for now. Frank, if you have some more time now, why don't we head back to our meeting room and talk about this case a little more?

Frank: Sure. Jeff will save a new thermostat for us.

Discussion

Notice that Patricia allows Frank to concentrate on the repair of the toaster without disruptions to his train of thought. Patricia focuses her questions on Frank's *actions*, on the *process* Frank follows. She needs to know where he starts and what he does at each step. Patricia does not interrupt to ask why Frank took various steps, what he would have done differently in other situations, or what he was thinking as he repaired the toaster. Such interruptions might have caused Frank to forget steps or to repeat steps that he had completed.

Case discussions during detailed investigation can consist of reviews of cases discussed during initial inquiry as well as full discussions of new cases. For example, Patricia Programmer could review the case discussion that appears in Dialog 3.1 and could ask Frank Fixit the questions she listed in her notebook under the heading *Topics for future discussion*.

In general, case discussions make it easy for experts to articulate the process by which they perform their tasks. Some experts, however, find it difficult to describe what they do—even when presented with a specific set of data. If a task consists primarily of mental activities, the expert may not follow a set series of steps. A financial analyst, for example, might study financial data about a company, become aware of important patterns in the data, and make recommendations and analyses on the basis of these patterns. But the analyst might not examine the data in any fixed order and might not look for possible problems in any fixed order. Some experts do not know how to begin a case discussion; sometimes case discussions bog down. If you encounter these problems, ask the expert to study the data that describe the case. Prompt the expert to discuss the case by asking:

What strikes you as important?

What strikes you as unusual?

What do you need to accomplish?

How do you plan to approach the problem?

What do you plan to do first?

5.2 Defining the Expert's Strategy

After each case discussion, the project team should check whether they can refine their current definition of the expert's procedure for performing the task. They should review the process the expert illustrated during the case discussion and compare it with their definition of the procedure. A case discussion might:

- Supply details about a step in the current definition

- Identify a step that is missing from the current definition

- Divide one step in the current definition into a number of substeps

- Identify new steps that are only relevant in situations similar to the case discussed

- Identify steps in the current definition that are *not* relevant in situations similar to the case discussed

The entire project team should discuss how the first several cases change the definition of the expert's strategy. Once the team has developed a fairly detailed description of the procedure, however, the knowledge engineers can review new cases by themselves. They will need to consult the expert only when they notice discrepancies between the new case and their current definition.

Dialog 5.2 illustrates how Patricia Programmer and Frank Fixit reviewed the case discussion that appears in Dialog 5.1.

Dialog 5.2 Reviewing the Definition of the Expert's Procedure

Setting

Patricia Programmer, Howard Hacker, and Frank Fixit have reconvened in their meeting room following the case discussion in Frank's service bay (Dialog 5.1). On the whiteboard, Patricia has written the current (high-level) definition of Frank's toaster-repair procedure:

Step 1. Look at the customer complaint and test the toaster.

Step 2. Track down the problem.

Step 3. Fix the problem that has been identified.

Step 4. Retest the toaster.

Dialog

Patricia: Frank, I've written your procedure for repairing toasters as you presented it at the beginning of the project. We're ready to flesh out the details of this procedure. I'd like to review the case we just discussed to see how it relates to this procedure. Let's start with step one. In this case, the customer complaint was "toast always burns." To test the toaster, you selected the lightest color setting and toasted a slice of bread.

Frank: That's right. That's my first step.

Patricia: Do you always test the toaster in the same way, or does the customer complaint influence how you test?

Frank: The customer complaint tells me how to test.

Patricia: Thanks. Let's move on to step two. This step covers quite a lot. To track down the problem, you tried to adjust the thermostat. That didn't make any difference so you knew you would have to replace it. Is that right?

Frank: Yes, that's right.

Patricia: Good. Now, in some of the cases we discussed earlier in the project, you followed a different procedure at this point. I believe you told us that the toaster problem, which you identified with the test in step one, guides your procedure for tracking down the problem.

Frank: That's right.

Patricia: OK. So for color problems, you first adjust the thermostat. If that fixes the problem, you are done. If not, you replace the thermostat.

Frank: That's right.

Patricia: My interpretation of this step is that you consider two possible causes for color problems. Either the thermostat is out of adjustment, or it is bad.

Frank nods.

When we discussed other types of problems, we saw that you sometimes have to consider as many as five or six possible causes.

Frank: Yes, I do.

Patricia: Well then, step two seems to boil down to a few substeps. First identify a set of possible causes for the problem. Next select one of these causes and try to repair it. Then test the toaster to see whether the problem is fixed. If it isn't fixed, go on to the next possible cause, and try to repair that one. Continue with each possible cause until the problem is fixed.

Frank: I've never thought about it that way, but I think that sounds right.

Patricia: Good. Does my description cover steps three and four?

Frank: Yes. After I try each repair, I always test the toaster to see whether I've fixed the problem.

Patricia: Thanks for reviewing this case with us, Frank. I think we've learned quite a lot about the procedure.

Patricia goes to the whiteboard.

Here's my understanding of your strategy for repairing a toaster.

Patricia presents the new definition of the procedure to Frank and Howard. As she describes each step, she writes it on the whiteboard.

Step 1: Select a test based on the customer complaint.

Step 2: Perform the test to identify the toaster problem.

Step 3: Deduce a set of possible causes based on the toaster problem.

Step 4: Select one of the possible causes, and perform the associated repair procedure.

Step 5: Test the toaster. If the repair fixes the problem, you're done. If not, return to step four, and pick another possible cause to check.

Frank: That's just what I do!

Discussion

The nature of this dialog is different from that of other dialogs we have discussed. In earlier dialogs, Patricia's goal was to *gather information* from Frank. She asked relatively brief questions and allowed Frank to do most of the talking. In this dialog, Patricia's goal is to *confirm her interpretation* of the information she has obtained. Patricia explains how she maps Frank's actions into the general procedure for performing the task. She identifies steps in the procedure that need to be refined, and she describes how the case discussion suggested more detailed substeps. Patricia's explanations are relatively long to ensure that she and Frank understand each other; Frank's responses are generally brief confirmations that he agrees with Patricia's analysis.

5.3 Testing the Generality of the Definition

After the project team members have discussed a case and have updated the definition of the expert's procedure for performing the task, they should discuss whether slight variations in the case would lead to changes in the procedure. The team may discuss hypothetical alternatives to the case or compare the case to other similar cases they have discussed before.

- After the first case discussion or if the case is substantially different from all other cases the team has discussed, the team should explore hypothetical alternatives. The knowledge engineers should pose "what if" questions to see whether small modifications to the case will result in differences in the expert's procedure. The project team can explore alternatives more quickly by considering what-if scenarios than by discussing entire cases from start to finish. Following each what-if scenario, the team can review the current definition of the expert's strategy and update the definition if necessary.

- If the project team has discussed other cases similar in some way to the new case, the team can compare the new case with these other similar cases. The knowledge engineers should look for differences between the expert's procedure in the cases and should check whether their current definition explains clearly why the procedure varied from case to case.

The same knowledge-acquisition approach can be used to compare a case with its hypothetical alternatives and with similar cases that have been discussed before. In Dialog 5.3, Patricia Programmer poses an hypothetical alternative to the case Frank Fixit described in Dialog 5.1.

Dialog 5.3 Exploring Hypothetical Alternatives to a Case

Setting

Patricia Programmer, Howard Hacker, and Frank Fixit have just agreed on a new definition of Frank's toaster-repair procedure. The whiteboard shows this definition.

Step 1. Select a test based on the customer complaint.

Step 2. Perform the test to identify the toaster problem.

Step 3. Deduce a set of possible causes based on the toaster problem.

Step 4. Select one of the possible causes, and perform the associated repair procedure.

Step 5. Test the toaster. If the repair does not fix the problem, return to Step 4.

Dialog

Patricia: Frank, before we leave this case, I'd like to see how your procedure might have been different for a toaster with a slightly different problem.

Frank: All right.

Patricia: Let's say that the customer had checked "toast too light." What would you have done differently?

Frank: Well, to confirm the problem, I would set the color control to medium and toast a slice of bread.

Patricia: OK. In step one, you choose a different test because the customer complaint is different. Let's suppose that the bread comes out very lightly toasted—about what you would have expected on a light setting, not on a medium one.

Frank: Well, that tells me we have a color problem. From there, I'd do the same as before. I'd adjust the thermostat, and if that didn't fix the problem, I'd replace the thermostat.

Patricia: OK. I'll review the full procedure; please tell me whether I've got it right. Step one: Because the complaint is "toast too light," you toast the bread with the color control set on medium. Step two: You perform the test, and the toast comes out light. You know you've got a color problem. Step three: You identify two possible causes—*thermostat out of adjustment* and *bad thermostat.* Step four: You select one possible cause—*thermostat out of adjustment*—and you perform the repair procedure.

Frank nods.

To adjust the thermostat, you turn the adjustment screw two full turns counterclockwise, and you

Frank: Wait a minute! That's wrong! In this case, I suspect a *minor* problem, so I'd only turn the adjustment screw about a quarter of a turn. Also this time the toast is *too light*, not *too dark*. So, I'd turn the screw *clockwise*.

Patricia: I think I see what I missed before. I thought both toasters had the same problem. Now it sounds as though you identified two different *kinds* of color problem in the two cases. In the original case—the toaster you showed us—the toast was *too dark*. In the case I made up, the toast was *too light*. Furthermore in the original case, the problem was *severe;* in my case, the problem was *minor*.

Frank looks fascinated by Patricia's dissection of his process. He nods.

Now, I'll call these two problems *severe too dark* and *minor too light*. Do you think in those terms?

Frank: Well, I never used those names before, but I'd say I do think in those terms. When I do the initial test, I want to find out whether there is a color problem, whether the toast comes out too light or too dark, and how serious the problem is.

Patricia: Good. Now I still need to know why your adjustment procedures were different in the two cases.

Frank: Well, you have to understand how the thermostat works. The thermostat regulates the color of the toast by controlling toasting time—the longer you toast the bread, the darker it's going to be. If the color is too dark, the thermostat is toasting for *too long* a time. If the color is too light, it's toasting for *too short* a time. If the problem is minor, I can almost always fix it by adjusting the thermostat. If it's severe, I'll probably have to replace the thermostat. But sometimes I can correct it with very large adjustments.

Patricia: That seems straightforward. Here's my understanding. In step three, you considered different possible causes for the two cases because you had identified different problems. In the original case, the first possible cause was a *severe* thermostat problem, heating for *too long* a time. The second possible cause was a bad thermostat. In my hypothetical case, the possible causes were *minor* thermostat problem, heating for *too short* a time, and bad thermostat.

Frank *(excited):* I like it! You make it sound so scientific. This is getting fun. What next?

Patricia: Let's move on to step four. Can you explain the difference in the adjustment procedures you used for the two cases?

Frank: Well, the adjustment screw is our way of controlling the toasting time. I turn it counterclockwise to shorten the toasting time and clockwise to lengthen toasting time.

Patricia: I think I see. In one case, you had to shorten the toasting time, and in the other, you had to lengthen it. Do you always use two complete turns for a severe problem and a quarter turn for a minor problem?

Frank: That's how I start. Then I toast another piece of bread and see if I'm done. If I didn't go far enough, I turn the adjustment screw a little farther. If I went too far, I turn back the other direction just a little.

Patricià: Good. We're down to step five. What would you do here?

Frank: Well, we've already tested the toaster as part of the adjustment procedure. This is your case—tell me what happens.

Patricia: Let's say the adjustment works this time.

Frank: OK. Like I said, we've already tested the toaster, so we're done. That's always going to happen when you have a thermostat problem. In general though, at step five, I've just made a repair—so I think I might have fixed the problem, and I test to see if I did. So I'd toast a slice of bread on medium.

Patricia: And you test the same way, regardless of the repair procedure?

Frank: That's right.

Discussion

Patricia's goal in this dialog is to test whether her current understanding of Frank's procedure is sufficiently general. If so, her definition of Frank's procedure will be consistent with Frank's actions for a wide variety of cases. Patricia asks Frank how he would repair a toaster if the customer complaint differed slightly from the complaint in the previous case discussion. Patricia looks for ways in which Frank's procedure differs for the two cases; when she identifies one such difference, she checks whether the variation in Frank's procedure is consistent with her definition. For example, Patricia notices that in step 1, Frank performs different tests for the two cases. This difference is consistent with her definition, which states that Frank chooses the test *on the basis of the customer complaint.* On the other hand, when Patricia learns that Frank adjusts the thermostat differently for two toasters that each have a color problem, she knows that she is missing important information.

In this dialog, Patricia learns that Frank omitted many details from his original description of the thermostat-adjustment process. Frank is so familiar with the operation of a toaster thermostat that these details seem obvious to him. Notice that Frank is able to describe how he uses the principles of thermostat operation to guide his adjustment procedures. Once Frank has explained the principles, Patricia and Howard can see how these principles could be applied in different cases—the team does not have to uncover variations through a long series of additional case discussions.

Note how Patricia and Frank invent a project vocabulary to facilitate their discussions of the new concepts they discover together. They have defined problems *severe too dark* and *minor too light*. Frank was certainly aware of different kinds of color problems, but he may have distinguished them only subconsciously. He never found a need to name them and to talk about them before.

5.4 Defining the Expert System's Procedure

Once the knowledge engineers understand how the expert performs the task, they need to translate the expert's strategy into the process by which the *expert system* can perform the same task. The knowledge engineers need to identify the input steps, the reasoning steps, and the output steps that the system should perform. They need to learn the order in which the system should perform its steps and the conditions under which it should perform the steps.

To define the procedure for the expert system, review the expert's procedure.

- Look for actions the expert takes that a computer program cannot take (for example, adjusting the toaster thermostat). Decide what steps should occur in place of these actions.

- Look for steps that someone other than the expert performs that the expert system should perform (for example, updating the toaster-part database).

- Look for steps the expert system should perform that no one performs currently. (For example, it might be useful for the toaster-repair advisor to keep historical data about specific toasters so it can identify recurrent problems or repairs that were unsuccessful.)

- Imagine how you would specify a computer program to perform the task. Identify boundary conditions the expert might not have mentioned, and discuss what the system should do in those situations.

Try to make the procedure as general as possible so it will require only minor modifications as the scope of the system is extended. Consider the range of cases you discussed during initial inquiry. Be sure that the procedure is general enough to handle the cases outside the scope of the current development increment.

In Dialog 5.4, Patricia Programmer defines the procedure for the toaster-repair advisor.

Dialog 5.4 Defining the Expert System's Procedure

Setting

Patricia Programmer, Howard Hacker, and Frank Fixit have defined the process by which Frank repairs toasters. They meet to define the process by which the *toaster-repair advisor* will assist with toaster repair. The whiteboard shows Frank's repair procedure.

Step 1. Select a test based on the customer complaint.

Step 2. Perform the test to identify the toaster problem.

Step 3. Deduce a set of possible causes based on the toaster problem.

Step 4. Select one of the possible causes and perform the associated repair procedure.

Step 5. Test the toaster. If the repair does not fix the problem, return to Step 4.

Dialog

Patricia: Frank, we have been talking about how *you* repair toasters. Now we're going to concentrate on the *expert system*—the system won't be able to repair the toasters itself. Instead it will assist the repair staff. We need to separate the steps the expert system will take from those the repair person will take. I'll refer to the person that the toaster-repair advisor helps as the *user*.

Frank: OK.

Patricia: I'll explain what I expect the system to do, and you can let me know whether it sounds correct. When I run into questions, I'll ask you what to do.

Frank: All right. Go on.

Patricia: In step one, you use the customer complaint to select the test. This sounds like two steps for the system: Get the complaint from the user, and decide what test is appropriate.

Frank nods.

In step two, the system can't perform the test. It will have to recommend the test procedure, wait for the user to perform the test, then get the test result from the user. Then on the basis of the test result, it will have to deduce the problem with the toaster.

Frank nods again.

That brings up my first question. Will you always find some problem?

Frank: I'm not sure I know what you mean.

Patricia: Can you ever perform the initial test and find nothing wrong?

Frank: I think I see what you're getting at. Is this the kind of thing you're talking about? Last June my brother-in-law, Mike, called me one Saturday. He said that his toaster wasn't working and asked if I'd fix it. I stopped by to take a look at it. He said the toaster had been working fine until Monday. On Monday morning, his toast burned; after that, the toast *always* came out burnt. I tested it like I showed you. I put the control on light, toasted a slice of bread, and it came out very light—just like it should have! I set the toaster on medium and tried again. The toast came out a nice golden brown. It looked fine to me, and Mike said that was just how he liked it. Mike couldn't figure out why the toaster had suddenly stopped working but then worked fine for me. You know what the problem was? His daughter, Jane, had come home from college the weekend before, and she had started a summer job on Monday. Jane had to leave for her job very early in the morning—before Mike was up. When she fixed her breakfast, Jane set the toaster on the darkest color—she likes her toast sort of burnt. Anyway, all year long Mike is the only one in the house who uses the toaster. He always leaves it on medium. When his toast burned on Monday, it never even occurred to him to check the color control!

Patricia, Howard, and Frank all laugh and shake their heads.

Patricia: That's a good example, Frank. That's just the kind of situation I wondered about. Do you often get a toaster like that—with no problem?

Frank: No. Not very often. Those cases are very difficult. The toaster could be fine, but then again, it might have a wiring problem that comes and goes.

Patricia: What do you think the expert system should do if the user doesn't find any problem?

Frank: I guess we'd need to have someone else look at the toaster. I'd hate to give it back to the customer without checking further.

Patricia: OK. Now, let's assume the user did find some problem. The system will need to check that the problem is something it can handle. For now, it will have to be a color problem. Also, we are going to be limited to two-slice toasters. So we'll need to get the make and model from the user so we can look up the toaster style. If the toaster style or the problem type are outside the current scope, the system will inform the user that it can't help and will terminate the interaction.

Frank: That sounds fine.

Patricia: In step three, the system will deduce a set of possible causes based on the toaster problem. In step four, it will select a possible cause. That's where I need help, Frank. Do you always try to adjust the thermostat before you try to replace it?

Frank: Yes, because that is a cheaper repair.

Patricia: We're only concerned about color problems for now, but I'd like to know if step four is more difficult for other problems. Do you always try the *cheapest* repair first?

Frank: Not always. With color problems, I do—even when I think the most likely cause is a bad thermostat. But for other problems, I'll try the *most likely* cause first. Or I might do the *quickest* repair first even if it's a little more expensive. It depends.

Patricia: I see. For a given problem, do you always try the possible causes *in the same order,* or do you have to figure out what to try first for the particular toaster?

Frank: I don't think I spend any time thinking about what to try first.

Patricia: For any particular problem, do you think you could give me a list of the repairs that you try in the order that you try them?

Frank: Yes, I would guess I could, but I need to think about it some more.

Patricia: Good. That's all I need to know for now. So the expert system will determine an ordered list of possible causes based on the toaster problem. The next step is to pick the first cause from the list and to decide what repair is appropriate.

Frank nods.

The expert system can't perform the repair so it has to instruct the user to carry out the repair procedure. This is where my next question comes up. When you described the thermostat-adjustment procedure, it sounded like a series of procedures, not just one. You make your first adjustment, then you test to see if you still have a problem. If so, you make another adjustment and test again. You repeat this process until the toast comes out the way you want.

Frank scowls but nods.

I need to know how much the expert system should guide the user through this procedure. Suppose a repair person had identified a color problem—say *minor too light*—and called you on the phone to find out what to do. What would you say?

Frank: It depends on who calls. Let's say it's Jeff; he's been working here for a couple years. I'd tell him to adjust the thermostat to lengthen the toasting time. That's all I'd have to tell him. He knows how to adjust thermostats. Now, if Dick called, I'd have to give more instructions. He just started a few weeks ago. I'd explain the whole procedure like I explained it to you. I'd suggest that he start by making just a quarter of a turn. After I explained the procedure, I'm sure Dick could carry it out. It might take him a few more adjustments than it would take Jeff or me. But that's fine—that's how Dick will learn to judge how far to turn the screw.

Patricia: So, you wouldn't ask Dick the result after each adjustment, and tell him how much to turn the screw the next time?

Frank: Oh, no! That would be a waste of my time and an insult to Dick.

Patricia: Thanks. That answers my question. Now, the other repair procedure we discussed was to replace the thermostat and then calibrate it. Should we treat that as two procedures or one?

Frank: I guess I think of each repair as a single procedure. If I were talking to Jeff on the phone, I'd just tell him to replace and calibrate the thermostat. Dick would need more instructions. Weren't we going to let new staff members ask the computer for instructions if they need to?

Patricia: Yes, but that will be the one of the last capabilities we add. For now, we can have the system ask the user to replace and calibrate the thermostat. Eventually, the user will be able to request a description of the replacement or calibration procedure.

Frank: That sounds fine.

Patricia: Great. To summarize this step then, the expert system would ask the user to perform a given repair procedure and to test the toaster. Then it would get the test result from the user. If there's no problem, the system would end the interaction. In later versions of the expert system, there will be additional steps: The system will have to update the toaster-part database and generate a bill for the customer.

Frank: That's right. And if there is still a problem, we go to the next possible cause and repeat the process.

Patricia: What happens when you run out of possible causes?

Frank: What do you mean?

Patricia: With the toasters we have discussed, you always found a repair that fixed the problem. You tried to repair each possible cause in turn until you found the right one. Do you ever try *all* possible causes without being able to fix the problem?

Frank: I guess that could happen, but it's rare. There are some problems we just can't fix. And sometimes, a repair person doesn't do the repair procedure correctly. When they run out of things to try, they come to see me. If that situation occurs, I guess the computer should just tell the user to see the senior member of the repair staff.

Patricia: That sounds good. Do you think we should make the same recommendation if the user has a problem outside the current scope—say, for example, a no-latch problem?

Frank: Yes, we want to be able to tell them what to do even if it's to ask someone else for help.

Patricia: Thanks, Frank. I think we've got the full procedure now.

Patricia goes to the whiteboard and describes the steps to Frank and Howard as she writes them on the board.

Step 1: Get the customer complaint from the user.

Step 2: Infer the appropriate test based on the customer complaint.

Step 3: Ask the user to perform the test.

Step 4: Get the test result from the user.

Step 5: Infer the toaster problem based on the test result.

Step 6: If the test found no problem, refer the user to the senior member of the repair staff, and end the interaction.

Step 7: Decide whether this case is within the scope of the system based on the toaster problem.

Hmm, I guess we need to know the toaster style, too. We need to get the make and model from the user.

Patricia erases the description of step 7.

Step 7: Get the toaster make and model from the user.

Frank: I think it's a little strange to ask for the make and model number here. It would make more sense to get that information right up front.

Patricia: Yes, of course. I'll add those questions to step 1.

Patricia erases and rewrites the description of step 1.

Step 1: Get the toaster make and model and the customer complaints.

Now, we're back to step 7.

Step 7: Infer the toaster style from the make and model.

Step 8: Decide whether this case is within the scope of the system based on the toaster problem and the toaster style.

Step 9: If the case is outside the current scope, refer the user to the senior member of the repair staff, and terminate the interaction.

Step 10: Infer an ordered list of possible causes based on the toaster problem.

Step 11: Select the first possible cause (or the next one if we've been through here before). If there are no possible causes left, refer the user to the senior member of the repair staff, and terminate the interaction.

Step 12: Infer the appropriate repair procedure based on the possible cause that we're considering.

Step 13: Ask the user to perform the procedure and to test the toaster.

Step 14: Get the test result from the user.

Step 15: If the test result shows no problem, terminate the interaction. Otherwise return to step 11.

Frank: Fifteen steps? It only took me five!

Patricia: You see? You're doing a lot more than you think!

Frank: I guess so.

Discussion

Patricia needs to define clearly what the expert system will do and what the user will do. Whereas Frank can *perform* tests himself and *observe* the results, the expert system can only *ask the user* to perform the tests, and it must rely on the user to *report the results*. Notice that Patricia investigates what the expert system should do in certain boundary conditions.

- The initial test finds no problem.

- The problem is outside the scope of the expert system.

- The system exhausts the list of possible causes without having fixed the toaster.

These possibilities are unusual enough that Frank did not think to mention them; Patricia must know what the expert system should do, however, in even the most unlikely circumstances.

Notice that Patricia considers problems outside the current scope; this practice will help her to ensure that she defines a procedure that can accommodate enhancements to the system. Although Frank considers possible causes *of color problems* in a fixed order, Patricia needs to know whether he *always* considers possible causes in a fixed order. If not, Patricia would need to add steps to the system's procedure. For example, at the beginning of step 11, the system might decide which possible cause to try next.

We have described how knowledge engineers can compose an *initial* definition of the expert system's procedure. Although the knowledge engineers turn their focus to other aspects of task performance, they may continue to learn about the expert's strategy. Very often, knowledge engineers refine the definition of the system's procedure as they learn more about the expert's reasoning process.

5.5 Points to Remember

Knowledge engineers face two major challenges during detailed investigation. First, they must obtain the knowledge *relevant to the expert system's task* and avoid getting sidetracked with the remainder of the expert's vast knowledge about the application subject area. Second, they must *learn the details that will enable them to implement an expert system*—details that expert may not consider important. Knowledge engineers can meet the first challenge by using case discussions to focus interviews on the knowledge relevant to the task. They can meet the second challenge by concentrating on the goals of detailed investigation.

The first of these goals is to understand the steps the expert takes in performing the task (Table 5.1). Knowledge engineers must understand this aspect of the expert's problem-solving process thoroughly enough to enable them to describe a method by which the *expert system* can perform the same task.

Table 5.1 Learning the Steps in the Task

Objective	Useful Activities
Learn the expert's strategy.	Discuss in detail the actions the expert would take to perform the task for specific cases.
	Do not interrupt the expert's train of thought; avoid questions about the expert's reasoning process or about alternative situations.
	Tape record the discussions for later review.

Table 5.1 (continued)

Objective	Useful Activities
Define the expert's strategy.	Draft a definition from the high-level description you obtained during initial inquiry. Review the cases you discuss against the current definition of the expert's strategy, and refine the definition as appropriate. • Obtain details about steps in the definition. • Identify new steps. • Define the circumstances under which steps are appropriate. • Divide steps in the current definition into substeps.
Test the generality of your definition.	Discuss what the expert would have done if there had been slight variations to the cases. Compare each case with other similar cases and with hypothetical alternatives. Find out *why* the expert's procedure varied in similar cases. Refine the definition to account for the variations in the expert's procedure in different circumstances. Check your definition against the cases you discussed during initial inquiry that are *outside the scope of the current development increment.* Be sure your definition will accommodate these cases when the system is enhanced in future cycles of development.
Define the *expert system's* procedure.	Identify actions the expert takes that a computer program cannot take. Pay particular attention to the expert's ability to observe and assess sensory data (sounds, smells, and so on). Identify steps someone other than the expert performs that the expert system should perform. Identify steps no one performs currently that the expert system should perform. Decide what input, reasoning, and output steps the expert system should take in place of these actions. Remember that the expert system must know what to do in *all* situations it encounters. Try to anticipate unlikely situations and to specify what the system should do. Make sure that the system will exit gracefully when it is not able to perform the task. Learn how to identify situations beyond the system's capabilities, and decide how the system should behave in those situations.

Chapter 6

Understanding the Expert's Reasoning Process

Patricia Programmer, Howard Hacker, and Frank Fixit are in the conceptual design stage of the first cycle of development for the toaster-repair advisor. To this point, Patricia and Howard have concentrated on the first goal of detailed investigation: to learn the steps in the toaster-repair task. They are now ready to begin to investigate the second goal: to understand how Frank reasons about toaster-repair problems.

When the knowledge engineers have learned the steps in the task, they can turn their attention to the expert's **reasoning process**—that is, the process by which the expert uses available information about a case to deduce additional facts and hypotheses about the case. For example, Frank Fixit is able to reason with data that he observes or finds in manuals. On the basis of these data, Frank makes conclusions about the possible toaster problems. He uses these conclusions plus additional observed data to make more conclusions and so on until he reaches the decisions that form the results of the repair task—namely the cause of the toaster malfunction and the repair procedure that will correct the problem.

Knowledge engineers do not have to wait until they have a *complete* definition of the expert's procedure before they begin to discuss the expert's reasoning. It is useful, however, for the team to discuss the expert's procedure for one case (or a series of cases) and then to review the expert's reasoning for the same case(s). During discussions of an expert's procedure for performing the task, knowledge engineers usually identify *reasoning steps* in which the expert makes decisions about the case. As we saw in Chapter 5, Patricia Programmer learned that Frank Fixit infers the appropriate initial test procedure, the toaster problem, the ordered list of possible causes, and so on. Patricia's next goal is to understand exactly *how* Frank decides on the initial test procedure, the toaster problem, and the list of possible causes *in a wide variety of situations*. Detailed discussions about the reasoning process often reveal that the expert makes additional intermediate conclusions that were not apparent in earlier discussions.

To understand an expert's reasoning process, knowledge engineers should first identify the conclusions that the expert makes and the information that forms the basis for these conclusions (Section 6.1). Then they should check whether the expert bases some of the decisions on additional hidden assumptions (Section 6.2). Finally they should investigate whether the expert system will need to reason with uncertainty (Section 6.3).

6.1 Identifying the Expert's Inferences

Each decision that adds to an expert's body of knowledge about a case is called an **inference** (Figure 6.1). An inference specifies a **condition** and a **conclusion** that can be made when the condition is true. The condition of an inference tests facts and hypotheses about **basis characteristics:** the characteristics of the case that the expert considers in making the decision. The conclusion specifies facts or hypotheses that the expert deduces about the **conclusion characteristic.** You can think of an inference as a single step in the expert's reasoning process. During that step, the basis characteristics of the inference are the input to the reasoning process, and the conclusion characteristic is the resulting output.

6.1.1 Recognizing Inferences

When knowledge engineers focus on the expert's reasoning process, they try to identify the knowledge that allows the expert to make decisions. They should look for:

- **Definitions** or well-established relationships between objects, processes, or concepts. A definition could constitute a guideline that relates a set of data to an abstraction of that data. (For example, in toaster models GA700 through GA720, a line voltage below 117 volts is *too low*.)

- **Formulas** or specifications of how to calculate certain numerical values from other values. (For example, the current in a part of an electrical circuit can be calculated by dividing the voltage by the resistance.)

- **Heuristics** or *rules of thumb* that guide the expert. (For example, if the customer complains that a model GA11569 toaster always burns the toast, the problem is usually that the toast will not pop up.) Typically heuristics are not based on hard, scientific evidence; rather they express relationships that the expert has found to hold true most of the time.

Figure 6.1 Components of an inference. An inference indicates how to use information about *basis characteristic(s)* to deduce information about *conclusion characteristic(s)*. For example (a), Frank Fixit infers the *ordered list of possible causes* of a toaster malfunction on the basis of the *toaster problem*. An inference specifies a *condition* about the basis characteristics and a *conclusion* that can be made if the condition is true. For example (b), if the toaster problem is *severe too dark*, Frank concludes that the possible causes are *severe thermostat problem, toasting for too long a time*, and *bad thermostat*.

BASIS CHARACTERISTIC		CONCLUSION CHARACTERISTIC
toaster problem	is used to infer	ordered possible causes

(a)

CONDITION		CONCLUSION
For severe too dark problems	infer ⟶	Possible causes are 1. Severe thermostat problem, toasting for too long a time 2. Bad thermostat
For minor too light problems	infer ⟶	Possible causes are 1. Minor thermostat problem, toasting for too short a time 2. Bad thermostat

(b)

Often, the condition in a definition or in a formula is implicit: The basis characteristics must be known. For example, in the formula:

$$current = voltage \div resistance$$

the basis characteristics are *voltage* and *resistance;* the conclusion characteristic is *current*. The formula specifies how to make a conclusion about *current*, but it does not specify a condition on the *voltage* and the *resistance*. If an expert system is to use this formula, however, the implicit condition is that the system must know the *voltage* and the *resistance* before it can calculate the *current*.

In contrast with a definition or a formula, an heuristic always specifies a condition. Because heuristics are not hard-and-fast rules, however, they often express some degree of uncertainty. An heuristic's conclusion may be qualified with words such as:

. . . probably is . . .

. . . might be . . .

. . . usually is . . .

6.1.2 Reviewing Case Discussions

A case discussion provides an ideal opportunity to learn how an expert reasons. Unfortunately, most experts become frustrated when their performance of a task is interrupted continually with questions about their reasoning process. We suggest therefore that you focus on the expert's reasoning process in a *review* of the original case discussion. In your initial discussion of a case, focus on the expert's strategy as we discussed in Chapter 5. Pay attention, however, for any indication that the expert has made a conclusion. If you find that you would like to ask a question, such as:

Why did you . . . ?

How did you decide . . . ?

What does . . . tell you?

write a note to yourself to raise the question in your second pass through the case.

When you are ready to discuss the expert's reasoning process, read through notes you took during the initial case discussion and list the kinds of inference the expert appeared to draw. To begin the review of the case discussion, explain that you would like to reconsider the case to understand how the expert made decisions. Present a synopsis of the case to establish the context for your questions. As you review the case, try to learn:

- *What* the expert was thinking

- *Why* this line of reasoning was important

- *How* the expert made each conclusion

- *When* the expert would make the same conclusion

- *When* the expert would make a different conclusion

Try to identify *all* the factors that make each decision valid. The expert may not think to mention all relevant factors so you should suggest slight variations to the case to see whether the expert would reach a different conclusion in different circumstances.

A tape recording of the original case discussion can facilitate your second pass through the case. If you recorded the original discussion, review the tape before you meet with the expert; write down the locations on the tape at which the discussion indicated that the expert had made a conclusion. When you interview the expert, play enough of the tape to establish the context for the discussion, then ask the necessary questions to obtain an indepth understanding of the expert's reasoning process.

Dialog 6.1 illustrates how Patricia Programmer reviews a recorded case discussion with Frank Fixit. The original case discussion appears in Dialog 5.1.

Dialog 6.1 Reviewing a Case to Learn the Expert's Reasoning Process

Setting

Patricia Programmer, Howard Hacker, and Frank Fixit meet to review Frank's reasoning process. Patricia has set up a tape recorder so she can replay the tape of an earlier case discussion. On the whiteboard, Patricia has listed the types of inference the team identified through their discussions of the toaster-repair procedure.[1]

- Infer the appropriate test based on the customer complaint.

- Infer the toaster problem based on the test result.

- Infer toaster style from make and model.

- Decide whether the case is within the scope of the expert system based on toaster problem and toaster style.

---

1. The types of inference were identified as reasoning steps that the toaster-repair advisor must perform; refer to the end of Dialog 5.4.

- Infer an ordered list of possible causes based on the toaster problem.

- Infer the appropriate repair procedure based on the possible cause currently under consideration.

Dialog

Patricia: Frank, I'd like to change our focus today. So far we have concentrated on the *actions* you take when you repair a toaster. Now I'd like to talk about the *decisions* you make during the repair process. I need to understand how you make these decisions. You remember that I recorded our session in the service department?

Frank: Yes. I've been wondering if you were going to use that tape.

Patricia: I sure am! Today's the day. You remember the case? The toast always burned, and you had to replace the thermostat.

Frank: Yes, I remember it.

Patricia: OK. I'll play the tape to remind us what you were doing, and I'll stop when I need to ask questions. I've made a list of the kinds of decisions you seem to make.

Patricia points to the list on the whiteboard. Frank scans the list and nods.

We'll probably discover more kinds of decisions as we investigate further. As we reach the point in the discussion where you appear to make one of those decisions, I'm going to stop the tape and try to find out the exact factors that allowed you to make the decision.

Frank: I'm ready. Roll the tape.

Patricia starts the tape. Patricia, Howard, and Frank listen to Patricia's introduction. She stops the tape after they hear Frank say, "I first look at the repair slip that is taped to the toaster. They only checked one complaint, 'toast always burns.' I'm going to test the toaster to see what the real problem is."

Patricia: Frank, you commented that the customer had only checked *one* complaint. Why was that significant?

Frank: Well as we discussed, I need to decide how to test the toaster. If they also had checked "toast doesn't pop up," I would have suspected a no-trip problem, and my test would have been a little different.

Patricia: I see. We really need to talk about customer *complaints*, plural, because they can check more than one.

Frank: Yes. We ask them to check *all* problems they have encountered. In this case, they only checked one problem. But, of course, they might just have overlooked the box for "toast does not pop up." I don't really know what's wrong until I do the test.

Patricia: It sounds to me as though you use customer complaints to make a guess about the toaster problem. I'll call your guess the "suspected toaster problem." Then you use the suspected toaster problem to select the test procedure. Does that sound right?

Frank: Yes, I guess that's what I do.

Patricia: In this case, what problem did you suspect?

Frank: Well, I guessed right. I suspected that the problem was *severe too dark*.

Patricia: Try to think of other occasions when you repaired a toaster with the complaint *toast always burns* and no other complaint. Did you suspect the problem *severe too dark* for *all* these toasters?

Frank: Well, I can't remember particular toasters—I've seen so many. But I guess it would depend on the model.

Frank flips through his notes.

This was a Toasts-Best, model TB10445. The thermostat on that model is prone to failure.

Patricia: Can you give me an example of a situation in which the customer just checks *toast always burns,* but you would suspect a problem other than *severe too dark?*

Frank: Well. Let me think—yes. If it was a Toasts-Best TB27713, I think I'd suspect a *minor too dark* problem, even though the customer said the toast *burns.* That model is brand new, and it uses a very reliable thermostat. Unfortunately, many of those toasters were assembled poorly— if you bump the toaster around on the kitchen counter a few times, the thermostat tends to get out of adjustment. So I would test the toaster with the color control on *medium,* not on light. I can think of another example, but it's not a color problem. Do you want to hear about it anyway?

Patricia: Yes. The system will need to decide whether the problem is a color problem so we need to know enough to make that judgment.

Frank: That's right. Anyway, if I got a General Appliance, model GA11569, and the repair slip just said toast always burns, I would suspect that the toast doesn't pop up even if they didn't check that box on the repair slip. We just see more no-trip problems with those toasters than color problems.

Patricia: So you use the toaster make and model as well as the customer complaints to decide the suspected toaster problem.

Frank: Yes, I guess I do.

Patricia: If I made a list of all the different toaster models and we assume that the repair slip just says toast always burns, could you tell me what problem you suspect?

Frank: No, I don't think I could tell you for *every* model—probably just a dozen or so of the most common models.

Patricia: So what would you do for a model that you don't see often?

Frank: Well, if I don't know anything about the particular model, I guess I'd assume that the problem was *severe too dark.*

Patricia: Thanks, Frank. Let's go on.

Patricia starts the tape. She stops it after they hear Frank say, "I plug the toaster in, OK. Now I put in a slice of bread. I turn the color knob down to the lightest setting, push down the operating lever, and wait to see what happens."

After you determine the suspected problem, you use the suspected problem to chose the test procedure. In this case you toasted a slice of bread on light. Can we use a short name for that test?

Frank: Sure. Let's call it *toast on light*.

Patricia: OK. If you suspect the problem *severe too dark*, do you always choose *toast on light* to test the toaster?

Frank: Yes. That's the way to test for *severe too dark*.

Patricia: You wouldn't have tried a different test for a different model?

Frank: Well, slight details of the test might vary from toaster to toaster, depending on the kind of color-control switch.

Patricia: Think about how you would tell Jeff or Dick to perform this test. Would your instructions differ across toasters?

Frank: Not the short instructions—I'd always tell Jeff the same thing. But if Dick requested detailed instructions, I'd want to tell him *exactly* what to do for the particular model. I'd like to show him a diagram of the toaster with an arrow pointing to the color-control switch and another arrow showing where he should set the switch.

Patricia: It sounds like we can decide the test from the suspected problem alone. We don't have to consider toaster model. But when the user requests detailed instructions for a procedure, we need to give different instructions based on both the procedure and the toaster model.

Frank: Yes, that's exactly right.

Patricia: Good. Let's go on.

Discussion

In this part of the dialog, Patricia investigates the first type of inference on her list: *Infer the appropriate test based on the customer complaint*. She discovers that this item comprises two distinct inferences. First, Frank infers the *suspected toaster problem* based on *customer complaints*, *toaster make*, and *toaster model*. Second, he infers the appropriate *initial test procedure* based on the *suspected toaster problem*. Note that Frank was not aware that he considered the toaster make and model until Patricia asked him to think about other cases.

In addition to identifying that Frank makes these the two types of inference, Patricia learns Frank's heuristics for making the first decision in three different circumstances—for customer complaint *toast always burns* and toasters *Toasts-Best TB10445*, *Toasts-Best TB27713*, and *General Appliance GA11569*. She also learns that if the customer complaint is *toast always burns* and Frank does not have extensive experience with a particular model, his *default* assumption is to suspect the problem *severe too dark*. Patricia knows that she will need to learn what problem Frank suspects for other combinations of customer complaints and toaster makes and models.

Patricia learned one example of Frank's second kind of inference. If he suspects the problem *severe too dark*, he performs the test *toast on light*. This guideline is more a definition than an heuristic, it is not based on Frank's unique experience. *Toast on light* is the generally accepted method for confirming the problem *severe too dark*. Patricia knows that she will need to ask Frank to list the methods for testing other suspected problems.

6.2 Checking for Hidden Assumptions

In a case discussion, the knowledge engineers must rely on the expert to identify the basis characteristics for each inference. For example, if Frank Fixit does not mention a piece of information when he and Patricia discuss a particular inference, Patricia will not realize that the information was part of the rationale for Frank's decision. As we discussed in Section 6.1, it is important to identify *all* factors that form the basis for an inference. To uncover the complete rationale for every decision, review the expert's inferences for hidden assumptions. Experts often neglect to mention factors that they consider *implicit* or *obvious*.

6.2.1 Checking for Implicit Assumptions

Once an expert and a knowledge engineer have discussed a particular characteristic of a case, the expert may use this characteristic as an implicit basis for some future decisions. For example, if Frank Fixit has mentioned that the toaster under discussion is made by Toasts-Best, he may not remember to tell Patricia Programmer that he uses this information when he decides how to repair a suspected problem. Patricia Programmer can identify which decisions depend on the toaster model by asking Frank what he would have done differently if the toaster had been made by General Appliance or some other manufacturer.

It is common for an expert to use limitations on the expert system's current scope as implicit assumptions behind many decisions. For example, when Frank Fixit tells Patricia Programmer that a decision is *always* valid, he might mean that it is valid *for all color problems* but not necessarily for no-latch problems. Or Frank might mean that the decision is valid *for all two-slice toasters* but not necessarily for other kinds of toasters. After Patricia has identified an inference, she should check whether it will be valid when the scope of the system is extended. If necessary, she could add a description of the current scope to the condition of the inference.

6.2.2 Checking for Obvious Assumptions

Experts often fail to mention information that is obvious to them— data that they can observe, feel, hear, or smell. Even the most observant knowledge engineers cannot detect *all* data that an expert perceives and uses in the process of performing the task. One way to discover exactly what information the expert uses in making decisions is to ask the expert to explain *over the telephone* how to perform the task for a particular case. The expert will have to ask the caller to examine and describe the situation; the expert's questions can identify information the expert might otherwise neglect to mention.

To make this kind of case discussion realistic, the knowledge engineers may need to enlist the assistance of a second professional in the expert's field. In many applications, the knowledge engineers are not familiar enough with the task to provide consistent answers to the expert's question. A professional in the expert's field, however, could prepare a complete case description for discussion.

If your project includes multiple experts, select one expert to discuss a case and a second expert to prepare a case description. If your project does not include multiple experts, try to find someone who is sufficiently knowledgeable about the application subject area to provide answers to the expert's questions about an hypothetical case. If possible, find someone who has access to data about actual situations in which the task was performed. In the interview, ask the expert and the person who prepared the case description to follow these ground rules.

- The expert may see neither the case description nor any physical objects relevant to the task.

- The expert should describe how to perform the task. When an action or decision depends on data about the case, the expert should request the data from the person who prepared the case description.

- The person who prepared the case description may supply data but may not make decisions about the case.

- The person who prepared the case description may not *volunteer* information.

- The expert should ask multiple-choice or yes/no questions wherever possible. To formulate a multiple-choice question, the expert will need to identify precisely what information is relevant. A multiple-choice question also limits the likelihood that the person who prepared the case description will inadvertently volunteer information.

You may want to tape record the case discussion to facilitate a future review of the case as we discussed in Section 6.1. Dialog 6.2 illustrates how Patricia Programmer used this technique with help from Barbara Burnt.

Dialog 6.2 Discussing a Case with Two Experts

Setting

Patricia Programmer asked Barbara Burnt to prepare a case description. Then she asked Barbara, Frank Fixit, and Howard Hacker to join her in a meeting to discuss the case. Patricia asked Barbara not to bring the toaster to the meeting but rather to bring a written description of the case and any manuals or notes that she used when she repaired the toaster.

Patricia set up a tape recorder (with Frank's and Barbara's approval) to record the interaction. Patricia started the recording by identifying the date of the meeting, the participants, and the content of the discussion. We join the interview after Patricia has explained the rules of the game to Barbara and Frank.

Dialog

Patricia: Let's begin. Frank, it might be easiest for you to pretend that Barbara has phoned you about a toaster problem. Barbara, remember that you're not supposed to be an expert. Make Frank tell you how to do everything. Everyone set?

Frank and Barbara both nod.

OK. Frank, you begin.

Frank: So Barbara, what's the matter with the toaster?

Barbara: I don't know, Frank. That's why I phoned you.

Frank *(chuckling):* Right. What kind of toaster do you have?

Barbara: It's a General Appliance, model GA98985.

Frank writes down the make and model number.

Frank: GA98985? Where did you find that? I don't think I've ever seen one.

Barbara *(smiling):* I didn't want to make this too easy for you.

Frank *(chuckling):* OK. Look on the repair slip and tell me what complaints are checked off.

Barbara glances at her notes.

Barbara: They checked "bread not toasted."

Frank: That doesn't tell me much.

(to Patricia)

This could mean that the thermostat is shot, a heating element is bad, or maybe there's a problem in the wiring.

(to Barbara)

Set the color selector on the darkest setting and toast a slice of bread.

Barbara: OK.

(to Patricia)

Should I just tell Frank what happened when I toasted the bread?

Patricia: No, I want to hear what Frank asks you. Frank, try to state your request for the test results as a multiple-choice question.

Frank: OK. Barbara, what color was the bread: white, light, medium, brown, or burnt?

Barbara: It was white.

Frank: Was the bread warm at all, or was it the same temperature as when you put it in?

Barbara: It was a little warm.

Frank *(to Patricia):* The bread is warm so that tells me the heating element is doing *something*. If the bread wasn't even warm, I would suspect a problem in the heating elements or maybe a problem in the wiring. Let's see. I don't know what kind of thermostat this toaster uses. It looks like Barbara brought the manuals. Can I look up this toaster, or should I ask Barbara?

Patricia: Go ahead and look in the manual yourself, but let us know what you're looking for.

Barbara hands Frank the manual.

Frank: Thanks. I need to see what kind of thermostat this toaster uses. General Appliance uses three or four different varieties, and the repair procedure is slightly different for each kind.

Frank flips through the manual.

OK. It uses a *class two* thermostat. Hmm. We've got a service bulletin. Barbara, would you look at the thermostat in the toaster and read me the part number?

Barbara *(looking at her notes):* It's an X77213.

Frank: OK. What you have to do next is to go to the store room and get a new thermostat, model X77215. Replace the old thermostat with that new part.

Patricia: So for this toaster, you don't try to adjust the thermostat first?

Frank: Well the service bulletin says that there is a serious problem in thermostat X77213. We're supposed to replace that part with the new part, X77215, anytime we see a toaster that still has the old thermostat even if the old thermostat still works fine. So, there's no point trying to adjust a part we have to replace.

(to Barbara)

Did you replace the part?

Barbara: Yes I did.

Frank: Good. And you calibrated the new thermostat?

Barbara nods.

Did that fix the problem?

Barbara: Yes it did.

Frank: OK. We're done.

Patricia: One quick question. You just asked Barbara whether the repair fixed the problem. After the user tries a repair procedure, is that all we need to ask: whether the problem is fixed?

Frank: Yes.

Patricia: You don't need to ask if the repair made the problem worse or introduced a new problem?

Frank: I don't think I've ever seen that happen. What do you think, Barbara?

Barbara: Most of the time the repair either makes no difference or fixes the problem. If we replaced a part and it didn't make any difference, I'd put the old part back in.

Frank: Yes, I agree.

Barbara: I think it's possible that a new problem could crop up, but that would be unusual. The most likely explanation would be that the repair person didn't carry out the procedure correctly. It's pretty obvious when that happens. I think most of our staff would realize they had made an error and would redo the procedure. They wouldn't even report that the procedure had introduced a new problem.

Frank: Barbara's right. I don't think the computer has to worry about the problem getting worse.

Patricia: I suppose if that situation ever occurred, the user could just start over and ask for advice about the new problem.

Frank: I think that would be fine. It shouldn't happen very often.

Discussion

Patricia learns details about toaster repair from this case discussion. She obtains specific guidelines about how to test and repair a particular customer complaint *(bread not toasted)* for a particular toaster make and model *(General Appliance GA98985)*. Patricia learns more from this case discussion, however, than she would have learned if Frank had prepared the case. She learns that Frank checks not only the *color* of the bread he toasts, but if the bread remains white, he also checks its *temperature*. In earlier case discussions, Frank never mentioned that he feels the temperature of untoasted bread. Patricia also learns that Frank pays attention to the particular *part number* of the thermostat. When Frank was able to glance at the thermostat in a toaster, he did so subconsciously. He never thought to tell Patricia that he had determined visually what *kind* of thermostat was used in the toaster.

6.3 Investigating the Use of Uncertainty

Most expert systems use inferences that are *exact:* the basis characteristics *provide definitive evidence* for the conclusion characteristics.

Some expert systems also use inferences that are *heuristic:* the basis characteristics *suggest values for* the conclusion characteristics, but *do not provide enough evidence for a definite conclusion.* If your expert system needs to use inferences that make uncertain or inexact conclusions, you will need to investigate these inferences to learn what the expert's uncertainty means and how the expert system should reason with uncertainty.

Review each kind of inference that you identified; check whether any of the inferences specify inexact reasoning. If conclusions of these inferences are qualified in some form, you will need to discuss two topics with your project expert:

1. How the expert system system should *make* inexact conclusions

2. How the expert system system should *use* inexact conclusions

6.3.1 Learning How to Make Inexact Conclusions

An expert system can make inexact conclusions about a characteristic in one of two ways. For any particular case:

1. The system may be able to use a *single inference* that provides all available evidence about the conclusion characteristic.

2. The system may need to use *many inferences* each of which provides evidence about the conclusion characteristic. The system must make its final assessment about the conclusion characteristic by combining evidence from the individual inferences.

Expert systems are easier to develop, test, and maintain if they *do not* need to accumulate evidence. Therefore you should try to express inferences about each conclusion characteristic in such a way that you avoid the need to accumulate evidence.

Review the collection of inferences for a given conclusion characteristic. Compare the conditions of the inferences to see whether more than one condition can be true at a given time. If only one condition can be true at a given time, the inferences are said to be *mutually exclusive.* Each inference specifies what to conclude *in a different situation,* so your expert system will not need to accumulate evidence. If your inferences are not mutually exclusive, try to enumerate all situations in which your system will need to infer the conclusion characteristic.

1. List all basis characteristics used in the conditions of the inferences.

2. List all possible values for each of the basis characteristics.[2]

3. If the number of characteristics and the number of possible values for each characteristic are both relatively small, enumerate all possible combinations of values for the different basis characteristics. Each combination represents a unique situation in which the expert system will need to make a decision about the conclusion characteristic.

4. Review the situations you have identified; ask the expert what the system can infer about the conclusion characteristic in each of these situations.

Figure 6.2 illustrates this process with a very simple example.

Unfortunately, real-life heuristics are not always as simple as the inferences shown in Figure 6.2. If the inferences for a conclusion characteristic consist of a collection of special-purpose heuristics, you may not be able to enumerate all possible situations in which a conclusion can be made. A classic example of such a characteristic can be found in MYCIN, one of the earliest expert systems.[3] MYCIN classified the type of a meningitis infection as *bacterial, fungal, viral,* or *tubercular.* The system's knowledge base contained 55 different inferences to conclude the type of infection. These inferences used a total of 31 basis characteristics.[4]

> 24 characteristics with 2 possible values
> 1 characteristic with 4 possible values
> 1 characteristic with 6 possible values
> 4 characteristics with 7 possible values
> 1 characteristic with 9 possible values

Thus MYCIN was able to decide the type of a meningitis infection in over 2 billion different situations.

$$2^{24} \times 4 \times 6 \times 7^4 \times 9 = 2,147,483,647$$

Because it was not feasible for the MYCIN expert to specify the type of infection for each possible situation, MYCIN had to accumulate small amounts of evidence from the individual inferences.

---

2. Section 7.1 describes techniques that can be used to identify all possible values for a characteristic.

3. For a description of the MYCIN system, see B. Buchanan and E. Shortliffe, eds., *Rule-Based Expert Systems.* Reading, Mass.: Addison-Wesley, 1986.

4. This example was obtained through examination of the MYCIN knowledge base.

Figure 6.2 Enumerating situations in which inexact conclusions can be made. A meteorology expert provided four inferences that could be used to decide whether it would be raining in an hour's time (a). These inferences were not mutually exclusive: The conditions of more than one inference could succeed at a given time. For example, if it is raining and rain clouds are visible, the conditions of the first two inferences both succeed. The expert's four inferences use three basis characteristics of a situation: *whether it is raining now, whether rain clouds are visible*, and *whether rain is predicted*. Each of these basis characteristics can have two possible values: *yes* and *no*. The knowledge engineer identified eight different situations in which the inferences could be used, by listing all possible combinations of the values for the three basis characteristics (b). When the knowledge engineer reviewed these situations with the expert, the expert was able to specify the likelihood of rain in an hour in each of the eight situations (c). As a result of this exercise, the knowledge engineer was able to replace the four inferences in (a) with eight mutually exclusive inferences corresponding to the rows of the table in (c). In any given case, the expert system will be able to use one of these inferences to assess the likelihood of rain in an hour. The expert system will not need to accumulate evidence from different individual inferences.

(a) 1. If it is raining now, it will probably be raining in an hour.

2. If rain clouds are visible, it might be raining in an hour.

3. If the weather forecast predicts rain, it might be raining in an hour.

4. If it is not raining now, no rain clouds are visible, and there is no forecast of rain, it probably will not be raining in an hour.

(b)

	Raining now?	Rain clouds visible?	Rain predicted?
1.	yes	yes	yes
2.	yes	yes	no
3.	yes	no	yes
4.	yes	no	no
5.	no	yes	yes
6.	no	yes	no
7.	no	no	yes
8.	no	no	no

(c)

	Raining now?	Rain clouds visible?	Rain predicted?	Likelihood of rain in an hour
1.	yes	yes	yes	probable
2.	yes	yes	no	probable
3.	yes	no	yes	probable
4.	yes	no	no	probable
5.	no	yes	yes	moderately likely
6.	no	yes	no	moderately likely
7.	no.	no	yes	moderately likely
8.	no	no	no	unlikely

If you are not able to enumerate all the circumstances in which the expert system will need to infer a particular conclusion characteristic, discuss this characteristic with the expert. Try to understand how the expert considers evidence about that characteristic; learn the process the expert follows to reach a decision about that characteristic. In Dialog 6.3, Patricia Programmer investigates how the toaster-repair advisor should conclude *suspected toaster problem*.

Dialog 6.3 Learning How the System Should Make Inexact Conclusions

Setting

Patricia Programmer, Howard Hacker, and Frank Fixit are reviewing the inferences that allow Frank to conclude *suspected toaster problem*. Frank has explained that he assumes that each toaster has a *single* problem. The evidence about a particular toaster, however, often indicates *more than one* possible problem.

Frank uses three basis characteristics to infer *suspected toaster problem: toaster make, toaster model*, and *customer complaints*. Patricia finds it not feasible to enumerate all possible combinations of values for these characteristics. In the first place, the number of toaster models is very large. In the second place, the customer can check any number of complaints on the repair slip.

Dialog

Patricia: Frank, I'd like to understand how you weigh the evidence for different possible problems to decide which problem to suspect.

Frank: Well, I'm not sure I can explain what I do.

Patricia: Let's talk about some particular examples. You said that if the customer checks both *toast too light* and *toast too dark*, there is probably a heating-element problem.

Frank nods.

And if they check *bread not toasted*, the problem is probably *severe too light*, but you might also have a heating-element problem.

Frank nods again.

Now suppose the customer checks all three of those complaints. How would you combine the evidence?

Frank: Well, the evidence for a heating-element problem really outweighs the evidence for a color problem.

Patricia: Good. How strongly would you suspect each of the two kinds of problem?

Frank: I don't think I'd even consider a color problem. If I've got evidence for a heating-element problem, I don't look any further.

Patricia: All right. Let's consider some other possibilities. Suppose the customer also checked *operating lever will not go down.*

Frank: I'd be pretty sure we have a no-latch problem.

Patricia: Even though you have other evidence that suggests a heating-element problem?

Frank: The evidence for *no-latch* is pretty conclusive. If the operating lever won't go down, you're not going to be able to toast bread. I guess I believe that complaint more than I do the others. Especially because the other complaints sound a little inconsistent. Maybe the customer was confused and just checked everything that had ever happened with the toaster.

Patricia: Are there any complaints that would outweigh *operating lever will not go down?*

Frank: Let me look at a repair slip.

Frank retrieves a repair slip from his papers and studies it.

No. If I see *operating lever will not go down* or *operating lever will not stay down,* I really don't care what else is checked. I'm pretty sure that there's a no-latch problem. The next possibility to consider is a no-trip problem. If they check "toast does not pop up," I'm pretty sure that there's a no-trip problem. After that, I consider heating-element problems. If they check "toasts on one side only," I'm pretty sure there's a heating-element problem. If they check either "bread not toasted" or "toast too light" and they also check either "toast too dark" or "toast always burns," I also suspect a heating-element problem, but I'm not so sure.

Patricia: It sounds as though you consider possible problems in a fixed order. As soon as you find evidence for one problem, you don't go any further.

Frank: Well, up to a point that's right. But if I don't find a heating-element problem, I don't really consider other problems in any particular order. I check to see what I know about the particular toaster model. If I have experience with the toaster model, I'm more sure than if I have to make a guess from the customer complaints alone.

Patricia: Would you say that you consider the *strongest* evidence first and then try successively weaker evidence until you decide what problem to suspect?

Frank: Yes. I think that describes what I do.

Patricia: If you consider the evidence in the appropriate order, can you always identify a *single* problem to suspect?

Frank: No. For example, if I don't know anything about the particular toaster, and they just checked "bread not toasted," I suspect both *severe too light* and *heating-element problem.*

Patricia: Oh, that's right. In this example, you seem to be making a single decision. The complaint *bread not toasted* enables you to identify two possible problems at once.

Frank: Yes, that's right.

Patricia: When you suspect more than one problem, do you always make a single decision that tells you all the possible problems? Or do you sometimes decide one problem for one reason and a different problem for a different reason then compare the two to see which is more likely?

Frank: I can't say for sure, but I don't think I make a lot of different decisions. I usually consider the complaints and decide which problems are likely.

Discussion

In this dialog, Patricia Programmer discovers that Frank Fixit considers evidence *in a fixed order*. She realizes that the toaster-repair advisor will be able to model this behavior. The system can try inferences in a fixed order. When one inference succeeds, the system can ignore the remaining inferences. By controlling the use of inferences in this way, Patricia can ensure that a single inference will be used in any given case. As a result, the toaster-repair advisor will not need to accumulate evidence.

6.3.2 Learning How to Use Inexact Conclusions

After you have decided whether your expert system will need to accumulate evidence, identify the consequences that can result when the expert system makes a decision with less than certainty. Find out how the conclusion characteristic will be used in the system's reasoning process. If the characteristic is not concluded with certainty, how will subsequent inferences be affected? Check whether the conclusion characteristic affects the sequence of steps that the system will take. If so, find out what course the system should take when it is uncertain about the characteristic.

Expert systems typically use inexact conclusions in one of three ways.

1. The system may use its assessment about the conclusion characteristic to make a *go or no-go* decision. For example, an expert system might use the likelihood of rain in an hour (Figure 6.2) to advise its user about whether to carry an umbrella. If there is sufficient evidence to suggest that it will rain, the system will recommend that the user carry an umbrella. Note that the system only needs to be able to compare likelihood with some threshold to decide whether there is sufficient evidence to warrant carrying an umbrella.

2. The system may conclude a number of alternative values for a characteristic; it may act on the alternatives differently depending on their *relative likelihood*. For example, the system may use only the single most likely alternative. Or it may act on each alternative in order of their decreasing likelihood.

3. The system may need to assess the *absolute strength* of the evidence for each alternative. It may take one action for very likely alternatives and a different action for moderately likely alternatives. The system may need to *propagate* uncertainty as it reasons. If it bases one decision on definite evidence and a second decision on likely evidence, the first decision should be given more certainty than the second.

In Dialog 6.4, Patricia Programmer and Frank Fixit discuss how the toaster-repair advisor will use its conclusions about *suspected toaster problem*.

Dialog 6.4 Learning How the System Should Use Inexact Conclusions

Setting

Patricia Programmer and Howard Hacker have just finished their discussion about how to make conclusions about *suspected toaster problem* (Dialog 6.3). They continue their dialog by discussing how the toaster-repair advisor should use these conclusions.

Dialog

Patricia: Now that we understand how the system will conclude *suspected toaster problem*, let's see how the system should use this information. As we've discussed, you use *suspected toaster problem* to select the initial test procedure.

Frank: Yes, that's right.

Patricia: Let's think about the case where you suspect two problems: *severe too light* and *heating-element problem*. How would you test the toaster?

Frank: Which problem is more likely?

Patricia: Let's say *severe too light*.

Frank: I guess I'd toast one slice on dark.

Patricia: That's your normal test for *severe too light*.

Frank nods.

So you wouldn't do anything different because you're also considering *heating-element problem*?

Frank: We *could* toast two slices on dark to try to distinguish between the two possible problems. But I really don't do that. I decide which problem is most likely and test for that problem.

Patricia: Whenever you suspect more than one problem, do you *always* test the most likely problem?

Frank: Yes.

Patricia: OK. Now suppose you have two toasters. For one toaster, you're virtually sure there's a heating-element problem—the user said that the bread toasts on one side. For the other toaster, *heating-element problem* is the most likely problem, but you're not sure—say they checked both "toast too light" and "toast too dark." Would you test both toasters in the same way?

Frank: Yes. It really doesn't matter how sure I am of the problem. If it's the most likely, it's what I'm going to check with the initial test.

Patricia: Thanks, Frank. Let's go back to the decisions you make about *suspected toaster problem*. You said you sometimes decide that more than one problem is likely.

Frank nods.

When you decide to suspect more than one problem, can you always specify which problem is the most likely?

Frank: Yes. That's how I think about the problem. I'll always come up with one, two, or three possibilities. And I can always tell you which is my first, second, and third choice.

Patricia: To summarize what we've discussed about *suspected toaster problem*, you can make a single decision that specifies all the problems you suspect and the relative likelihood of these alternatives. You use the *most likely* problem to conclude the initial toaster problem. When you make this conclusion, you don't care *how* likely the suspected toaster problem is as long as it's the most likely problem.

Frank: That sounds right to me.

Patricia: If you only use the *most likely* problem, is there any reason why the system should conclude *all* problems that you suspect?

Frank: Hmm. That's a good point. There's only one reason I can think of. It would be instructive if the system could show an inexperienced repair person what it's thinking. But I don't know if we'll be able to do that.

Patricia: Later in the project, we have time in the schedule to add a capability for the user to request descriptions of repair procedures. When we get to that point in the project, we may find that we are able to include additional explanation capabilities. I propose that we have the system to conclude *all* likely problems. For now, it will only use the most likely. Later in the project, the system may use the additional problems in explanations.

Frank: Good idea.

Patricia: Let's assume we will have time to add the ability for the system to explain its conclusions. Should the system just explain what problems it suspects with their order of likelihood, or should it try to describe how likely it considers each alternative?

Frank: Could you give me an example? I'm not sure what you're asking.

Patricia: Sure. Let's say that the complaint is *bread not toasted.* The system suspects two problems: *severe too light* and *heating-element problem.* I need to know how the system should explain this conclusion. Should the explanation just list the two possible problems, or should it say that *severe too light* is very likely and *heating-element problem* is moderately likely?

Frank: I see what you mean. I think all we need to say is that *severe too light* is the most likely and *heating-element problem* is also a possibility. We don't need to try to describe how strongly we believe each possibility.

Discussion

In this interview, Patricia Programmer learns that the toaster-repair advisor will need to know the relative likelihoods of the different possible values for *suspected toaster problem*. The relative likelihood will enable the system to select the most likely problem and to use this problem to determine the initial test procedure. Patricia learns that Frank Fixit makes the same decisions and takes the same actions regardless of how sure he is that he has identified the correct toaster problem. So Patricia knows that the toaster-repair advisor will not need to *quantify* the likelihood of each possible problem.

After you have identified the ways in which your expert system will make and use inexact conclusions, you may need to discuss one or two additional topics with your expert (Figure 6.3).

1. How to *label* the different degrees of certainty

2. How to *combine* different degrees of certainty

Notice that it is unnecessary to discuss these topics if a characteristic can be concluded with a single inference and that characteristic is used to make a go or no-go decision or to rank-order alternatives.

- The meteorology example in Figure 6.2 illustrates a characteristic that is used to *make a go or no-go decision*. The likelihood of rain is used to decide whether to carry an umbrella. The threshold of *sufficient evidence* can be implicit in the definition of the conclusion characteristic. In other words, a conclusion of *yes* for the characteristic *rain is likely* could mean *there is sufficient evidence that it will rain in an hour to assume that it will rain in an hour*. A conclusion of *no* for the characteristic would mean that there is insufficient evidence. Thus the inferences about the characteristic *rain is likely* would not need to specify a particular likelihood.

- Dialog 6.4 illustrates conclusions that are used to *rank-order alternatives*. The toaster-repair advisor could conclude the possible problems as a list of problems ordered by decreasing likelihood. The relative likelihood of an alternative would be implicit in the order of that alternative within the list. The system would be able to use the first element of the list (the most likely problem) to conclude *initial test procedure*.

Bear in mind that a single characteristic may be used for more than one purpose. Be sure to consider *all* uses when you decide whether to define labels for different strengths of certainty. Dialog 6.4 illustrated this point. Patricia Programmer considered not only how *suspected toaster problem* would be used to infer *initial test procedure* but also how it would be used in explanations. If Frank had wanted more detailed explanations, it would have been necessary to label the certainty of each possible problem.

Figure 6.3 Collecting information about degrees of certainty. The kinds of information a knowledge engineer should obtain about degrees of certainty depend on two factors.

1. The number of inferences that expert system can use in any given case to conclude a particular characteristic

2. The ways in which the expert system will use this characteristic

In some applications, the system will need to *label* certainties of different strengths. For example, the expert may express the strength of certainty with descriptive labels such as *definite, probable, possible, unlikely*. Alternatively, the expert may use numbers to label the strength of certainty, for example, 5 might label the strongest and 1 might label the weakest degree of certainty. In addition to labeling the strength of certainty, some systems will need to *combine* certainties of different strengths to determine the cumulative certainty from a number of individual inferences.

	Number of Inferences	
Use of Conclusions	**One inference**	**Many inferences**
To make a go or no-go decision		Label Combine
To rank-order likely alternatives		Label Combine
To assess the strength of evidence	Label	Label Combine

Legend:

Label   The system will need to label different strengths of certainty.

Combine   The system will need to combine certainties of different strengths into a cumulative certainty.

6.3.3 Learning How to Label Different Degrees of Certainty

If your system will need to label the strength of certainty for its conclusions, work with the expert to devise a simple labeling scheme. Pick
a small number of strengths (three to five) that are meaningful to the
expert. Ask the expert to provide an example of evidence of each strength.
The collection of examples can serve as a scale to ensure that the labels
are used consistently. Although the toaster-repair advisor will not need
to label degrees of certainty, Figure 6.4 illustrates a scale that Frank
Fixit could have developed to guide him in labeling the degrees of
certainty for inexact conclusions.

6.3.4 Learning How to Combine Different Degrees of Certainty

If your expert system will need to accumulate evidence, find out how
the expert system should combine different degrees of certainty to
derive a cumulative measure of certainty. Review the inferences for a
particular conclusion characteristic, and identify several different situations in which the system will need to use two or more inferences.
Describe each situation to the expert, and ask for the final assessment
of the conclusion characteristic. Ask the expert:

- What values should the system conclude in that situation?

- What degree of certainty should be assigned to each value?

Figure 6.4 Scale for labeling degrees of certainty. If the toaster-repair
advisor had needed to label the strength of certainty in its conclusions,
Frank Fixit might have devised this scale. The scale indicates that Frank
would consider three different strengths of certainty, which he would
label *definite, probable,* and *possible.* Whenever Frank needed to label
the degree of certainty for a conclusion, he would refer to the examples
in this scale. The examples quantify (for Frank) the amount of evidence
that corresponds to each of the three labels.

Strength	Example
Definite	If *customer complaints* include *toast does not pop up,* then *suspected toaster problem* definitely is *no-trip.*
Probable	If *customer complaints* include *bread not toasted,* then *suspected toaster problem* probably is *severe too light.*
Possible	If *customer complaints* include *bread not toasted,* then *suspected toaster problem* possibly is *heating-element.*

Compare this assessment with the degrees of certainty from the individual inferences. Try to devise guidelines that describe how the expert appears to combine evidence. For example, you might learn that three *possible* certainties add up to *very likely*. Your goal in reviewing these situations with the expert is to verify that:

- The expert has used the certainty labels consistently

- The expert has consistent expectations about how the certainties should be combined

---

Table 6.1 Understanding the Expert's Reasoning Process

Objective	Useful Activities
Identify the expert's inferences.	Define a *kind of inference* by the characteristic whose value is concluded. List the kinds of inference that the expert appeared to make during case discussions. Review a case discussion with the expert. Identify parts of the discussion in which the expert appears to have made a conclusion. Ask *why* the expert made the conclusion. Identify the factors that form the basis for each kind of inference.
Check for hidden assumptions.	Compare similar cases. Distinguish *all* the factors that go into each decision by discussing what the expert would have concluded in slightly different cases. Find out *why* the expert would make different decisions in similar cases. Check for implicit assumptions that restrict the validity of a decision (such as the current scope limitations). Identify information that the expert uses subconsciously. Ask the expert to *request* all information about a case from the second person.
Investigate the use of uncertainty.	If inferences about any conclusion characteristic specified inexact conclusions, find out whether the system can infer that characteristic with a single inference or whether it will have to accumulate evidence from multiple inferences. Find out how the system will use the conclusion characteristic in its reasoning process or to control its actions. If the system must assess the amount of certainty associated with an hypothesis or if the system must accumulate evidence, learn how the expert labels different degrees of certainty. If the system must accumulate evidence, learn how the expert combines evidence into a final assessment about the conclusion characteristic.

If your expert system will need to accumulate and combine evidence, we advise *against* trying to devise your own mechanism for combining certainties. Instead, we recommend that you select an expert-system shell that provides a built-in mechanism for accumulating certainty or that you implement a well-understood method for combining certainties.[5]

6.4 Points to Remember

The second goal of detailed investigation is to understand the expert's *reasoning process* in enough depth to design an expert system that can perform similar reasoning steps (Table 6.1). Knowledge engineers must identify inferences that the expert makes, learn the factors on which these inferences are based, and understand the expert's degree of confidence in each inference.

---

5. For more information about the use of uncertainty in expert systems, refer to the Additional Reading section.

Chapter 7

Defining Important Characteristics of a Case

Patricia Programmer and Howard Hacker are trying to understand how Frank Fixit repairs color problems in simple two-slice toasters. They have learned the strategy that guides Frank's actions, and they have defined the procedure that the toaster-repair advisor should follow. They understand the reasoning steps that system must perform and have identified the definitions, formulas, and heuristics that will enable the system to reason. Now Patricia and Howard must obtain a more comprehensive grasp of the characteristics of a toaster-repair case that Frank considers when he repairs a toaster.

The final goal of detailed investigation is to learn about the **general characteristics** of the case that are relevant to performance of the task. We use the generic terms *characteristic* and *factor* to indicate some particular type of information about the case. Through discussions of the expert's procedure and reasoning process, the knowledge engineers identify certain general characteristics of a case: the input data the expert system will obtain from the user or from other sources, the output results the system will produce, and the intermediate conclusions the system will reach as it reasons from its input data to its output results (Figure 7.1).

Figure 7.1 General characteristics of a toaster-repair case. Patricia Programmer has learned that the toaster-repair advisor will need to use several general characteristics of a toaster-repair case. It will ask the user for input data that describe the toaster and its current operation; it will use this information to conclude additional information about the toaster. Some of these conclusions will be intermediate steps in the reasoning process; other conclusions will be communicated to the user as output.

Patricia gives each general characteristic a name. If a name consists of more than one word, she joins the words with underscores to indicate that the group of words made up a single name.[1] Notice that Patricia uses descriptive names rather than terse abbreviations. Notice also Patricia's convention of giving each yes/no characteristic a name that ends with a question mark (for example, repair_fixed_the_problem?).

Input Data	Intermediate Conclusions	Output Results
toaster_make	toaster_style	initial_test_procedure
toaster_model	suspected_toaster_problem	repair_procedure
customer_complaints	toaster_problem	(for the possible
result_of_initial_test	(confirmed by initial test)	cause currently
repair_fixed_the_problem?	problem_within_scope?	under consideration)
thermostat_part_number	ordered_possible_causes	
	possible_cause_currently_ under_consideration	

As the expert system performs its task in a given situation, it must accumulate information about that situation. This information consists of facts and hypotheses that the system learns or concludes; facts and hypotheses identify *specific examples* of the various general characteristics. Many knowledge engineers find it convenient to think of a general characteristic as a *variable* of the case and of the specific example as the *value* for that variable. For instance, the toaster-repair advisor can learn that the toaster make for a particular case is *Toasts-Best*, the toaster model is *TB10445*, and the customer had a single complaint: *toast always burns*. The system can use this information to conclude that the toaster's style is *simple two-slice* and that the suspected problem is *severe too dark*. It can use its conclusions to recommend *toast on light* as the initial test.

Knowledge engineers need to obtain a detailed *definition* of each general characteristic they identify. The definition of a characteristic

---

1. In the remainder of this book, we shall adopt Patricia's notation and join words with underscores to denote that we are using a term in the toaster-repair advisor project vocabulary.

provides details about the specific examples of the characteristic (Section 7.1) and the method for learning which of these specific examples are relevant to a given case (Section 7.2). For instance, when Patricia Programmer obtains a definition of *toaster_make*, she will learn all the possible toaster manufacturers (General Appliance, Toasts-Best, CrustMaster, and so on) and the method by which the system will learn which manufacturer is relevant to a particular case (it will ask the user for the make of the toaster to be repaired). General characteristics that represent input to, or output from, the system require additional investigation. The definition of an input datum requires details that will allow the system to obtain the relevant information from the appropriate source (Section 7.3). The definition of an output result must identify the recipient of the result and must specify how the information should be communicated (Section 7.4).

7.1 Identifying the Specific Examples

After knowledge engineers have identified general characteristics of a case, they should learn what range of values each characteristic can have. The general characteristics define the *dimensions* of the problem space within which the expert system will perform its task; the range of values of these characteristics define the *size* of the problem space. Knowledge engineers need to know the size of the problem space so they can verify that they have obtained adequate knowledge from the expert and so they can test the system thoroughly.

To begin your investigation of the general characteristics of a case, make a table like the one in Figure 7.1.

1. List all the characteristics the expert mentioned in earlier case discussions. To identify important characteristics of a case, review the sentences the expert used to describe a case. Look for the factors of the case that the expert mentioned.

2. Next list the specific examples (or values) for these characteristics that were mentioned in the case discussions (Figure 7.2). To identify specific examples, review *what the expert said about the general characteristics* in each case.

To identify the specific examples of a general characteristic, you need to answer three questions.

1. *What kind of value* constitutes a specific example of this characteristic? Many characteristics have descriptive values. For instance, the characteristic *suspected_toaster_problem* has the descriptive values *severe_too_dark* and *minor_too_light*. Other characteristics

Figure 7.2 Specific examples of the characteristics of a toaster-repair case. Patricia Programmer listed the general characteristics of a toaster-repair case in the approximate order in which they would be used by the system. Patricia then reviewed the cases the project team had discussed and made a list of all the examples of these characteristics that Frank Fixit had mentioned in case discussions. Patricia named each specific example, following the naming conventions she had established for general characteristics.

General Characteristic	Specific Examples (Values)
toaster_make	Toasts_Best, General_Appliance, CrustMaster,...
toaster_model	GA00952, GA11569, GA98985,..., TB10445, TB27713, TB80601,...
customer_complaints	toast_always_burns, toast_too_light, toast_too_dark, toast_does_not_pop_up, bread_not_toasted,...
suspected_toaster_problem	severe_too_dark, minor_too_light, no_latch, no_trip, heating_element_problem,...
initial_test_procedure	toast_on_light, toast_on_medium, toast_on_dark
result_of_initial_test	toast_burnt, toast_too_light, toast_white, toast_warm, toast_right_color
toaster_problem (confirmed by initial test)	severe_too_dark, minor_too_light, no_latch, no_trip, heating_element_problem,...
toaster_style	simple_two_slice, four_slice, two_slice_with_bakery_switch, under_cabinet, toaster_oven
problem_within_scope?	yes, no
ordered_possible_causes	(1. severe_thermostat_problem_heating_too_long, 2. bad_thermostat), (1. minor_thermostat_problem_heating_too_short, 2. bad_thermostat)
possible_cause_currently_under_consideration	severe_thermostat_problem_heating_too_long, minor_thermostat_problem_heating_too_short, bad_thermostat
repair_procedure (for possible cause currently under consideration)	adjust_thermostat, replace_and_calibrate_thermostat
thermostat_part_number	X77213, X77215,...
repair_fixed_the_problem?	yes, no

can be numeric. The characteristic *room_temperature* might have the value *72.5 degrees Fahrenheit;* the characteristic *toasting_time* might have the value *60 seconds.* Some characteristics are logical (or true/false). The characteristic *problem_within_scope?* has two possible values, *yes* and *no*. Characteristics can have more complex values. For instance, each specific example of the characteristic *ordered_possible_causes* is an ordered list of descriptive values.

2. *How many values of this characteristic can a particular case have?* A case can have any number of values for the characteristic *customer_complaints*, corresponding to the number of complaints the customer checked on the repair slip. In contrast, a given toaster can have only one make and one model. So any case can have a single value for each of the characteristics *toaster_make* and *toaster_model*. Note that Patricia Programmer gives a characteristic a *plural* name *(customer_complaints)* to indicate that it can have more than one value.

3. *What are all the specific examples* of this characteristic? If the values for a characteristic are numeric, try to identify a legal range. For instance, Patricia Programmer learns that Frank Fixit sometimes needs to measure the line voltage to a toaster. When she investigates the definition of *line_voltage*, she learns that the voltage for a toaster can be between 110 and 150 volts. If the values for the characteristic are descriptive, try to obtain a list of the possible values. If you cannot enumerate all possible values, try to obtain a description of what would constitute a legal value. For instance, the toaster-repair advisor will need to know the customer's name to prepare a bill. The name could be any text string that consists of two names, possibly preceded by a title, and possibly with a middle initial.

You will generally be able to answer the first two questions by examining the list of specific examples you identified through case discussions. To answer the third question, you will need to obtain from the expert the full set of possible values for each characteristic. Start with characteristics that represent physical properties or well-understood concepts.

> The characteristics *toaster_make* and *toaster_model* represent physical properties of a toaster. Patricia Programmer asks Frank Fixit for a list of all possible toaster makes and models; he responds that Patricia can find these lists in his repair manuals. The characteristic *customer_complaints* is a well-understood concept. When Patricia asks Frank for the possible customer complaints, he shows her a repair slip that lists all the complaints customers can check.

If a characteristic represents a concept you identified through case discussions or a concept whose meaning is vague, it will be easiest to identify the possible values by reviewing a case discussion. In the course of the discussion, you may find that the expert really considers a number of more precise characteristics. Dialog 7.1 illustrates how

Patricia Programmer prompted Frank Fixit for specific examples of imprecise characteristics.

Dialog 7.1 Learning the Possible Values for Imprecise Characteristics

Setting

Patricia Programmer, Howard Hacker, and Frank Fixit meet to discuss the range of possible values for the characteristics of a toaster-repair case. The whiteboard shows the characteristics and values listed in Figure 7.2. Patricia has set up a tape recorder so she can replay the tape of an earlier case discussion.[2]

Dialog

Patricia: Frank, I want to make sure I know all the possible variations of toaster problems we are likely to encounter. I need your help to fill in the table on the whiteboard with as many specific examples as you can think of.

Frank glances at the table on the whiteboard and nods.

I'm going to review the case we discussed with Barbara. Whenever we get to a question that you asked, I would like you to try to think of all the different answers Barbara might have given. Also I want to find out if there are any other questions you might have needed to ask in different circumstances. I'll skip over the beginning of the tape. Your first questions were about the make and model and the customer complaints. We have already discussed how I can find the possible answers to those questions. After you ask for those three pieces of information, you decide the suspected toaster problem. Are there other problems we should add to the list?

Frank looks at the whiteboard and studies the list of examples of suspected_toaster_problem.

Frank: Well, you can add two color problems: *minor_too_dark* and *severe_too_light*. I think we can also break down the other kinds of problem—no-latch, no-trip, and so on. But I'd have to think about those some more.

Patricia: For now, we can use the general problems. When we add no-trip problems to the system, you can tell me the more specific problems as you did for color problems. And we can do the same thing when we get to the other types of problem.

Frank: Good.

Patricia goes to the whiteboard and adds minor_too_dark *and* severe_too_light *to the list of examples of* suspected_toaster_problem.

---

2. The original case discussion appears in Dialog 6.2.

Patricia: Do you consider any color problems beside these four?

Frank: No. That's the full list.

Patricia: And this is the same set of problems you might confirm (or identify) with the initial test?

Frank: That's right.

Patricia adds the two new examples to the list for the characteristic toaster problem *(confirmed by initial test). She then points to the characteristic* initial_test_procedure.

Patricia: After you have decided what problem you suspect, you recommend an initial test.

Frank nods.

I'd like to list all the different tests you might suggest.

Patricia advances the tape to the point at which she wants to ask her first question.

Here we are.

Patricia plays the tape. The group listens as Frank says, "Set the color selector on the darkest setting and toast a slice of bread."

Frank, you always seem to toast a slice of bread for your initial test.

Frank nods.

Sometimes you set the color control on full light, sometimes on medium, and sometimes on full dark.

Frank nods again.

Do you ever set the color control somewhere between medium and full light or between medium and full dark?

Frank: No, I wouldn't do that.

Patricia: Are there other adjustments you might make to the toaster before the initial test?

Frank: We're just talking about simple two-slice toasters, right?

Patricia nods.

There's really nothing else to adjust.

Patricia: That gives us three possible tests—toast on light, medium, and dark. Do you *always* use one of those three tests?

Frank: Yes.

Patricia: Review the list of suspected problems. Can you think of any circumstance in which you'd perform a different test?

Frank glances at the whiteboard.

Frank: Well, if I suspect a problem with the heating elements, I like to toast *two* slices of bread. Sometimes one slot toasts fine, and the other slot toasts on one side only. I can save myself some time if I toast two slices at once.

Patricia: When you toast two slices, do you sometimes toast them on light, sometimes on medium, and sometimes on dark?

Frank: Hmm. I usually toast two slices when the customer says that the bread only gets toasted on one side. If they don't check *any* complaints, I don't have any clue what's wrong; so I toast two slices. I guess I always toast the two slices on medium.

Patricia: Can you think of any reason why you might toast two slices on light?

Frank: No. Never.

Patricia: On dark?

Frank: Well, I could have told Barbara to toast two slices in this toaster. You see, she set the color control on dark to see if there was a problem with the thermostat. If the bread had come out dark, I guess I would have told her to toast another slice in the other slot. This second test would have checked whether there was a problem with one of the heating elements. I could have told her to toast two slices to begin with. That would have saved a little time by testing for both a thermostat problem and a heating-element problem at the same time. But I don't think I'd ever really do that.

Patricia: So you have four different tests for two-slice toasters: *toast_one_slice on_light*, *toast_one_slice_on_medium*, *toast_one_slice_on_dark*, and *toast_two_slices_on_medium*.

Frank: Yes. I think that covers it. I hope I'm not forgetting anything! What happens if I realize that I do something different with some toasters?

Patricia: We can always add more tests later if we need to.

Frank: Good.

Patricia: Before I go on with the tape, I want to follow up on a comment you made. You said that if Barbara's toast had come out the way it should have (dark), you would have asked her to toast another slice of bread in the other slot.

Frank: That's right.

Patricia: If the initial test involves only one slice and the bread comes out the right color for the setting, should the system *always* ask the user to toast a slice in the other slot?

Frank: Yes, I guess we should test the other slot. If both slots toast OK, we can refer them to the senior staff member. But we might find a problem in one side only. There's a slight complication about checking the second slot though. On some toasters, if you want to toast one slice at a time, you have to use a particular slot. For those toasters, we'll have to ask the user to toast two slices.

Patricia: Thanks, I think I've got that. I'll ask you later which toasters have this restriction on toasting one slice at a time. For now, let's get back to the tape. You just asked Barbara to perform the initial test. The next step is to ask for the test results. I'd like to get a list of *all* the possible test results you might encounter, but I suspect that the idea of "test result" is too general. The result might consist of a number of different factors.

Patricia plays the recording. Frank first asks Barbara the color of the bread; then he asks whether the bread is warm.

In this case, you needed two questions to get the test results. You wanted to know the color of the bread and its temperature. Now, consider all the possible problems you might suspect. Suppose that you're talking to Barbara over the phone. You can't see the toaster. Are there any other questions you might need to ask to confirm any of those problems?

Frank studies the list of suspected problems on the whiteboard.

Frank: Well, for the color problems, I'd always want to know the color. If the bread came out white, I'd need to know if it was warm. I suppose that I might need to ask if the bread was toasted on just one side. Of course, if they toasted *two* slices, I'd need to know if both were the same, and if not, how they were different.

Patricia: What kind of differences would you consider?

Frank: Mainly I look for one slice that's fine and the other slice that's toasted on one side only. Or maybe they both are toasted only on the outside. That would tell me that I have a problem with one of the heating elements.

Patricia: What about the no-latch problems?

Frank: I'd also need to know if Barbara was able to push the operating lever down—the lever might be stuck. Then if it did go down, I'd want to know if the bread stayed down.

Patricia: Any other questions you'd ask?

Frank: Not for no-latch. For no-trip, I'd need to ask if the toast popped up. I think that should be all the questions.

Patricia: Thanks. Let's go on.

Discussion

Before the meeting, Patricia lists the characteristics of a toaster-repair case in the order in which they appear in a case discussion. This order allows her to go through the list systematically as she reviews a case discussion with Frank. Patricia needs to ask questions that will be difficult for Frank to answer in the abstract; she uses the context of a case discussion to make it clear to Frank what information she needs to obtain.

Notice that Patricia asks some questions in a variety of ways, to be sure Frank has not overlooked anything. Although Frank says that he *always* uses one of three initial tests, Patricia asks him to think of circumstances in which he might vary the tests. Her second question allows her to learn that Frank might toast *two* slices of bread rather than one.

In this discussion, Patricia's focus is to identify specific examples of the general characteristics of a toaster-repair case. However, she learns details about Frank's procedure for repairing toasters and his reasoning process as well. Patricia takes a slight digression to learn a refinement to the expert system's procedure: If the initial test finds no problem, the system should recommend a second test before it refers the user to the senior staff member. Note that Patricia's digression does not interrupt Frank's train of thought. Patricia finishes the discussion of initial tests before she starts the digression. At the end of the digression, she uses the tape recording to reorient Frank to the case discussion.

When Patricia investigates the characteristic *result_of_initial_test*, she identifies a collection of characteristics that constitute a test result. Frank himself thinks of the test result as a single concept. When he is not able to perform the test himself, however, he has to ask several questions to learn the test result.

7.2 Learning How the System Should Obtain Information

Knowledge engineers must know exactly how the expert system will obtain each piece of information about a case. Some information will come from an outside source. For example, the user of the toaster-repair advisor will enter the toaster make and model. Other information will be concluded by the expert system itself. For example, the toaster-repair advisor will conclude the suspected toaster problem. Some information can come from a variety of sources. The knowledge engineers, therefore, must review the list of characteristics with the expert to learn:

- How will the expert system determine this characteristic of a particular case?

- Should the system use different methods to determine this characteristic in different cases?

- Are there alternative means for determining this characteristic of a case if the standard method fails?

- What should the system do if it is unable to determine this characteristic for a case?

The knowledge engineers should identify a *general* method the system can use to determine the value of a characteristic. If necessary, they can obtain details about the method in separate discussions.[3] In

---

3. In Section 6.2, we discussed how to learn details about the method for concluding the value of a characteristic; in Section 7.3 we shall discuss how to learn details about the method for obtaining data from an external source.

Dialog 7.2, Patricia Programmer learns how the toaster-repair advisor should find out each characteristic of a case.

Dialog 7.2 Defining Methods for Obtaining Information

Setting

> Patricia Programmer, Howard Hacker, and Frank Fixit meet to discuss the methods by which the toaster-repair advisor should obtain information. On the whiteboard is Patricia's list of general characteristics and their specific examples (shown in Figure 7.2).

Dialog

Patricia: Frank, I'd like to review this list quickly to be sure I know how the expert system should obtain each piece of information it will need. Let's start with toaster make. We'll ask the user to enter the toaster make.

> *Frank nods.*

What happens if they don't enter any answer?

Frank: They've got to. I have to know the make and model, or I won't know what to do. It doesn't make sense that the user wouldn't know this— you can look at the toaster and read the make and model. You might have to search for the model number, but all our staff members should know how to find it.

Patricia: So we should *require* the user to enter a make and model?

Frank: Yes. If they don't know it, we can tell them to see the senior staff member.

Patricia: Good. What about customer complaints? We'll ask the user to enter all the complaints that were checked on the repair slip. What if they don't enter any complaints?

Frank: That can happen. Sometimes the customer doesn't check anything. Sometimes they write notes that you can't read. When I don't know the complaint, I toast two slices on medium. That will tell me what the problem is.

Patricia: Good. Next comes the suspected problem. What would you do if you weren't able to figure out what problem to suspect?

Frank: That's just like not knowing the customer complaints. If I don't know what to suspect, I always toast two slices on medium.

> *Patricia and Frank continue in this manner until they come to the characteristic* thermostat_part_number.

Patricia: You said that you first decide the general repair procedure. Then you get the specific details for the particular toaster.

> *Frank nods.*

So when you tell the user to replace a thermostat, you have to specify the part number of the thermostat they should use.

Frank nods again.

How do you know what part number to recommend?

Frank: Well, I would first check the service bulletins for this model toaster. That might tell me that I should use a specific part or it might give me a list of part numbers to choose from. If I didn't find a service bulletin, I would check the toaster-part database. I'd look up this toaster model and find what thermostat I should use. Again, it might give me one part number or several numbers to choose from.

Patricia: When you find more than one part number, how do you decide which one to use?

Frank: I use whichever part I can find in stock.

Patricia: What should the system recommend when it finds several possible part numbers?

Frank: Well, I think it should tell the user *all* the numbers. That gives the user flexibility to use whichever parts are in stock. The computer won't know exactly what's in stock. It could get an idea by looking up the inventory information in the toaster-part database, but the database might be wrong. Or someone else might have just taken the last part.

Patricia: What happens if we can't find a part number in the service bulletins or in the database?

Frank: That would be pretty rare. In that situation, I read the part number from the thermostat that's in the toaster. I replace the old thermostat with a new one with the same part number.

Patricia: Thanks.

7.3 Defining Input Data

To obtain a complete definition of the characteristics that constitute an expert system's input data, knowledge engineers must learn details about the *source* and the *reliability* of the data.

7.3.1 Identifying the Source of the Data

Before they can implement an expert system, knowledge engineers must know precisely how to obtain data from external sources. Table 7.1 summarizes the information they must gather. Note that the expert will not be able to provide all this information. For example, when Patricia Programmer and Howard Hacker need to know how to obtain part numbers from the toaster-part database, they will have to talk to the database administrator, not to Frank Fixit.

The expert will be able to suggest how to phrase questions for the users, whether to request related data on a single form or through a series of questions, and whether to include diagrams with the prompts for information. At this stage of system development, the knowledge engineers should learn enough to develop a user interface that will suffice for testing the expert system. Once they have a running version of the system, they can fine tune the interface with help from users as we shall discuss in Chapter 11. In most applications, the expert system's procedure for performing the task will evolve as the expert tests and refines the system. Some questions that are asked in the initial implementation will be removed or replaced by different questions. Knowledge engineers can waste valuable project time by putting too much effort into the wording of questions and the design of forms and diagrams before they have implemented the expert system.

7.3.2 Investigating the Reliability of the Data

Knowledge engineers need to understand how reliable the expert considers each input datum. They need to learn how the expert compensates for unreliable data so the expert system can make similar adjustments. For example, a particular sensor might not provide completely reliable data. The expert might know this and might read the sensor several times within a small interval of time. The expert system could be designed to obtain a number of readings and to take the average reading or the reading that appeared most frequently. In addition, the expert might gather other data to confirm the sensor reading. The expert system could gather these same data and could use them to decide whether the sensor reading is reliable.

Many expert systems have to depend on their users to provide in-

---

Table 7.1 Understanding the Source of Input Data

Source of Data	Questions to Answer
User	What kind of request will the user be able to understand?
Database	What database, table within the database, and field within the table will contain the information? What is the proper form for database queries? How can the expert system access the database (or the database-management system)?
File	What file contains the information? What is the format of the file? Where within the file can the information be found?
Sensor	What sensor will provide the information? In what form will the sensor provide the information? How can the expert system obtain sensor readings?

formation that a human expert can collect directly. The expert must judge what information the users can provide reliably. For example, the toaster-repair advisor must ask the user whether a repair actually corrected the toaster problem. Frank Fixit is capable of observing a test result and deciding whether the problem is fixed. But can *all* members of the repair staff make this judgment? When Patricia Programmer raises this question, she finds that Frank is sure that any member of the repair staff would be able to judge whether a toaster has been fixed.

The toaster-repair advisor project does not encounter problems with reliability of data from the user. As Dialog 7.3 illustrates, experts sometimes decide that the expert system should be responsible to assess data, rather than having to rely on the user's judgment. The system may need to collect more elementary data from the user and to draw its own conclusions from these data.

Dialog 7.3 Investigating the Reliability of Input Data

Setting

Deborah is an expert at trouble-shooting problems in a manufacturing plant. Lucy is a knowledge engineer who is working with Deborah to develop an expert system that will help plant operators to correct problems. Lucy is investigating the reliability of input data.

Dialog

Lucy: When you are tracking down a problem, you need to know whether there is a gas leak in the plant. *You* can tell that there is a gas leak, but the *expert system* will need to ask the operator.

Deborah: That's right.

Lucy: Do you think most operators can detect a gas leak?

Deborah: I hadn't thought of that! I'd say that most operators *can't* detect a gas leak. We've had several serious problems that would have been minor if the operator had known there was a gas leak.

Lucy: So do you think the expert system should ask whether there is a gas leak?

Deborah: It depends on who we're asking. We've got some very sharp operators who would be able to answer the question.

Lucy: Can you think of a particular operator who is about average—*not* someone who is unusually good at identifying problems?

Deborah: I'd say that Mike is about average.

Lucy: Suppose Mike telephoned you for advise. How could you identify a gas leak over the phone?

Deborah: First I'd ask Mike if there's a leak. If he said yes, I'd believe him. If he said no, I wouldn't be sure. I'd ask him to check the gas-flow gauge.

If the flow is unusually low, I'd suspect a leak. But I'd also ask him to walk by the primary gas pipes and tell me whether he could hear a hissing noise or could smell gas.

Lucy: We could have the expert system follow the steps you just outlined. First, it could ask whether there is a gas leak. If the operator says no, we could have the system judge for itself. It could ask the operator about the gas flow, the hissing noise, and the smell of gas; then the system could use the answers to decide whether there is a gas leak.

Deborah: Yes, I think that would give us more dependable information.

7.4 Defining Output Results

Just as knowledge engineers need details about the sources of input data, they also need details about the destinations for output results (Table 7.2), and they must obtain many of these details from people other than the project expert. For example, Patricia Programmer and

Table 7.2 Understanding the Destination of Output Results

Output Destination	Questions to Answer
User	What level of detail does the user want (or need)?
	What format would make the output easiest to understand and use?
Database	Into what database, table within the database, and field within the table should the information be written?
	What is the proper form for database-update requests?
	Should the database be locked while the expert system updates it?
	What should the system do if the database is already locked by some other user?
	How can the expert system access the database (or the database-management system)?
File	Into what file should the information be written?
	What is the format of the file?
	Where within the file should the information be written?
Printer (or other device)	What format would make the output easiest to understand and use?
	How can the expert system send information to the device?

Howard Hacker will need to talk to the database administrator to find out how to update the inventory fields of the toaster-part database.

Output to the user includes not only the expert system's *conclusions* but also *help text* that explains how to use the system. In some applications, the output may include *explanations* of the system's reasoning. The knowledge engineers should ask the expert to suggest how to phrase and format output but should not spend time fine tuning the contents of the display before the system is implemented. When they test the system (Chapter 11), they can obtain recommendations from both the users and the expert on the precise form and content of the output.

7.5 Points to Remember

The final goal of detailed investigation is to identify and define the characteristics that distinguish one case from another (Table 7.3). Each characteristic represents a kind of information relevant to the expert system's task. In general, knowledge engineers will identify many important characteristics when they investigate the steps in the task and the expert's reasoning process. Later they will interview the expert to discuss the details that define these characteristics. The knowledge

---

Table 7.3 Defining the Important Characteristics of a Case

Objective	Useful Activities
Identify the general characteristics.	Review sentences the expert used to describe the case; those sentences should indicate what factors of the case the expert considers important.
Define the range of specific examples of each characteristic.	Make a list of specific examples by reviewing what the expert said about the general characteristic during case discussions.
	Review the examples to define the *kind of value* the characteristic can have (descriptive, numeric, and so on).
	Review the case discussions to learn whether a case can have a single value for the characteristic or many values (or a specific number of values). If you are not sure whether a case can have multiple values for the characteristic, ask the expert.
	Ask the expert to list all the possible values for the characteristics that represent physical properties and well-defined concepts.
	Review case discussions to learn the full range of values for other characteristics. For each characteristic the expert mentioned in a case discussion, ask what other values might be possible.

Table 7.3 (continued)

Objective	Useful Activities
Define the method for finding each characteristic of a case.	Identify the method by which the expert system obtained this characteristic of each case discussed (by asking the user, by inference, and so on). Find out whether the information can be obtained by different methods in different circumstances. Find out whether this characteristic is essential to performance of the task. If not, learn what the system should do when it is unable determine this characteristic of a case. Ask whether the system can assume some default value.
Define how to obtain input data.	If a characteristic can be obtained from an external source, find out exactly how the information should be obtained. (The project expert will not be able to supply all the information about communication with on-line sources.) Wait until the expert system is implemented to obtain a detailed definition of how to collect data from a user.
Investigate the reliability of input data.	Find out whether the expert doubts the reliability of any input characteristic. If so, discuss how the system can compensate for this unreliability. Ask how the expert would request information over the telephone. This practice will help to define which decisions the *user* should make and which ones the *expert system* should make.
Define how to transmit output results.	If a characteristic should be communicated to an external destination, find out exactly how and in what form the information should be transmitted. (The project expert will not be able to supply all the information about communication with on-line destinations.) Wait until the expert system is implemented to obtain a detailed definition of how to display results to a user.

engineers should learn the *legal values* for each characteristic, the method by which the expert system will *obtain* this piece of information, and the ways in which the system will *use* the information. During these latter discussions, the knowledge engineers may identify additional characteristics.

Chapter 8

Organizing the Knowledge

After an interview early in the development phase of the toaster-repair advisor project, Howard Hacker tells Patricia Programmer, "I have pages and pages of detailed notes from our meetings with Frank. When we are ready to start implementation, I know that my project notebook will contain the information I need—I'm just not sure whether I'll be able to find it all. Today we talked about the procedure for adjusting a thermostat. But I also have notes about thermostat adjustment from two earlier meetings. When the time comes to implement Frank's knowledge about thermostat adjustment, I'm afraid I might overlook some vital notes." Patricia explains that knowledge acquisition is more than just obtaining knowledge from the expert. She tells Howard, "You can't say that you've *acquired* knowledge until you're sure that you *understand* it completely. The first step toward verifying your understanding is to organize the knowledge."

After knowledge engineers have collected information from an expert, they must use it to design and implement an expert system. As a result, it is not sufficient for the knowledge engineers to *record the contents* of interviews; they also must *organize their written records* of the meetings in such a way that they can find information when they need it. In the process of organizing information, knowledge engineers often identify topics for further knowledge-acquisition sessions. When they collect and consolidate knowledge from various interviews, the knowledge engineers may discover that they do not understand some topics completely. They may notice apparent inconsistencies between their notes from different interviews. As organization gives rise to further knowledge acquisition, the knowledge engineers refine their understanding of the expert's knowledge.

No single method of organization is best for all knowledge engineers or for all projects. At one extreme, some knowledge engineers prefer to transcribe all information into on-line files that are organized by topic. At the other extreme, some knowledge engineers prefer to create simple lists by which they can index their handwritten interview notes. In most projects, the knowledge engineers use a combination of these two approaches. They create an on-line description for any subject that they have discussed frequently; they keep printed copies of these descriptions in binders, ordered in a manner that permits easy retrieval. They create an index into their interview notes to enable them to look up subjects they have discussed only occasionally. In this chapter, we recommend a method of organizing information into project documents that combines the two approaches.

Knowledge engineers can begin to organize information by creating:

- A *project dictionary* of standard terminology the project team will use (Section 8.1)

- A *library of the cases* they have discussed with the expert (Section 8.2)

As we shall see in Chapter 9, knowledge engineers continue the organization process when they analyze the knowledge to create a conceptual model.

8.1 Creating a Project Dictionary

Each project develops its own vocabulary, which combines standard terms of the application subject area with project-specific words or phrases that emerge when the knowledge engineers describe the expert's strategy and reasoning process.

- Before knowledge engineers can understand how the project expert performs a task, they must understand the concepts of the expert's field and the terminology the expert uses to name and to describe these concepts. In the early project interviews, the knowledge engineers identify the key concepts and terms relevant to the task.

- As a project progresses, the members of the project team often invent new terms to label some of the concepts with which the expert system must reason. For example, we saw in Chapter 7 that the members of the toaster-repair advisor project use the term *severe_too_light* as a short label for the problem *the toaster toasts bread very much lighter than is appropriate for the color setting.*

The terms in a project vocabulary represent concepts relevant to the expert system's task. Over time, the knowledge engineers' understanding of these concepts may change. Quite often, the project team will discuss a concept over the course of several interviews before the knowledge engineers fully comprehend the concept. As the team members discuss different cases, the meaning of a project-specific term may evolve or the term itself may change. When the project vocabulary is in a state of flux, confusion and misunderstandings may result. More serious problems occur when the knowledge engineers use different terms for a single concept in different parts of the conceptual model. The two terms may be carried along into the implementation design and finally into the knowledge base. Inconsistent names in the knowledge base can cause subtle performance problems in the expert system. Such problems can be difficult to track down because the entries in the knowledge base all appear correct. It often takes side-by-side comparison of different knowledge-base entries to discover inconsistencies in terminology.

Knowledge engineers can standardize their terminology by developing a **project dictionary,** an alphabetized list of the terms in the project vocabulary with a description of the concept that each term represents. The exact content of the dictionary will vary from project to project. In some projects, the dictionary will contain only terms new to the knowledge engineers. For example, Patricia Programmer does not include the word *toaster* in her project dictionary, even though this word represents a concept that is central to the toaster-repair advisor project. Other knowledge engineers prefer to record all project-related terms, even the most obvious. At the very least, the dictionary should include the terms the project team will use to describe the general characteristics of a case and the specific examples of these characteristics (see Chapter 7).

We suggest that you keep your project dictionary on-line to facilitate modification. Use whatever form you find most convenient, for example, a text file that you create with a word processor, a spreadsheet, or a database. Start your project dictionary as soon as you identify new terms. After each interview, review the concepts you discussed and the words and phrases with which the team members described each concept. If necessary, add new terms to the dictionary, or update existing descriptions of the terms. A single knowledge engineer should be responsible for maintaining the project dictionary.

Some terms will need more complete explanations than will others (Figure 8.1). Decide on a word-by-word basis how detailed a definition to include. Remember that the purpose of the dictionary is to help *members of the project team;* it does not have to explain project terminology with wording that people outside the project can understand. The dictionary should serve two purposes.

1. It should specify which terms are part of the standard project vocabulary and which are not. For example, Figure 8.1 shows that the toaster-repair advisor project dictionary includes common synonyms that are not standard for the project *(coils)* and old terms that have been replaced and are therefore no longer standard for the project *(possible_cause_currently_under_consideration).*

Figure 8.1 Entries in the toaster-repair advisor project dictionary. The project dictionary indicates which terms are part of the standard project vocabulary and reminds project members how the terms relate to the expert system.

coil	DO NOT USE: Use *heating_element* instead. Frank uses this term occasionally to refer to a heating element.
current_possible_cause	After the system concludes an ordered set of possible causes of the toaster problem, it considers these causes one at a time. This term denotes the possible cause that is currently under consideration.
heating_element	Part of a toaster.
no_trip	Kind of toaster problem: The toast gets stuck inside the toaster and does not pop up.
possible_cause_currently_ under_consideration	DO NOT USE: Use *current_possible_cause* instead. We used to use this term, but it was too long!
problem_within_scope?	Yes/no characteristic of a case: If yes, the toaster problem is within the current system scope.
severe_too_dark	Toaster problem: The toaster toasts the bread much too dark for the color setting.
severe_thermostat_problem_ heating_too_long	Possible cause of a toaster problem.
simple_two_slice	Style of toaster: The toaster has two bread slots and no fancy features (like a bakery switch).
thermostat	Part of a toaster.

2. It should define any term whose definition is not obvious. Notice in Figure 8.1 that the description of *current_possible_cause* explains what this term means and the context in which it is important. On the other hand, the term *severe_thermostat_problem_heating_too_long* is sufficiently descriptive that the project members do not need a separate definition.

8.2 Creating a Case Library

As we saw in chapters 5, 6, and 7, a single case can serve as the focus for several different interviews. During initial inquiry, the knowledge engineers may ask the expert to discuss the case at a general level. During detailed investigation, the knowledge engineers may return to the case to obtain a more complete understanding of the process by which the expert performs the task. They may review the same case to learn about the expert's reasoning process or to identify the facts and hypotheses with which the expert reasons. The collection of information that the knowledge engineers obtained about a single case provides a concrete and indepth example of the expert's reasoning and problem-solving processes. Similar collections of information for different cases provide additional examples. If knowledge acquisition has been thorough, these case examples should span the range of situations in which the expert system should be able to perform its task; the full array of case examples should provide an organized description of the processes the expert system should perform.

This section explains how to collect and to organize information about cases. Section 8.2.1 describes the kinds of information you should collect about each case. Section 8.2.2 illustrates methods for organizing a written report of the expert system's intended performance for a case. Section 8.2.3 describes how to organize the case reports. Section 8.2.4 discusses how to maintain your collection of case reports to allow retrieval of cases when they are pertinent to development activities.

8.2.1 Collecting Information Relevant to a Case

The information relevant to a case consists of the *expert's knowledge* that you obtained during discussions of the case and *auxiliary information* that serves to organize the cases and to make case reports easy to use during the development of an expert system.

First, *construct a complete description of the expert system's actions as it performs the task for each case.* Review all the information you learned from the expert in your various discussions about the case, then integrate this information into a single coherent description. Your description should specify:

- The input data the expert system will need together with the source of each input characteristic

- The output results the system should produce together with the destination of each output characteristic

- The time-sequence of input, reasoning, and output steps the system should take as it performs its task for the case

Next, *give each case a unique reference name or number* (or both). Names are more descriptive; a well-chosen name can remind both expert and knowledge engineers of the details of the case. Many projects, however, accumulate so many cases that it becomes difficult for the team members to recall case names. Reference numbers can replace or augment case names as an easy means of distinguishing cases.

Finally, *write a brief summary of the case.* The project members should be able to use the summary to decide when a case is relevant to a particular design discussion. Include at least the most important inputs and the major results for the case. State what aspect of the task this case illustrates. For example, is the case a prototypical example of a common class of situations in which the task can be performed? Does it correspond to a particularly difficult or unusual situation? Is it unique in some way?

8.2.2 Designing a Case Report

Once you have collected relevant information for a case, use this information to create a **case report,** a written account of the intended behavior of the expert system for a particular case. Each case report should consist of a *complete description of system performance* for the case and a *cover sheet* with auxiliary information. Different projects will find different information useful so design your cover sheet to include any information you think will be important when you develop the expert system. A typical cover sheet might include:

- *Identifying information* about the case: the reference name or number and the brief summary

- *Project-tracking information* that tells how, when, and why the case report has been changed

- *Cross references* to other sources of information about the case (such as interview notes and corporate records about historical cases)

- *Status information* for use during implementation and testing of the expert system. This information can indicate how closely the expert system's actual performance for the case matches the intended performance shown in this case report.

When you have decided what information to include, devise a format for your cover sheets. Use this format consistently as you create a case report for each case you discuss with the expert.

> Patricia Programmer and Howard Hacker meet to discuss what information to include in their case reports and how to format these reports. They decide to identify each case with a unique reference number. They agree that case summaries for the toaster-repair advisor should specify the type of toaster, the customer complaints, the correct repair for the problem, and the type of problem this case illustrates. For project-tracking purposes, Patricia suggests that they record the name of the person who last modified the case report and the date on which the modification occurred.
>
> To document the source of the information in the report, Patricia suggests that they include the *repair order number* if the case corresponds to a toaster repaired in the service department. If necessary, the repair order number could be used to find the company files on that toaster. Patricia also thinks the case record should include cross references to the notebooks and tapes that record case discussions. Patricia and Howard use their initials to label their project notebooks. Patricia labels her notebook *PP1;* when she fills this notebook and begins a new one, she will label the new notebook *PP2* and so on. Howard labels his notebook *HH1.* Patricia and Howard number the pages in their notebooks. At the beginning of an interview, they both record the date in their notebooks. Patricia and Howard can use dates and page numbers to locate notes relevant to a particular case. Patricia numbers the tapes she uses when she tape records an interview. If any discussions of a given case were tape recorded, the cover sheet of the case report can indicate the relevant tape numbers.
>
> Although the toaster-repair advisor is not yet implemented, Patricia and Howard outline the status information that will be helpful when they start to implement and test the system. They will want to know whether the system performs correctly on the case, the date on which the case was last tested, and the version of the toaster-repair advisor on which the test was run. If the system does not handle the case correctly, they will want to keep a list of relevant bug reports.
>
> Figure 8.2 contains an example of the case-report cover sheet Patricia and Howard designed for the toaster-repair advisor.

The most important element of a case report is the complete description of the expert system's intended performance for the case. The form of the description will vary from application to application. Select a form that includes all the relevant information and is easy for the project team to understand. A description of system performance for a case can follow one of two general styles.

1. **A performance outline** presents a concise description (using project terminology) of the sequence of actions and decisions the expert

system should execute for the case. A performance outline specifies *what* the expert system should do but not *how* the system should interact with its environment. A performance outline is used only by the project members; its concise form facilitates their review of the case report.

2. An **annotated interaction log** describes the system's performance by illustrating how it will interact with its environment. Annotations explain any of the system's reasoning steps that are not apparent from a record of the system's interactions. An annotated interaction log uses terminology the system's intended users can understand not special project terminology. The knowledge engi-

---

Figure 8.2 Cover sheet for a case report. The cover sheet identifies the case by its reference number and gives a brief summary of the important features of the case. Additional information on a cover sheet can be used to track changes to the case report, to find relevant information on which the case report is based, and to record the expert system's status as it is tested on this case.

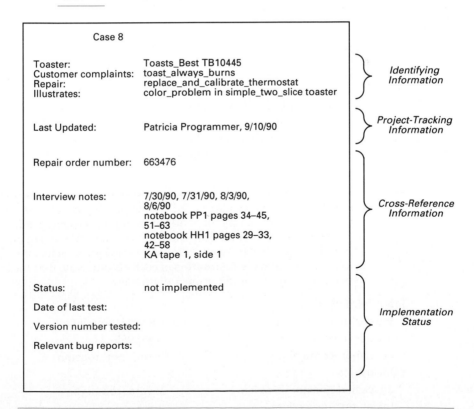

Case 8

Toaster: Toasts_Best TB10445
Customer complaints: toast_always_burns   Identifying
Repair: replace_and_calibrate_thermostat   Information
Illustrates: color_problem in simple_two_slice toaster

Last Updated: Patricia Programmer, 9/10/90   Project-Tracking
                                                                     Information

Repair order number: 663476

Interview notes: 7/30/90, 7/31/90, 8/3/90,
                         8/6/90
                         notebook PP1 pages 34–45,   Cross-Reference
                         51–63   Information
                         notebook HH1 pages 29–33,
                         42–58
                         KA tape 1, side 1

Status: not implemented

Date of last test: Implementation
                                                                     Status
Version number tested:

Relevant bug reports:

neers may use annotated interaction logs to explain the system's intended functions to people outside the project or to solicit suggestions about the user interface from some of the system's intended users.

We suggest that each project use annotated interaction logs in at least one or two case reports. Use more if the interaction varies greatly from case to case. These logs can serve as specifications for the format in which the system will accept its input and write its output. For an interactive expert system, the knowledge engineers can use the logs to guide the design of the user interface.

> Patricia Programmer and Howard Hacker create *performance outlines* to describe system performance for each case (Figure 8.3). They also create *annotated interaction logs* for a few cases and include these logs (along with the performance outlines) in the corresponding case reports. An annotated interaction log for the toaster-repair advisor consists of two parts. The first part shows the interaction that should occur between the toaster-repair advisor and the repair person (Figure 8.4). The second part shows the intended interactions between the system and the billing clerk—namely, the customer bill that the system should create (Figure 8.5).

8.2.3 Organizing the Case Reports

As soon as you have discussed your first few cases, design a format for case reports and start your **case library,** an organized collection of case reports. You can adapt the format over time if necessary. We suggest you develop case reports with a word processor. Use a standard naming convention for the files that contain your reports. Each file name should identify both the case and the contents of the file (if you use more than

---

Figure 8.3 Performance outline for the toaster-repair advisor. This description states succinctly the sequence of input, reasoning, and output steps the toaster-repair advisor should perform for the particular case. The outline specifies the source of each input, the conclusions of each reasoning step, and the destination of each output. Note that the outline uses terminology from the project dictionary.

Input from user:

toaster_make	General_Appliance
toaster_model	GA98985
customer_complaints	bread_not_toasted

Conclusions:

suspected_toaster_problem	severe_too_light
initial_test_procedure	toast_one_slice_on_dark

Figure 8.3 (continued)

Output to user:

   request the test procedure
      toast_one_slice_on_dark

Input from user:

operating_lever_was_lowered?	yes
operating_lever_stayed_down?	yes
toast_popped_up?	yes
both_sides_toasted_equally?	yes
toast_color	white
bread_warm?	yes

Conclusions:

toaster_problem	severe_thermostat_problem_ heating_too_short
toaster_style	simple_two_slice
problem_within_scope?	yes

Input from database:

thermostat_type	class_2

Input from user:

part_number of the thermostat	X77213

Conclusions:

ordered_possible_causes	(1. bad_thermostat)
current_possible_cause	bad_thermostat
repair_procedure	replace_and_calibrate_thermostat
acceptable_part_numbers	X77215

Output to user:

   request the repair procedure
      replace_and_calibrate_thermostat
      using part number X77215

Input from user:

repair_fixed_problem?	yes

Output to database:

   reduce inventory count
      of part X77215 by 1

Input from database:

price of part X77215	1.25

Conclusions:

sales_tax	.88
repair_cost	7.00
total_repair_charge	9.13

Output to printer:

   customer bill

Figure 8.4 Annotated interaction log for the toaster-repair advisor, part 1. The first part of an annotated interaction log for the toaster-repair advisor shows the intended interactions between the expert system and the repair person. User input is underlined. Annotations in *italics* explain any actions and decisions that are not obvious from the interaction alone. Annotations also explain transactions between the toaster-repair advisor and the toaster-part database.

Toaster Manufacturer: Toasts-Best   Model Number: TB10445

Customer complaints (check all that apply)

___bread not toasted   ___toast does not pop up

___operating lever will not go down   ___toast too dark

___operating lever will not stay down   ___toast too light

_X_toast always burns   ___toasts on one side only

On the basis of the toaster manufacturer and model number and the customer's complaints, suspect a severe too-dark color problem. The appropriate initial test for this problem is to toast one slice on the lightest color setting.

Please set the color control on the lightest setting and toast one slice of bread, then answer the following questions.

Could you lower the operating lever?	yes
Did the operating lever stay down?	yes
Did the toast pop up?	yes
Were both sides of the bread toasted equally?	yes
What was the toast's color?	burnt

On the basis of the results of the initial test, conclude that the toaster has a severe too-dark color problem. The possible causes are (1) a severe thermostat problem heating for too long or (2) a bad thermostat. Investigate these possibilities one at a time.

Try to adjust the thermostat to shorten the toasting time.
(Make a large initial adjustment: two full turns counterclockwise.)

Were you able to adjust the toaster to correct the problem?   no

The repair failed to correct the problem; go on to the next possible cause (bad thermostat).

Retrieve the part numbers of thermostats that can be used in this model toaster.

Please replace the thermostat. Use a new thermostat with any of the following part numbers:

R71993

R71994

R71995

R71998

Figure 8.4 (continued)

Calibrate the new thermostat.

    Does the toaster function correctly with the new thermostat?   <u>yes</u>

    Please enter the part number of the replacement thermostat.   <u>R71995</u>

    Reduce inventory count of R71995 by 1.

Updating the toaster-parts database...done.

Please enter the following information for the customer's bill:

    Customer Name: <u>P. R. Jones</u>   Repaired by: <u>Frank</u>

    Repair order number: <u>663476</u>

    Retrieve price of R71995 from database. Price is $1.25. Compute total repair charge.

Printing the customer bill...done.

---

one file per case report). Project members will generally find it most convenient to refer to printed copies of the case reports. Keep the printed copies organized and stored where they will be accessible to all team members. For example, keep case reports in folders in a filing cabinet or in a three-ring binder. Order the case reports by reference name or number. Whenever you modify a case report, print the updated file(s), and replace the old copy in your case filing cabinet or binder.

Figure 8.5 Annotated interaction log for the toaster-repair advisor, part 2. The second part of an annotated interaction log for the toaster-repair advisor illustrates the intended interactions between the expert system and the billing clerk. The system will prepare a customer bill for the billing clerk and will send it to the printer in the reception area of the service department.

Customer Name: P. R. Jones   Repair order number: 663476

Repaired by: Frank   Date: 7/30/90

Toasts-Best TB10445

Description of repair:

  Replaced thermostat with new part #R71995

	Parts		
		R71995	1.25
	Subtotal		1.25
	Tax		.88
	Labor		7.00
	Total		$9.13

To make cases easy to find when they are relevant to a particular discussion, create a *table of contents* for your case library. The table of contents should have a one-line summary of the salient features of the case. Include the reference name or number for the case and important inputs, outputs, or other classifications. In order to make concise descriptions of the important characteristics of cases, you may find it necessary to define abbreviations or short terms to use in the table of contents. If you do devise new terms for your table of contents, be sure to add them to your project dictionary. Use the same abbreviations or short terms consistently throughout the table of contents.

> Patricia Programmer and Howard Hacker create two files for each case report: one containing the cover sheet and one containing the performance outline. For a few cases, they create two additional files corresponding to the two-part annotated interaction log. They select basic file names that indicate the case number and file-name extensions that indicate the type of file (Table 8.1). Patricia and Howard assemble copies of case reports into a binder. They separate the individual case reports with index tabs and create a table of contents for the binder (Figure 8.6).

8.2.4 Maintaining the Case Library

The easiest way to maintain a case library is to update it after each interview. After you first discuss a particular case, create a new case report. Be sure to consult the notes made by *all* the project knowledge engineers when you write the description of system performance. Refer to the project dictionary to be sure your case reports make consistent use of standard project terminology. Distribute a draft of your report to all project members (including the expert of course). Collect comments and corrections from your teammates, and update the draft as necessary.

Table 8.1 File-Naming Conventions for the Toaster-Repair Advisor Case Library

Type of File	Basic File Name	File-Name Extension	Example File Name
Cover sheet	Case reference number	cov	case001.cov
Performance outline	Case reference number	per	case001.per
Annotated interaction log, part 1 (interaction with repair person)	Case reference number	log	case012.log
Annotated interaction log, part 1 (bill for billing clerk)	Case reference number	bil	case012.bil

After you discuss a case already in your library, update the case report to incorporate any new information you obtained. Very often, the information you learn in a discussion about one case will be relevant to other cases. Refer to the table of contents for your case library to see what other case reports might be affected. Review the reports for those cases, and update them as appropriate. Try to keep all cases in the library as up to date as possible. If your project team includes more than one knowledge engineer, select one person to take responsibility for maintenance of the case library.

Figure 8.6 Table of contents for the toaster-repair advisor case library. The table of contents provides a quick summary of the cases in the library. It lists important features of each case; project members can use the table of contents to identify the cases that are pertinent to design discussions or testing activities. To make the table of contents easier to read, Patricia Programmer does not join words with underscores; the format of the table makes it clear that groups of words name a single concept. To make the case summaries concise, Patricia uses shortened forms of standard project terminology in the *Style* and *Repair* columns. For example, she uses *2-slice* instead of *simple_two_slice* and *replace thermostat* instead of *replace_and_calibrate_thermostat*.

Case #	Toaster	Style	Complaints	Repair
1	TB80601	2-slice	Toast too dark	Replace thermostat
2	TB10445	2-slice	Toast too light	Adjust thermostat
3	GA77786	4-slice	Toast too dark	Adjust thermostat
4	TB10445	2-slice	Toasts on one side	Replace heating element
5	TB23435	2-slice	Toast always burns, Toast will not pop up	Clean and file vertical shaft
6	GA00952	2-slice	Toast will not pop up	Clean and file vertical shaft
7	TB88654	2-slice	Operating lever will not go down	Replace carriage assembly
8	TB10445	2-slice	Toast always burns	Replace thermostat
9	TB88654	2-slice	Toast always burns	Adjust thermostat
10	GA98985	2-slice	Bread not toasted	Replace thermostat
11	TB10049	2-slice	Toast too light	Adjust thermostat
12	GA00952	2-slice	Bread not toasted	Adjust thermostat
13	TB10048	2-slice	(None specified)	Adjust thermostat
14	GA01912	2-slice	Toast always burns	Replace thermostat

In the toaster-repair advisor project, Howard Hacker keeps the case library up to date. After each interview, Howard collects his and Patricia Programmer's notebooks and the tape recordings of the interview (if any). He reviews this material then creates new case reports and updates existing reports as appropriate. Howard checks his reports against the project dictionary to be sure he has used standard project terminology consistently. Howard asks Patricia Programmer and Frank Fixit to review new case reports and those that required significant modification. After Howard has incorporated Frank's and Patricia's comments and corrections into the case reports, he updates the table of contents. He then makes new copies of the files that have changed and uses these to update the project case binder.

When Howard needs to update case reports, he checks carefully whether notes from the current interview are consistent with existing case reports. If he encounters inconsistencies or if he is unsure how to consolidate new information with existing case reports, he discusses these problems with Patricia. If Patricia and Howard are not able to resolve these problems, they add them to the agenda for the next knowledge-acquisition interview.

The number of cases in a case library varies greatly from project to project; it is common, however, for the case library in a large project to contain hundreds of cases. As the number of cases in a library increases, maintenance becomes more time consuming and often more difficult. If your project accumulates so many cases that it becomes difficult to find relevant cases when you need them, you may want to employ additional measures to facilitate maintenance. The utilities you create will depend on the needs of your project. The following ideas may be useful.

- If the table of contents does not provide all the information you need to find cases, keep a separate binder with the cover pages of the case reports. It will be quicker for project members to flip through cover pages than to search through the entire collection of case reports.

- Create a database of cases that records the important features of each case. Use database queries to identify the cases relevant to your design or testing activities.

- Use whatever string-search facilities are available in your computing environment. For example, if Howard Hacker needs to update all case reports in which the suspected problem is *severe_too_dark*, he can use an operating-system utility to search all the performance-outline files for the string *severe_too_dark*.

8.3 Points to Remember

After each interview, knowledge engineers should organize the information they obtained and should integrate this information with related information they obtained in earlier interviews. This practice serves three purposes.

1. It tests whether the knowledge engineers have a complete understanding of the topics that were discussed in the interview.

2. It helps the knowledge engineers to recognize when they need to ask the expert to clear up their misunderstandings and to resolve apparent inconsistencies.

3. It produces project documents that will make the expert's knowledge accessible when it is needed during subsequent system-development activities.

The project documents that result from the initial organization efforts are

- A *project dictionary* that records the standard project vocabulary. The project team members should use the terms in this dictionary when they speak or write notes about the project.

Table 8.2 Initial Project Documents

Document	Suggested Contents
All	Cross references to notebooks and recordings of relevant interviews
	Cross references to other project documents
	Cross references to corporate files, textbooks, manuals, and so on
	Project-tracking information (audit trail of modifications)
	Implementation and testing status
Project dictionary	Special terms of the application subject area with definitions
	Terms the project members use to label concepts relevant to the expert system's task
	Definitions of project-specific terms not completely self-descriptive
	Warnings about synonyms and old project terminology *not* considered standard
Case library	A table of contents with a one-line summary of each case
	A cover sheet for each case report that includes the unique reference name or number and a brief summary of the important features of the case
	A description of the sequence of the input, reasoning, and output steps that the expert system should take when it performs its task for each case
	A few annotated logs of the intended interactions between the expert system and its environment

- A *library of case reports* each of which provides a detailed example of the intended performance of the expert system

The exact form and content of these document will vary across projects. The knowledge engineers on a project team should develop a set of formats they can use to capture the information that they will need when they design, implement, and test their expert system. The knowledge engineers should balance flexibility with consistency so their project documents contain all the information they need in a form that is easy to understand and use. Table 8.2 suggests the kinds of information that might be included in each kind of project document.

Chapter 9

Developing a Conceptual Model of the Expert System

Howard Hacker tells Patricia Programmer, "Now I think we understand how Frank repairs toasters—at least how he fixes color problems in two-slice toasters. I guess we're ready to start implementation—right?" Patricia explains they are ready to start their *design*, not their implementation. She reminds Howard, "The knowledge base of the toaster-repair advisor will require continual updates long after you and I complete this project. Each month, the information in new service bulletins will have to be added, and information from expired service bulletins will have to be removed. The knowledge base must keep pace with the industry as new toasters are manufactured and as new test equipment is developed. The time you and I spend now to design our knowledge base will make it easier for other knowledge engineers to keep the system up to date in the future. Our next step is to *analyze* the knowledge we've obtained from Frank. We have to understand and describe how the expert system will *use* Frank's knowledge to perform its task."

As we discussed in Chapter 1, knowledge-acquisition activities are interconnected with all the other activities that go into the development of an expert system. Expert-system *design* is an integral part of the knowledge acquisition process: As knowledge engineers design the system, they uncover topics for future interviews. During much of the

detailed investigation stage, design activities drive knowledge-acquisition activities.

The design of an expert system's knowledge base consists of two
steps: *conceptual* design and *implementation* design. In the conceptual-
design step, the knowledge engineers examine each piece of knowledge
to identify its *function* within the knowledge base. For example, as
Patricia Programmer and Howard Hacker review the knowledge they
have learned from Frank Fixit, they will specify how each piece of
knowledge affects the process of giving advice about the repair of a
toaster. The result of the knowledge engineers' careful analysis of the
expert's knowledge is a conceptual model of the expert system. A **conceptual model** shows the sequence of steps by which an expert system
will perform its task, the inferences it will perform, and the information
it will use. In other words, a conceptual model describes *how and when
the expert's knowledge will come into play as the expert system performs
its task.* As we shall see in Chapter 10, the evolving conceptual model
guides both subsequent knowledge acquisition and the implementation of the expert system.

Knowledge engineers create a conceptual model by using notations
and diagrams that allow them to express the function of the knowledge.
We refer to these notations as **intermediate representations** because
they should be completely independent of the representation formalisms used in any particular expert-system shell. In the *implementation
design* step, the knowledge engineers will translate their conceptual
model into an implementation design. Only at that point should the
knowledge engineers concern themselves with the representation formalisms of their chosen shell.

The creation of a conceptual model is a continuation of the organization process we discussed in Chapter 8. In that chapter, we saw how
knowledge engineers create two project documents: a project dictionary and a case library. In this chapter, we shall see how they create a
third document: a project **design document**, which contains an organized collection of the intermediate representations that make up the
conceptual model.

Chapters 5 through 9 present a three-step knowledge-acquisition
process: The knowledge engineers *obtain* knowledge from the expert,
they *organize* this knowledge, and they *analyze* it to produce a conceptual model. In practice, these three steps are not performed in their
entirety one after another (see Figure 1.5). Rather the knowledge engineers obtain some information in an interview. They organize this
knowledge to create the project documents that we discussed in Chapter 8. Then they analyze the knowledge and start to sketch the intermediate representations of their conceptual model. Finally they create
a design document to contain these intermediate representations. In

the next interview, the knowledge engineers obtain additional knowledge. They organize this knowledge and consolidate it with their project documents. They refine their intermediate representations and update their design document again. This process continues until the knowledge engineers have a conceptual model that is sufficiently complete to guide their implementation design.

The knowledge-acquisition process *could* proceed without the creation of a conceptual model. Knowledge engineers could analyze the knowledge they obtain to create an *implementation design* for their chosen shell and could use the implementation design to drive future interviews. Unfortunately, many knowledge engineers have followed this practice, often with dismal results. Projects that neglect the conceptual-design step often produce expert systems that are prohibitively difficult to extend or maintain.

Ease of maintenance is a frequently cited advantage of the expert-system architecture over traditional program architectures:

> In an expert system, the knowledge is separate from the program that uses it. Knowledge in an expert system is represented in a *declarative* form—that is, the representation states what is known but does not specify how to use this knowledge. In a traditional program, on the other hand, the knowledge is an integral part of the complex program logic. To extend an expert system's functionality, one need only add modular entries (such as *rules* or *frames*) to the knowledge base. A similar extension to a traditional program might require pervasive modifications instead of one localized addition.

This argument is valid up to a point: *If the knowledge base of an expert system is well designed*, the system will be easier to extend and maintain than is a traditional program. A well-designed program, however, might be considerably easier to maintain than is an expert system with a poorly-designed knowledge base. Knowledge engineers who map the knowledge they acquire directly into the *rules, frames,* or other representations of their favorite shell often do so without careful consideration (or complete understanding) of the *function* that the knowledge should serve. The result is a poorly-designed, unmaintainable expert system. Because a sound conceptual model is crucial to the long-term success of an expert-system project, this chapter will focus on the *creation* of a conceptual model. In Chapter 10, we shall describe how to *use* the conceptual model to guide knowledge acquisition.

To begin the conceptual-design process, knowledge engineers analyze how the expert system will use its knowledge; they classify the knowledge according to function.

- **Strategic knowledge** specifies what to do—that is, the sequence of steps the expert system should follow to perform its task.

- **Judgmental knowledge** specifies how the expert system can add to its current information about a case.

- **Factual knowledge** specifies what is true (or believed) about the world in general and about the particular case for which the task is being performed.

In Chapters 5, 6, and 7 we saw that Patricia Programmer and Howard Hacker followed a top-down approach to the collection of information about toaster repair. They first identified the steps in Frank Fixit's problem-solving strategy. Next they investigated the reasoning Frank uses in performing the different steps. Finally they defined the characteristics Frank uses and concludes as he reasons. In this chapter, we describe the parallel process by which the knowledge engineers develop their conceptual model. First they analyze the strategic knowledge, which specifies the sequence of input, reasoning, and output steps the system will take as it performs its task (Section 9.1). Next they analyze the judgmental knowledge that will guide the expert system in its reasoning steps (Section 9.2). Finally they analyze the factual knowledge the system will use and will conclude as it performs its task (Section 9.3). As the knowledge engineers develop the intermediate representations of their conceptual model, they will organize these definitions and diagrams into their project design document (Section 9.4). In subsequent cycles of development, they will enhance and refine their conceptual model (Section 9.5).

9.1 Analyzing Strategic Knowledge

The first step toward creation of a conceptual model is the analysis of the expert's strategic knowledge. Knowledge engineers analyze the strategic knowledge to produce a clear definition of:

- The modular steps that make up the expert system's task

- The flow of control that should occur within the expert system

The knowledge engineers first identify the high-level steps that the system should perform, the order in which it should take these steps, and the conditions under which it should perform each step (Section 9.1.1). Next, the knowledge engineers break the high-level steps into substeps as necessary (Section 9.1.2). If the expert system's task is complex, several levels of substeps will be needed. Finally the knowledge engineers describe the sequence of input, reasoning, and output actions that the expert system must take within each of the lowest-level substeps (Section 9.1.3).

9.1.1 Defining High-Level Control

In Chapter 5, we discussed the interview activities through which knowledge engineers can define the procedure an expert system should follow. Interviews identify a very detailed sequence of actions for the expert system to perform. (For an example, see the sequence of steps outlined at the end of Dialog 5.4.) To begin your analysis, review the low-level actions you identified. Try to describe, at a very general level, what your expert system will do. Your description should include *actions meaningful to the expert*. Each action should be a *unit of functionality you might implement and test separately*. The actions in your description correspond to the high-level steps the expert system will perform.

> Patricia Programmer describes the toaster-repair advisor's actions as follows. "The system should first identify the problem with the toaster then infer an ordered list of possible causes for that problem. It should try to repair each of these possible causes in order until either the toaster is fixed or the system runs out of possible causes."

Number the steps you identified in your description, then draw a flow chart to illustrate the sequence in which the expert system should perform these steps. If the current cycle of development does not cover the entire task, be sure your flow chart includes the omitted subtasks. For example, Figure 9.1 shows the high-level control for the toaster-repair advisor. The flow chart includes the steps Patricia Programmer identified in her description of the system's actions as well as the subtasks that will be added in later cycles of development.

9.1.2 Identifying Substeps of the Task

After you have defined the high-level steps the expert system will perform, focus on each of those steps in turn. Review your interview notes to understand *what the expert system must do* in the step. Subdivide any step that consists of more than a small number of input, reasoning, and output actions. For example, Patricia Programmer decides to subdivide Steps 1 and 3 of the toaster-repair advisor. To subdivide a step, repeat the process described in Section 9.1.1.

- Describe what the expert system should do in the step.

- Identify substeps corresponding to the actions in your description.

- Number the substeps.

- Draw a flow chart for the step to illustrate the sequence in which the expert system should perform the substeps.

Figure 9.1 Flow chart of high-level control in the toaster-repair advisor. Patricia Programmer and Howard Hacker identified five high-level steps for the toaster-repair advisor. In the first cycle of development, they will implement Steps 1, 2, and 3.

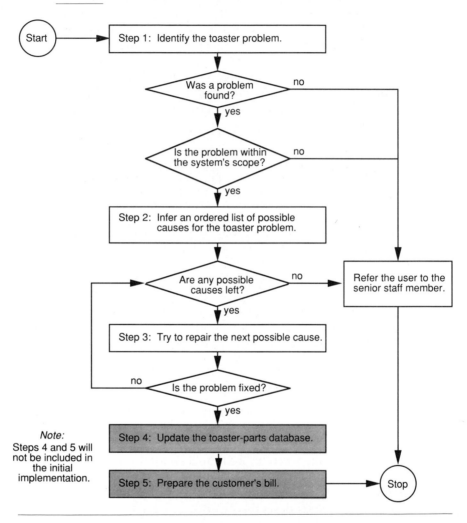

Review each of the substeps that you identify to see whether they need to be broken down further. If so, repeat the process. Define as many levels of substeps as you need. Figure 9.2 shows the substeps Patricia Programmer identified.

Figure 9.2 Substeps for the toaster-repair advisor. Patricia Programmer identified three substeps (a) for Step 1 and three substeps (b) for Step 3. (Patricia did not further subdivide any of these substeps.)

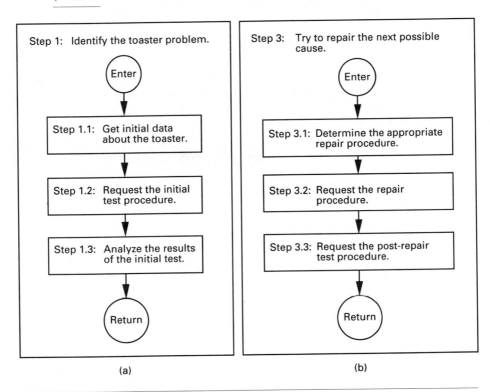

(a)   (b)

If you define many levels of substeps for your expert system, you may want to draw a functional-decomposition tree (Figure 9.3) to illustrate how the expert system's task can be broken into smaller steps. Start the tree with a node that corresponds to the complete task of the expert system. At the next level, show the high-level steps that make up this task. Under each step, list its substeps, and so on.

9.1.3 Defining the Substeps

After you have divided your expert system's task into modular steps, define the steps that make up the leaves of your functional decomposition tree (that is, the steps not further subdivided). The definition of a step should specify:

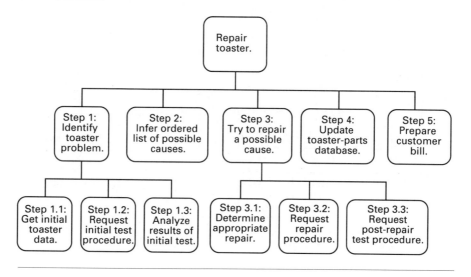

Figure 9.3 Functional-decomposition tree for the toaster-repair advisor. Patricia Programmer draws this tree to illustrate the modular steps that make up the task of the toaster-repair advisor.

- The purpose of the step
- The information that should be available to the system before it enters the step
- The sequence of input, reasoning, and output actions that should be performed in the step
- For each input action the source of the input
- For each reasoning action all information that is required as the basis of the inference and all information that will be concluded by the inference
- For each output action the destination of the output

Devise a standard format for the definitions of your system's steps. Include auxiliary information that will be useful in future design, implementation, and testing activities. For example, leave a space in the definition for the names of corresponding entries in the knowledge base, for references to other sources of information, and for implementation and testing status. As you write your step definitions, be careful to use project terminology consistently. Refer to your project dictionary (Section 8.1) to be sure you use standard terminology. Figure 9.4 shows definitions of the first two substeps the toaster-repair advisor will perform.

Figure 9.4 Definition of low-level steps for the toaster-repair advisor. When Patricia Programmer defines a step at the lowest level of the functional decomposition tree, she describes the individual input, reasoning, and output actions that the system should take within the step.

Step 1.1 Get initial data about the toaster.

Name(s) in knowledge-base: *(not implemented yet)*

Purpose: Start the interaction with the toaster-repair advisor by collecting the basic information that is needed to guide the repair process.

Required information: none

Actions: 1.1.1 (input) Get toaster_make from the user.
1.1.2 (input) Get toaster_model from the user.
1.1.3 (input) Get customer_complaints from the user.

Interview notes: 6/15/90, 8/3/90
notebook PP1 pages 5, 53

Implementation status: not implemented

Step 1.2 Request the initial test procedure.

Name(s) in knowledge base: *(not implemented yet)*

Purpose: The system must ask the user to test the toaster, and must use the result of this initial test to decide what problem needs to be repaired. In this step, the system decides what initial test procedure is appropriate, then asks the user to perform that procedure.

Required information: toaster_make, toaster_model, customer_complaints

Actions: 1.2.1 (reasoning) Infer suspected_toaster_problem.
Basis Characteristics: Conclusion Characteristic:
toaster_make
toaster_model ———► suspected_toaster_problem
customer_complaints

1.2.2 (reasoning) Infer initial_test_procedure.
Basis Characteristic: Conclusion Characteristic:
suspected_toaster_problem ———► initial_test_procedure

1.2.3 (output) Request the initial_test_procedure.
Display the short_description of the test procedure to the user.

Interview notes: 7/30/90, 8/6/90
notebook PP1 pages 34–36, 59–61
notebook HH1 pages 29, 56–57

Implementation status: not implemented

9.2 Analyzing Judgmental Knowledge

The second activity in the creation of a conceptual model is the analysis of the expert's judgmental knowledge, which specifies how the expert system can use currently known facts and currently believed hypotheses about the case to conclude new facts and hypotheses. Knowledge engineers analyze the judgmental knowledge within the context of the task the system will perform. They must understand *how the expert system will use its judgmental knowledge.* Their analysis should produce detailed definitions of each reasoning step the expert system will perform. A reasoning step may indicate that the system should *conclude* a specific characteristic (Section 9.2.1) or that it should *use* a specific characteristic to infer new information (Section 9.2.2). After the knowledge engineers have defined the individual reasoning steps, they should summarize the overall structure of the system's inferences (Section 9.2.3).

9.2.1 Understanding How to Make Conclusions

Examine each of the reasoning steps you identified in your analysis of the expert's strategic knowledge. If a reasoning step specifies that the system should infer a particular characteristic (for example, *infer the ordered list of possible causes for the toaster problem*), define how the system can infer this characteristic in all possible circumstances.

- Identify the characteristics that can form the basis for this kind of inference.

- See whether inferences of this kind follow a standard structure. Do the same characteristics form the basis of *all* these inferences?

- Select an intermediate representation that illustrates how the expert system should make this type of inference.

In the remainder of this section, we describe some intermediate representations that are can be used to organize and to illustrate judgmental knowledge.

General Decision Tables

As we saw in Figure 6.1, an inference consists of a *condition* and a *conclusion.* The characteristics used in the condition of an inference are called the *basis characteristics* because they form the basis for the decision. The characteristic in the conclusion is called the *conclusion characteristic.*[1] Examine the inferences for a particular conclusion char-

---

1. A single inference can conclude more than one characteristic; for simplicity, however, we refer to a single conclusion characteristic.

acteristic to see whether the conditions of these inferences follow a standard structure.

- The conditions all test the same basis characteristics.

- Each condition specifies a value (or a range of values) for each basis characteristic.

In other words, the inferences should all have the form:

If   *basis characteristic 1*   = *value 1* and
        basis characteristic 2   = *value 2* and
        . . . and
        basis characteristic N   = *value N*
then   *conclusion characteristic* = *value M*

   If all inferences have this form, a **decision table** can capture this standard inference structure. A decision table enumerates all possible combinations of values for the basis characteristics and indicates what conclusion can be made for each combination of values. We will look at two forms of decision table: the *general* decision table that can be used for inferences with any number of basis characteristics and the *two-basis* decision table that can be used for inferences with exactly two basis characteristics.

   In Chapter 6, we discussed the process of identifying all situations in which a characteristic could be concluded by enumerating all combinations of values for basis characteristics. The table we saw in Figure 6.2(c) is a decision table with three basis characteristics. Each column in the table corresponds to a characteristic; the right column corresponds to the conclusion characteristic and all the other columns correspond to basis characteristics. Each cell in a column contains a value (or range of values) for the indicated characteristic.

   When Patricia Programmer analyzes Frank Fixit's method for concluding the ordered list of possible causes of a toaster problem (Step 2 in Figure 9.1), she finds that Frank decides the list of causes on the basis of a single characteristic, *toaster_problem*. Patricia creates a decision table (Figure 9.5a) to illustrate how the toaster-repair advisor should infer the list of possible causes. In the first cycle of development, Patricia limits the entries in her table to color problems.
   Although the initial implementation of the toaster-repair advisor will not produce a customer bill, Patricia Programmer organizes the information she has obtained about how the system should conclude the *repair_cost* for a repair on the basis of *toaster_style* and *repair_procedure* (Figure 9.5b). She will add rows to this table in future cycles of development.

   As the examples in Figure 9.5 illustrate, a decision table can specify at a glance how the expert system should infer the conclusion char-

Figure 9.5 Decision tables for the toaster-repair advisor. Patricia Programmer uses table (a) to describe how the toaster-repair advisor will conclude *ordered_possible_causes* on the basis of *toaster_problem*. Each row in the table is a guideline for inferring the list of possible causes. According to the first row, for example, if the toaster problem is *minor_too_dark*, the possible causes are first *minor_thermostat_problem_heating_too_long* and second *bad_thermostat*. Table (b) shows how the toaster-repair advisor will conclude a repair cost on the basis of the toaster style and the repair procedure.

Toaster_Problem	Ordered_Possible_Causes
minor_too_dark	1. minor_thermostat_problem_toasting_too_long 2. bad_thermostat
severe_too_dark	1. severe_thermostat_problem_toasting_too_long 2. bad_thermostat
minor_too_light	1. minor_thermostat_problem_toasting_too_short 2. bad_thermostat
severe_too_light	1. severe_thermostat_problem_toasting_too_short 2. bad_thermostat

(a)

Toaster_Style	Repair_Procedure	Repair_Cost
simple_two_slice	adjust_thermostat	5.00
simple_two_slice	replace_and_calibrate_thermostat	7.00
four_slice	adjust_thermostat	5.00
four_slice	replace_and_calibrate_thermostat	8.00

(b)

acteristic in the full range of circumstances the system may encounter. The general form of a decision table is shown in Figure 9.6.

Decision tables of the form illustrated in Figure 9.6 are most appropriate when conclusions are based on a small number of characteristics, each of which has a small number of possible examples. If the number of basis characteristics for a particular kind of conclusion is large, the table can be broken into a collection of subtables. For example, the table in Figure 9.6 could be broken into subtables, one for each of the *P* different values of *basis characteristic 1*. Each table would show how to infer the *conclusion characteristic* for a given value of *basis characteristic 1*. The table would contain columns for the remaining basis characteristics (*basis characteristic 2* through *basis characteristic N*) and for *conclusion characteristic*.

Figure 9.6 Structure of a general decision table. A general decision table illustrates how an expert system should infer a particular conclusion characteristic. The column headings name the characteristics that form the basis for inferences and the characteristic to be concluded. Each column contains values of the characteristic whose name appears in the heading of that column. Thus *basis characteristic 1* has *P* possible values, named *value 1.1* through *value 1.P*. Similarly *basis characteristic 2* has *Q* different values, and *basis characteristic N* has *R* different values. A decision table should contain *all* possible combinations of examples of the basis characteristics. The values for *conclusion characteristic* are named *conclusion A, conclusion B,* and so on. These values are not necessarily unique; the same value might be concluded in different circumstances.

Every row in the table indicates how the expert system can make an inference in a particular circumstance. The elements in the first *N* columns specify the condition of the inference as a combination of values for the basis characteristics. The right column in the row contains the value to be concluded for the conclusion characteristic.

Basic Characteristic 1	Basic Characteristic 2	...	Basic Characteristic N	Conclusion Characteristic
value 1.1	value 2.1	:	value N.1	conclusion A
			value N.2	conclusion B
			:	:
			value N.R	conclusion C
	:	:	:	:
	value 2.Q	:	value N.1	conclusion D
			value N.2	conclusion E
			:	:
			value N.R	conclusion F
:	:	:	:	:
value 1.P	value 2.1	:	value N.1	conclusion G
			value N.2	conclusion H
			:	:
			value N.R	conclusion J
	:	:	:	:
	value 2.Q	:	value N.1	conclusion K
			value N.2	conclusion L
			:	:
			value N.R	conclusion M

Note: Eash of the letters A through R represents a small integer.

Two-Basis Decision Tables

If a particular kind of inference is made *on the basis of exactly two characteristics* and these two characteristics each has a small number of specific examples, it is often convenient to use a **two-basis decision table** (Figure 9.7).

> To calibrate a replacement thermostat, Frank Fixit installs the thermostat in the toaster, then he measures the toasting time with the color control set on medium. Frank uses this measured toasting time together with the room temperature to judge whether the thermostat should be adjusted. Frank classifies the thermostat's toasting time as *too short*, *OK*, and *too long*. Patricia Programmer creates a two-basis decision table (Figure 9.8) to describe how Frank makes this decision.

Figure 9.7 Structure of a two-basis decision table. A two-basis decision table is appropriate for a characteristic that is inferred on the basis of exactly two other characteristics. The columns of the table correspond to values for one basis characteristic; the rows correspond to values of the other basis characteristic. Each cell in the table indicates how the expert system can make an inference in a particular circumstance. The row heading and column heading define this circumstance; the cell itself contains the value of the conclusion characteristic the system should conclude.

The cell in the first row and first column is equivalent to the inference:

If   basis characteristic   = *value 1.1* and
              basis characteristic 2   = *value 2.1*
then   conclusion characteristic = *conclusion A*

		Basis Characteristic 1			
		value 1.1	value 1.2	...	value 1.P
	value 2.1	conclusion A	conclusion B	...	conclusion C
Basis Characteristic 2	value 2.2	conclusion D	conclusion E	...	conclusion F
	⋮	⋮	⋮	⋮	⋮
	value 2.Q	conclusion G	conclusion H	...	conclusion J

Note: Each of the letters A through Q represents a small integer.

Pseudorules

We have seen that decision tables can present a succinct summary of the expert's method for inferring a particular conclusion characteristic, *provided the inferences all have the same simple structure*. This restriction points out the major limitations of decision tables.

- They are not appropriate for expressing *complex conditions* on the basis characteristics.

- They are not appropriate if *different inferences use different collections of basis characteristics*.

- They are not appropriate if the *form of the condition on the basis characteristics varies* in different circumstances.

Figure 9.8 Two-basis decision table for the toaster-repair advisor. Patricia Programmer uses this table to specify how the toaster-repair advisor will assess a replacement thermostat's toasting time on the basis of the room temperature and the measured toasting time. Each cell in the table is a guideline for inferring the status of the thermostat toasting time. For example, the cell in the first column and first row indicates that a toasting time of *less than 60 seconds* in a room whose temperature is *at least 50° but less than 60° Fahrenheit* is *too short*. Notice that a decision table can specify *ranges of values* for the basis characteristics as well as discrete values. However, the ranges of values *should not overlap*. Any value should match exactly one range.

Room_Temperature (degrees Fahrenheit)	Toasting_Time (seconds)				
	time < 60	60 ≤ time < 65	65 ≤ time < 70	70 ≤ time < 75	75 ≤ time
50 ≤ temp < 60	too_short	too_short	OK	OK	too_long
60 ≤ temp < 70	too_short	too_short	OK	too_long	too_long
70 ≤ temp < 80	too_short	OK	OK	too_long	too_long
80 ≤ temp < 90	too_short	OK	OK	too_long	too_long
90 ≤ temp < 100	too_short	OK	too_long	too_long	too_long

Decision tables are inadequate for representing some kinds of inference. Experts sometime use a variety of special-purpose heuristics to make a given kind of inference in different situations. For example, to track down a particularly difficult problem in one toaster model, Frank Fixit might make a decision based on whether he hears a rattle when he shakes the toaster. For a different toaster model, Frank might base the same decision on the age of the toaster or the time since its last repair. For a third toaster model, Frank might base the decision on whether he observes rust on a particular toaster part. When experts use special-purpose heuristics to make a particular kind of inference, knowledge engineers can record these heuristics as pseudorules. A **pseudorule** is a statement of the form:

If   *condition*
then *conclusion*

that specifies how the expert makes an inference in a particular situation. We use the term *pseudorule* to distinguish this intermediate representation from the *rule* representations of any particular expert-system shell. Notice that we have not specified the *form* of the condition of a pseudorule. Because their form is flexible, pseudorules can be used when decision tables are inappropriate or cumbersome. In addition, many knowledge engineers prefer a small collection of pseudorules in place of a very sparse decision table. That is, if very few combinations of value for the basis characteristics are meaningful, it is simpler to write pseudorules for the meaningful combinations rather than to create a table with many empty conclusion cells.

When Patricia Programmer analyzes the knowledge Frank Fixit uses to infer *suspected_toaster_problem* (Dialog 6.1), she finds that the basis characteristics are *toaster_make, toaster_model,* and *customer_complaints*. Patricia recognizes that the two characteristics *toaster_make* and *toaster_model* are related: A given model number is particular to one specific manufacturer. Conceptually, therefore, Frank decides the *suspected_toaster_problem* on the basis of *toaster_model* and *customer_complaints*. Patricia quickly realizes that a decision table is impractical for this kind of inference. The toaster-repair advisor will need to handle 41 models of simple two-slice toasters (Dialog 4.3). It will need to accept 8 possible customer complaints (these complaints are illustrated in Figure 8.4). So the decision table would need to represent 328 combinations of a particular toaster model and a particular customer complaint. But even such a table would be inadequate—the user can enter any number (including zero) of customer complaints. So the table would need to include *combinations of customer complaints* as well as single complaints. Luckily for Patricia, there is no need for the toaster-repair advisor to represent all possible combinations of toaster models and customer complaints. As Frank explained in Dialog 6.1, he recognizes a few special situations, and he makes default as-

Figure 9.9 Pseudorules for the toaster-repair advisor. Patricia Programmer uses these pseudorules to specify how the toaster-repair advisor will infer the suspected toaster problem.

If   toaster_model is TB10443, TB10445, TB10446, or TB10448 and
        customer_complaints include only toast_always_burns,
then   suspected_toaster_problem probably is severe_too_dark.

If   toaster_model is GA11569 and customer_complaints include only
        toast_always_burns,
then   suspected_toaster_problem probably is no_trip.

If   customer_complaints include either toast_too_light or
        bread_not_toasted and either toast_always_burns or
        toast_too_dark,
then   suspected_toaster_problem probably is heating_element.

If   customer_complaints include toast_does_not_pop_up,
then   suspected_toaster_problem definitely is no_trip.

If   customer_complaints include bread_not_toasted,
then   suspected_toaster_problem probably is severe_too_light and
        possibly is heating_element.

$\vdots$

sumptions in other situations. Patricia Programmer uses pseudorules to define Frank Fixit's judgmental knowledge about *suspected_toaster_problem*. Figure 9.9 illustrates a few of these pseudorules.

As Figure 9.9 illustrates, pseudorules can be written in a combination of English (or another natural language) and special project terminology. Pseudorules can include any combination of logical operators *(and, or, not, for all, there exists)*. Pseudorules can capture the expert's inexact reasoning. Notice that the conclusions of some of the pseudorules in Figure 9.9 include the qualifiers *probably* and *possibly*.[2] The main guidelines to follow when you write pseudorules are:

- Keep the language simple.

- Use consistent language and format.

Decision Trees

If you are not able to identify a standard structure for inferences about a conclusion characteristic and if you find it confusing to express the

---

2. As we saw in Section 6.3, the toaster-repair advisor does not actually need to label the degree of certainty of its conclusions for *suspected_toaster_problem*. Patricia Programmer could have written the pseudorules without qualifying their certainty. We included labels for degrees of certainty only to illustrate how such labels might appear in pseudorules.

expert's reasoning in a number of independent pseudorules, you can use a decision tree to represent the expert's logic. A **decision tree** illustrates the *process* by which the expert reasons. Each nonleaf node in the tree corresponds to a question. The branches from that node correspond to the possible answers to the question. Each path through the tree corresponds to a particular situation the expert system might encounter; the leaf node on this branch specifies the conclusion that the system should make in that situation.

> Patricia Programmer analyzes the method by which Frank Fixit infers the toaster problem from the results of the initial test. She finds that Frank's logic is too complicated to capture in a decision table. Pseudorules do not give a clear picture of Frank's reasoning process. Frank gathers different information about the test results in different situations. In the simplest case, Frank can determine the toaster problem after a single question. Patricia notes that Frank asks a different set of questions depending on what initial test was performed. Patricia draws a decision tree (Figure 9.10) for each possible initial test procedure to illustrate how the toaster-repair advisor should interpret the results of that test.

Note that a decision tree often includes *strategic* knowledge as well as *judgmental* knowledge: A decision tree can specify *a sequence of input or reasoning steps* that the expert system should take as it attempts to infer the conclusion characteristic. For example, the decision tree in Figure 9.10 shows not only how the toaster-repair advisor should decide *toaster_problem* but also the order in which the system should request data and the circumstances under which the system should perform these input steps. Thus if the user says the operating lever did not go down, the system should not ask whether the operating lever stayed down. If your expert system should make decisions *in the order* in which they appear as you traverse the tree, be aware that your tree includes both judgmental and strategic knowledge. When you implement the inferences that appear in the tree, you will also need to implement the strategic knowledge to control the system's decision process.

Formula Definitions

In many applications, the expert will calculate certain numeric characteristics of a case from other numeric characteristics. The expert may use a single formula in all cases or may use a small number of formulas each of which is appropriate in a different range of circumstances. Formulas do not fit naturally into decision tables, pseudorules, or decision trees. We recommend that knowledge engineers record all information about a particular formula in a definition of that formula (Table 9.1).

Develop a standard format for your formula definitions, and create definitions for the formulas your expert system will use. Figure 9.11 shows two formula definitions Patricia Programmer created for the toaster-repair advisor.

Figure 9.10 Decision tree for the toaster-repair advisor. Patricia Programmer uses this decision tree to illustrate how the toaster-repair advisor should infer the conclusion characteristic *toaster_problem* from the results of the initial test procedure, *toast_one_slice_on_dark*. Each node in the tree tests the value of some basis characteristic; the name of the characteristic appears in parentheses. Each arrow from the node corresponds to one of the possible values for the basis characteristic. Each path from the root node to a leaf node indicates an inference; the leaf node specifies the conclusion of that inference. For example, the path indicated by the heavy arrows corresponds to the inference: *If the operating lever went down and stayed down and the toast did not pop up, then the toaster has a no-trip problem.*

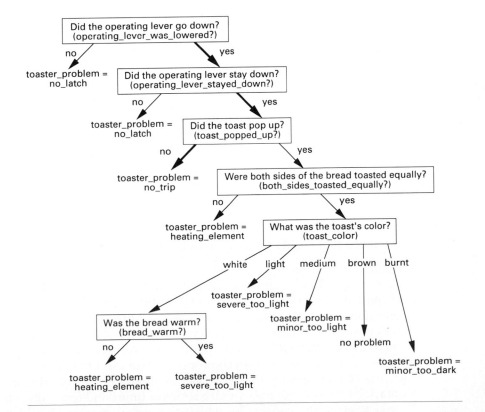

Table 9.1 Contents of a Formula Definition

Information	Description
Conclusion characteristic	Identify the conclusion characteristic that can be calculated with this formula.
Formula	Give the mathematical formula or algorithm the expert system should use to calculate the conclusion characteristic.
Description	If the formula is complex, explain the principles on which the formula is based, and give the rationale for the calculation. If the formula is experimental or if it produces an approximation, you may want to cite a literature reference that justifies the validity of the formula.
Basis characteristics	List the basis characteristics that are used in the formula. This list specifies the information that must be available before the formula can be applied.
Precision	Specify the precision with which the number should be calculated (for example, dollar amounts should be calculated to two decimal places).
Restrictions	If the formula is valid only in certain situations, describe restrictions on the formula's use. Many formulas are valid only for a specific range of a given basis characteristic. For example, if a basis characteristic is used as a divisor, the formula would not be valid when that characteristic is zero.
Cross-reference information	Include references to interview notes, cases in which the formula is used, and other related formulas.
Implementation status	Give the names of knowledge-base entries that implement this formula. Indicate whether the expert system's use of the formula has been tested and whether the implemented formula works as intended.

Procedures that Guide the Use of Judgmental Knowledge

Judgmental knowledge alone may not be sufficient to specify how the expert system should infer a particular characteristic. As we have seen, decision trees often capture both judgmental knowledge and strategic knowledge. Similarly when the judgmental knowledge is expressed as pseudorules, the expert system may need to try these pseudorules in a fixed order. Alternatively, the judgmental knowledge about a characteristic may be used within the context of an established procedure. The expert may specify that the system should try to obtain the information by following a particular series of input and reasoning steps. As you analyze the process by which the expert system should infer

Figure 9.11 Formula definitions for the toaster-repair advisor. Patricia Programmer defines these two formulas to describe how the toaster-repair advisor should calculate the total repair cost for the customer bill.

Formula for Total_Part_Cost

Name(s) in knowledge base:	*(not implemented yet)*
Used to calculate:	total_part_cost
Basis Characteristics:	repair_procedure, list_of_replacement_parts, price of each replacement part
Formula:	total = 0 for each part in list_of_replacement_parts total = total + price of this part end for each total_part_cost = total
Description:	Calculate the total part cost as the sum of the prices of the individual replacement parts.
Precision:	2 decimal places
Restrictions:	none
Interview notes:	8/7/90: notebook PP1, page 62
Implementation status:	not implemented

Formula for Total_Repair_Cost

Name(s) in knowledge base:	*(not implemented yet)*
Used to calculate:	total_repair_cost
Basis Characteristics:	repair_cost, total_part_cost
Formula:	total_repair_cost = repair_cost + (total_part_cost × 1.07)
Description:	The total cost is the sum of the cost of the repair procedure and the total part cost plus 7 per cent sales tax on the parts.
Precision:	2 decimal places
Restrictions:	none
Interview notes:	8/7/90: notebook PP1, page 62, 63
Implementation status:	not implemented

each characteristic, check whether this process consists of more than one step. If so, create a definition (Section 9.1.3) of the process or if necessary a flow chart (Section 9.1.1).

Frank Fixit considers evidence for *suspected_toaster_problem* in a fixed order (see Dialog 6.3). Frank considers some evidence a more conclusive indication of a problem than other evidence. For example, the customer complaints that indicate a no-latch problem always outweigh evidence for any other problem. If the customer has checked one of these complaints, Frank assumes the toaster has a no-latch problem (even if the customer checked additional complaints). The complaints that indicate no-trip problems outweigh the other remaining complaints followed by the complaints and combinations of complaints that indicate heating-element problems. The remaining customer complaints are not uniquely indicative of toaster problems. Frank uses these complaints in conjunction with his knowledge of specific toaster models. If Frank is unfamiliar with a particular model, he will decide the suspected problem on the basis of these "weak" customer complaints alone.

Patricia Programmer defines a procedure that the toaster-repair advisor should follow to infer *suspected_toaster_problem* (Figure 9.12), then she classifies the pseudorules to indicate when they should be used (Figure 9.13).

When Patricia Programmer examines the process by which the toaster-repair advisor should infer the acceptable part numbers for a replacement thermostat (Dialog 7.2), she finds that the system will not always infer this information. In some cases, the acceptable part numbers will be input data rather than intermediate conclusions. Patricia defines the procedure the system should follow to obtain this information (Figure 9.14).

Figure 9.12 Procedure to guide an inference step. Patricia Programmer defines a new step for the toaster-repair advisor to control the order in which it applies its judgmental knowledge to infer *suspected_toaster_problem*.

Step 1.2.1 Infer Suspected_Toaster_Problem

Name(s) in knowledge-base: *(not implemented yet)*

Purpose: Determine what toaster problem is likely based on the customer complaints and the toaster model. This information will be used to select the appropriate initial test procedure.

Required Information: toaster_make, toaster_model, customer_complaints

Actions: Try each of the following actions until one succeeds in concluding the suspected_toaster_problem.

1.2.1.1 (reasoning)	Check for no-latch problems.
1.2.1.2 (reasoning)	Check for no-trip problems.
1.2.1.3 (reasoning)	Check for heating-element problems.
1.2.1.4 (reasoning)	Check for model-specific problems.
1.2.1.5 (reasoning)	Check for default complaint-specific problems.

Rationale: This procedure uses the "strongest" evidence first. Indications of a no-latch problem are stronger than indications of a no-trip problem and so on. Model-specific information is stronger than default assumptions.

Interview notes: 8/6/90
notebook PP1 pages 59–61

Status: not implemented

Figure 9.13 Rules grouped according to steps in the inference process. Patricia Programmer categorizes the pseudorules that conclude *suspected_toaster_problem* to indicate when they should be used.

No-Latch Rules (Step 1.2.1.1)

If   customer_complaints include either
         operating_lever_will_not_go_down or
         operating_lever_will_not_stay_down,
then suspected_toaster_problem definitely is no_latch.

No-Trip Rules (Step 1.2.1.2)

If   customer_complaints include toast_does_not_pop_up,
then suspected_toaster_problem definitely is no_trip.

Heating-Element Rules (Step 1.2.1.3)

If   customer_complaints include toasts_on_one_side_only,
then suspected_toaster_problem definitely is heating_element.

If   customer_complaints include either toast_too_light or
         bread_not_toasted and either toast_always_burns or
         toast_too_dark,
then suspected_toaster_problem probably is heating_element.

Model-Specific Rules (Step 1.2.1.4)

If   toaster_model is TB27713 and
         customer_complaints include toast_always_burns,
then suspected_toaster_problem probably is minor_too_dark.

If   toaster_model is TB10443, TB10445, TB10446, or TB10448 and
         customer_complaints include toast_always_burns,
then suspected_toaster_problem probably is severe_too_dark.

If   toaster_model is GA11569 and
         customer_complaints include toast_always_burns,
then suspected_toaster_problem probably is no_trip.

                                 ⋮

Default Complaint-Specific Rules (Step 1.2.1.5)

If   customer_complaints include toast_always_burns,
then suspected_problem probably is severe_too_dark.

If   customer_complaints include toast_too_light,
then suspected_toaster_problem probably is minor_too_light.

If   customer_complaints include bread_not_toasted,
then suspected_toaster problem probably is severe_too_light and
         possibly is heating_element.

                                 ⋮

Figure 9.14 Procedure for obtaining a characteristic. Patricia Programmer defines a new step for the toaster-repair advisor to control the reasoning and input steps that may be necessary when the system needs to find *acceptable_part_numbers* for a replacement part.

Step 3.1.2 Find Acceptable_Part_Numbers for Replacement Parts

Name(s) in knowledge-base: *(not implemented yet)*

Purpose: This step is relevant when the repair procedure involves replacing one or more toaster parts. In this step, the system determines what part numbers can be used for each of the replacement parts. This information is used to customize the instructions that request the user to perform the repair procedure.

Required Information: list_of_replacement_parts, toaster_model, part_type of each replacement part

Actions: For each part in list_of_replacement_parts, try the following actions until one succeeds.

   3.1.2.1 (reasoning) Check recent service bulletins for this model and part type.

   3.1.2.2 (reasoning) Use model-specific preferences.

   3.1.2.3 (input)   Look up acceptable part numbers in the toaster-part database.

   3.1.2.4 (input)   Ask the user what part number is currently used in the toaster.

Rationale: This procedure uses the most specific guidelines first and the most general guidelines last.

Interview notes: 8/3/90
                   notebook PP1 pages 52–54

Status: not implemented

9.2.2 Understanding How to React to New Information

In Section 9.2.1, we discussed one form of reasoning step—namely, a step in which the expert system infers a particular characteristic. All of the reasoning steps for the toaster-repair advisor have this form. Some expert systems, on the other hand, must *react immediately* to input data they receive or to conclusions they make. In those systems, some reasoning steps will specify that the system should *infer the consequences of a new piece of data or a recent conclusion*. For example, an expert system that monitors sensors in a processing plant will not infer a standard set of characteristics each time it reads data from the sensors. Rather it will compare the sensor data against normal measurements to detect unusual conditions. When it detects an abnormal condition, it will infer characteristics about the plant that are consequences of the abnormal condition (Figure 9.15).

In a reasoning step like Step 3 in Figure 9.15, information about some basis characteristic triggers the inference process; we call this characteristic a **trigger characteristic.** When you analyze a reasoning step that specifies a trigger characteristic, describe how the system should infer the consequences of this trigger characteristic in all possible circumstances.

- Identify all conclusion characteristics that might be inferred on the basis of the trigger characteristic.

- See what other basis characteristics are needed in conjunction with the trigger characteristic.

- See whether inferences that use the trigger characteristic follow a standard structure.

Figure 9.15 Flow chart of high-level control in a simple monitoring application. Step 3 is a reasoning step that specifies an important *basis* characteristic but not a specific *conclusion* characteristic. Depending on the condition identified, the system may infer different conclusion characteristics in Step 3.

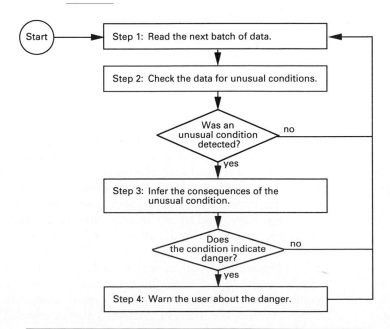

- Select intermediate representations that illustrate how the expert system should infer the consequences of the trigger characteristic.

The intermediate representations we described in Section 9.2.1 are equally relevant for judgmental knowledge that is triggered when the expert system receives information. Instead of grouping the inferences by the *conclusion* characteristic, however, you should group them by the *trigger* characteristic.

- If the trigger characteristic (and a small number of additional basis characteristics) are used to conclude a fixed set of conclusion characteristics, use decision tables.

- If the system must make very different kinds of inferences in different circumstances, use pseudorules.

- If you need to consider certain characteristics in a specified order, use a decision tree.

- If the characteristic is used to calculate other characteristics, use formula definitions to describe the calculations.

- If necessary, create a step definition (Section 9.1.3) to describe a procedure that the expert system should follow as it infers the consequences of the trigger characteristic.

9.2.3 Describing the Inference Structure

If your expert system makes several levels of intermediate conclusions between the input data and the output conclusions, an inference network can help you understand the interdependencies among the characteristics of a case. An **inference network** is a directed graph that shows the overall structure of inferences within an expert system (Figure 9.16). The network illustrates how the different characteristics of a case are concluded and used during the system's inference process. Each node in the graph is a characteristic. Each arrow from one characteristic to a second characteristic indicates that the first characteristic can be used as a basis for concluding the second characteristic.

If your expert system reasons about a large number of characteristics, you may need to use several inference networks to illustrate the inference structure for the entire expert system.

Because an inference network provides an overview of the interdependencies in a conceptual model, this representation is a particularly useful tool during the extension and refinement of an expert system. When knowledge engineers need to modify the definition of a characteristic, the inference network shows what other characteristics might be affected by the modification.

In a later cycle of development for the toaster-repair advisor, Patricia Programmer finds she needs to modify the definition of the characteristic *ordered_possible_causes*. In order to implement the modification, Patricia must change the values the system can conclude for the characteristic *toaster_problem*. The inference network shows Patricia that the characteristic *toaster_problem* is also used to conclude *problem_within_scope?* as well as *ordered_possible_problems*. As a result, Patricia knows that she must review the judgmental knowledge for concluding *problem_within_scope?* She may need to modify this judgmental knowledge to accommodate the new set of legal values for *toaster_problem*.

9.3 Analyzing Factual Knowledge

The final step in the development of a conceptual model is the analysis of factual knowledge. The expert's factual knowledge encompasses information the expert system will know *a priori* about the application subject area as well as information the system will learn or deduce about a specific case as it performs its task.

Analyze your expert system's factual knowledge as follows:

1. Organize the information you collected about each general characteristic into a written definition of the characteristic (Section 9.3.1).

Figure 9.16 Inference network for toaster-repair advisor. Patricia Programmer draws this network to illustrate the overall structure of inferences within the expert system. Arrows point from basis characteristics to conclusion characteristics.

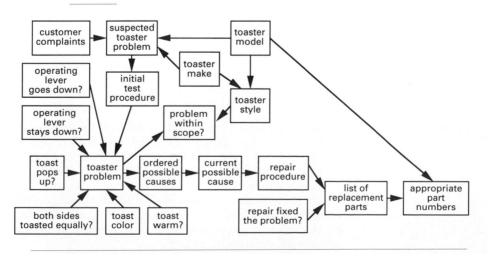

2. Classify the characteristics that are important to your application (Section 9.3.2).

3. Organize facts about the application area that relate to objects, processes, or conceptual entities that are *independent of* the particular case (Section 9.3.3).

4. Define interrelationships among the objects, processes, and other conceptual entities you identified in Step 3 (Section 9.3.4).

9.3.1 Creating Definitions for Characteristics of a Case

General characteristics are features of a case that the expert system uses as input data, intermediate conclusions, or output results. In Chapter 7, we described how to obtain the information that constitutes the definition of a general characteristic. As you collect information about a characteristic, organize it into a written definition. Table 9.2

Table 9.2 Contents of a Characteristic Definition

Information	Description
Name	The standard project term that names this characteristic
Description	A brief explanation of the feature of a case that this characteristic represents
Type of value	The kind of value that can constitute a specific example of this characteristic (numeric, descriptive, logical, and so on) The units for numerical values (for example, inches, seconds, volts) The precision for numerical values (for example, 4 decimal places)
Range of values	A list of possible descriptive values A range of numeric values A description of the legal syntax or structure of a value
Number of values per case	The number of values for this characteristic that a single case can have (usually *one* or *many*)
Source	The method by which the expert system will find out about this characteristic of a case (the sources from which it will try to obtain a value for the characteristic, the order in which it will try each source, and the circumstances in which it should try each source) The action the system should take if it is unable to determine this characteristic of a case (for example, assume a default, proceed without the information, or terminate the interaction with an informative message)

Table 9.2 (continued)

Information	Description
Details about the method for obtaining this information	For input from a user, the text and diagrams that should be displayed to prompt for the information For input from another source, details about the source and the format of the data For input data, a description of how to check the input for legality (if necessary) For characteristics that are inferred, cross references to descriptions of the relevant judgmental knowledge (see Section 9.2) Default value, if any
Reliability (input data)	If the input is not always reliable, a description of the method by which the system can compensate for unreliable data
Use	Notes that describe how the expert system will use this characteristic (as the basis for inferences, to control the sequence of actions the system performs, and so on) Cross references to other entries in the design document that describe the use of this characteristic
Format (output results)	If the output will be displayed to a user, the format of the text and diagrams that should be used to communicate this characteristic to the user If the output will be transmitted to a file or device, details about the destination and the format of the output For numeric characteristics, the precision and format with which values should be printed
Supporting material	References to the documents and interviews that provided information about this characteristic

describes the information you should include in the definition of a characteristic.

Develop a format for definitions of characteristics that will show you what information you have obtained, and what additional information you need to obtain in future interviews. Although you should try to standardize the format of your definitions as much as possible, keep the format flexible. As Table 9.2 describes, you will need different details about different characteristics. For example, the definition of one input datum might contain a question for the user; the definition of a different datum might contain a database query. Sometimes knowledge engineers who develop a standard form for definitions tend to overlook information that does not fit into the form; be careful to avoid this problem. The definition of a characteristic should include *all* information you obtain about the characteristic. If you learn details that do not fit into your standard format, modify the format.

As you develop a format for definitions, try to anticipate what information will be helpful when you begin to implement and test the expert system. For example, you might include space in the definition for:

Figure 9.17 Definition of a characteristic of a toaster-repair case. Patricia Programmer and Howard Hacker create a definition like this for each characteristic of a case. The format of a definition guides the knowledge engineers to collect all the important information about each characteristic. It also reminds them of functionality that they must implement. For example, the toaster-repair advisor must check the legality of some user input; it must terminate interactions gracefully when required information is not available.

Characteristic: Toaster_Model

Name in knowledge base:	*(not implemented yet)*
Description:	The manufacturer's identifying number for the particular model of toaster
Type of value:	Alphanumeric; usually two or three letters followed by four to six digits (e.g., TB10445)
Range of values:	Any model number that can be found in the toaster-part database
Number of values per case:	One (Each interaction deals with a single toaster; each toaster has a single model number.)
Source:	Ask the user.
Details:	The initial form should include an input field, labeled "Model Number:" The system should read keyboard input when cursor is in this input field.
Check legality of answer?	Yes
Is answer always reliable?	Yes
Is an answer required?	Yes
Default:	(None)
Use:	Obtained at the beginning of an interaction. Many details of the repair are customized according to the model number. Also used to check whether a case is within the system's current scope.
Interview notes:	6/15/90, 7/30/90 Notebook PP1 pages 5, 36
Implementation status:	Not implemented

- The name used for the characteristic in the knowledge base

- A list of cases in which the characteristic is important (if the characteristic does not figure into every case)

- Notes on whether the expert system is currently able to use the characteristic as intended

A well-designed definition can guide design and implementation as well as future knowledge-acquisition sessions.

> After each interview in the toaster-repair advisor project, Patricia Programmer and Howard Hacker meet to review the information they obtained and to decide what modifications and additions they should make to the definitions of characteristics in their design document. As they update each definition, they refer to the project dictionary to be sure they use standard terminology. Figure 9.17 illustrates the form in which Patricia and Howard record the definitions of characteristics of a toaster-repair case.
>
> The toaster-repair advisor will need to check some of the answers it obtains from the user. For example, the toaster repair advisor will not be able to perform its task without certain key data about the toaster. The definition of each characteristic can indicate whether that characteristic is required for performance of the task. As another example, the system will need to ensure that the user enters a recognized toaster model number. Although Patricia and Howard do not plan to implement the data-checking capability until later in the project, a characteristic's definition can indicate whether the answer should be checked.
>
> After Patricia and Howard create or update a definition, they check whether they have obtained a *complete* definition of the characteristic. If not, they make a summary of the kinds of information they lack, and they use this summary to guide future knowledge-acquisition interviews. As Figure 9.18 illustrates, a definition can include the knowledge engineers' notes about the information they must obtain about a characteristic.

9.3.2 Classifying the Characteristics

Typically each characteristic corresponds to a specific piece of information about some particular type of object, process, or other conceptual entity. (For simplicity, we shall use the term *object* to refer to any kind of physical object, process, or conceptual entity.)[3] You can use these object types to organize the characteristics.

---

3. We have chosen the word *object* for its generality. We do not mean to imply any necessary correlation between objects identified in a conceptual model and *objects* that would be implemented in a shell that employs object-oriented programming.

Figure 9.18 Incomplete characteristic definition. Patricia Programmer and Howard Hacker have obtained a general understanding of the method by which the toaster-repair advisor should find the acceptable part numbers for a replacement part, as described under the headings *Source* and *Details*. The knowledge engineers use the definition itself as a reminder that they must obtain additional details before they can specify how the expert system will decide what part numbers to recommend: At the end of the *Details* section, they list the questions that remain to be answered.

Characteristic: Acceptable_Part_Numbers

Name in knowledge base: *(Not implemented yet)*

Description: The part numbers that can be used for a replacement part

Type of values: Alphanumeric; usually one or two letters followed by four to six digits (e.g., R71995)

Range of values: Any part number that can be found in the toaster-part database

Number of values per case: Many (Several different parts of a particular type (thermostat, heating element, and so on) are compatible with any given toaster model.)

Source: Infer, lookup in database, or ask the user

Details: First check recent service bulletins to see whether specific parts are recommended for the toaster model. If no relevant service bulletins are found, select the best part numbers for the particular toaster model (based on Frank's experience). If Frank did not give us specific information about the particular toaster model and part type, retrieve the compatible part numbers from the database. If all else fails, ask the user what part number is currently used in the toaster, and use that part number.

Remaining questions:

Do we have all the current service bulletins relevant to replacement thermostats?

Is the thermostat the only part that might be replaced to fix a color problem in a simple two-slice toaster?

Have we collected all Frank's model-specific preferences for replacement parts?

What is the correct form of the database query?

How should the system ask for the part number?

Check legality of answer? Only user answers—we assume the database has valid information

Is answer always reliable? Yes

Is an answer required? Yes

Default: (None)

Use: If a repair procedure requires the user to replace one or more parts of the toaster, the system should specify which part

Figure 9.18 (continued)

numbers can be used for the replacement parts. The user is then free to use any acceptable part number that is available in inventory.

Interview notes: 8/3/90
Notebook PP1 pages 52–54

Implementation status: Not implemented

---

1. Identify the type of object that each characteristic describes.

2. Group together characteristics that provide information about a similar type of object.

3. Give each type of object a name, and add this name to your project dictionary.

4. Review the characteristics of each object type. Check whether you can classify these characteristics further by categorizing the types of object. Identify as many levels of classification as you need.

> When Patricia Programmer reviews the characteristics of a toaster case, she finds that some characteristics provide information about the toaster itself, for example, *toaster_make, toaster_model, toaster_style,* and *customer_complaints.* Other characteristics provide information about specific parts of the toaster. For example, the toaster-repair advisor may need to know the *price* and the *part_number* of a replacement thermostat (or a replacement carriage assembly or other replacement part). Still other characteristics provide information about procedures that the user should perform. For example, the system will display the *short_description* of a repair procedure or test procedure when it asks the user to perform the procedure. It will display the *long_description* of the procedure if the user requests a description of the procedure. If a repair procedure fixes the toaster problem, the system will need to use the *repair_cost* of the procedure to calculate charges for the customer bill. Thus Patricia identifies three types of object that serve to classify the characteristics of a toaster-repair case; she names these object types *toaster, toaster_part,* and *procedure.* Note that the object type *procedure* corresponds to a type of process rather than a type of physical object.
>
> Patricia Programmer identifies two categories of *toaster_part:* A *current_toaster_part* is a part currently used in the toaster, and a *replacement_part* is a new part to be used in the toaster. The toaster-repair advisor may use the *part_number* of either type of part; however, it will need to use the *price* of a replacement *_part* only. The system may need to know some characteristics of a *current_toaster_part* that are not relevant for a *replacement_part.* For example, the system may need to ask the user to check whether a particular part is *rusty.*
>
> Patricia classifies each *procedure* object as either a *test_procedure* or a *repair_procedure.* The system will need to use a *short_description* and

a *long_description* of both types of procedure; the characteristics that constitute results of a procedure, however, will be relevant to a *test_ procedure* but not to a *repair_procedure*. On the other hand, the system will need the *repair_cost* of a *repair_procedure* but not of a *test_procedure*.[4] Patricia further divides *test_procedure* into *initial_test_procedure* and *post_repair_test_procedure*.

Select an intermediate representation to illustrate how you have organized the characteristics your expert system will use. If your organization is simple, a list of object types may be sufficient. If you have organized the characteristics into a multilevel classification, you may prefer a collection of classification hierarchies (Figure 9.19).

Define each type of object you identified. Specify which characteristics are relevant to objects of that type. If the object type is part of a multilevel classification, its definition should contain cross references to both more general and more specific object types. Figure 9.20 shows definitions of two types of object that are relevant to the toaster-repair advisor.

9.3.3 Organizing Case-Independent Facts

Up to this point, we have said that an expert system reasons with facts and hypotheses about characteristics *of a case*. Most expert systems, however, also use facts about the application subject areas that are *independent of any specific case*. For example, the toaster-repair advisor will use facts such as *part number R71995 is a thermostat* and *the price of part number R71995 is $1.25*. Notice that both these two facts concern a particular object: *part number R71995*. Just as a type of object (for example, *toaster_part*) served to organize characteristics, objects themselves (such as *part number R71995*) can serve to organize case-independent facts.

To organize case-independent facts:

1. Review your interview notes and identify case-independent facts that specify characteristics of objects. Consider only facts *the expert system will use when it performs its task*.

2. Identify the object, process, or other entity to which each fact pertains. For example, the fact *part number R71995 is a thermostat* specifies a value for the characteristic *part_type* of the object *part number R71995*.

---

4. As Frank Fixit explained in his introductory overview, the customer is not billed for labor hours but is charged a fixed price for a given repair procedure on a given type of toaster. See point 1.c in the outline in Figure 2.2.

Figure 9.19 Classification of characteristics. Patricia Programmer classifies the characteristics of a toaster-repair case according to the types of object they describe (a). Some characteristics provide information about the *toaster*. Others provide information about particular parts of a toaster *(toaster_part)*. Still other characteristics provide information about a *procedure* the system will ask the user to perform.

Patricia uses classification *hierarchies* to show how the object types *toaster_part* (b) and *procedure* (c) can be categorized into parts or procedures of different types. In a hierarchy, the most general classification appears as the root node. If a classification can be subdivided, the node for that classification is the parent of nodes for the more specific classifications. Thus *current_part* and *replacement_part* are more specific classifications of *toaster_part*. Whereas certain characteristics are general to any kind of part, some characteristics are specific to parts that are currently used in the toaster *(current_part)*, and other characteristics are specific to new parts that will be put into the toaster during a repair procedure *(replacement_part)*.

(a)   Types of object: toaster, toaster_part, procedure

(b)

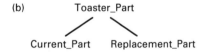

(c)

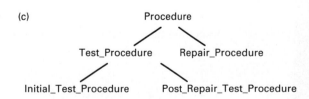

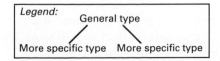

Figure 9.20 Definitions of object types. Patricia Programmer creates a definition of each type of object that she uses to classify the characteristics of a toaster-repair case.

Object Type: Procedure

Name(s) in knowledge base: *(not implemented yet)*

Description: A procedure is a method for testing or repairing a toaster. The system will ask the user to perform the procedure by using the short_description. A user may ask for additional details; to respond to such a request, the system will display the long_description. Either form of description may need to be customized for a particular case. The supporting_characteristics are the characteristics of the case needed to customize the descriptions.

Characteristics: short_description, long_description, supporting_characteristics

More general object type: none

More specific object types: test_procedure, repair_procedure

Notes: 8/9/90, notebook PP1 pages 72–74

Implementation status: not implemented

Object Type: Repair_Procedure

Name(s) in knowledge base: *(not implemented yet)*

Description: A repair procedure is a method for repairing a toaster. The system will ask the user to perform the procedure. The characteristic repair_fixed_the_problem? indicates whether this repair procedure was successful in correcting the toaster problem. The characteristic repair_cost specifies the cost of the repair procedure (used to calculate charges for the customer bill).

Characteristics: repair_fixed_the_problem?, repair_cost

More general object type: procedure

More specific object types: none

Notes: 8/9/90, notebook PP1 pages 72–74

Implementation status: not implemented

---

3. Group facts according to the objects to which they pertain. For example, collect all facts about *part number R71995*.

4. Collect groups of facts that pertain to the same *type* of object. For example, collect the facts about *part number R71995* with the facts about other toaster parts.

5. List the characteristics that the facts specify about each kind of object. For example, the facts about toaster parts specify values for the characteristics *part_number, part_type, price,* and *number_in_inventory.*

6. Develop intermediate representations to summarize related collections of facts.

In this section, we describe two intermediate representations for related facts: fact tables and object definitions.

Fact Tables

You can organize facts about objects of a particular type into a fact table if:

- The expert system will use the *same facts* about different objects of this type.

- The system will use a *small number* of facts about objects of this type.

- The individual facts are relatively *concise.*

A **fact table** is a tabular collection of facts about objects of a particular type. Each row of the fact table corresponds to a specific object, and each column corresponds to a different characteristic of that object. The cells in the table contain values of the characteristics. Figure 9.21(a) shows the general form of a fact table; Figure 9.21(b) gives an example.

Object Definitions

When the information about an object is too verbose to fit conveniently in the row of a fact table, you can create a definition for each individual object. An **object definition** is a description of the object; the definition specifies all the facts the expert system will need to know about the object. For each type of object relevant to your expert system, devise a standard definition form that includes space for all case-independent facts you will need to specify about objects of that type.

> Patricia Programmer reviews facts about repair procedures that the toaster-repair advisor will ask the user to perform. She finds that these facts specify values for three characteristics of the repair procedures:
>
> - *Short_description:* A brief description of the procedure to be displayed when the toaster-repair advisor asks the repair person to perform the procedure

Figure 9.21 Fact tables. A fact table contains a collection of facts about objects of a certain type; the facts are arrayed in the format illustrated in (a). The column headings name characteristics of the objects. By convention, the first column contains a unique identification name or number for the object. Each row corresponds to a particular object. The object's unique name or number appears in the first column of the row. The remaining columns describe the object in terms of values of the characteristics whose names appear in the column headings. For example (b), the toaster-repair advisor will use facts about toaster parts. Each part has an identifying *part_number*. The toaster-repair advisor will use three different characteristics of a toaster part: *part_type, price,* and *number_in_inventory* (the number of these parts currently in the service department's inventory). The first row of the table indicates that part *R71995* is a *thermostat,* priced at *$1.25,* and that *147* of these parts are currently in inventory.

Object Name	Characteristic 1	Characteristic 2	···	Characteristic N
Object 1	value 1.1	value 2.1	···	value N.1
Object 2	value 1.2	value 2.2	···	value N.2
Object 3	value 1.3	value 2.3	···	value N.3
⋮	⋮	⋮	⋮	⋮
Object M	value 1.M	value 2.M	···	value N.M

Note: The letters N and M each represent a small integer.

(a)

Part_Number	Part_Type	Price	Number_In_Inventory
R71995	thermostat	1.25	147
H00987	thermostat	1.15	29
R88797	thermostat	1.25	3
S11223	heating_element	2.10	118
⋮	⋮	⋮	⋮

(b)

- *Long_description:* A more detailed description of the procedure to be displayed when the repair person requests instructions on how to perform the procedure

- *Supporting_characteristics:* The characteristics of the case used to customize the description in the *short_description* or the instructions in the *long_description*

The values for the first two characteristics are long pieces of text. As a result, it would not be practical to specify values for these characteristics in a fact table. Patricia develops a standard format for the definition of a repair procedure (Figure 9.22).

9.3.4 Organizing Case-Independent Relationships

In Section 9.3.2, we described case-independent facts that each specify the value of a characteristic of a particular object. These facts have the form *general characteristic of object is value*, for instance, *price of R71995 is $1.25*. Many expert systems also use case-independent facts that express *relationships* among different objects. A relationship

---

Figure 9.22 Definition of a toaster-repair procedure. Patricia Programmer collects the facts about each toaster-repair procedure into a definition of the repair procedure. The definition specifies three case-independent facts about the repair procedure: the values of its *short_description*, its *long_description*, and its *supporting_characteristics*.

Note that an object's definition can contain notes about the definition's completeness. Under the heading *Status*, Patricia indicates that the facts that specify values for the characteristics *long_description* and *supporting_characteristics* of this repair procedure may need to be modified in the future.

- The value of *long_description* will need to indicate how it can be customized, and it may need to be augmented with diagrams.

- The value of *supporting_characteristics* will have to include *toaster_make* and *toaster_model* to indicate that these two characteristics of a case can be used to customize the repair procedure's *long_description*.

Repair Procedure: Replace_and_Calibrate_Thermostat

Name in knowledge base: *(not implemented yet)*

Use: This repair procedure is generally the last repair the system will recommend when the initial test confirms a thermostat problem.

Case-Independent facts:

Short_description: Please replace the thermostat. Use a new thermostat with any of the following part numbers:
(list the appropriate_part_numbers)
Calibrate the new thermostat.

Figure 9.22 (continued)

Long_description:

1. Open the crumb tray on the bottom of the toaster.
2. Detach the color-adjustment spring from the thermostat.
3. Remove the clip that holds the thermostat in place.
4. Remove the old thermostat and replace it with a new one.
5. Insert the holding clip to secure the new thermostat.
6. Attach the color-adjustment spring.
7. Calibrate the thermostat.
   [For more details on thermostat calibration, click the Describe Procedure button.]
8. Close the crumb tray.

Supporting_characteristics: appropriate_part_numbers

Interview notes: 6/29/90, 7/30/90
notebook PP1 pages 37–40
notebook HH1 pages 32–33

Status: not implemented
We will probably need to review this definition when we add the ability to describe repair procedures. The long description may need to be customized for toaster_make and toaster_model. We will probably also need to include diagrams as well as a text description of the procedure.

---

can be expressed in the form, *object1 relation object2* (for example, *element_wire is_connected_to bus_bar*). Alternatively, a relationship can have the form, *relation between object1 and object2 is value* (for instance, *distance between trip_wire and trigger is .125 inches*).

Review your interview notes to identify relationships your expert system will use in its reasoning process.

1. Identify facts that specify relationships among objects. In particular, look for the expert's statements regarding *taxonomy, structure, topology, causality, function,* or *chronology* (Table 9.3).

2. Group together facts that specify the same kind of relationship.

3. Check each of these relationships against the strategic and judgmental knowledge you have accumulated. Separate the relationships your expert system *will use* from additional relationships that enable you to understand the rationale for the system's actions. Check whether the relationships are already captured in your intermediate representations of judgmental knowledge.

4. Develop intermediate representations to illustrate the relationships that your *expert system will use* and that are *not already captured* in your intermediate representations of judgmental knowledge.

The most useful representations for relationships are graphs and trees in which the nodes correspond to objects and the arcs correspond

---

Table 9.3 Relationships that Are Common in Expert Systems

Type of Relationship	Description	Examples
Taxonomic	A *taxonomic* relationship classifies a general object or concept into a number of more specific objects or concepts.	A is a B. An A can be classified as a B, a C, or a D.
Structural	A *structural* relationship describes how an object or a system of objects can be decomposed into parts or subsystems.	A is a part of B. An A is composed of a B, a C, and a D.
Topological	A *topological* relationship describes the spatial arrangement of physical objects and the interconnections among these objects.	A is next to B. A is to the left of B. A is to the right of B. A is above B. A is below B. A is inside B. A contains B. A intersects B. A is connected to B. A is in contact with B.
Causal	A *causal* relationship describes how certain states or actions induce other states or actions.	A causes B. A is caused by B.
Functional	A *functional* relationship describes conditions under which actions can occur and the reactions and consequences that can result from the actions.	A enables B. A requires B. A triggers B.
Chronological	A *chronological* relationship describes the temporal sequence in which events occur.	A happens before B. A happens after B. A and B happen at the same time. A happens during B. A begins before B ends.

to relationships. In general, each graph should illustrate a single kind of relationship (for example *part_of* or *causes*). Use arrows to indicate the direction of an asymmetric relationship. For example, if one action causes a second, draw an arrow from the first to the second action. If one event occurs before another, draw an arrow from the earlier to the later event.

Figure 9.23 contains a tree that Patricia Programmer uses to represent a taxonomic relationship the toaster-repair advisor will use. Figures 9.24 through 9.27 contain intermediate representations of additional relationships that Patricia Programmer and Howard Hacker learned through their interviews with Frank Fixit. These latter figures are included for illustrative purposes only; the toaster-repair advisor will not actually reason about any of these relationships so the knowledge engineers would not have needed to develop representations for them.

Figure 9.23 Tree representation of a taxonomy. Patricia Programmer draws this tree to illustrate the taxonomic classification of toaster problems. Toaster problems are categorized as no-latch, no-trip, color problems, and heating-element problems. The first cycle of development addresses color problems only; the tree shows that these problems can be classified as *minor_too_dark, severe_too_dark, minor_too_light,* and *severe_too_light*. In future cycles of development, Patricia will add more specific no-latch, no-trip, and heating-element problems to the tree.

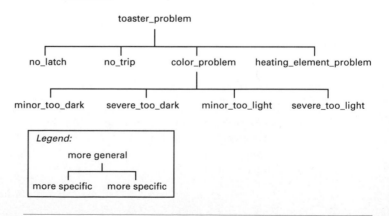

9.4 Creating a Design Document

An expert-system *design document* is an organized collection of the intermediate representations in the conceptual model of the system.

Figure 9.24 Tree representation of structural relationships. A toaster is made up of a number of components, for example, the carriage assembly, the body, and the element assembly. Each of these components is made up of additional components. This tree describes the structural decomposition of a toaster.

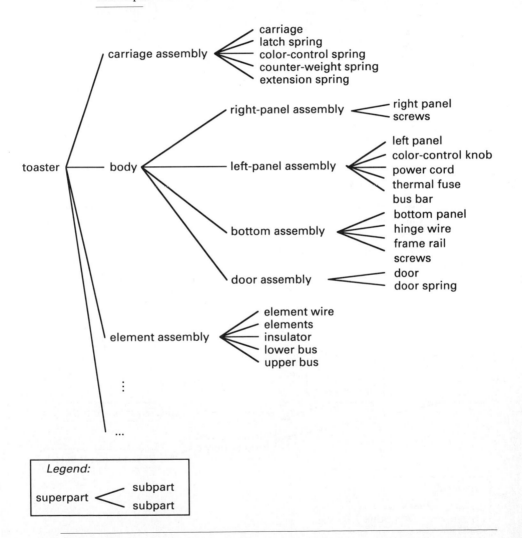

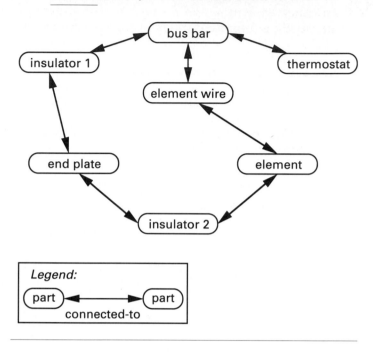

Figure 9.25 Graph representation of a topological relationship. This graph shows how the parts in the thermostat assembly are interconnected.

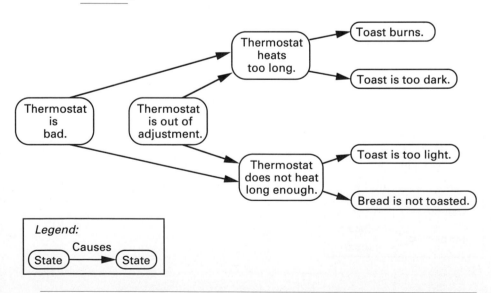

Figure 9.26 Graph representation of a causal relation. This graph illustrates how conditions or states in a toaster can cause other states, including observable behavior.

Figure 9.27 Graph representation of a functional relationship. This graph illustrates the normal function of a toaster. Notice that chronological relationships are also implicit in this graph. If one action triggers or enables a second action, the first action must occur *before* the second action.

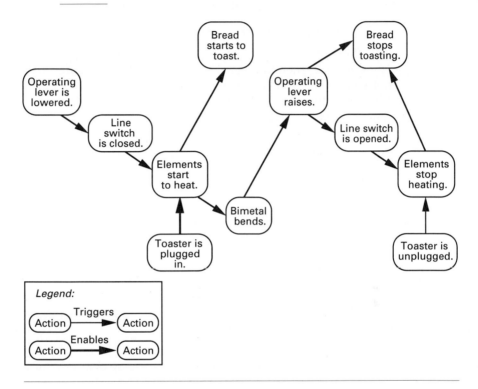

As you create each intermediate representation, integrate it into your design document. Organize the definitions and illustrations in your document in an order that will make them easy to retrieve. This section describes one method for organizing a design document.

1. Group all the information you have obtained about a particular characteristic. Create a *complete description of each characteristic* by collecting all the intermediate representations relevant to that characteristic (Figure 9.28).

2. Organize these descriptions according to the classification of characteristics that you developed (Section 9.3.1). Create a *description of each object type* in your classification (Figure 9.29).

Figure 9.28 Outline for the complete description of a characteristic. A complete description of a characteristic includes the definition of the characteristic as well as the strategic and judgmental knowledge pertinent to the conclusion or the use of this characteristic. To create the description of a characteristic, assemble your intermediate representations in the order indicated in this outline.

Type of Representation	Description	Examples
1. Definition of the characteristic	Section 9.3.1	Figures 9.17, 9.18
2. Strategic knowledge to guide the collection of information about this characteristic	Section 9.2.1 Section 9.2.1	Figures 9.12, 9.14 Figures 9.5, 9.8–9.11, 9.13
3. Judgmental knowledge to conclude this characteristic		
4. Strategic knowledge to guide the process of inferring the consequences of this characteristic	Section 9.2.2	
5. Judgmental knowledge to infer the consequences of this characteristic	Section 9.2.2	

3. Organize your knowledge according to function (strategic, judgmental, or factual) to create *a four-part design document* (Figure 9.30).

Figure 9.29 Outline for the complete description of an object type. If you are able to classify the characteristics in your applications according to the type of object a characteristic describes, use this classification to organize the descriptions of characteristics. A complete description of a classification object type includes a definition of the object type itself, the case-independent facts about objects of that types, and descriptions of the characteristics of objects of that type. Create the description of an object type by collecting your intermediate representations in the order specified in this outline.

Type of Representation	Description	Examples
1. Definition of the object type	Section 9.3.2	Figure 9.20
2. Facts about objects of this type	Section 9.3.3	Figures 9.21, 9.22
3. Complete description of each characteristic of this type of object	Section 9.4	Figure 9.28

9.5 Refining the Conceptual Model

As we saw in Chapters 3 and 4, knowledge engineers identify the full scope of an expert system during initial inquiry. They discuss a variety of cases to obtain a general understanding of the system's task throughout the breadth of its scope. In the first cycle of development, knowledge engineers focus on a particular development increment, *but they also consider the full scope they identified during initial inquiry.* For example, in Dialog 5.4, we saw that Patricia Programmer considered cases outside the initial scope of color problems in simple two-slice toasters. Patricia explored beyond the limits of the first development increment to ensure that she could define a general procedure for the toaster-repair advisor that would accommodate enhancements. Patricia acquired a complete enough understanding of the task to enable her to create a conceptual model that would accommodate extensions in subsequent cycles of development.

Figure 9.30 Outline for an expert-system design document. Assemble the definitions and diagrams that make up your conceptual model in the order indicated in this outline to create a design document that explains what the expert system will do and how it will apply knowledge to perform its task.

Type of Representation	Description	Examples
1. Strategic knowledge		
a. Flow chart of the expert system's task (and possibly flow charts of substeps)	Section 9.1.1	Figures 9.1, 9.2, 9.15
b. Functional decomposition tree that identifies substeps	Section 9.1.2	Figure 9.3
c. Definitions of low-level steps	Section 9.1.3	Figure 9.4
2. Overview of judgmental knowledge		
a. Inference network	Section 9.2.3	Figure 9.16
3. Overview of factual knowledge		
a. Classification of characteristics	Section 9.3.2	Figure 9.19
b. Important relationships	Section 9.3.4	Figures 9.23–9.27
4. Detailed factual and judgmental knowledge		
a. Complete description of each object type used to classify characteristics	Section 9.4	Figure 9.29

A conceptual model can be thought of as a *framework* and a collection of *details* within the framework (Figure 9.31). In the first cycle of development, knowledge engineers create a framework that spans the full scope of the expert system; they fill in details relevant to the first development increment. In each subsequent cycle of development, the knowledge engineers fill in the details relevant to the new development increment. If the knowledge engineers do a careful job in the initial cycle, modifications to the framework in later cycles of development should be few in number and minor in extent.

9.6 Points to Remember

The success of most expert-system projects depends on the long-term extensibility and maintainability of the expert system. Knowledge engineers who develop an expert system can ensure that the system is easy to extend and maintain by creating a complete and accurate *conceptual model* of the expert system. To create a conceptual model, knowledge engineers analyze:

Figure 9.31 Framework and details of a conceptual model. The *framework* of a conceptual model consists of *high-level descriptions of the task* the expert system will perform and *a classification of the characteristics* that describe a situation in which the task can be performed. The *details* within this framework are definitions of low-level steps of the task and descriptions of the factual and judgmental knowledge the system will use as it performs the task.

1. *Strategic knowledge*
   a. **Flow chart of the expert system's task (and possibly flow charts of substeps)**
   b. **Functional decomposition tree that identifies substeps**
   c. Definitions of low-level steps

2. *Overview of judgmental knowledge*
   a. Inference network

3. *Overview of factual knowledge*
   a. **Classification of characteristics**
   b. Important relationships

4. *Detailed factual and judgmental knowledge*
   a. Complete description of each object type that is used to classify characteristics

---

Legend:
Element of the framework
Details within the framework

- The *strategic knowledge* that specifies the procedure the expert system should follow as it performs its task (Table 9.4)

- The *judgmental knowledge* that will enable the expert system to infer information about a case (Table 9.5)

- The *factual knowledge* about which the expert system will reason (Table 9.6)

A conceptual model consists of a number of *intermediate representations* of the expert's knowledge that illustrate:

- The sequence of steps by which the expert system will perform its task

- The inference the system will perform

- The information the system will use

The knowledge engineers collect and organize these intermediate representations into a *design document* for the expert system.

Many different intermediate representations are available for use

---

Table 9.4 Analyzing Strategic Knowledge

Action	Details
Define the high-level control in the expert system.	To create a robust conceptual model that will accommodate extensions, consider the *full scope* of the expert system when you define the task the expert system will perform.
	Identify the high-level steps that make up the expert system's task. Each step should be meaningful to the expert. Each step should be a unit of functionality that could be implemented and tested separately.
	Define the sequence in which the expert system should perform its steps and the conditions under which it should perform each step.
Identify modular substeps.	Subdivide any high-level step that consists of more than a few input, reasoning, and output actions.
	Identify as many levels of substep as necessary.
Define the substeps at the lowest level of functionality.	State the purpose for the step.
	Identify the information the expert system must have before it undertakes the step.
	Describe the sequence of input, reasoning, and output actions that constitute the step.

Table 9.5 Analyzing Judgmental Knowledge

Action	Details
Define reasoning steps in which the system concludes a particular characteristic.	Identify the characteristics that can form the basis of this kind of inference.
	Check whether inferences that conclude this characteristic all use the same basis characteristics.
	If necessary, define the procedure the expert system should follow to find out the conclusion characteristic.
Define reasoning steps in which the system uses a particular trigger characteristic as the basis for inferences.	Identify the conclusion characteristics that can be inferred on the basis of the trigger characteristic.
	Identify the other basis characteristics needed in conjunction with the trigger characteristic.
	Look for groups of inferences that use the same set of basis characteristics to conclude the same characteristic.
	If necessary, define the procedure that the expert system should follow when it infers the consequences of the trigger characteristic.
Describe the overall inference structure of the expert system.	Map out the flow of information to show which characteristics are used to infer which other characteristics.

Table 9.6 Analyzing Factual Knowledge

Action	Details
Classify the characteristics relevant to the expert system's task.	Identify the type of object (physical object, process, or conceptual entity) the characteristic describes.
	Group together characteristics that describe the same type of object.
Organize case-independent facts that specify characteristics.	Identify the particular object each fact describes.
	Group together facts that specify characteristics of the same object.
	Organize these groups of facts by the type of object they describe.
Organize case-independent facts that specify relationships.	Identify the particular type of relationship each fact describes.
	Group together facts concerning the same kind of relationship.

in a design document (Table 9.7). Not all these representations will be needed in every conceptual model. Knowledge engineers should select the representations that can clearly and accurately illustrate the knowledge of their applications.

Table 9.7 Intermediate Representations

Intermediate Representation	Type of Knowledge	Purpose
Flow chart	Strategic	Illustrate the order in which the expert system should perform the steps in its task and the conditions under which it should perform these steps.
Functional-decomposition tree	Strategic	Illustrate how the system's task can be broken down into modular steps and substeps.
Definition of procedural step	Strategic	Describe in detail the individual input, reasoning, and output actions the expert system should take in a step. Explain why the step is necessary. List the prerequisites for performing the step.
General decision table	Judgmental	Describe how the expert system can use a fixed set of basis characteristics to infer a particular conclusion characteristic.
Two-basis decision table	Judgmental	Describe how the expert system can use two basis characteristics to infer a particular conclusion characteristic.
Pseudorule	Judgmental	Describe an inference that entails complex logic. Describe the expert's inexact heuristics. Describe a collection of related special-purpose guidelines that do not follow a standard structure.
Decision tree	Judgmental, strategic	Illustrate a complex decision-making process. Illustrate how the expert system should collect supporting evidence as it tries to infer a particular conclusion characteristic.
Formula definition	Judgmental	Explain how to calculate a numeric characteristic.

Table 9.7 (continued)

Intermediate Representation	Type of Knowledge	Purpose
Inference network	Judgmental	Describe how the expert system will reason from input data through intermediate conclusions to output results.
Definition of characteristic	Factual	Define a characteristic of a case. Describe in detail all the information that will affect the expert system's use of this characteristic.
Definition of object type	Factual	Describe a class of objects relevant to the system's task. Identify the characteristics that describe objects of that class.
Fact table	Factual	Collect a group of similar facts about objects of a particular type.
Definition of object	Factual	Describe the facts an expert system will need to know about a particular object.
Tree	Factual	Illustrate hierarchies of object types used to classify the characteristics important to the expert system's task. Illustrate hierarchical (one to many) relationships among objects, in particular taxonomic relationships and structural decomposition of parts into subparts.
Graph	Factual	Illustrate any relationship among objects, especially topological, causal, functional, and chronological relationships.

Chapter 10

Using the Conceptual Model

Patricia Programmer and Howard Hacker are in the conceptual design step of their first cycle of development. They have begun to create a conceptual model of the toaster-repair advisor. Now Patricia and Howard are ready to review their conceptual model with Frank Fixit. They will use the model to guide further knowledge acquisition; as they acquire more knowledge, Patricia and Howard will refine their conceptual model. Ultimately, the conceptual model will drive the implementation of their expert system.

During the development phase of an expert-system project, the conceptual model is critical for both knowledge acquisition and the development of the expert system. In this chapter, we shall concentrate on the use of a conceptual model for knowledge acquisition.

- An evolving conceptual model enables knowledge engineers to illustrate their understanding of the expert's knowledge; it allows the expert to identify the knowledge engineers' misconceptions (Section 10.1).

- The intermediate representations of a conceptual model provide a structure for knowledge. Knowledge engineers may find that they cannot fill this structure completely, because they have not acquired all the knowledge the expert system will need. Thus an evolving conceptual model pinpoints the additional information knowledge engineers must obtain (Section 10.2).

For completeness, we shall mention briefly how knowledge engineers use a conceptual model to guide the implementation of the expert system.

- The conceptual model specifies what an expert system must do; it establishes requirements for system implementation. These requirements can guide the knowledge engineers to select (or to design) an appropriate expert-system shell for the project (Section 10.3).

- The conceptual model serves as a specification that can direct the knowledge engineers as they implement the expert system (Section 10.4).

10.1 Reviewing your Understanding with the Expert

Before knowledge engineers can use their conceptual model to guide the implementation of an expert system, they must verify that the model accurately captures the expert's knowledge. During the review of an intermediate representation, the expert sees for the first time what knowledge engineers plan *to do* with the knowledge. As a result, this review is a challenge for the knowledge engineer's interview skills.

- The knowledge engineer must communicate clearly what the intermediate representation means *without confusing the expert*.

- The knowledge engineer must present a simple and concise description of the expert's knowledge *without implying that this knowledge is trivial*.

- The knowledge engineer must explain how the intermediate representation organizes the expert's knowledge *without implying that the expert should use the same organization*.

- The knowledge engineer must describe how the expert system will use the intermediate representation *without implying that the expert's own actions can be reduced to a straightforward algorithm*.

- The knowledge engineer must *encourage the expert to criticize* the intermediate representation and to express uncertainties or reservations without fear of offending the knowledge engineer.

- If the expert is uncomfortable with the intermediate representation, the knowledge engineer must work with the expert to define alternative representations that serve the knowledge engineer's purpose and *are natural to the expert.*

Each review of an intermediate representation should consist of a careful *presentation* of the representation (Section 10.1.1) followed by an *evaluation* of the representation (Section 10.1.2).

10.1.1 Presenting an Intermediate Representation

To prepare for an interview in which you will review an intermediate representation, write a brief description that explains what the representation shows and how it will be used. Follow this description with the intermediate representation itself. Make a copy of this material for each person who will attend the interview, but *do not distribute the copies before the interview.* At the interview, you will explain how to interpret the representation. If you were to distribute copies of the representation beforehand, the expert might waste time and become confused trying to puzzle out what you mean by the columns and rows in a table or by the arcs in a graph.

Introduce your presentation of an intermediate representation by explaining *what* the representation illustrates and *why* you need to illustrate this information. Present the representation slowly and carefully. *Do not distribute your written description until you have finished your presentation.* The written material might distract the expert's attention from your presentation.

As you present each component of the intermediate representation, draw this component on a whiteboard or flip chart that is easily visible to the entire group. Make sure the expert understands what you have drawn before you proceed to the next component. When you have finished explaining the structure of your representation and you are sure the expert has understood this structure, hand out the written copies of the representation. Give the group time to read through the representation before you proceed with a discussion of its content.

In Dialog 10.1, Patricia Programmer begins to review her intermediate representation of the judgmental knowledge she has gathered about thermostat calibration.

Dialog 10.1 Presenting an Intermediate Representation

Setting

Patricia Programmer, Howard Hacker, and Frank Fixit are seated at a table in their meeting room. A whiteboard is on the wall. On the table in front of Patricia are three sheets of paper. On the front of each sheet is a copy of the decision table shown in Figure 9.8; the sheets are lying face down so the decision table is not visible.

Dialog

Patricia: Frank, since our last meeting Howard and I have outlined our understanding of the decisions you make when you calibrate a new thermostat. Today we'd like to review our understanding with you to find out whether we're missing anything. We found it helpful to organize the information into a table. The table lets us see at a glance what decisions you would make in different situations.

Patricia walks to the whiteboard.

First let me describe our organization. You seem to use the toasting time and the room temperature to assess whether the thermostat toasts for too short a time, too long a time, or the right length of time.

Frank nods and watches intently while Patricia labels the top and left side of the table (Figure 10.1a).

I'm going to label the columns with different lengths of toasting time. I'll label the rows with different room temperatures.

Patricia adds the column and row headings to her table (Figure 10.1b).

Now, I'm not sure about these ranges. In the few cases we discussed, you seemed to draw distinctions between cases where the toasting times differed by five minutes or where the room temperatures differed by ten degrees. So I picked five-minute intervals for the toasting time and 10° intervals for the temperature. I'll want to review these ranges later, but for now, I want to make sure that you understand what the table means.

Frank nods.

Each cell in the table corresponds to a different kind of situation. I'm going to look in the cell to tell me how to assess the thermostat time in that situation.

Patricia fills in the first row of the table (Figure 10.1c), then she points to the cell in the first row and first column.

This square tells me how to assess the thermostat time when the toasting time is less than 60 seconds and the room temperature is between 50° and 60°. In that situation, the toasting time is too short. The thermostat should be adjusted to lengthen the toasting time.

Patricia draws her finger across the first row of the table.

If the room temperature is between 50° and 60°, any toasting time less than 65 seconds is too short; 75 seconds or more is too long, and anything in between is just right.

Frank scowls slightly.

Frank: I see how the table works, but I'm not sure it's right.

Patricia: Good! Then we should get on with our discussion of the table.

Patricia hands Howard and Frank their copies of the decision table.

Now that you understand what the table means, Frank, I'd like you to help us improve it. We want the table to be an accurate reflection of

Figure 10.1 Presenting an intermediate representation to the expert. To present this decision table to Frank Fixit (Dialog 10.1), Patricia Programmer first explained that the columns correspond to toasting times and the rows correspond to room temperatures (a). Then she filled in the column and row headings and explained that each different cell in the table corresponds to a different situation (b). Finally she filled in the first row and explained how the table can be used to assess the thermostat time in different situations. When Patricia was sure that Frank understood the meaning of this intermediate representation, she showed him the complete table (see Figure 9.8).

(a)

Room_Temperature (degrees Fahrenheit) | Toasting_Time (seconds)

(b)

Room_Temperature (degrees Fahrenheit)	Toasting_Time (seconds)				
	time < 60	60 ≤ time < 65	65 ≤ time < 70	70 ≤ time < 75	75 ≤ time
50 ≤ temp < 60					
60 ≤ temp < 70					
70 ≤ temp < 80					
80 ≤ temp < 90					
90 ≤ temp < 100					

(c)

Room_Temperature (degrees Fahrenheit)	Toasting_Time (seconds)				
	time < 60	60 ≤ time < 65	65 ≤ time < 70	70 ≤ time < 75	75 ≤ time
50 ≤ temp < 60	too_short	too_short	OK	OK	too_long
60 ≤ temp < 70					
70 ≤ temp < 80					
80 ≤ temp < 90					
90 ≤ temp < 100					

your knowledge. I filled it out as best I could from my interview notes, but I'm sure I made some mistakes. Why don't you take a few minutes to look over the table, then we can start to discuss it.

Discussion

This is the first time Patricia Programmer has shown Frank Fixit this kind of decision table. Before she lets him see the table, she explains step by step what the columns and the rows represent and how to interpret the cells in the table. In the future, when Patricia shows Frank a different decision table with a similar format, she will not need to introduce the table with such a long explanation; if necessary, she can give Frank a brief reminder of what the format means. On the other hand, when Patricia presents a different kind of intermediate representation for the first time (for example, a functional decomposition tree), she will need to introduce the structure and the interpretation of that representation carefully beforehand just as she did in this dialog.

10.1.2 Evaluating an Intermediate Representation

An intermediate representation serves two purposes: First it is a vehicle for communication between the knowledge engineers and the expert; second it is a specification of the intended behavior of the expert system. Your review with the project expert should evaluate the ability of an intermediate representation to serve both purposes.

- As a vehicle for communication, an intermediate representation should reflect *the expert's way of structuring knowledge*. In many applications, however, the expert system needs to use knowledge that the expert has never before analyzed and organized into any structure. By necessity, the intermediate representation will impose a structure on the expert's knowledge; it is important that the structure be one *natural to the expert's way of thinking*. The minimum requirement for an intermediate representation is that the expert should be *comfortable with the form in which it presents the knowledge*.

- As a specification of expert-system behavior, the contents of an intermediate representation must be accurate, complete, and internally consistent. In this section, we discuss the accuracy of the representation; in Section 10.2, we shall discuss completeness and consistency.

After you have presented an intermediate representation to the expert, ask for the expert's comments and corrections. Make sure that expert realizes you want and need criticism. Sometimes an expert will balk at the *form* of an intermediate representation; as a result, the expert will be unable or unwilling to comment on the *content* of the representation. If the expert seems uneasy with your representation, work together to modify it into a more appropriate structure. Encourage the expert to redraw the representation to present the information in a more natural way. Review the content of the intermediate representation, and make sure the expert understands how it will be used by the expert system. Ask the expert whether the information in the representation is correct.

Dialog 10.2 is a continuation of Dialog 10.1. Patricia Programmer asks Frank Fixit to evaluate her representation of the judgmental knowledge about thermostat calibration.

Dialog 10.2 Evaluating an Intermediate Representation

Setting

Patricia Programmer has introduced the decision table for assessment of thermostat timing (Dialog 10.1). Frank has just finished studying the decision table in Patricia's handout.

Dialog

Frank *(hesitantly):* I guess this table will work OK.

Patricia: Don't be bashful about telling us what's wrong with the table. This is just a first pass, and we need your help to get it right.

Frank *(smiling):* OK. What kind of feed-back do you want?

Patricia: We want your comments on the *form* of the table, and its *content.* As far as form goes, we're using this table to show you how we understand your knowledge. I'd like you to be able to look at the table and immediately think, "That makes sense." If you have to twist the table around mentally before you can evaluate it, the form is wrong, and we need you to help us to reshape it into a form that doesn't require any mental reorganization.

As for the content of the table, the expert system is going to use this information. When you review the contents of the table, I want you to believe that the table can guide the system to make the right decisions. If it can't, we need to figure out what's wrong in the table and how to fix it.

Frank: Well, I'll give you my comments, but I don't know if they'll be organized the way you want.

Patricia: No organization is necessary. Just tell us what you think. Let us hear all your reactions to the table.

Frank: Well I understand what you're trying to show and, like I said, it's OK. I remember the examples of calibration we talked about, and I can see why you built the table this way. The problem is that the table doesn't account for line voltage. I know I didn't mention line voltage in those examples. I guess I was trying to simplify my description. Sorry!

Patricia: Don't apologize! We expect you to simplify things so we can follow you. That's why we do this kind of review—to make sure we've got the full picture.

So tell us about line voltage.

Frank: Right. Your table isn't bad for an average line voltage, but the right way to calibrate the thermostat is to measure both the line voltage to the toaster and the room temperature. The voltage is generally going to be anywhere from 117 to—I'd say 122 volts. A toasting time that's just right for 122 volts would be too short for 117 volts.

Patricia: I see. We're missing an important factor in this table—line voltage.

Patricia walks to the whiteboard. She erases her outline of the decision table and draws the outline for a general decision table with columns for three basis characteristics (Figure 10.2a).

Suppose we format the table like so. Each row will tell us what to do in a particular situation. The first column will have the room temperature; the second, the line voltage; and the third, the toasting time. The fourth column will tell us how to assess the thermostat time. I've filled in the first row to show how the table would work. The numbers are probably wrong.

Frank scowls at the new table on the whiteboard.

Frank: I'm not sure whether I like this table any better than the last one. It's good because it includes line voltage—you've got to include line voltage—but I think it's a little confusing. I don't know if I could do any better, but I think I'm going to have to work to figure out this table.

Patricia: Frank, why don't you go to the board and explain what you do after you measure the voltage and the temperature. Draw any diagrams that will help your explanation.

Frank walks to the whiteboard and erases Patricia's outline. He stares at the blank board for a few seconds then turns to face Patricia and Howard and begins to talk.

Frank: I measure the line voltage and the room temperature. Then I measure the toasting time, and I think, "Is this time OK, too short, or too long?" For a given voltage and temperature, I know what range of toasting time I should see. Hmm, that gives me an idea.

Frank turns to the board and starts to write. After a few false starts, he creates the outline of a new decision table (Figure 10.2b).

This is more like the way I think about thermostat calibration. I don't know if this table will work for you—it doesn't show the assessment of thermostat time like yours does.

Patricia: The table is fine. It shows us the range for an assessment of *OK*. So it's clear from the table that a toasting time below that range is *too_short* and a time above the range is *too_long*. I like the table.

Howard nods emphatically.

How do you feel about it, Frank?

Frank turns to the board, looks at the table, and nods.

Figure 10.2 Exploring alternative representations. When Patricia Programmer learned that the two-basis decision table of Figure 9.8 needed an additional basis characteristic *(line_voltage)*, she outlined a general decision table (a) to replace the two-basis table. Frank Fixit was not comfortable with Patricia's new table. Although it captured the important information, this information was not structured in a form natural to Frank. Frank proposed a different representation (b). The cells in Frank's table contain the range of acceptable toasting times (measured in seconds). When Patricia Programmer adopts Frank's table, she will ask Frank to specify the ranges of room temperature and toasting time more precisely. For example, Frank specified a temperature range as *70–80.°* Patricia must find out whether this range includes the end points *70* and *80*.

(a)

Room_Temperature (degrees Fahrenheit)	Toasting_Time (seconds)	Line_Voltage (volts)	Thermostat_Time_Assessment
50 ≤ temp < 60	time < 60	120	too_short

(b)

Room_Temperature (degrees Fahrenheit)	Line_Voltage (volts)						acceptable toasting times (in seconds)
	117	118	119	120	121	122	
50–60	70–80	70–75	65–75	65–75	65–70	65–70	
60–70							
70–80							
80–90							
90–100							

Frank: I like it. I think it shows all the information your table had, but it's a lot easier for me to understand.

Patricia: Yes, it's simpler than my table.

Frank: Does this mean I'm a knowledge engineer now?

Patricia, Howard, and Frank laugh.

Patricia: You're well on your way! All right, I think we're all happy with the form of the table so let's move on to its content. Do you think you could fill out the table for us, Frank?

Frank: Sure! Do you want me to fill it out now?

Patricia: Your choice.

Frank: I'd like to give it some thought and to check my manuals. I'll do it between now and our next meeting.

Patricia: Thanks, Frank. That will be great.

Frank studies that table outline on the whiteboard. He bites his lower lip and taps his fingers on the table.

Frank: You know, there's another complication. I've been thinking about what you said before, Patricia. If the computer follows this table, will it do the right thing? I think we are going to need a different table for each different manufacturer. One table should be fine for all the simple two-slice toasters that Toasts-Best makes. But I'm going to need a different table for General Appliance toasters. They're almost the same—maybe it's too small a difference to worry about—but I'd feel better knowing that the computer is using a table that's *exactly right* for the particular toaster.

Patricia: I agree, Frank. If it takes multiple tables to do the job right, we should use them. Will we need different tables for four-slice toasters?

Frank: I'm afraid so.

Patricia: What about for different models of toaster?

Frank: I think the toaster style and the manufacturer will give us all the information we need. There's not too much variation among different models of the same style from the same manufacturer. I'll definitely get you the table for Toasts-Best by our next meeting. It may take me till the end of next week to get all the tables for simple two-slice toasters.

Patricia: That will be fine.

Discussion

Frank Fixit's hesitant reaction to the decision table tells Patricia Programmer that Frank is not satisfied with the table. When Patricia learns that the table is missing an important basis characteristic *(line_voltage)*, she knows that a two-basis table is an inadequate representation. Patricia suggests an alternative representation. Although the general decision table that Patricia proposes will capture all the necessary information, Frank is not comfortable with the table. It is not an accurate reflection of the way he thinks about thermostat calibration.

Frank himself proposes the form for a better representation by adapting and combining components of the two tables Patricia has shown him.

Notice how the right intermediate representation simplifies future knowledge acquisition. Once Frank feels comfortable with the decision-table format for knowledge about thermostat calibration, he can supply the necessary knowledge by filling in these tables. Patricia and Howard do not have to interview him to obtain this information.

Some experts do not like to work with intermediate representations. If your expert is not comfortable with an intermediate representation, try to find a more appropriate alternative representation as illustrated in Dialog 10.2. If several alternatives all fail to satisfy the expert, drop the topic and proceed to a different matter. For the purpose of specifying the behavior of your expert system, select the intermediate representation you think best captures the expert's knowledge. However, *do not use the intermediate representation as a vehicle for communicating with the expert.* Try writing a detailed description of the knowledge and how it will be used, and ask the expert to review the text. If that approach fails, you will have to verify the contents of your representation through a series of interviews. Describe each component of the representation verbally, and ask for the expert's confirmation or correction. For example, if you use a decision table, describe each inference in the table separately, and ask for the expert's comments and criticisms.

10.2 Focusing Knowledge Acquisition

Each intermediate representation in a conceptual model is an organized collection of related information. As such, the conceptual model facilitates the knowledge engineers' review of the knowledge they have acquired. An evolving conceptual model can focus future knowledge-acquisition interviews in two ways. First the knowledge engineers can review the conceptual model by themselves to identify *topics for discussion* in subsequent interviews with the expert. Second the intermediate representations can *establish the context for discussions* in which the knowledge engineer and the expert review the conceptual model together.

Before discussing the conceptual model with the expert, review the model to check whether you have achieved a complete and consistent understanding of the expert's knowledge. For each intermediate representation, ask yourself:

- Does this representation include *all* the information that will be needed to implement the desired behavior, or is information missing?

- Is all the information in this representation *consistent,* and is it consistent with information in other intermediate representations?

- Will the expert system actually *use* all this information, or is some information extraneous to the system's task?

Table 10.1 describes how to use the answers to these questions.

The remainder of this section describes the topics you should discuss with the expert as you review the completeness and consistency of the system's strategic (Section 10.2.1), judgmental (Section 10.2.2), and factual (Section 10.2.3) knowledge.

10.2.1 Discussing Strategic Knowledge

To begin your review of the conceptual model, discuss the strategic knowledge with your project expert. Use your intermediate representations of strategic knowledge to describe the procedure the system

---

Table 10.1 Using the Conceptual Model to Focus Knowledge Acquisition

Observed Problem	Corrective Actions
Missing information	Use the intermediate representation to explain to the expert what information you need.
	Ask the expert to fill out the representation for you, or use the representation to guide your collection of information in interviews.
Apparent contradictions	Use the intermediate representations to explain the inconsistency to the expert.
	Discuss the problem with the expert to resolve the inconsistency.
Extraneous information	Use the intermediate representation to identify the extraneous information for the expert.
	Review the conceptual model with the expert to illustrate that the model does not show how the information will be used by the expert system.
	Find out whether the system should use the information.
	If the information is not needed, keep the intermediate representation as part of the conceptual model. (As the scope of the expert system is extended, the information may be needed after all.)
	Annotate the intermediate representation to indicate that the information will not be needed by the expert system.
	Do not implement the information unless you can anticipate how it will be used in future versions of the system.

will follow as it performs its task. Trace the procedure, as described by the conceptual model, to ensure that your understanding of the procedure is complete and consistent (Table 10.2).

If the expert system is interactive, discuss how the system should interact with its user. Are the correct input and output steps reflected in the conceptual model? Review the need for explanations or justifications. If the system will be used to train relatively inexperienced personnel, it may need to explain what it is doing and why. If the system will be used as a job aid for experts or near-experts, it may need to justify its actions.

- Find out which steps require an explanation or a justification.

- Gather the text and the diagrams that the system should display to explain or justify its actions.

Table 10.2 Checking the Strategic Knowledge

Intermediate Representation	Review Process
Flow chart	Check whether the flow chart specifies what the system should do in *all* circumstances.
	If a branch in control is made on the basis of some characteristic, find out what the system should do if this characteristic is unknown.
	Review each unconditional arrow. Find out whether there are any circumstances in which the system should *not* take the indicated action.
Functional-decomposition tree	Make sure that every step in the tree makes sense to the expert.
	Check whether the collection of lowest-level steps captures every action the expert system should take.
Definition of procedural step	Look at the *required information* for this step (see Figure 9.4). Make sure that earlier steps in the process guarantee that the required information will be available at the beginning of this step.
	For each input action, review the definition of the input characteristic. Check that the definition specifies *how* the expert system should obtain the input.
	For each reasoning action, check the judgmental knowledge to be sure that it specifies what inferences should be made *in all situations* within the current scope of the system.
	For each output action, review the definition of the output characteristic. Check that the definition specifies *how* and *where* the characteristic should be written.

- Find out whether the system should present its explanations or justifications as a matter of course. If so, add the necessary output steps to the conceptual model. If not, update the conceptual model to illustrate how and when the user can request an explanation or a justification.

10.2.2 Discussing Judgmental Knowledge

In most expert systems, the majority of the conceptual model concerns the system's judgmental knowledge. The review of this portion of the conceptual model is generally the most time consuming. Knowledge

---

Table 10.3 Checking the Judgmental Knowledge

Intermediate Representation	Review Process
Decision table (general or two-basis)	Check whether the table includes all the necessary basis characteristics.
	Make sure that the table specifies *all* possible values for the basis characteristics.
	Find out what should happen if any of the basis characteristics is unknown.
	Find out whether some combinations of values for the basis characteristic represent impossible or unrealistic situations.
	Make sure that the table specifies a conclusion for *all realistic combinations* of values for the basis characteristics.
Pseudorules	Check whether the pseudorules that conclude a particular characteristic are mutually exclusive. (Rules are mutually exclusive if the condition of only one rule can be true at a given time.)
	If the rules are not mutually exclusive, review rules that can succeed at the same time. Should the system use *all* these inferences? If not, should the rules be tried in a particular order to prevent interactions?
	Check whether any groups of rules appear to contradict one another.
	If the rules specify inexact conclusions, find out how the system should *use* these conclusions. Should it act on all possible values or only on the most likely value? Does the system need to combine uncertain evidence concluded by different rules? If the system is uncertain about the basis characteristics, should this uncertainty affect the degree of certainty of the conclusion?

Table 10.3 (continued)

Intermediate Representation	Review Process
Decision tree	Make sure that the branches from each node specify all possible values for the characteristic tested in that node.
	Find out what the system should do if any of these characteristics is unknown.
Formula definition	If the definition specifies *restrictions* (see Table 9.1), make sure that other formulas are defined to cover alternative situations.
	Check the definitions of the basis characteristics to see whether any characteristic needs a default value. For example, if the formula calculates a sum of several characteristics, certain of these characteristics may be optional. An optional characteristic should have a default value of zero.
Inference network	Check for cycles in the network (that is, a sequence of nodes and arcs that indicate A is used to infer B, which is used to infer C, . . . , which is used to infer A.) Review the relevant judgmental and strategic knowledge to see whether situations exist that might lead to circular reasoning. If so, modify the representations to eliminate this circular reasoning.
	Check whether the network indicates *all* ways in which each characteristic can be used in the inference process.
	Check whether each path through the graph leads to a node for a characteristic that will be used as output. If you find a path that does not lead to output, check whether the inferences are necessary.

engineers can use the procedure that the expert system will follow to organize the discussion of judgmental knowledge.

Refer to the appropriate representations of strategic knowledge (flow chart or step definitions) to identify a reasoning step for the expert. Discuss the context in which the expert system will need to perform this reasoning step. Then review the intermediate representations of the judgmental knowledge that will guide the system's decisions during this step (Table 10.3). Find out whether the expert system will need to explain or to justify any of its decisions. If so, gather the text and the diagrams the system should display to explain or to justify its decisions, and incorporate this information into the appropriate intermediate representations.

In Dialog 10.3, Patricia Programmer uses intermediate representations to focus the discussion about the completeness and consistency of her conceptual model.

Dialog 10.3 Checking the Completeness and Consistency of a Conceptual Model

Setting

Frank Fixit has filled out the new decision table for assessing thermostat timing in Toasts-Best toasters. (The outline of the decision table is shown in Figure 10.2b.) Patricia Programmer and Howard Hacker are meeting with Frank to review this table. Patricia has prepared three copies of Frank's decision table and three copies of the definition of the repair procedure *replace_and_calibrate_thermostat* (Figure 9.22).

Dialog

Patricia distributes the copies of Frank's decision table.

Patricia: Thanks for filling out this table for us, Frank. Before we get into the details of the table, I'd like to review how the expert system will use it. Let's look at our current definition of the thermostat replacement procedure to see where this table fits in.

Patricia hands out the copies of the definition of replace_and_calibrate_thermostat. *Howard and Frank review the definition.*

Frank, do you remember how we're planning to use these definitions?

Frank: Yes I do. Hmm. When we were talking about the table before, I envisioned that the system should ask for the room temperature and the line voltage then ask the user to measure the toasting time. Then the system would check the decision table, and tell the user whether to adjust the new thermostat. Now that I look at our definition of the repair procedure, I remember I told you that we'd just tell the user to replace and calibrate the thermostat. Maybe we don't need the table after all.

Patricia: It sounds as though we won't need the table when the user is familiar with this repair procedure.

Frank nods.

What if the user is inexperienced? How much guidance would you like the system to provide?

Frank looks at the definition of the repair procedure.

Frank: Let's see. The system prints this short description. If the user asks for details, it prints the long description. Now, the user can ask for details about the calibration procedure.

Patricia: Should we have a standard description, or should we use the table to tailor the description for the user?

Frank: Could we print out the whole table?

Patricia: Sure. We could have a description of the procedure that explains how to use the table, then we could print the appropriate table, depending on the make and style of the toaster.

Frank: That would be good. You know what I think would be better? This might be too complicated, but here's how I think we should lead the user through this procedure. First we print an overview of the calibration procedure. This lets the user know why the line voltage and room temperature are important. Then we ask the user to measure the voltage and the temperature and to enter those two numbers. We tell the user to set the color control on medium and measure the toasting time. We look in the table to assess the toasting time. Then we say that the thermostat is calibrated just right, or we tell the user to shorten or lengthen the toasting time. If necessary, the user can request a description of the adjustment procedure.

Patricia: Should we ever show the user the entire table?

Frank: Let me think. If the system can look up the assessment, there's no need to ask the user to look it up.

Patricia: Should the system be able to explain how it assessed the toasting time?

Frank: If it could, that would be great! If a user is curious, the table would be a good way to show what to do.

Patricia: As I recall the project plan, we're going to finish the major problems in two- and four-slice toasters first, then we'll add the ability to describe repair procedures for inexperienced repair personnel. I think it's very possible that we'll have enough time in the schedule to implement the kind of interaction you described, including the ability to explain the assessment by showing the decision table. We'll have to see when we get there.

Frank: If we just print a general description and the table, it will be good enough. But if we have time to do more, we should. The more information the system can give to a new staff member, the more valuable it will be.

Patricia: I agree. To sum up our discussion so far, we decided that the system *will* use this table in one way or another, but not until we add the capability to describe repair procedures. I've got a few questions about the table. They can wait until later in the project when we're ready to use the table. We do have enough time in our schedule to discuss them now though. Frank, would you prefer to go over the table while it's fresh in your mind, or should we go on to a new topic?

Frank: Let's continue with the table.

Patricia: OK. I just need to make the tables a little more precise. Let's look at the row headings. The first one is *50 to 60*, and the second one is *60 to 70*. Which table should we use if the room temperature is 60°?

Frank *(studying the table):* I guess it doesn't really matter.

Patricia: We need to label the rows so the system will know which row to use. How about if I include the lower bound on each row but not the upper bound? So we'll use the first row if the temperature is 50, but the second row if the temperature is 60, the third row if the temperature is 70, and so on.

Frank: That's fine.

Patricia: What happens if the temperature is below 50? Or if it's 100 or more?

Frank: I bet we'd close the shop and all go home!

Patricia, Howard, and Frank laugh.

Patricia: If the temperature is out of the range covered in this table, should the system say that it can't describe the calibration procedure?

Frank: I guess we should describe the procedure in general terms and tell them to do the calibration when the temperature is in a reasonable range.

Patricia: What about the line voltage? What should the system do if the measured voltage is below 117 or above 122?

Frank: I suppose that could happen. If the voltage is so far off, we should refer them to the senior staff member.

Patricia: OK. One last question. Let's look at the ranges for acceptable toasting time. The first cell in the table gives the range as *70° to 80°*. Does that mean that 70 and 80 are both OK? Or is 70 too low and 80 too high?

Frank: They're both OK. The same goes for all the temperature ranges in the table.

Patricia: Thanks, Frank. That does it for this table. Why don't we take a break before we go on?

Discussion

When Patricia Programmer reviewed her understanding of the process that the toaster-repair advisor will follow, she noticed that the assessment of thermostat toasting time did not appear to fit into this process. Therefore Patricia begins this interview by investigating whether the system will actually use the tables that describe how to assess thermostat toasting times.

Contrast this dialog with dialogs that took place earlier in the project. Patricia's questions are much simpler now. Frank Fixit is well integrated into the project team and understands what the knowledge engineers want to accomplish. Patricia does not need to explain in detail what she is trying to find out. Frank is able to review the intermediate representations and to see what questions must be answered; Patricia does not need to prompt him for the necessary information.

Note also that Frank has begun to identify with the expert system. Frank wants the toaster-repair advisor to give the assistance that he himself could provide. Frank uses the word "we" to describe what the system should do because he thinks of himself and the system performing the same task.

10.2.3 Discussing Factual Knowledge

The final step in the review of a conceptual model consists of checking the completeness and consistency of the factual knowledge (Table 10.4). Review your representations of factual knowledge to ensure that:

- Your definitions of characteristics include all the details you will need to know when you implement your expert system

- You have obtained all the case-independent facts your system will need

This step is usually the most straightforward because experts are generally able to articulate facts more easily than they can articulate their problem-solving strategies and reasoning processes. By the time you are ready to review your conceptual model, you will probably find you have obtained most of the information you need about factual knowledge.

When you discuss case-independent facts, investigate whether the facts that you need are available in some written or on-line form. Often the information that is easily represented in a fact table is available in tabular form in a manual or a database. For example, Patricia Programmer will not need to gather facts about toaster parts from Frank Fixit because these facts are available in the toaster-part database. The toaster-repair advisor will not need to duplicate these facts in its knowledge base but will be able to retrieve the facts it needs directly from the database.

10.3 Analyzing Requirements for Implementation

In Sections 10.1 and 10.2, we saw how knowledge engineers use the evolving conceptual model to guide knowledge acquisition. After the

---

Table 10.4 Checking the Factual Knowledge

Intermediate Representation	Review Process
Definition of a characteristic	Check that the definition contains all the necessary information (refer to Table 9.2).
Fact table	Check whether the system needs additional facts about the objects in the table. Make sure that the system will *use* all the facts in the table. Verify that the table contains a row for *every* object of the correct type.
Object definition	Check whether the system needs additional facts about the object. Make sure that the system will *use* all the facts in the definition. Check whether the conceptual model includes a definition of every relevant object.
Graph or tree of a relationship	Check whether the graph or tree specifies the relationship for all relevant objects. Make sure that the system will *use* the relationship.

knowledge engineers have obtained enough information to begin implementation of the expert system, the conceptual model continues to guide their efforts. Implementation of an expert system requires an expert-system shell that provides the representation formalisms in which the knowledge base can be encoded and the inference and control mechanisms that can interpret the knowledge base to perform the desired task. A conceptual model enables knowledge engineers to select (or to implement) a shell that meets the requirements of their application.

Project teams can find themselves in three different situations with respect to the selection of an expert-system shell.

1. *Knowledge engineers select a suitable shell.* The toaster-repair advisor project illustrates the first situation. After Patricia Programmer and Howard Hacker have developed their conceptual model, they will choose an expert-system shell that best satisfies the needs of their application.

2. *The knowledge engineers design a specialized shell.* In the second situation, the knowledge engineers will design and implement an expert-system shell customized to the particular needs of their application.

3. *The knowledge engineers must make do with an available shell.* In the third situation, the choice of expert-system shell is made *before* the knowledge engineers develop their conceptual model. For example, the knowledge engineers might work for a company that has purchased a single expert-system shell for use in all applications. Project management is another factor that may put a project team in this situation. The management group who funds the project may require the knowledge engineers to specify what shell they will use as part of their project plan—before they know enough about the application to be able to predict all its requirements.

In all three situations, the knowledge engineers should review their conceptual model to determine what requirements this model places on the expert-system shell they use. The basic requirements for an expert-system shell are:

- The ability to represent the strategic, judgmental, and factual knowledge the expert system will use

- The ability to effect the necessary inference, following the correct sequence of steps

Although the evaluation and selection of expert-system shells is beyond the scope of this book, we present a summary (Table 10.5) of the factors knowledge engineers should consider in determining their application's requirements for a shell.[1] They must analyze:

Table 10.5 Analyzing Requirements of a Conceptual Model

Requirements	Questions
Representation of strategic knowledge Control mechanisms	Does the expert system perform a standard sequence of steps? If not, does the system "decide" what steps are appropriate, or does a user (or calling program) govern the steps the system should take? Does the system need to iterate through a sequence of steps? Does the system need to execute some steps conditionally? Does the system need to perform operations that are best implemented through recursion? Does the system need to explain or to justify the steps it takes in performing the task? Are explanations and justifications needed only at the time when an action is taken? Or must the system record reasons for its actions (for explanation later in the interaction)?
Representation of judgmental knowledge Inference mechanisms	What kinds of conditions does the system need to test (for example: *equal, not equal, greater than, less than, before, after, during, element of, subset of,* and *substring of*)? How does the system need to combine simple conditions? Does it need to allow all possible combinations of the logical operators *and, or,* and *not?* Does the system need to test quantified conditions (for example: *there exists* . . . and *for all* . . .)? Does the system need to reason with uncertainty? Must it accumulate evidence for and against hypotheses? Must the strength of a conclusion be modified by the system's degree of certainty about the basis characteristics? What kinds of expressions must the system use to specify values for characteristics (for example, arithmetic expressions, date arithmetic, construction and decomposition of text strings, and construction and decomposition of lists)? Will the system ever need to change an hypothesis that it has made? If so, will it need to "undo" all inferences that used that hypothesis as a basis? Does the system need to explain or to justify its decisions? Are explanations and justifications needed only at the time when a decision is made? Or must the system record reasons for its decisions (for explanation later in the interaction)?

---

1. For additional information about the selection of an expert-system shell, refer to the Additional Reading section.

Table 10.5 (continued)

Requirements	Questions
Representation of factual knowledge	What kinds of data does the system need to represent (for example: numeric values, symbolic values, lists of values, dates or times, or complex record structures)?
	Does the system need to represent characteristics that can have multiple values at the same time? (For example, the customer can check a number of different complaints on the repair slip.)
	Are all facts definite, or does the system need to represent hypotheses with varying degrees of certainty?
	Does the system need to represent both positive and negative evidence or just positive evidence?
	Does the system need to represent relationships among objects in addition to simple facts and hypotheses about characteristics?
	Does the system need to be able to provide the user with definitions of the terms it uses?

- The system's strategic knowledge to determine the shell's requirements for *representation of strategic knowledge* and for *control mechanisms*

- The system's judgmental knowledge to determine the shell's requirements for *representation of judgmental knowledge* and for *inference mechanisms*

- The system's factual knowledge to determine the shell's requirements for *representation of factual knowledge*

The requirements for representation, inference, and control are key elements in the selection of an expert-system shell; they are not the only elements, however. Knowledge engineers must also consider the shell's ability to address the application's integration and performance requirements.

Once the knowledge engineers have assessed all requirements for the expert system shell, they proceed to use the results of their analysis.

1. The knowledge engineers can select a shell that satisfies their requirements.

2. They can design and implement a shell that meets their needs.

3. If they must use a preselected available shell, they should compare their requirements against the capabilities of that shell. If the shell cannot satisfy all requirements, the knowledge engineers must plan

how they will deal with the shell's limitations. For example, they may be able to implement additional functionality in computer programs that can be used in conjunction with the shell. In some applications, however, the knowledge engineers must review the limitations of the available shell with their project managers and redefine the task of the expert system in light of these limitations.

10.4 Implementing the Knowledge Base

Once an expert-system shell has been selected, the conceptual model guides the implementation of the expert system. The knowledge engineers create an *implementation design* by mapping their conceptual model onto capabilities of the shell. The implementation design in turn directs the implementation of a working expert system. Whereas the conceptual model specifies *what* the expert system will do, the implementation design specifies *how* the desired behavior can be achieved, given the shell's representation formalisms and its inference and control mechanisms.

In many applications, the expert-system project consists of knowledge-engineering activities that develop a conceptual model and software-engineering activities that assess the requirements for integration. To develop an implementation design, the knowledge engineers must merge the requirements of the conceptual model with the constraints of the operating environment and the need for integration.

A given conceptual model can produce very different implementation designs for different expert-system shells.

- Some shells provide formalisms for the explicit representation of strategic knowledge (for example, *methods, procedures, control blocks,* or *rules*). In other shells, strategic knowledge will be implicit in the ordering of rules in the knowledge base or of clauses within the conditions of rules.

- A unit of judgmental knowledge may be represented in one shell as a *rule* or a *formula*. In some shells, judgmental knowledge can be implicit in a hierarchical relationship that will be used by the inference engine's built-in inheritance mechanism.

- A fact about a case may be represented in one shell as the *value* of an *expression*. In another shell, the same fact may be represented as the *value* of an *attribute* of an *object*. In yet a third shell, the fact may be represented as the *contents* of a *slot* of a *frame*.

To develop an implementation design, the knowledge engineers must understand the built-in control and inference mechanisms of the chosen shell. They must understand how the system's inference engine will *use* the knowledge in its knowledge base. For example, most shells support some form of *rule* to represent judgmental knowledge. But different inference engines use rules in different ways.

- Some inference engines try rules in a fixed order. Others try rules in different orders in different cases.

- Some inference engines check the individual clauses in the condition of a rule in a fixed order. Others try the clauses in different orders in different cases.

- Some inference engines will try a given rule only once for any case. Others may try the same rule many times for a single case.

- Different inference engines have different termination criteria to control when they stop trying rules in a particular set.

You will be ready to develop the implementation design for your expert system after you develop a conceptual model, select an expert-system shell, and learn how the shell can represent knowledge and how its inference engine will use the knowledge. The process of developing an implementation design consists of the following steps.

1. Review the *content* of each element of knowledge in your conceptual model.

2. Identify all the shell's representation formalisms that could be used to represent this knowledge.

3. Review the *function* of this knowledge as indicated by your conceptual model. Consider all ways in which the expert system will use this knowledge.

4. Review how the shell's inference engine will use each of the representation formalisms you identified in 2.

5. Select the representation(s) that the inference engine can use to produce behavior consistent with the intended function of this knowledge.

    If the knowledge should be used in multiple ways, try to select a representation that will permit multiple uses. If your shell requires you to duplicate the knowledge in different representations to accomplish all the necessary functions, document any such duplicate representation. If you later need to modify the knowledge, your documentation will help to ensure that you update all duplicate representations.

    When you choose an implementation, *consider whether the knowledge will need to be kept up to date.* If so, select a representation that facilitates update. For example, the knowledge base of the toaster-repair advisor must incorporate information that appears in service bulletins. This information must be kept current as new bulletins are issued and old bulletins expire. Patricia Programmer will encode the information in a service bulletin using representations that can be added and removed without necessitating other modifications to the knowledge base.

When you choose an implementation, *consider the complete data-processing environment* in which your system will operate. You may find you can best implement certain desired functionality *outside the expert system*. For example, it may be most efficient to implement some calculations in a program that the expert system calls; it may be advantageous to store large tables of facts in a database rather than in the knowledge base of the expert system. (Databases are particularly appropriate for information that is expected to change over time.)

6. Update the *implementation status* fields in your intermediate representations to document how the knowledge will be implemented.

The more closely your implementation design reflects your conceptual model, the clearer your knowledge base will be. Knowledge represented *explicitly* is easier to understand than implicit knowledge that relies on a thorough understanding of the inference engine. For example, Patricia Programmer must implement an expert system that iterates through a list of possible causes of the toaster problem. Her knowledge base will be easy to understand if she can represent this strategic knowledge explicitly in a *rule, procedure,* or *method* that directs the system to perform the iteration. On the other hand, the knowledge base will be less clear if the iterative control is a *side effect* of the way in which the inference engine uses various entries in the knowledge base. When the capabilities of your chosen shell do not permit a straightforward encoding of your conceptual model, use careful naming conventions and document your knowledge base so that other knowledge engineers will understand what actions should result when the inference engine uses your knowledge base entries and why these actions are important.

10.5 Points to Remember

During the development phase of an expert-system project, the evolving conceptual model serves as a catalyst for knowledge acquisition. The intermediate representations of the conceptual model illustrate the knowledge engineers' understanding of the expert's knowledge. Knowledge engineers can use these representations as vehicles for com-

Table 10.6 Reviewing an Intermediate Representation

Do	Don't
Explain clearly what the representation shows and how it will be used.	Make the expert try to figure out how to interpret the representation.
Present the representation piece by piece. Make sure the expert understands each piece before you proceed with the next piece.	Imply that the expert should use the same organization that appears in the representation.
Encourage the expert to criticize.	Imply that the expert's knowledge is trivial or that his or her actions can be reduced to a straightforward algorithm.
Make sure the expert is comfortable with the form of the representation before you start to discuss its content.	
Work with the expert to develop a representation the expert finds natural.	Insist on communicating via an intermediate representation if the expert does not like to work with intermediate representations.

munication with the project expert. Table 10.6 presents guidelines for reviewing an intermediate representation with an expert.

The conceptual model can focus interviews through which knowledge engineers ensure that they have obtained a complete and consistent understanding of the expert's knowledge. As the expert and the knowledge engineers review the conceptual model together, they refine and correct the knowledge engineers' understanding of the knowledge the expert system will use to perform its task.

A conceptual model is critical for system development as well as for knowledge acquisition. When the knowledge engineers have obtained the detailed information that will enable them to implement the expert system, they use their conceptual model to guide implementation.

- The knowledge engineers analyze the conceptual model to identify the system's requirements for representation, inference, and control.

- They use these requirements to guide their selection (or implementation) of an expert-system shell that provides the necessary capabilities.

- They use the conceptual model as a specification to guide implementation. They design a knowledge base that the shell's inference engine can use to achieve the behavior described in the conceptual model.

Chapter 11

Reviewing the Performance of the Expert System

Patricia Programmer and Howard Hacker are in the implementation step of their first cycle of development. They have obtained and have analyzed Frank Fixit's knowledge about the repair of color problems in simple two-slice toasters. They have created a conceptual model of the toaster-repair advisor and have used this model to guide their selection of an expert-system shell and their implementation of the knowledge base. They have just built a prototype toaster-repair advisor and have run the system on a few cases from their case library. Howard tells Patricia, "I'm thrilled to see our system in action, and I'm eager to show it to Frank. But do you think he'll like it? It can only handle one or two cases now, and the user interface is very rough. Should we let him see it now or wait until it's more polished?" Patricia responds that they should demonstrate the system in its current state. Frank's feedback on the demonstration will provide them with valuable information on what improvements are necessary.

When an expert system is implemented, a new knowledge-acquisition activity becomes available to the knowledge engineers: a **review of the expert system** itself. In a review, one or more **evaluators** assess the system's performance of its task. In many reviews, the project expert is an evaluator. Other typical evaluators are members of management, potential users of the expert system, and experts who are not associated with the project. Often a review reveals minor problems with the system that the project team did not anticipate. A review also may uncover more serious problems if it tests aspects of the task that were not discussed thoroughly in earlier knowledge-acquisition sessions.

In this chapter, we look at reviews from two perspectives: the *form* in which the evaluator reviews the expert system and the aspect of the system's performance that is the *focus* of the review. We consider two different forms of review.

1. In a *demonstration* review, the expert (or other evaluator) reviews the system while it performs its task (Section 11.1).

2. In a *typescript* review, the evaluator reviews a written record of the system's past performance of the task (Section 11.2).

Regardless of the form of a review, the review can focus on one or both of two different aspects of the system's performance (Figure 11.1).

1. A review of the *results* evaluates the correctness of the expert system's problem-solving behavior (Section 11.3).

2. For an interactive expert system, a review of the *interaction* evaluates the manner in which the system interacts with its user (Section 11.4).

Finally we consider the role of reviews within the life cycle of the expert system. The review of an expert system should be an on-going process. As additions and modifications are made to the system, the knowledge engineers should ensure that these changes do not degrade those aspects of the system's performance that have already been evaluated. Early in the development phase, therefore, the knowledge engineers should prepare for *recurrent testing* of the expert system's performance (Section 11.5).

11.1 Demonstrating the Expert System

The first demonstration of an expert system to the project expert is an exciting occasion for the knowledge engineers and the expert alike. This demonstration represents a turning point for many projects. For the first time, the expert gains a concrete grasp of the project's aim. Many experts are stimulated when they see their own knowledge made operational; their enthusiasm for the project increases as they imagine how the initial prototype will be transformed into the finished product. From this point forward, the evolving system becomes the expert's tangible measure of progress.

Figure 11.1 Focus for the review of an expert system. A review of an expert system can focus on the *results* that the system produces (a). For the toaster-repair advisor, a review of results would assess whether the system correctly identifies the cause of the toaster malfunctions, recommends an appropriate repair, updates the toaster-part database, and prepares a customer bill. If the expert system is interactive, a second focus for review is possible: the *interaction* between the expert system and its user(s). For the toaster-repair advisor, a review of interaction would evaluate the ease and clarity of the interaction through which the system requests data from the repair person and presents its results.

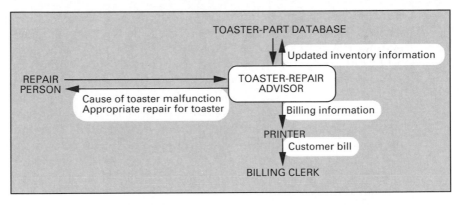

(a)

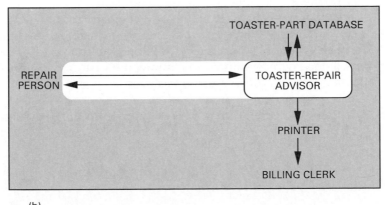

(b)

Legend:
☐ aspects of performance that are the focus of the review
▨ aspects of performance that are ignored in the review

An evaluation of the system's performance is an evaluation of the knowledge engineer's understanding of the expert's knowledge. The expert's evaluation of the system therefore provides the ultimate test of knowledge acquisition. As Frank Fixit watches the first demonstration of the toaster-repair advisor, Patricia Programmer and Howard Hacker wait anxiously for the answer to the pivotal question: *Did we understand Frank well enough to implement his problem-solving process correctly?*

11.1.1 Introducing a Demonstration

As a knowledge-acquisition activity, a demonstration provides a means by which knowledge engineers can fine tune the knowledge they have acquired. A demonstration is a vehicle for learning what corrections, additions, and refinements should be made to the existing system. To ensure that a demonstration will be productive, knowledge engineers should *introduce the demonstration carefully*. In any review (as Figure 11.1 illustrates), the evaluator should *focus on certain aspects of the system's performance* and ignore other aspects. This fact presents a major challenge for the knowledge engineers. If a demonstration is not introduced properly, the evaluator may focus on the wrong aspects of performance. As a result, the evaluator may fail to provide the information the knowledge engineers seek. In short, a poor introduction can result in a wasted interview session, leading to frustration for both the knowledge engineers and the evaluator. A good introduction is especially important early in the project when the knowledge engineers have implemented only part of the system's intended functionality. Many an expert has become disillusioned with a project because the knowledge engineers failed to explain the system's limitations.

When you introduce a demonstration:

- Explain what the evaluator can expect from the demonstration; describe current limitations to the system's knowledge, integration, interface, and efficiency.

- Describe the aspects of the system's performance that you would like the evaluator to assess.

11.1.2 Presenting a Demonstration

In a successful demonstration, the knowledge engineers *explain* clearly what they are demonstrating. The evaluator should understand throughout the demonstration what the expert system is doing. More complete explanations are necessary for an evaluator who is not familiar with the computer equipment you use; more detailed explanations are necessary for the first demonstration to a particular evaluator.

The first demonstration to the project expert is particularly important. This demonstration can serve to teach the expert how to use the expert system. Experts often enjoy being able to test the system by themselves. In many projects, the expert's use of the system is a boon to knowledge acquisition. For example, the expert's independent tests may uncover situations the project team had overlooked. After such tests, it is common for the expert to arrive at knowledge-acquisition sessions with a list of necessary modifications and additions to the knowledge base.

During a demonstration:

- Tell the evaluator where to look and what to expect. For example, explain where on the screen the system will display prompts for input, recommendations, help text, explanations, and so on.

- Describe what the expert system is doing whenever its actions are not obvious.

- If you expect the final version of the system to behave differently from the current implementation, point out these differences to the evaluator.

- If you interact with the system, explain what you are doing.

Use your tone of voice to guide the evaluator during a demonstration. Act less interested in those details you want the evaluator to ignore; speak with excitement about those details you want to emphasize. When the system exhibits behavior on which you would like the evaluator's comments, explain that you have reached an important point in the demonstration, and ask the questions you have prepared. Make sure that your manner conveys your openness to criticisms and suggestions.

In your first demonstration to the project expert, encourage the expert to run the system (but do not *insist* if the expert is reluctant). When the expert is ready to use the system, provide whatever instruction is necessary. You will need to provide more assistance if your system is interactive or if the expert has had limited experience with computers. Explain clearly how to use the keyboard, mouse, or other input devices and how to interpret and respond to the system's output.

Dialog 11.1 illustrates how Patricia Programmer and Howard Hacker first demonstrated the toaster-repair advisor for Frank Fixit.

Dialog 11.1 Demonstrating an Expert System

Setting

Patricia Programmer, Howard Hacker, and Frank Fixit are seated at the table in their meeting room. On a small table in the corner of the room is a personal computer with a video display screen, a keyboard, and a mouse.

Dialog

Patricia: Frank, we're ready to show you our initial implementation of the toaster-repair advisor.

Frank: Great! I've been looking forward to seeing what you two have been working on.

Patricia: The system is not complete, so before we start, I'd like to explain what it can do. We've implemented the portion of the knowledge base that deals with the customer complaint *toast_always_burns*. If you enter any other complaint, it won't be able to help you. We plan to add the rest of the knowledge about color problems this week.

Frank: That's fine.

Patricia: I have to warn you that the interaction with the system is going to look very rough. We plan to develop a user-interface that will be easy for the repair staff to use. But so far, Howard has implemented just enough to let us test the system. So the user will have to do more typing than we'd like, the questions probably won't be phrased well, and the displays won't be pretty.

Frank: I understand.

Patricia: The other thing you'll notice is that we haven't hooked up to the toaster-part database. The system will ask for information it should be able to find in the database. You'll see some questions that start with the word *Database* in parentheses. That's our way of indicating that the system really should look in the database instead of asking the question.

Frank: OK.

Patricia: Well let's get started!

Patricia, Frank, and Howard walk to the personal computer. Howard sits in front of computer and types the commands to start the expert system. Patricia and Frank pull chairs over and sit down where they can see the screen.

Frank, I'd like you to try to overlook the rough interface and to concentrate on whether the system asks the right questions, makes the right decisions, and prints the right advice.

Frank: OK.

Patricia: But please feel free to make *any* suggestions that come to mind. If you have ideas about the interface, please give them to us. We need you to tell us what the expert system should do and how you'd like it to behave. At this point, we can change anything. When you see something you don't like, let us know. We *want* your criticisms. Of course, we'd also like to hear compliments if you have any!

Frank, Howard, and Patricia laugh.

Would you like to run the system?

Frank: No. Let me watch.

Patricia: All right. Howard, why don't you begin? I'll write down all Frank's suggestions. Frank, you can interrupt with questions or comments at any time. The purpose of this demo is for us to get your reactions to the system so don't hold anything back.

Frank: OK, but remember that you asked for it!

Howard points to the screen as he describes the display.

Howard: I've just started the system. As you can see, this first form has three questions for me to fill in: the toaster make, the model number, and the customer complaints. Let me explain how I enter the answers.

Howard points to the mouse.

This device is called a *mouse;* I can use it to point to different locations on the screen. Watch the arrow on the screen; as I move the mouse, the arrow moves. Now I place the arrow over *Toaster Manufacturer,* and I click the mouse button. You see the list of manufacturers?

Frank nods.

We call the list a *menu.* I can use the mouse to position the arrow over the answer I want. Now I'll click the button on the mouse. You see how the answer gets filled into the form?

Frank: So you don't have to type the answer. That's great!

Howard: Glad you like it. I don't have menus for all the questions yet. We still have to type some of the answers. For example, I'll type in the model number. Next we have the customer complaints. As you can see, all the possible complaints are listed on the screen. I can click any of these complaints with the mouse. When I do, an *X* appears in front of the complaint. If the customer checked several complaints on the repair slip, I would click on all of those complaints.

Frank: I see. What happens if you make a mistake?

Howard: Good question. If I chose the wrong complaint, I just click that complaint again and the *X* disappears.

Howard demonstrates how to correct mistakes. Frank nods. Then Howard points to the bottom of the screen.

You should watch this lower section of the display. That's where the system will print its instructions and recommendations.

Howard enters the customer complaints as Patricia and Frank watch.

Do you recognize this case, Frank?

Frank: Yes, it's the toaster I showed you in the service department.

Frank reads the text displayed on the computer screen.

It's asking you to toast a slice of bread on light—good. So now it asks about the results—you tell it that the toast burned—OK.

Howard: Now the system is asking me to adjust the thermostat to decrease the toasting time. I plan to add a button—that's a little square on the screen that you can click with the mouse. The label on the button will say *Describe Procedure*. Suppose I don't know how to adjust the thermostat. If the button were implemented, I could just click it, and the system would describe the procedure for me.

Frank: That sounds good. Now it wants to know whether you fixed the problem. Let me watch again how you use the mouse.

Howard slowly moves the mouse so that the arrow is over the answer "no" on the screen, then he clicks the mouse button.

Thanks. I see how it works.

Howard: Now it's asking me what thermostat part numbers can be used in this model toaster. You see the label *Database* in this question?

Frank nods.

The system shouldn't ask this question. It should look up the part numbers in the database. I don't know the right answer, so I'll just make up some numbers.

Frank *(chuckling):* I'll pretend I didn't see that question.

Howard points to the screen.

Howard: Now the system is asking me to get a replacement thermostat; the instructions tell me what part numbers to look for. It uses the same part numbers I just typed in. Of course, it should use part numbers from the database.

Frank reads the text that is displayed on the computer screen.

Frank: So it wants you to replace and calibrate the thermostat, then test whether that fixed the problem—good. You enter *yes*, so we're done. Wait a minute! What's this other question? Why is it asking for the part number of the replacement thermostat?

Howard: The system doesn't use this information now. Eventually we'll use the answer to update the inventory information in the toaster-part database and to generate a customer bill.

Frank: I see. Well, it looks pretty good! Can I drive now?

Patricia: Sure!

Howard and Frank change places.

Howard: To start the system, just type T-R-A, then press the key labeled *Return*.

Frank types the command.

Frank: OK. What does T-R-A mean?

Howard: That's just the name I gave the program. It stands for *Toaster-Repair Advisor.*

> *Frank moves the mouse and watches the arrow move on the screen.*

Frank: I think I get the hang of this. So now I can just enter the make and model?

Howard: That's right.

Discussion

Early demonstrations present three challenges for the knowledge engineers. Patricia Programmer must *set realistic expectations* for Frank Fixit, *encourage him to be open with his comments and criticism,* and *focus his attention* on the aspects of system performance she wants him to evaluate. This dialog illustrates how Patricia meets these challenges.

1. Before this demonstration, Frank Fixit may have envisioned a near-perfect system that does everything Frank himself would do. Patricia Programmer carefully explains the system's current limitations so that Frank will not be disappointed by the demonstration. Patricia reassures Frank that, with his help, the toaster-repair advisor will evolve into the system he imagines.

2. Frank Fixit knows that Patricia Programmer and Howard Hacker have worked long and hard to prepare the system for this demonstration. When he sees the demonstration, he may be hesitant to express his true reactions for fear of hurting Patricia's and Howard's feelings. Patricia lets Frank know that she *expects, wants,* and *needs* his criticism.

3. Notice *how* Patricia asks Frank to focus his attention. On the one hand, she asks him to overlook the system's limitations and to concentrate his comments on those aspects of system performance on which she needs feedback. On the other hand, Patricia does not inhibit Frank from making suggestions about other aspects of the system.

We close this section with a word of caution. When an evaluator uncovers a fairly simple error during a demonstration, knowledge engineers often are tempted to correct the error immediately. Too frequently, knowledge engineers have wasted an evaluator's time in their attempt to demonstrate how quickly they can modify an expert system. Sometimes a modification takes longer than the knowledge engineers anticipate. And sometimes a quick modification introduces new problems. In general, it is better to *delay the modification until after the demonstration.* When the knowledge engineers are free from the pressures of the demonstration, they can review the problem carefully. Instead of making a quick local correction, they can review their conceptual model to identify ramifications of potential modifications. They can decide how to correct the error without introducing new problems.

We suggest that you make modifications during a demonstration *only* if all the following statements are true.

1. The change will make a major difference in the remainder of the demonstration.

2. The *evaluator* believes that the demonstration should not be continued without the modification.

3. You are certain that you can make the change in less than a minute.

4. You are certain that the change is isolated—that making the modification will not introduce unexpected behavior in other portions of the expert system.

11.1.3 Correcting Problems with the Presentation

If you follow the recommendations of Sections 11.1.1 and 11.1.2, you will avoid the majority of problems that can occur in expert-system demonstrations. Unfortunately, however, occasional problems are inevitable. In some demonstrations, for example, the evaluator concentrates on the wrong issues or is not able to see past current limitations of the system.

If you encounter problems, the most important rule is to remain calm. Do not communicate (verbally or nonverbally) frustration, irritation, or impatience with the evaluator.[1] Politely remind the evaluator of your objectives for the demonstration, and try to steer the conversation back to relevant topics.[2] If you are unable to lead the evaluator to provide the information you seek, end the demonstration early. Be sure to thank the evaluator for taking time to view the demonstration and for providing helpful suggestions (even if the suggestions were not what you wanted). If the evaluator was troubled by limitations of the system, apologize for scheduling a demonstration too soon. Tell the evaluator that you think a demonstration would be more effective later in the project when the system's development is more advanced.

You may find that demonstration reviews with a particular evaluator are not productive. If so, try to obtain the information you need with a typescript review; if all else fails, relay on comments from other evaluators.

---

1. Chapter 13 describes the importance of nonverbal communication and presents guidelines for interacting with an expert. These guidelines are equally relevant for interactions with any evaluator.

2. Chapter 17 describes how to redirect unproductive discussions.

11.2 Reviewing Typescripts

Demonstrations are not sufficient for assessing noninteractive expert systems. Consider, for example, a system that examines applications for life insurance and recommends whether to accept or to reject the applications. The system may obtain all the information about an applicant from a database; it may write its recommendations into the same database and may produce an on-line summary of its recommendations for later review by a senior underwriter. The evaluators of this system would not be able to judge its performance by observing a demonstration; they would need to review a written summary that shows what input the system used for each case and what recommendations it made.

Although demonstrations are an effective method of evaluating many interactive expert systems, they can be time consuming. A thorough evaluation of the system requires that its performance be tested on a wide range of cases. To streamline the review process, knowledge engineers can ask the evaluator to assess typescripts of the system's performance. A **typescript** is a written record of the expert system's performance of its task for a particular case. A typescript may be an actual log of the system's interactions or a summary of the system's performance prepared specifically for the purpose of review. A complete typescript shows:

- All input data the expert system used

- The source of each input

- All output the system produced

- The destination of each output

- The time sequence in which the input and output actions occurred

Many experts find it more convenient to review a typescript than to observe the performance of the expert system.

> When Frank Fixit reviews the toaster-repair advisor's results, he prefers to review typescripts of the system's performance on various cases. If Frank needs to compare input the system receives at the beginning of its interaction with the results it produces at the end, he can flip between pages of the typescript or can look at two pages side by side. If Frank Fixit needs to discuss a case with Barbara Burnt, he can easily take the typescript to Barbara's service bay. Frank does not need to ask Barbara to watch him interact with the system. He can schedule the discussion at a time convenient for Barbara regardless of the availability of the expert system. Similarly, if Frank needs to refer to documents in the service department library when he reviews a case, he can carry the typescript of the system's performance with him to the library.

11.2.1 Creating Typescripts

Some expert system shells provide a facility for logging interactions to a file, and some operating systems provide a facility for recording terminal interactions. If a project develops an interactive expert system with such a shell or such an operating system, the knowledge engineers can use these facilities to create typescript files. If no built-in logging facility is available or if the expert system is not interactive, the knowledge engineers may be able to design an expert system so that it can record its inputs and outputs to a file. For some reviews of an expert system's results, typescripts should include important intermediate conclusions. Some shells provide facilities that allow an expert system to display a trace of its conclusions. The use of such a trace facility with a built-in logging facility can produce typescripts that include intermediate conclusions. If knowledge engineers implement their own logging facility, they may choose to log critical intermediate conclusions as well as input and output.

> Patricia Programmer and Howard Hacker implement a *recording mode* for the toaster-repair advisor. When they run the system in recording mode, all keyboard inputs, text displays, and database transactions are written to a file (Figure 11.2). With each major addition to the system's scope, Patricia and Howard run the toaster-repair advisor in recording mode for several cases within the new scope addition. They then ask Frank Fixit to review the typescripts of those cases when his time permits.

In general, typescripts are most useful for reviews of an expert system's *results* rather than its *interaction*. For some expert systems, however, typescripts can be used to evaluate certain aspects of the user interface. For example, evaluators could be asked to review a typescript and to comment on the wording of the system's questions, recommendations, and so on. If the interface uses graphics or forms, the knowledge engineers could create a typescript that consists of screen images. They could ask the evaluator to comment on the layout and the organization of the screens and the clarity of diagrams and graphs.

11.2.2 Preparing for a Typescript Review

A typescript review is an effective method for evaluating the expert system's performance on a variety of cases. To ensure that you obtain the comments you want on all evaluation cases, create an *evaluation form*. The form should list each question, followed by sufficient space for the evaluator's answer. The questions you ask will depend on whether you are reviewing the expert system's results, its interaction, or both. (In Section 11.3, we shall see the questions that would appear on an evaluation form for a review of results.) When you have designed an

Figure 11.2 Typescript of an interaction with the toaster-repair advisor. When Patricia Programmer asks Frank Fixit to review this typescript, she explains that any text inside square brackets [ ] indicates an intermediate conclusion that was not displayed to the user. All other text in the typescript appeared on the computer screen during the interaction with the toaster-repair advisor. Underlined text in the typescript indicates user input; the remaining text was printed by the expert system.

Toaster Manufacturer: Toasts-Best   Model Number: TB10445

Customer complaints (check all that apply)

____ bread not toasted   ____ toast does not pop up

____ operating lever will not go down   ____ toast too dark

____ operating lever will not stay down   ____ toast too light

 X toast always burns   ____ toasts on one side only

Please set the color control on the lightest setting and toast one slice of bread, then answer the following questions.

Could you lower the operating lever?   yes

Did the operating lever stay down?   yes

Did the toast pop up?   yes

Were both sides of the bread toasted equally?   yes

What was the toast's color?   burnt

[conclusion: severe thermostat problem, toasting for too long a time]

Try to adjust the thermostat to shorten the toasting time.
(Make a large initial adjustment: two full turns counterclockwise.)

Were you able to adjust the toaster to correct the problem?   no

Please replace the thermostat. Use a new thermostat with any of the following part numbers:
    R71993
    R71994
    R71995
    R71998
Calibrate the new thermostat.

Does the toaster function correctly with the new thermostat?   yes

Please enter the part number of the replacement thermostat.   R71995 evaluation form, assemble the evaluation materials: the typescripts you want the evaluator to assess and a copy of the evaluation form for each typescript.

If you plan to ask an evaluator to review several typescripts, find out whether the evaluator would prefer to review the typescripts all at once or one at a time. Develop a review schedule with the evaluator. The schedule should begin with a meeting at which you deliver and explain the evaluation materials. You may also want to schedule a meeting to discuss the results of the review.

11.2.3 Conducting a Typescript Review

Initiate a review of typescripts in a brief meeting with the evaluator. Give the evaluator the typescripts and the evaluation forms you have prepared. Read through one typescript with the evaluator and explain how the typescript reflects the expert system's performance. Encourage the evaluator to question you about the content of the typescript, and make sure that the evaluator understands how to interpret the information it presents. Next read through the evaluation form together. Make sure that the evaluator understands what information you expect in the answer to each question. Finally verify that your planned review schedule is still agreeable to the evaluator. If not, agree on a time when the evaluator will return the completed review materials.

After the initial meeting, the evaluator should be able to conduct the review independently. Be prepared, however, to answer any questions that may come up. Let the evaluator know how to contact you (or another project member) during the evaluation period. Plan to keep in touch with the evaluator during a long evaluation period. For example, if you have asked an evaluator to review more than two or three typescripts or if the evaluator will not be able to complete the review within two weeks, check occasionally on the progress of the evaluation.

> Patricia Programmer gives Frank Fixit 20 typescripts to review. He says he should be able to finish the review within four weeks. After the end of the second week, Patricia telephones Frank. She asks him whether he has encountered any questions about the typescripts. She asks whether Frank has been able to find enough time for the review or whether he thinks he will need more than two weeks to complete the review. In her telephone conversation, Patricia is able to check on Frank's progress and to remind him that she needs the evaluation results. She phrases her inquiries to emphasize her concern for *Frank's* schedule. In this way, Patricia avoids giving the impression that she is nagging Frank to complete his review.

11.3 Reviewing an Expert System's Results

A review of the expert system's results evaluates whether the expert system performs its task correctly. Throughout the development phase of a project, the knowledge engineers can test the system on the cases in their case library and can compare the systems results to the expected results shown in the performance outlines.[3] Periodically throughout the development phase, it is a good idea for the project expert to evaluate the expert system's results on additional cases. These reviews allow the project team to discover whether they have obtained a *sufficiently general definition* of the system's task as well as a *sufficiently detailed understanding* of the expert's problem-solving behavior. At the end of the development phase, reviews should verify that the system behaves correctly for all cases discussed during development. In many projects, the user group or the funding agency will require a more formal evaluation of the system before it is deployed. A formal evaluation may be restricted to cases discussed during system development or may include additional cases.

In a review of the expert system's results, the knowledge engineers should ask the evaluator to answer the following questions.

- Does the system perform the correct sequence of actions?

- Does the system make correct decisions?

- Does the system gather appropriate data?

- Does the system produce the correct output results?

- Are all the system's actions and decisions *necessary* to its task?

These questions can be customized for the particular application. For example, Figure 11.3 shows the questions Patricia Programmer will ask evaluators who review the toaster-repair advisor's results.

When a review identifies a problem in the expert system's performance, knowledge engineers must locate the source of the problem. They should ask:

- Is knowledge missing from the knowledge base?

- Is some entry in the knowledge base incorrect?

- Did the knowledge engineers misunderstand how the inference engine would use a certain knowledge-base entry?

---

3. Case libraries and performance outlines are described in Section 8.2.

SELECTION OF AN INITIAL TEST PROCEDURE

1. Would you have tested the toaster in the same manner as the system recommended?
   If not, please answer questions a, b, and c.

   a. How would you have tested the toaster?

   b. Do you consider the system's test procedure an acceptable alternative to your own?
      If not, please explain why not.

   c. Why do you prefer your test procedure?

INTERPRETATION OF THE TEST RESULTS

2. Did the system ask any unnecessary questions about the results of the initial test?
   If so, which questions do you consider unnecessary and why?

3. Did the system's questions provide all the necessary information for you to assess the test results?
   If not, what additional questions would you have asked?

4. Did the system interpret the test results correctly to identify the toaster problem?
   If not, what problem(s) did the test results suggest to you and why?

SELECTION OF THE REPAIR PROCEDURES

5. Would you have performed the sequence of repair procedures the system recommended?
   If not, please answer questions a, b, and c.

   a. Were any of the repair procedures unnecessary?
      If so, which procedures do you consider unnecessary and why?

   b. Would you have performed additional procedures?
      If so, what additional procedures would you have performed and why?

   c. Would you have performed the repair procedures in a different order?
      List the repair procedures in the order in which you would have tried them.
      Explain why you prefer this order.

The final step in the review process is to modify the expert system as necessary to correct the problems. When the system has been modified, it should be tested to verify that the problems were fixed.

11.4 Reviewing Interactions with an Expert System

Knowledge engineers need to ensure that the user interface of an interactive expert system provides effective communication between the user and the system. Knowledge engineers should ask the expert and a small number of potential users of the system to observe demonstrations, to interact with the expert system, and to evaluate its interface. It is important to ask *users* to review interactions because the expert may not have an accurate model of the needs of users. The expert may have misconceptions about what the users know, what they need the expert system to explain, or how they will respond to the system's presentation of its questions and recommendations.

A review of an expert system's interaction should supply answers to the following questions.

- Does the system perform the appropriate sequence of input-output activities? Are questions asked in a logical order? Are instructions provided when they are needed?

- Are questions, explanations, instructions, and recommendations phrased clearly? Do they provide the appropriate level of detail?

- Are text and diagrams arranged on the screen in a layout that is understandable and helpful to the user?

- Are graphs, diagrams, and other illustrations clearly drawn and labeled so that users can understand them? Would additional illustrations be helpful?

- Is interaction with the system self-explanatory? Is on-line help adequate?

In Dialog 11.2, Patricia Programmer and Howard Hacker obtain valuable comments about the interface of the toaster-repair advisor.

Dialog 11.2 Evaluating the User Interface of an Expert System

Setting

The toaster-repair advisor project is approaching the end of the implementation step in the first cycle of development. The system's knowledge base now covers the full range of color problems in two-slice toasters. The system is able to retrieve information from the toaster-part database. An initial version of the user interface is fully functional. The time has come to show the interface to members of the repair staff.

A personal computer has been installed in Frank Fixit's service bay so that he can test the toaster-repair advisor. Frank has asked his colleague, Jeff Johnson, to help with the evaluation of the expert system. Frank has explained to Jeff that his suggestions will enable the knowledge engineers to refine the interface before they make the system available for regular use. The current dialog takes place in Frank's service bay; Jeff and Frank are meeting with Patricia Programmer and Howard Hacker. Jeff has brought two toasters with color problems. Patricia starts the meeting with an explanation of the purpose of the review. She asks Jeff to provide any comments and criticisms that might help them to transform the toaster-repair advisor into a tool that Jeff would like to use. Patricia also asks Frank to make any suggestions that occur to him. Next Howard describes the layout of the screen and shows Jeff how to use the keyboard and the mouse.

As we join the dialog, Jeff is seated in front of the personal computer. Frank is seated next to him. Patricia and Howard are seated behind Jeff and Frank where they can observe and take notes.

Dialog

Jeff: Should I start now?

Patricia: Yes. Go ahead and see how the system helps you to repair one of the toasters you brought. As you work with the system, please give us all your reactions to it. Let us know what you like and what you don't like.

Jeff studies the screen.

Jeff: Well, it looks OK so far. I need to enter the make, the model, and the customer complaints.

Jeff removes the repair slip from one of his toasters. He reads the repair slip and enters the make and model number. He then glances back and forth between the screen and the repair slip.

I can't find the complaint I want to check.

Howard: They're in alphabetical order.

Jeff: OK. I see it now. You know, it would be a lot easier if you put the complaints in the same order as the list on the repair slip. I know that *toast too light* is in the middle of the list on the repair slip so that's where I looked on the screen.

Howard: OK. That should be easy enough. Can I look at the repair slip a minute?

Jeff: Sure.

Jeff hands Howard the repair slip. Howard looks at the repair slip, then at the screen.

Howard: Would you like it better if I moved the fields for make and model so that the layout is similar to the repair slip?

Jeff: Well, it's fine like you have it. But I guess it would be a good idea to make the screen look as much like the repair slip as you can.

Frank: I agree.

Jeff continues with the interaction without comment until the system instructs him to perform a repair procedure. Jeff reads the text displayed on the screen.

Jeff: These instructions are pretty clear, but it took me a while to read them. If you put up a schematic, it would be a lot quicker for me to see what the computer wants me to do.

Frank *(looking at the screen):* I didn't think to suggest a diagram here, but Jeff is right. Tell you what—after this meeting, Jeff and I will discuss the issue. By tomorrow or the next day, I'll give you a diagram and some text to put in place of these instructions.

Patricia: That would be great!

Frank: I had an idea while I was watching Jeff use the system. I think it would be nice for the system to explain what it's considering as it goes along. That way, new staff members could learn from it.

Patricia: Jeff, what do you think of Frank's idea?

Jeff: I don't know—I'm not sure what kind of explanation Frank wants.

Frank: Well, for example, after you entered the results of your initial test, the system could have told you that the test results indicate a thermostat problem.

Jeff: I like Frank's idea. When I saw the message to adjust the thermostat, I said to myself, "OK, it knows that I've got a thermostat problem." I felt a little left out of the repair process because I had to figure out for myself the reason for the repair procedure. I'd like it better if the computer would tell me *why* it's asking me to do a particular procedure. And like Frank said, these explanations would be especially good for some of our less experienced people.

Patricia: Frank, should we have the system print out *all* its conclusions?

Frank: I'm not sure.

Patricia: I'll make a list of the conclusions we don't currently display. You can go over the list and let me know which ones you'd like us to display and how we should word the messages. Also, I'd like you to think about *where* you'd like us to display this information. We'll need the answers to a few questions. Should we write these messages in the same area where we display instructions? Or would you prefer that we use a special area of the screen for conclusions? Should we try to keep these messages visible throughout the interaction, or should they disappear after the user responds to the instructions?

Frank: OK. When you get me the list of conclusions, I'll give the matter some thought. Jeff, would you like to help Patricia and me decide what to do about these explanations?

Jeff: Sure, I'd be happy to.

⋮

[Jeff has just finished using the toaster-repair advisor to help him repair the second toaster he brought to the meeting.]

Jeff: Can I run it again and just make up some answers?

Patricia: Of course! Do whatever you want. If you'd like, see if you can break the system. We need to exercise the system thoroughly so we can fix as many problems as much as possible before we put it into use.

Jeff: How did you know I wanted to see if I could break it?

They all laugh.

OK. Here goes.

Jeff enters the make, model number, and customer complaints. The system asks him to perform an initial test procedure, then prompts him for the results. Jeff enters the test results and reads the text displayed on the screen.

So *now* it tells me it can't help with a four-slice toaster! Why didn't it tell me that right away?

Patricia: Oops! We can fix that. If you're interested, I can explain what we did wrong.

Jeff: Yes, I'd like to hear how it works. I thought I was going to break the program by giving it a four-slice toaster. It did better than I expected.

Patricia: Well, we have the system figure out whether the toaster problem is something it can handle. I guess Frank explained that it's currently limited to color problems with simple two-slice toasters.

Jeff nods.

The system can't tell whether the toaster has a *color problem* until after you perform the initial test. I guess that's why we decided to wait until the system gets the test results before it decides whether it can help with the problem. What we *should* do is to replace that one decision with two separate decisions. First, the system should decide whether it can handle this particular *toaster*. As you pointed out, it can make that decision as soon as you enter the make and model. Second, the system should decide whether it can handle the *problem* with the toaster. It can make this decision when you enter the results of the initial test.

Discussion

It is important to involve potential users of an expert system in the design and evaluation of the system's interface. Jeff identified a problem with the layout of the first form the toaster-repair advisor displays. None of the members of the project team noticed a problem with this form because they do not look at repair slips on a daily basis. Even Frank, who frequently looks at repair slips, had no problem using the form. Frank first saw the form's layout before the interface was fully developed. At that time, he was asked to ignore the interface. By the time the knowledge engineers asked Frank to comment on the interface, he had learned the layout of the form, and he found it easy to use.

A project expert's opinions do not always reflect the preferences of the system's intended users. When Frank suggests adding more explanations to the output, notice that Patricia asks what *Jeff* thinks about Frank's suggestion. If Jeff had answered that explanations would be superfluous or annoying, Patricia would have decided not to act on Frank's recommendation.

As a result of this dialog, the project team will design two modifications to the interface of the toaster-repair advisor. First, the system will use a diagram in place of a lengthy text instruction. Second, the system will display more of its conclusions to the user. For both of these modifications, *Jeff* will be involved in deciding what exact changes should be made.

Although the focus of this review is to obtain comments about the system's interface, notice that Patricia also learns how the system's *knowledge* should be modified. Patricia will add a new characteristic to the system: *toaster_style_within_scope?* The system will infer this characteristic as soon as the user has entered the toaster make and model. If the toaster is outside the current scope, the system will terminate the interaction with an informative message. Patricia will modify the system to infer the current characteristic, *problem_within_scope?* on the basis of *toaster_problem* but not on the basis of *toaster_make* and *toaster_model*.

11.5 Preparing for Recurrent Testing of an Expert System

When knowledge engineers test an expert system, they not only validate the system's performance, they also identify topics for future knowledge acquisition sessions. When the system does not perform as expected, the knowledge engineers often discover that they did not understand the expert correctly or that the expert omitted important details from earlier interviews. Recurrent testing leads to refinement of the knowledge engineer's understanding of the expert's knowledge as well as improvement in the system's performance.

As we discussed in Chapter 1, the development of an expert system typically consists of a cyclic repetition of steps; in each cycle, the scope of the expert system is extended. The extensions to an expert system in different cycles are *not always independent* of one another. For example, in their second cycle of development, Patricia Programmer and Howard Hacker will extend the toaster-repair advisor to handle color problems in four-slice toasters. As they do so, they may make minor modifications to portions of the knowledge base that concern two-slice toasters. Alternatively, some of their additions may affect the system's performance on two-slice toasters in ways that Patricia and Howard do not anticipate. At the end of the cycle, a review of the system's performance for color problems in *four-slice toasters* will not be sufficient. Patricia and Howard must also *retest* performance on color problems in two-slice toasters. They must check whether their modifications to the system cause unexpected behavior when the system is tested on earlier cases. If so, Patricia and Howard must identify and correct these problems before they proceed with development.

A project case library (Section 8.2) can play an important role in the recurrent testing of an expert system. As the project progresses, the project team members should discuss new cases; the case library should grow to contain a representative cross section of the situations in which the expert system should be able to perform its task. Any new case that is used in a review of the system's results should be added to the case library. At the end of each cycle of development, the knowledge engineers should test the expert system on *the entire collection of cases in the library.*

Although thorough periodic testing is necessary, it can be a very time-consuming activity. The knowledge engineers should try to automate or streamline the test process. A case library can be adapted to form a *suite of test cases* that is used by an automated testing facility. Some expert system shells provide testing facilities that allow an expert system to save user input to a case file and to rerun the case by reading input from the saved case file. Some operating systems provide facilities for comparing files; these facilities can be used to find differences between a saved typescript that has been certified "correct" and a new typescript from a recent test run. If such built-in facilities are not available, the knowledge engineers may be able to implement extensions to the expert system to speed the testing process.

> Patricia Programmer and Howard Hacker implement a *testing mode* for the toaster-repair advisor that allows them to run tests without terminal interaction. In testing mode, the system reads inputs from a file instead of from the terminal. It creates a typescript file but does not display any information to the computer screen. Whenever Frank Fixit reviews the system's performance on a new case, Patricia and Howard add that case to their test suite. They create an *input file* for the case and a *baseline typescript file* that shows the system's correct performance. They also add the case to their case library. They create a cover sheet for the case report and use the baseline typescript in place of a performance outline (see Section 8.2.2).
>
> Howard writes a program to automate the test procedure. This test program runs the toaster-repair advisor in testing mode on each case in the test suite. The program then uses an operating-system utility to create files that record the differences between the baseline typescripts and the new typescripts produced by the test run.
>
> When the time comes to test a new release of the toaster-repair advisor, Howard runs the test program overnight. The next morning, he reviews the difference files; if the test found discrepancies between the system's current performance and its correct performance, Patricia and Howard investigate these discrepancies. If a discrepancy indicates an *improvement* in the system's performance, Howard updates the baseline typescript file. If a discrepancy indicates a *problem* with current performance, Patricia and Howard investigate and correct the problem.

When they have corrected all problems, Howard reruns the test program to ensure that their changes did not introduce new problems.

11.6 Points to Remember

After the initial implementation of an expert system, the review of the system's performance becomes an important knowledge-acquisition activity. Reviews can pinpoint topics for future interviews. The project expert or another evaluator can review either a *demonstration* of the system or a *typescript* that records the system's performance (Table 11.1).

A review of the expert system can focus on the *results* the system produces or on the *manner in which the system interacts* with its user (Table 11.2). Either typescripts or demonstrations can be used to evaluate the results of an expert system or its manner of interaction. Demonstrations, however, are generally more effective for obtaining

---

Table 11.1 Guidelines for Conducting a Review of an Expert System

Form of Review	Review Procedure
Demonstration	Explain what the evaluator should expect from the demonstration. Set realistic expectations; describe any current limitations to the system's knowledge, interface, integration, and efficiency.
	Encourage the evaluator to provide criticisms and suggestions at any time during the demonstration.
	Focus the evaluator's attention on the aspects of performance you would like appraised.
	During the demonstration, make sure the evaluator understands all the system's actions and all your actions.
	Record all comments the evaluator makes during the demonstration.
Typescript	Prepare the typescripts.
	Prepare an evaluation form with the questions you would like the evaluator to answer.
	Review a typescript with the evaluator. Make sure the evaluator understands how the typescript reflects the behavior of the expert system.
	Review the evaluation form with the evaluator. Make sure the evaluator understands the questions on the form.
	Schedule a completion time for the evaluation.
	Check on the evaluator's progress during the evaluation.

Table 11.2 Information to Obtain from a Review of an Expert System

Focus of Review	Questions to Answer
Results the expert system produces	Does the system perform the correct sequence of actions? Does it make correct decisions? Does it gather appropriate data? Does it produce the correct results? Are all its actions and decisions necessary to the performance of its task?
Interaction between the system and its user	Does the system perform the appropriate sequence of input–output activities? Are questions asked in a logical order? Are instructions provided when they are needed? Are questions, explanations, instructions, and recommendations phrased clearly? Do they provide the appropriate level of detail? Are graphs, diagrams, and other illustrations clearly drawn and labeled so users can understand them? Is interaction with the system self-explanatory? Is on-line help adequate?

comments on the form of the interaction whereas typescript reviews are more effective for obtaining comments on the system's results.

An evolving expert system should be tested periodically to ensure that enhancements to the system do not introduce unanticipated problems. A project's case library can be adapted into a suite of test cases that form the foundation for a program of regular testing. The project team can develop an automated testing procedure and can use this procedure to evaluate the expert system against the test suite whenever major modifications are made to the expert system. If this evaluation uncovers performance problems, the knowledge engineers can work with the project expert to resolve these problems before they continue with further development of the system.

Part 2

Interviewing Activities

We now shift our attention from knowledge engineering to interviewing. Part 1 described *what* information knowledge engineers need to obtain; we now focus on *how* the knowledge engineers conduct the dialogs through which they obtain information from an expert. In Part 2, we present the general interviewing techniques that are useful through both initial inquiry and detailed investigation. In Part 1, we described the goals of the two stages of knowledge acquisition: initial inquiry and detailed investigation. Although the different goals of the two stages dictate different contents for interviews, the techniques we present in this part are equally helpful in both stages. To emphasize this point, the chapters in Part 2 include examples from both stages of knowledge acquisition.

In Part 2, we look at the interviewing activities within the toaster-repair advisor project. We go back to the beginning of the project and trace the improvement of Howard Hacker's interviewing skills as the project progresses. Each chapter introduces a set of skills that Howard must master before he can play a more active role in the knowledge-acquisition interviews.

- Chapter 12 looks at knowledge acquisition as an interviewing endeavor. It defines what we mean by an interview, explains how knowledge acquisition is unique among interviewing endeavors, and identifies goals for knowledge acquisition that will increase the productivity of interviews.

- Chapter 13 explains how to interact with the expert and with other knowledge engineers during an interview.

- Chapter 14 explains how to plan an interview and prepare the participants.

- Chapter 15 describes the transfer of information in an interview. It explains how to structure an interview to make the communication most productive and how to record information during an interview.

- Chapter 16 focuses on the interview dialog. It introduces techniques for asking questions and for understanding and responding to the expert's answers.

- Chapter 17 explains how to keep the discussions in an interview focused on the constructive topics.

As you read the dialogs in this part, concentrate on the *form* of the discussions. Observe how the knowledge engineers *interact with the experts*, how they *phrase questions*, how they *respond to the expert's answers*, and how they *guide the flow of the discussions*.

An interview is a form of conversation; because conversations are a common element of the human experience, we expect that readers will find that many of the interviewing guidelines in Part 2 are obvious. We have included a discussion of these guidelines precisely because they *are* obvious. In our experience, novice knowledge engineers are often overwhelmed by the challenge of leading experts to articulate their knowledge. When novices concentrate their efforts on meeting this challenge, they often overlook the more obvious aspects of interpersonal interactions. In short, the behavior that seems to be common sense when one *reads about* an interview is not necessarily the behavior knowledge engineers *exhibit* in their first interviews. As you read Part 2, let the guidelines that seem obvious serve as reminders to *observe these guidelines when you interview an expert*.

Chapter 12

Knowledge Acquisition and Interviewing

When the toaster-repair advisor project first began, Patricia Programmer and Howard Hacker needed to learn how Frank Fixit repairs toasters. They had to obtain the necessary information from Frank through a series of interviews. Howard had never participated in a knowledge-engineering project before. He had never conducted an interview and was not quite sure what to expect. When Howard expressed these anxieties, Patricia assured him that he was more familiar with interviews than he thought. She told him that he had probably participated in several interviews and had observed other interviews on TV. As a job applicant, he had been interviewed by several recruiters. In the past, he may have been interviewed by a doctor about some sickness. He had probably seen movies or television shows in which police officers interviewed suspects; most likely he had watched talk-show hosts interview guests.

The diverse activities Patricia Programmer mentioned share common elements.

- All interviews consist of person-to-person interactions between two parties or individuals. One party obtains information by asking questions; the second party supplies information by answering the questions.

• Each interview is conducted for a specific purpose.

The *purposes* behind the different interviews vary quite a bit. Patricia Programmer aims to develop a computer program. A recruiter needs to determine whether to hire the candidate. A doctor hopes to establish the cause of the patient's illness. A police officer tries to decide whether to arrest the suspect. A talk-show host wants the dialog to inform and entertain the television audience. These disparate underlying goals lead to differences in the interviewing activities.

The character of a knowledge-acquisition interview reflects its purpose. In many other kinds of interview, questions can specify clearly what information the interviewer wants to obtain; the questions are easy for the respondent to understand and to answer.

Describe your responsibilities at your previous job.

How long have you suffered from back pain?

Where were you on the night of March fifteenth?

Tell us about your experiences as a corporate spy.

In contrast, knowledge engineers are challenged to pose questions the expert will understand. For example, a knowledge engineer must obtain answers to such questions as:

What steps do you take when you perform the task?

What decisions do you make?

How did you make that decision?

What information do you use when you perform the task?

How can we divide this task into subtasks?

How can we classify different situations in which you might perform this task?

Unfortunately, however, many experts find it difficult to understand or answer these particular questions. The knowledge engineer typically cannot ask these questions directly but must employ the techniques we described in Part 1 to lead the expert to formulate and express the answers to the questions.

The objective of an interview affects not only the content of the discussions but also the precision with which the participants must communicate (Section 12.1) and the relationship between interviewer and interviewee (Section 12.2). In this chapter, we describe how the goal of creating an expert system influences knowledge-acquisition interviews and how knowledge acquisition differs from other interviewing activities.

12.1 Effective Communication

The purpose of an interview is to exchange information. In any dialog, some discrepancy can be expected between the meaning the speaker intends to convey and the meaning the listener understands. The smaller this discrepancy, the more accurately the parties understand each other and the more effective their exchange of information. Communication is more likely to be effective when the speaker and the listener share the same language, culture, educational background, point of reference, and familiarity with the subject matter. In many interviews, however, the participants lack this common background. The knowledge engineer and talk-show host are at the biggest disadvantage in this respect. By the very nature of their jobs, they are usually less familiar with the subject matter than is their expert or guest. Consequently, initially they may not know the right questions to ask, and they may have difficulty understanding the answers.

For the talk-show host, this situation is not a serious problem. While the host and the television viewers should understand the gist of what the guest describes, no harm will be done if they miss a few details or if they completely misinterpret some information. For the knowledge engineer, on the other hand, completeness and accuracy are crucial; every detail is important. To implement an expert system, the knowledge engineer must have a precise and indepth grasp of all the specifics.

When a knowledge engineer and an expert first start to work together on a project, their communication is ineffective. The potential for misunderstanding is high because of differences in experience and education between the knowledge engineer and the expert. At the start of the toaster-repair project, for example, all Patricia Programmer and Howard Hacker know about toasters is how to use them to toast bread. Much of Frank Fixit's terminology is foreign to them. They are completely unaware of the simplest facts that Frank takes to be common knowledge. Communication problems are especially dangerous when the knowledge engineer and expert are unaware of discrepancies between intended and perceived meanings. An interview may proceed for an hour or more before either party detects a misunderstanding. The longer the inconsistency in meanings persists, the more serious the misunderstanding is likely to be.

Patricia Programmer can counteract ineffectual communication in two ways. First, she and Howard Hacker can learn Frank Fixit's terminology; when they speak, they can be careful to choose terms he will understand. When the team has established a common vocabulary, their communication pattern will become more effective. Second, Patricia and Howard can identify and correct misunderstandings as soon as they occur. They should check continually that what they *think* Frank is saying is what he actually means.

12.1.1 Common Vocabulary

Initially, Frank Fixit's descriptions may sound like a foreign language to Patricia Programmer and Howard Hacker. They will need to stop him periodically to ask for definitions of unfamiliar words and explanations of unfamiliar concepts. While these interruptions are necessary, Frank may find them distracting and frustrating. As time goes on, Patricia and Howard need to learn Frank's terminology so they can minimize these distractions. Chapter 16 includes techniques for learning the expert's vocabulary.

At the beginning of the project, Frank will not understand what Patricia and Howard need to know. He might omit necessary details, assuming that Patricia and Howard would not be interested. Alternatively, he might try to be thorough and might include a full discussion about toaster manufacturing that is completely irrelevant to the task of repairing toasters. As the project progresses, Patricia and Howard should teach Frank what they need to know and why. They should introduce knowledge-engineering terminology only when this will help Frank understand what they need to know from him.

12.1.2 Confirmation of Comprehension

Patricia Programmer and Howard Hacker aim to build an expert system from Frank Fixit's knowledge. This requires a clear understanding of the role each fact, decision, and action plays in the process of repairing a toaster. As we saw in Part 1, knowledge acquisition is a cyclic activity (Figure 12.1). After each interview, Patricia and Howard should discuss and analyze the information they obtained. They should decide how each piece of information fits into their understanding of the process of repairing toasters and how the information will be used in the expert system. The post-interview analysis will give Patricia and Howard a clearer understanding of what Frank said, but it is subject to error. What they analyze is *their interpretation* of Frank's knowledge. Before they use this, they should review their analysis with Frank to ensure that their interpretation is correct.

The cycle illustrated in Figure 12.1 occurs on a smaller scale within each knowledge-acquisition interview. After Patricia asks Frank a question, she should listen to his answer and try to comprehend fully what he says. As Patricia reflects on what she hears, she should decide whether she understands Frank's answer. If not, she should ask for elaboration or clarification. If she thinks she understands the answer, she should repeat her understanding and ask for Frank's confirmation. Chapter 16 describes interviewing techniques knowledge engineers can use to ask questions, to analyze the expert's responses, and to review their understanding with the expert.

12.2 Relationship between Participants

The relationship between the participants in an interview can be examined along several dimensions. In Sections 12.2.1 through 12.2.5, we will describe five key dimensions of the relationship.

1. *Duration*—the amount of time the participants spend in interviews

2. *Shared goals*—the degree to which the interviewee shares the interviewer's goals

3. *Trust*—the extent to which the parties trust each other

4. *Cooperation* and *conflict*—the amount of cooperation or conflict between the parties

Figure 12.1
Knowledge-acquisition cycle. Knowledge acquisition consists of a cycle of three steps. First, the knowledge engineers interview the expert to obtain information. Second, they analyze and organize this information to see how it will be used in the expert system. Third, they review their analysis with the expert to ensure that their understanding is correct. This review may uncover misunderstandings; if so, a new cycle begins.

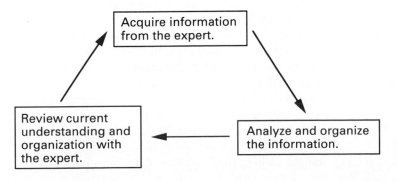

5. *Influence*—the degree to which the interviewee can contribute toward achieving the goal of the interview

The ideal relationship between knowledge engineer and expert has a particular profile against these dimensions.

12.2.1 Duration of the Relationship

Frank Fixit uses a vast amount of knowledge in repairing toasters, far too much to be captured in a single interview. The cyclic nature of expert-system development further necessitates a series of interviews spread out over time. This lengthy process is the norm; depending on the size and complexity of an expert system, knowledge acquisition can be expected to last from a few weeks to several years. The interview process necessitates a long-term relationship between knowledge engineer and expert. For the recruiter, police officer, and talk-show host, on the other hand, the norm is to conduct a single interview with any given individual. The relationship between interviewer and interviewee may be just an hour or two in duration.

12.2.2 Shared Goals between Participants

Experts and the knowledge engineers are equally important participants in the development of an expert system. In a successful project, both parties work together toward a common goal. Patricia Programmer, for example, would like Frank Fixit to be as eager as are she and Howard Hacker to see the system develop. Frank should view himself as a critical part of the team, a necessary contributor to the success of the project. Sharing goals does not imply sharing motivations. Patricia and Howard might be motivated by a desire to demonstrate the usefulness of knowledge engineering so that their management will support future projects. Frank might be motivated by a belief that he is being "immortalized" in the expert system. He might feel that the system will allow him to leave the company with his job "wrapped up neatly" so that his departure does not disrupt smooth operations. Whatever his motivations, his ultimate goal should be the same as is that of the knowledge engineers—to see the expert system working successfully.

While it might seem that all successful interviews rely on shared goals, this is not necessarily true. The recruiter's goal is to make the right decision; the job applicant's goal is to be hired. A talk-show host's goal might be to have good ratings while the guest's goal might be to make a public statement or simply to earn money.

12.2.3 Trust between Participants

Trust between the parties in an interview has two components. The interviewer must trust the interviewee to provide accurate information. The interviewee must trust the interviewer to use this information appropriately. Patricia Programmer and Howard Hacker depend on Frank Fixit to provide them with knowledge about toaster repair. He is a recognized expert in this field, and they trust the information that he gives them. A successful project also requires Frank to trust Patricia and Howard. He needs to feel that they will treat him fairly in all their dealings. He needs to know that they will not disclose anything that he tells them in confidence. He needs to believe that the expert system will be used in the manner they have described.

Mutual trust is desirable in all types of interview. It is less typical in interviews between police officer and suspect; the very word "suspect" implies distrust. With a television talk show, trust is less important than in other interviews because the information provided during the interview is not used in any way after the show. The only purpose behind the interview is to share the information.

12.2.4 Cooperation and Conflict between Participants

In order to achieve their shared goals, Frank Fixit, Patricia Programmer, and Howard Hacker need to cooperate. Because they will have to work together over a period of time, conflict should be kept at a minimum. Although good cooperation and lack of conflict are beneficial for all interviews, these qualities are less important in some settings. The police officer and suspect, for example, often regard each other as adversaries; conflict is common. While a cooperative suspect might facilitate the interview, the police officer might distrust a suspect who seems unusually cooperative. Conflict can make a talk show more exciting to watch; the host might encourage a certain level of conflict. In both of these examples, the participants do not need to worry that conflict in today's interaction will damage their ability to work together in the future.

12.2.5 Influence of the Interviewee on Achievement of Goals

The last dimension we look at is how strong an influence the *interviewee* can have on the achievement of the goal of the interview. At one extreme, the patient, job applicant, and suspect have relatively small influence. These interviewees provide the information, but the doctor, recruiter, and police officer must rely on their own decision-making abilities to interpret this information correctly. An intermediate situation occurs on a talk show. The guest can contribute to the success of the program; some guests are more amusing and entertaining than others. Two guests could provide the same information but in such a different manner that one show flops while the other is a big hit. The influence of an expert in knowledge-acquisition interviews is the highest. Frank Fixit must be involved in almost every stage of development not only to supply information but also to verify that the knowledge engineers have used his know-how correctly in the expert system.

12.2.6 Development of the Relationship

Patricia Programmer is responsible for establishing a relationship with Frank Fixit that fits the profile shown in Figure 12.2(a). Two of the characteristics of the profile are inherent in the knowledge acquisition process: the interaction will last over a period of time and Frank will have a strong influence on the realization of the goal. The other four dimensions are particularly important to Patricia. She must show Frank that the expert system is important *to him* so that he will share the goal to develop the system. She must earn Frank's trust and cooperation. In short, she must make sure Frank feels like a member of the project team. Patricia's primary goal in early interviews will be to establish this relationship with Frank. The entire project depends on successful interviews, and a good working relationship with Frank is vital for successful interviews. Chapter 13 presents guidelines for interacting with the expert that can contribute to developing a good working relationship.

12.3 Points to Remember

Chapter 1 identified three *information-gathering* goals for the initial inquiry stage of knowledge acquisition. Those goals—defining what the expert system will do, learning how the expert performs the task, and deciding how the full coverage of the system can be subdivided— lay the groundwork for the development of an expert system. This chapter adds two *team-building* goals that lay the groundwork for successful interviews lasting throughout the project.

1. Establish a good working relationship with the expert.

2. Develop a shared vocabulary for communicating about the project.

An interview is a person-to-person interaction between two parties in which one party obtains information by questioning the other party. Each interview has a specific purpose; the purpose of knowledge-acquisition interviews is to obtain the information needed for the development of an expert system. The purpose behind an interview affects the content of the discussions, the degree of precision with which the interviewer and interviewee must communicate, and the nature of the relationship between the participants.

The content of knowledge-acquisition interviews includes the proc-

Figure 12.2 Relationship between knowledge engineer and expert. The ideal profile for the relationship between a knowledge engineer and an expert (a) is distinct from the profiles for the relationships between interviewers and interviewees in other activities—(b) through (e). The relationship between knowledge engineer and expert lasts over a period of time, the two participants share goals for the outcome of the interviews. Their relationship is characterized by a high degree of trust, good cooperation, and little conflict. The expert has a strong influence on the achievement of the shared goals.

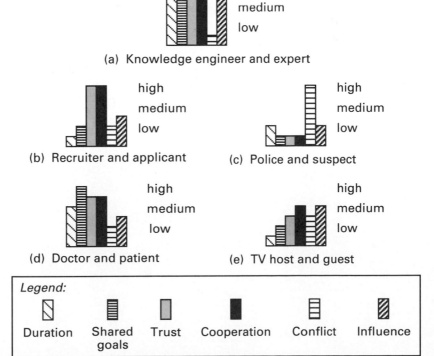

ess by which the expert performs the task, the reasons behind each of the expert's actions and decisions, and the facts needed to perform the selected task. A major challenge of knowledge acquisition is to request this information in ways the expert can understand.

Communication between knowledge engineers and experts must be *detailed* and *precise*. Knowledge engineers can facilitate indepth communication by developing a shared vocabulary with the expert. They can ensure a valid interpretation of the expert's knowledge by repeating their understanding for confirmation. Knowledge acquisition therefore is a cycle of three steps.

1. Acquiring information from the expert

2. Analyzing and organizing this information

3. Reviewing the current understanding and organization with the expert

Each cycle gives the knowledge engineers a clearer and more accurate understanding of what the expert does.

The knowledge engineers and experts on a project must develop a cooperative relationship based on mutual trust and respect that lasts over a period of time. They must share the goal of creating a successful expert system.

Chapter 13

Interview Participants

After Howard Hacker had discussed interviews with Patricia Programmer, he became comfortable with the idea of interviewing, but he was not sure what *he* should do during the interviews. Patricia explained that she and Howard would act as an interviewing team. Patricia would lead the initial interviews, but as Howard developed and improved his interviewing skills, he would be able to play an increasingly active role. Patricia told Howard to observe her during the interviews. She said Howard should learn how to interact with Frank Fixit and how to work cooperatively with Patricia.

Each participant in a knowledge-acquisition interview plays a particular role, and the appropriate interaction among the participants is crucial to the success of the interview. Howard's first three lessons in interviewing will teach him:

1. The roles he, Patricia, and Frank should play (Section 13.1)

2. How he and Patricia should interact with Frank (Section 13.2)

3. How he and Patricia should interact with each other (Section 13.3)

13.1 Knowledge-Acquisition Roles

The simplest knowledge-acquisition interview has two participants: a knowledge engineer and an expert. The knowledge engineer plays the role of *interviewer*, and the expert plays the role of *interviewee*. Many project teams include more than one knowledge engineer. When teams of knowledge engineers interview an expert, they must work together so the presence of multiple interviewers does not make the expert uneasy. In each interview, one knowledge engineer should be the **lead interviewer.** Depending on their interviewing skills, other knowledge engineers in the team can play the roles of **silent observer, secondary questioner,** or **acting interviewer.**

> In the initial interviews with Frank Fixit, Patricia Programmer is the *lead interviewer*. She plans the agenda and asks most of the questions. She is responsible for keeping the dialog focused and productive. However, Hacker is a *silent observer*. He watches, listens, and takes notes, but he rarely participates in the discussions. In addition to learning from Frank how to repair toasters, Howard learns from Patricia how to conduct interviews.
>
> As the project progresses, Howard learns how to interact with Frank, to ask questions, to interpret the responses, and to keep the discussion on track. Howard starts to practice these interviewing skills as the *secondary questioner*. In this role, he asks follow-up questions that expand on topics Patricia introduces. He explains his understanding of an answer to Frank and asks for confirmation.
>
> When Howard is proficient, he becomes the *acting interviewer*. In this role, Howard plans the agenda; he leads the interviews, asks most of the questions, and keeps the dialog productive. Patricia is on hand to help him if he encounters difficulties he cannot manage. Before Howard assumes the acting interviewer role, he and Patricia work out signals by which Howard can ask for help inconspicuously. Patricia also has signals to indicate she is taking control of an interview. Patricia can use these signals to resume the lead unobtrusively if she perceives problems with Howard's approach. As acting interviewer, Howard agrees to defer to Patricia's judgment during interviews. These signals enable Patricia to take over from Howard so smoothly that Frank is not aware that any change has occurred. If necessary, Patricia and Howard discuss problems and air their disagreements in a separate discussion after the interview. When Patricia thinks Howard is competent to conduct interviews on his own, she lets him play the role of lead interviewer in most of the remaining interviews.

13.2 Interactions between Knowledge Engineer and Expert

The way in which knowledge engineers interact with the expert during interviews can make or break a project. It is through this interaction that they establish a good working relationship with the expert. Early interactions with the expert are particularly important. If knowledge engineers get off to a bad start with an expert, it may be impossible to repair the damage. The main guideline in conducting an interview is to *keep the expert comfortable throughout the interview*. Maintaining the expert's comfort requires effort in the first few interviews.

> At the start of the toaster-repair project, Frank Fixit does not know what to expect from knowledge acquisition. He does not know what Patricia Programmer and Howard Hacker want from him. This uncertainty leads to anxiety. Patricia eases Frank's apprehensions by explaining what is required of him and why she needs his help. She makes sure Frank understands the aims of the project and the role he is to play. In each interview, Patricia is careful to explain the relevance of the interview topics and of her questions. As the project progresses, Frank becomes familiar with the interview process. As Frank's familiarity with the process increases, Patricia and Howard find it easier to keep Frank comfortable with a particular interview and with the project in general.

Each expert is an individual; the best way to interact with one expert will not be best for interacting with a different expert. You need to *be sensitive to your expert* and to adapt your style accordingly. Throughout Part 2, we shall use dialog examples to illustrate good and bad knowledge-acquisition techniques. Our examples introduce a variety of experts and knowledge engineers to show the importance of individual differences.

As you interact with an expert, be sensitive to:

- The expert's feelings (Section 13.2.1)

- The expert's nonverbal communication (Section 13.2.2)

- Cultural differences between yourself and the expert (Section 13.2.3)

Section 13.2.4 contains dialog examples that illustrate how the knowledge engineer's style of interaction can influence the success of an interview. We close this section with a survey of additional points to consider in interactions that involve multiple knowledge engineers or multiple experts (Section 13.2.5).

13.2.1 Sensitivity to the Expert's Feelings

Sensitivity to the expert's feelings will guide you to treat the expert as *you* would like to be treated. Be sure to *include* the expert in all discussions and to behave in a manner that shows *respect* and *patience*.

Inclusion

An important goal of knowledge acquisition is to encourage the expert to become a full member of the project team and to be enthusiastic about contributing to the system's development. To further this goal, you should *ensure that the expert is included in the entire process*. Include the expert in all meetings with management that affect the direction of the project. Make sure that the expert is aware of the overall project plan and schedule. At the close of an interview, let the expert contribute as much as possible to planning the content and the schedule for subsequent interviews.

Treat interviews and other project discussions as *mutual problem-solving sessions* in which the knowledge engineers and the expert work together to find a solution. During interviews, confine your discussions to topics that require the expert's input. Make sure the expert understands *why* you want to discuss each topic. When you need to use knowledge-engineering terminology or to discuss how the expert system works, take the time to be sure the expert understands you.

If your team occasionally goes out to lunch together or if you have parties after reaching major milestones in the project, invite the expert to share in these social activities.

Respect

You can make interactions comfortable by showing regard for the expert as an individual and as a talented member of the team. *Show respect for the expert's knowledge, skill, and expertise.* In other words, treat the expert like an expert.

> Patricia Programmer and Howard Hacker show their respect by explaining to Frank Fixit that his unique skills and abilities are precisely what make him important to the project. They are particularly careful to emphasize Frank's importance at the beginning of the project. Frank is not familiar with computers; he does not see how a computer could possibly do his job. He thinks computers can be programmed to perform only simple tasks. Patricia and Howard take pains to acknowledge the difference between what Frank can do and what they expect the expert system to do. Even more important, they conscientiously avoid giving Frank the impression that they think his job is easy. Patricia and Howard let Frank know that they are eager to learn from him and that he has something important to teach them. Throughout the project, they show Frank that they value his contribution and that he is crucial to the success of the project.

You should also *respect the expert's wishes*. If you would like to make audio or video recordings of interview sessions, do so only with the expert's permission. Follow any restrictions the expert places on who can listen to or view the tapes. If you want to share the tape with anyone other than the attendees at the interview, be sure that you obtain the expert's approval beforehand.

In a successful project, the expert respects the knowledge engineers. You can earn the expert's respect if you make effective use of the expert's time, display your competence and commitment to the project, and demonstrate progress in developing the expert system.

Patience

Be patient with the expert; show that you appreciate the difficulty of the expert's role. Knowledge acquisition can be frustrating for *both* parties. As a knowledge engineer, you need to obtain particular information in order to build an expert system. When the expert fails to provide this information, you may be frustrated. When you ask the same question in a number of different ways without getting a satisfactory answer, you may become impatient. That is the perfect time to stop and look at knowledge acquisition *from the expert's perspective.*

> Before the start of the toaster-repair project, Frank Fixit had never been asked to explain how he repairs a toaster. When Frank sees a toaster problem, he knows automatically what to do. He performs the necessary actions without stopping to think about what steps he should take or why he chooses one action over another. Knowledge acquisition will be a discovery process for Frank as he analyzes his actions. Frank will not be able to provide immediate answers to all Patricia Programmer's questions. Instead, he will need time for introspection to explore what actions he takes and why he takes them. Patricia understands the process Frank must go through and will be patient with him in all interviews.

The point to remember is to be patient *while you are with the expert.* You need to suppress your impatience during the interview itself. Once the interview is over, however, and you are away from the expert, if you need to let off steam, you can vent your frustrations confidentially to a colleague or friend.

13.2.2 Sensitivity to Nonverbal Communication

The purpose of an interview is to communicate with the expert. Speech is only one part of communication; effective communication requires that you *notice, understand, and respond to the expert's nonverbal messages.* Facial expressions, vocal inflection, speaking rate, pauses, hand gestures, body movements, and posture also convey information. As you interact with an expert, pay attention to these nonverbal messages, decide what these messages mean, and respond appropriately. Become conscious of the nonverbal signals you send, and make sure these signals convey the messages you intend.

In the remainder of this section, we explore the steps you can take to improve nonverbal communication. In your early interaction with an expert:

- Determine the expert's normal communication style.

- Learn to interpret deviations from the normal style.

During all interviews:

- Be aware of the nonverbal messages you send.

- Notice how the expert reacts to your nonverbal signals.

- Watch for discrepancies between verbal and nonverbal messages.

Expert's Normal Communication Style

Become familiar with the expert's communication style. In the first few interviews, try to learn what is normal for *this* expert. Look for the pattern of behavior that tells you everything is going well. This pattern includes the expert's usual flow of speech, common facial expressions, and frequent gestures. Variations from this pattern deserve closer attention; they indicate something out of the ordinary. As you become familiar with the expert's communication style, you can start to identify deviations from the normal pattern and to learn how to interpret these deviations.

For example, consider two experts, Mark Miller and Gloria Green. They have very different communication styles; what is normal for Mark indicates problems for Gloria and vice versa. The knowledge engineers who work with these two experts must observe the experts and learn to interpret their nonverbal messages.

Mark normally responds to a question with an initial silence, followed by slow and deliberate speech, and ending with a quizzical expression. He habitually plays with his pen, rotating it end over end as he talks. Mark's silence indicates that he considers a question important and that he is trying to formulate a clear and comprehensive answer. The quizzical expression is Mark's way of signaling that his answer is complete; it asks the knowledge engineers whether they understand and whether they need more information.

Occasionally, Mark answers a question immediately and speaks more quickly than usual; instead of rotating his pen, he taps it lightly on the table. This pattern indicates that Mark does not want to talk about the current topic. Instead of pausing to think through his response, he tries to dismiss the question as soon as possible; he taps his pen to signal impatience to get on to a different topic. Instead of the quizzical look that asks, *What next?* Mark's matter-of-fact expression indicates, *That's all I have to say.*

Gloria generally answers questions immediately with no initial pause; she speaks quickly and looks at the knowledge engineers as she responds. Gloria's fast response indicates that she has understood the question and is eager to provide an answer.

After certain questions, Gloria is silent for a while. Then she folds her arms in front of her chest and answers the question, speaking more slowly than usual and looking down at the table in front of her. At the end of her answer, she looks up from the table with a quizzical expression. Gloria's initial silence means she does not understand the question and is reluctant to answer; she speaks slowly because she is unsure what is expected of her. Her quizzical expression means, *I have no idea what you were trying to ask; did I answer your question?*

Knowledge engineers working with Mark quickly learn to ignore his initial silence, quizzical looks, and rotating pen. This normal pattern means the interview is proceeding smoothly; they worry when this pattern changes. Knowledge engineers working with Gloria, on the other hand, worry when they notice initial silence after a question and a quizzical look after an answer.

Deviations from the Normal Communication Style

When you are familiar with your expert's normal communication style, you will be able to detect deviations from this style. Learn how to interpret different kinds of deviation so you can respond appropriately. Try to discern signals that tell you when the expert is tired, uneasy about the topic under discussion, frustrated, enthusiastic, unsure of information, worried, or pleased. Watch for these indicators during interviews, and take appropriate actions. For example, if the expert appears tired or distracted, call a break and consider ending the meeting early. If the expert seems to be frustrated with the current line of questioning or uneasy about the current topic, take a break or change the subject. You can return to the current discussion at a later date.

Try to sense when the expert is unsure of an answer or less confident than usual about some information. Ask whether it would be best to delay a detailed discussion until after the expert has had more time to think about the topic or to confer with colleagues. Pay attention to how your expert reacts when additional people attend an interview. If the expert is unusually quiet when a manager or colleague is in the room, try to limit all interviews to the project team.

When you notice deviations from the normal style, judge whether they indicate a positive feeling or a negative one. Try to encourage positive feelings; try to identify the cause of negative feelings and to correct them. For example, if the expert seems especially enthusiastic about a particular topic, you may want to pursue it in more detail than you initially planned. Remember, however, to limit the discussion to information that will be needed by the expert system. On the other hand if the expert seems worried, express your concern and try to find the cause. Do what you can to reassure the expert and to remove the source of anxiety.

Your Nonverbal Messages

Remember that *your* facial expressions, movements, speaking rate, and so on convey information. Learn to control these indicators to send the messages you want to send. Avoid sending the expert negative messages. At some time during knowledge acquisition, you can expect to feel tired, bored, frustrated, or impatient. Without thinking, you may shift restlessly in your seat and glance frequently at your watch, yawn, sigh, or speak more sharply than usual, letting a tone of irritation creep into your voice. Such behavior can impede the productivity of an interview. In the early meetings, it could undermine your ability to establish a good relationship with the expert.

It is important for you to be conscious of these negative feelings when they occur. As soon as you become aware of a problem, take steps to correct it. While you are doing so, make a special effort to prevent your actions from conveying your feelings. For example, if you are tired, suggest a break; other people in the team may be ready for one too. It may even be appropriate to end the meeting early. If you need to finish discussing certain topics before you adjourn, concentrate on the dialog, and suppress the urge to check your watch or glance at the clock. If you find yourself getting bored, make a conscious effort to appear interested. Lean forward attentively. Stifle yawns as inconspicuously as possible. Take extra care in writing notes; pay attention to what the expert stresses even if it does not seem important to you. When you feel frustrated or irritable, call a break or switch to a more productive topic of discussion. Make a note to return to the current topic at a later time.

Be aware that your mood affects the nonverbal signals you send. If you are upset because of personal problems, a family emergency, or difficulties with your boss, you may unconsciously convey negative signals during interviews. These can give the impression that you are having problems with *the expert*. If you are unable to control your emotions during times of personal difficulty, explain the situation so the expert does not get the wrong impression.

Expert Reaction to Your Nonverbal Messages

Although you can keep yourself from exhibiting negative feelings, you cannot keep the expert from misinterpreting actions that indicate your positive or neutral feelings. Instead you must notice when the expert perceives a negative signal. In the future, be careful to avoid the action that was misinterpreted. If necessary, clear up the immediate misunderstanding by calling attention to your action and explaining what it really meant. The following example indicates how to detect and correct a misunderstanding.

> When knowledge engineer Bob Smith interviews expert Alice Jones, he notices that from time to time Alice scowls then sits up particularly straight and raises her voice slightly. He wonders what Alice's actions mean but is unable to correlate them with changes in the topic of discussion.

Bob suffers from occasional lower back pain especially when he sits for long periods of time. He has learned he can get temporary relief by putting his hands behind his head then arching his back as he leans backward in his chair. During an interview, Bob develops a mild back-ache and adopts this posture. Alice immediately sits up straight and raises her voice.

Alice apparently thinks Bob's actions indicate that his interest is waning. Her upright posture and raised voice signal Bob to start paying attention. As soon as Bob realizes Alice has misinterpreted his action, he sits up and says, "That feels better. These chairs don't give my back enough support; when my back starts to ache, I have to lean back like that." In subsequent interviews with Alice, when Bob's back starts to hurt, he changes his posture much more subtly, without putting his hands behind his head as he does so.

Mixed Signals

Watch for **mixed signals**, discrepancies between verbal and nonverbal messages. As you learn to interpret the expert's nonverbal signals, you will be able to spot actions, facial expressions, or vocal inflections that appear to contradict the expert's spoken words. As Dialog 13.1 illustrates, it is best to respond to the *nonverbal* message.

Dialog 13.1 Responding to a Mixed Message

Setting

Bob Smith is interviewing Alice Jones. They are approaching the end of the time they had scheduled for their current meeting.

Dialog

Bob *(looking at the clock on the wall):* I can see that we won't be able to finish discussing this case today. Have we completed the current step?

Alice: Yes. There's only one step left to talk about, but I agree that we don't have time to finish today.

Bob: Let's stop here then and discuss the final step in this case next week. Is that all right with you?

Alice *(confidently):* Next week will be fine. The same time and place?

Bob: Yes. It won't take us too long to finish up our discussion of this case so why don't you bring descriptions of one or two more cases.

Alice *(hesitantly):* Oh, OK.

Bob: Can you prepare new case descriptions by next week?

Alice's voice rises in pitch as she talks. She looks down at her left hand as she continually twists her wedding ring around on her finger.

Alice: Yes, I should be able to. I think I'll have enough time by next week.

Bob: I guess one week doesn't give you very much time. Maybe we should just plan to have a short meeting next week to finish up the current case. At that meeting, you give me an estimate of when you think you'll have the other case descriptions ready. We can schedule a separate meeting to discuss the new cases.

Alice *(eagerly):* I think that *would* be better. I have to prepare a presentation for a staff meeting on Friday so I don't have very much time this week.

Discussion

When Alice agrees to meet with Bob in a week's time, she thinks they will simply complete today's discussion. She does not count on having to prepare additional case descriptions. She initially agrees to prepare the case descriptions because she feels she has already committed to a meeting time.

Bob notices Alice's hesitation when she agrees to bring new case descriptions so he tries to verify that she will have time to prepare them. Alice's answer to this question sends a mixed message. Her words say that she *will* have enough time, but her rising voice, her halting speech, and her nervous hand movements are inconsistent with this affirmative answer. Bob senses that Alice's actions are telling him that she will *not* have enough time to prepare the cases. Rather than believing Alice's words, Bob responds to her actions.

A final word of caution: Make sure *your own* nonverbal signals are congruent with what you say. If you send mixed messages, the expert is likely to listen to your actions, not to your words.

13.2.3 Sensitivity to Cultural Differences

Issues of cultural differences are particularly important for knowledge engineers who work as consultants and develop expert systems with experts in different companies. Although less common, subtle differences in work cultures also exist between different groups in a single company. You must be aware of cultural differences between yourself and the expert and adjust your behavior in deference to your expert's cultural expectations. What seems normal, customary, and comfortable to you may seem alien and uncomfortable to an expert from a different country, a different region in your own country, a different company, or a different profession. It is your responsibility to *notice and accommodate the expert's preferences.* You can anticipate cultural differences when working with an expert from a different geographical area. Even when you work with an expert from your own company and do not expect to encounter cultural differences, you should pay careful attention to the expert's normal behavior. Look also for the expert's reactions to your behavior. Try to adapt to the expert's norm in the areas of formality, dress, and personal space.

Formality

People vary in the degree of formality they expect in interactions with others. You need to be attuned to the level of formality or familiarity your expert prefers and to adjust your normal conduct as necessary. The customary manner of address differs from one region to another. For example, many people in California prefer to be called by their first names and are accustomed to calling other people by their first names. After knowledge engineer Bob Smith is introduced to expert Alice Jones, both find it perfectly natural to use the names "Bob" and "Alice." They would find "Mr. Smith" and "Dr. Jones" stuffy or pretentious. On the other hand, many people in the eastern United States (and in other countries) expect relative strangers to address them with a title and last name. To them, "Bob" and "Alice" would be rude or impertinent forms of address; they would prefer "Mr. Smith" and "Dr. Jones." Regional differences in formality extend to language and posture. Some people may feel more comfortable using slang and informal language occasionally; others may want to use more formal language at all times.

Dress

You should decide what manner of dress is most comfortable to your expert and wear the corresponding level of casual or professional attire to interviews. If the expert prefers wearing a suit to interviews, you should wear a suit; if the expert prefers to dress more casually, you should dress casually. Many experts prefer to wear their normal work clothes to interviews, but this is not always so. For example, a stock broker who normally wears a suit or tailored dress to work might prefer to wear casual slacks to an all-day interview when she does not need to go to her own office. On the other hand, a mechanic who usually dresses casually might look forward to the opportunity to wear a business suit.

At the first meeting, you can judge (or discuss among the team) how to dress for subsequent interviews. The only challenge, therefore, is to select the correct attire for the first meeting. The aim is to avoid two possible problems. If you dress too casually, you may insult the expert. On the other hand, if you wear business clothes when the expert does not do so, you may make the expert feel uncomfortable and inappropriately dressed. As a general rule, err on the side of more formal dress for your first meeting. Wear a suit so you can adjust to a more casual look by taking off your jacket. It is acceptable to suggest less formal attire as the norm for subsequent interviews if that seems appropriate.

> Patricia Programmer, Howard Hacker, and Frank Fixit all wear suits to their first interview. From time to time during the introductions,

Frank puts his index finger between his shirt collar and his neck, then he draws his finger around his neck, pulling outward on the collar. He adjusts his tie frequently and pulls at the cuffs of his shirt. It is clear to both Patricia and Howard that Frank is uncomfortable in his suit. To put Frank at ease, Patricia suggests that they all get comfortable before starting the interview. Howard asks if anyone would mind if he took off his jacket and tie. Frank, much relieved, also removes his jacket and tie. Patricia follows up by letting Frank know that he need not wear a suit for subsequent interviews.

Personal Space

Different cultures have different standards for the comfortable distance between individuals. The average North American, for example, feels comfortable standing 3 or 4 feet away from other people in an uncrowded room. This distance defines the radius of an individual's personal space in the North American culture. When one person stands closer to a second person for no apparent reason, the second person usually reacts by backing away. When working with an expert from a different country, watch for this behavior. If the expert frequently backs away from you, you may be standing too close. Observe how close the expert normally stands to you, and get into the habit of allowing the expert more room. On the other hand, if you find the expert tends to stand uncomfortably close to you, try to resist the urge to move away. The expert might find that insulting or at least disconcerting.

13.2.4 Dialog Examples

Dialog 13.2[1] illustrates how a knowledge engineer's style of interacting with an expert can affect the success of an interview. This example consists of two parts: a dialog in which the knowledge engineers encounter difficulties and a dialog in which they avoid these difficulties. Read this example critically; try to identify good and bad interviewing techniques.

Dialog 13.2 Interviewing a Reluctant Expert

Setting

Larry Lamont is the manager of the accounting department of a large company. Joe Johnson is a knowledge engineer in the advanced development group of the information services department of the same com-

---

1. Dialog 13.2 contains adaptations of dialogs that appear on the "Knowledge Acquisition Problems and Solutions" videotape used in the *Knowledge Acquisition Workshop* at Cimflex Teknowledge Corporation.

pany. Larry has asked Joe to develop an expert system to help accountants with the classification of fixed assets. Larry is very enthusiastic about the system. He prepared descriptions of a few cases to give Joe a general idea of what the system should do. Larry explained that he has had little experience in this particular area. For a detailed discussion, Joe needs to meet with Robert Rankin, the company's expert in the area of fixed assets.

Larry called Robert into the meeting and told him that the company has decided to build an "expert accountant program." He introduced Joe and asked Robert to schedule some time to explain fixed assets to Joe. They agreed on a meeting time the following week.

Robert is a little upset about this meeting. Larry's request came out of the blue. Robert is not sure what an "expert accountant program" is; he is worried that if the system is built he will lose his job.

Dialog with Problems

Robert arrives at the meeting dressed in his normal work attire, a suit. Joe arrives wearing jeans and a T-shirt—his normal working attire. Robert scowls at Joe's unprofessional appearance.

They go to the table. Robert sits upright. Joe slouches and pushes his feet against the table so that his chair leans back. Robert's scowl deepens as he observes Joe's actions.

Joe: Hi Robert. I'd like to discuss the case descriptions Larry gave us last week. Did you have a chance to look at them?

Robert: I glanced at them, but it didn't seem like an efficient use of my time.

Joe *(disappointed):* Oh! That's too bad! We have a lot of material to go through, and we have a pretty tight schedule. Well, lets just go ahead with them now.

Robert *(interrupting):* To be perfectly frank, I'm very skeptical about this whole project. It's taken me years to develop my proficiency, and I don't see how a computer can handle the complexity of dealing with fixed assets.

Joe *(confidently):* There's really nothing to worry about! We've got knowledge-representation schemes, inference methods, and software techniques that are *excellent* for capturing the kinds of expertise that people normally think is difficult. I'm sure we won't have any problems. Let's just go ahead with the first case.

Joe picks up a case description and starts flipping through it. Robert frowns.

For example, this lists a "PrintMaster" laser printer. How would you go about classifying that?

Robert: That would be computing equipment.

Joe: Why? What about it makes it computing equipment?

Robert looks at his watch.

Robert: It just is. This is a pretty straightforward example.

Joe: Well you must have some sort of rules or ideas about what puts something into the "computer equipment" category.

Robert *(exasperated):* Yes, but they're very complex—every situation is different—you can't just write it down on a piece of paper—it's very involved—it's in my head.

Joe *(a little impatient):* Yes, but it *got into* your head somehow! So *obviously*
there's something objective we can put down.

Robert: I just don't see how. I'm very busy, and I simply don't see the point
in all this.

Before you read further, think about the previous dialog.
    This interview takes place during the initial inquiry stage
of knowledge acquisition. As we discussed in Chapter 12,
this stage has information-gathering and team-building
goals. How does Joe fare at achieving the two types of goal?
    Review the guidelines for interacting with an expert that
appear in Sections 13.2.1 through 13.2.3. Which of these
guidelines does Joe follow? Which does he violate?
    What is wrong with Joe's approach? What would you
have done differently?

Dialog without Problems

Robert and Joe, both dressed in suits, arrive at the meeting room at the
appointed time.

Joe: Hi Robert. It's good to see you again.

Joe extends his hand to Robert. They shake hands then go to the table
and sit down.

Thanks for taking the time to talk with me. I'd like to spend today's
meeting discussing the case descriptions that Larry gave us last week.
This will help me start to learn how you analyze fixed assets. Did you
have a chance to read through the case descriptions?

Robert: I glanced at them, but it didn't seem like an efficient use of my time.

Joe *(sympathetically):* I understand that you're very busy, and we appreciate
the time you can give us. One of the reasons we wanted to include you
in this project is that Larry says you're one of the most valued people
in the accounting department. I will do all I can to make sure that we
don't waste your time.

Robert: Well, Joe, I am not totally convinced that your project can work. It's
taken me years to develop my proficiency, and I don't see how a computer can handle the complexity of dealing with fixed assets.

Joe *(nodding):* I can understand that. From looking at some of the initial
material Larry and I discussed, it's clear to me that classifying fixed
assets is a very intricate process. That's exactly why we wanted to build
this system. There's so much for you to remember and even more for
a new accountant with the company.
    I'm sure that we won't be able to duplicate the originality and cre-
ativity that goes into all aspects of your job. What we'd *like* to do is to
build a system that will help you and others. You can think of it as an

intelligent job aid, something that will take the burden of the more mundane, day-to-day work off your shoulders. You will still oversee that work, but it will be automated as much as possible. We want the system to allow you to spend your time helping people with the more interesting and complicated cases.

Robert: Well I can see some possibilities there. A certain amount of it *is* repetitious.

Joe: As we go through these cases, let's try to look for places where a computer system could relieve you from the more straightforward tasks. This would free you to spend your time on the more challenging aspects of your job.

Robert: I'm certainly willing to experiment with you on this.

Joe: Good. Let's start working through this first case so I can get a better feel for the process you use in classifying fixed assets. It will also give you a better idea of the kinds of things I am interested in learning from you.

Joe picks up a copy of the case description.

This mentions a "PrintMaster" laser printer. Let's take a look at that. How would you classify that?

Robert: We'd classify that as computing equipment.

Joe: What in particular about the PrintMaster makes it computing equipment?

Robert: Actually, we get a list from the people who run the information services department. Anything that's on the list I classify as computing equipment.

Discussion

Robert is not a willing participant in this project; his boss, Larry, essentially ordered him to help. Larry is already convinced that the expert system will be of benefit to the company, but Robert sees no evidence that it will be of any benefit *to him*. On the contrary, Robert views the system as a threat. This perspective places an extra burden on Joe to win Robert's trust and cooperation.

Joe's *information-gathering* goal in this interview is to get an overview of how Robert classifies fixed assets. Equally important is the *team-building* goal of establishing a good working relationship with Robert. In the first dialog, Joe neglects the team-building goal. He starts the meeting on the wrong foot by ignoring the differences between the work cultures of an engineer and an accountant within his corporation. Joe's casual dress and posture are both perfectly acceptable in his own office. To Robert, however, Joe's informality is completely inappropriate even insulting. Robert was leery of the project after he first heard about it; Joe needs to do everything possible to make Robert want to be a part of the team that is building the expert system. Instead he further alienates Robert before they even begin their first discussion.

Joe's verbal skills do nothing to counteract Robert's initial negative impression. Joe starts the interview abruptly by saying what he wants to do but not why he wants to do it. Robert does not know what they need to discuss about the case descriptions or why Joe wants to have these discussions.

When Robert expresses reservations about the project, Joe waves them aside with jargon that is meaningless to Robert. Although an introduction to knowledge-engineering technology is not called for at this point, a careful explanation of the techniques might have helped to assuage Robert's fears. Instead of taking the time to define his terminology, however, Joe sprinkles buzz words through his sentence like magic powder into a cauldron. To Robert, who does not recognize any magical force in these words, Joe seems to imply that Robert's job is trivial. In this interchange, Joe has violated two guidelines for interacting with an expert. First his use of unfamiliar jargon excludes Robert from the conversation. Second he fails to show respect for Robert's expertise.

Joe's final error is to show his impatience when Robert is unable to explain why he classifies a PrintMaster as computing equipment. As frustration takes hold of his speech, Joe becomes almost belligerent. Robert can hardly be expected to continue the interaction.

In the second dialog, Joe adapts his dress and behavior to the more formal style with which Robert is comfortable. He takes a little time at the beginning of the meeting to express his appreciation for Robert's help and to explain what they will discuss and his reasons for that discussion.

Joe shows concern about, and understanding of, Robert's skepticism about the system. In doing so, he acknowledges the difficulty and complexity of Robert's specialty. Joe addresses Robert's real concern—that of losing his job—by making clear the purpose of the expert system. Joe presents the system in terms of its potential benefit to Robert himself. In doing so, he emphasizes Robert's continuing importance to the company. When Robert realizes that the system will not replace him but may even make his own job more interesting, he stops viewing it as a threat. Although still unsure that a useful system can be developed, Robert is willing to explore this possibility with Joe.

Joe includes Robert in the discovery process when he says, "As we go through these cases, *let's* try to look for. . . ." He starts to show Robert that he wants the two of them to work together to build the system. In this second dialog, Joe makes important progress toward the goal of building a cooperative relationship with Robert.

13.2.5 Group Interactions

As we have seen, knowledge engineers must show sensitivity to the experts they interview. Although the same guidelines apply in interactions that include multiple knowledge engineers or multiple experts, it is often more difficult for the knowledge engineers to follow these guidelines in group interactions.

Interactions with Multiple Knowledge Engineers

If interviews are somewhat threatening for experts, team interviews can be downright intimidating. The larger the interviewing team, the greater the likelihood that problems will arise. Try to limit the number of questioners in each interview. As a general rule, one or two knowledge engineers should ask most of the questions in an interview. *Occasional* questions from other team members are permissible. If you find that your expert is unusually quiet in team interviews, limit the interviewing team to two members. If the expert still seems uncomfortable, abandon team interviews, and let a single knowledge engineer interview the expert.

In a team interview, *be particularly mindful to keep the expert comfortable.* In an interview between a single knowledge engineer and a single expert, the knowledge engineer can focus on the expert. This focus often prompts the knowledge engineer to be sensitive to the expert. Unfortunately, the knowledge engineer's focus is diffused in a team interview. When knowledge engineers outnumber the expert, they often forget the importance of sensitivity. Keep this point in mind during a team interview.

- Do not digress into technical discussions in front of the expert; save these discussions for after the interview.

- If cultural differences exist between the knowledge engineers and the expert, do not force the expert to adapt to the majority culture in a team interview.

Be careful not to overwhelm the expert. Keep the pace of the interview comfortable for the expert. Watch for signs that you are going too fast or are tiring the expert. Remember to give the expert time to rest. While you and the other questioners can alternate asking questions, the expert has to provide *all* the answers. What seems like a comfortable rate to you may be exhausting for the expert.

Before you ask a question, give the expert time to answer the previous question. If you think a team member's question was not phrased well, see how the expert answers it before you rephrase the question in your own way. When several questioners repeat the same question in different words without waiting for an answer, they give the impression of "ganging up" on the expert.

Interactions with Multiple Experts

If your project team includes more than one expert, you will need to establish a good working relationship with each expert. Pay particular attention to individual differences. You may need to develop different styles for working with the different experts. Each interaction with project experts will be complicated by the fact that the project includes multiple experts. The nature of the complication will depend on the nature of the interaction.

- *Successive individual interviews.* Many knowledge-acquisition interviews will focus on a single area and include a single expert. The complication with a series of individual interviews is to remember each particular expert's interaction style. Be especially sensitive to individual differences when you interview different experts in quick succession. *Be sure your behavior is appropriate for the expert you are interviewing currently.*

- *Group discussions.* When you focus on an aspect of the task in which the knowledge of multiple experts must interact, you will need to discuss the issues with all concerned experts present. (Section 2.8 provides guidelines for conducting group discussions.) You may find it necessary to act as an interpreter, explaining one expert's view in a light that a second expert can understand. When you conduct meetings that include more than one expert, *try to keep all experts comfortable throughout the meeting.*

  If disagreements arise, play the moderator; *be careful not to give the impression that you side with any expert in a dispute.* Try to settle the problems; do what you can to facilitate understanding and agreement among the experts. If you anticipate conflicts between particular experts in your project, try to interview each independently *before* the group meeting. Present the views of each in the manner that will be easiest for the others to understand and to accept.

- *Interviews with multiple experts.* If your project includes experts who work in teams, or experts who share an area of expertise (options 2a and 2b of Figure 2.6), you may need to interview multiple experts in a single session. This kind of interview is subject to the difficulties of individual interviews as well as group discussions. You will need to keep all the experts comfortable and to pay attention to individual differences. You may have to adapt your interaction style *with each question.* (In Chapter 17, we shall examine how to correct problems that can occur when experts argue among themselves.)

13.3 Interactions among Knowledge Engineers

During interviews, the interactions among the knowledge engineers should be cordial and cooperative, never quarrelsome. As the name *interviewing team* implies, the knowledge engineers who participate in an interview should work together as a team. If more than one person asks questions, teamwork is particularly important. Each question should follow naturally from the preceding question and its answer as though a single person were asking all the questions. All questioners should follow the lead of the primary interviewer.

If differences of opinion arise, they should be discussed politely. The lead interviewer should decide which alternative is preferable, and the remaining knowledge engineers should defer to this decision. If necessary, the knowledge engineers can air their disagreements after the meeting when the expert is not present. Under no circumstances should knowledge engineers argue among themselves during an interview. Such arguments waste time and can make the interview unpleasant for the expert (as well as for the knowledge engineers). Arguments can undermine the expert's confidence in the project and respect for the knowledge engineers.

Dialog 13.3[2] illustrates the importance of teamwork among knowledge engineers. Read this example critically; try to identify good and bad interactions among the knowledge engineers.

Dialog 13.3 Team Interviewing

Setting

David is an expert television repairman. Jim and Mary are knowledge engineers developing an expert system to help repair personnel with the diagnosis and repair of television sets. Jim is the project leader and the more senior knowledge engineer.

In this interview, Jim and Mary are trying to get a general understanding of the task of television repair. David has just given an overview in which he explained that his approach in repairing televisions differs between sets with vacuum tubes and those with solid-state circuitry. The vacuum-tube sets are simpler to repair.

Dialog with Problems

Jim: Thank you for that overview, David. Now can you tell us about a particular television you repaired recently.

David *(hesitantly):* Well, I really can't think of a *particular* set. I've repaired so many.

Jim: That's OK. You said tube TVs are easier to repair. Do you still see many of these sets?

David: Yes, you'd be surprised at the number of people who still have these old TVs. They watch a more modern TV most of the time, but they use the old TVs in their back rooms, workshops, or kitchens.

Jim: Well then, let's suppose I am a customer. I bring you a tube TV to fix. What is the first thing you would do.

David *(confidently):* I'd ask you what is wrong with the TV.

---

2. Dialog 13.3 was inspired by dialogs on videotapes used in two Cimflex Teknowledge Corporation training courses: the *Knowledge Acquisition Workshop* and the *Diagnosis Seminar.*

Jim: When I turn it on, nothing happens. No sound. No picture.

Mary *(interrupting Jim):* This example is too difficult to start with—everything is broken. It would be better if we started with an example where only one thing has gone wrong. I'm not even sure this example makes sense.

The two knowledge engineers ignore the expert as they quibble between themselves.

Jim: I'm sure we had problems like this with the TV my family had when I was a kid. It can't be *that* unusual.

David *(interrupting hesitantly):* I do see televisions like that fairly often. You turn the TV on, and all you see is a bunch of snow—little white and black dots all over the screen. The only sound you get is a hum or a lot of crackling.

Jim glares at Mary triumphantly.

Jim: So what do you do in a case like this?

David: Well, I try to locate the component of the TV that has a problem. The video component controls the picture. The audio component controls the sound. In this case, both the picture and the sound failed. Usually, only one thing goes wrong at a time so I look for the place where both the audio and the video signals originate.

Jim: Where would that be?

David: My first guess would be the tuner, but you also might have a problem with the I-Fs, the internal-frequency amplifiers.

Jim: So what would you do next?

Mary: Before you go further, David, what would you have done if the picture had been good but the sound was bad?

David *(puzzled):* That sounds like a problem with the audio amp—you're talking about a different TV, right?

Mary: Yes. I'm interested in the different problems you might see.

Jim *(interrupting):* Let's concentrate on one case at a time. You said you suspected the tuner.

David *(confused and frustrated):* Now are we talking about the first TV again?

Jim nods.

The most likely problem is the tuner. I would try to replace the R-F amp to see if that fixed the problem.

Mary: Is the R-F amp similar to the audio amp?

David *(scowling slightly):* I'm not sure what you mean. Both amplifiers are tubes. The R-F amp—that's the radio-frequency amplifier—is in the tuner. The audio amplifier circuit might contain one or two tubes depending on the TV. Some TVs have an amp and a preamp. Did that answer your question?

Mary: Yes. If the problem had been . . .

Jim *(interrupting and glowering at Mary):* Let's get back to the TV we've been discussing. David, suppose you replaced the radio-frequency amplifier, but the problem didn't go away. Can that happen?

David: Yes. Then I would try replacing each of the I-F tubes.

> Before you read further, think about the previous dialog.
> Review the interviewer roles described in Section 13.1. What role does Jim play? What role does Mary play? Do they follow the guidelines for team interviews?
> What problems can you identify? What would you have done differently?

Dialog without Problems

Jim: Let's suppose I am a customer. I bring you a tube TV to fix. What is the first thing you would do?

David *(confidently):* I'd ask you what is wrong with the TV.

Jim: OK. I tell you that when I turn the TV on nothing happens. No sound. No picture.

David: Then I'd turn on the TV to see for myself. Let's say I turn it on and see a bunch of snow—little white and black dots all over the screen. The only sound I hear is a crackling noise.

Jim: What does this tell you?

David: Both the picture and the sound failed. Usually only one thing goes wrong at a time so I look for the place where both the audio and the video signals originate.

Jim: Where would that be?

David: My first guess would be the tuner, but you also might have a problem with the I-Fs, the internal-frequency amplifiers.

Jim nods and writes in his notebook.

Mary: So what would you do next?

David: The most likely problem is the tuner. I would try to replace the R-F amp to see if that fixed the problem.

Mary: David, would you please explain what you mean by *R-F amp?*

David: The R-F amp is the the radio-frequency amplifier; it's a tube in the tuner.

Mary: Thank you. You had just told us that you would try to replace the R-F amp.

David: That's right. I would pull out the tube, look for the identification number, get a new tube with the same number, and pop it in. Then I'd turn on the set. If the picture and sound are good now, I'm done.

Jim: David, suppose you replaced the radio-frequency amplifier, but the problem didn't go away. Can that happen?

David: Yes. Then I would try replacing each of the I-F tubes—there are usually three of these tubes. I'd replace them one at a time—just like I did with the R-F amp—until I found the bad tube. I'd say that in 90 to 95 percent of the TVs with this kind of problem, one of those four tubes is to blame.

Mary: Let me see if I have understood correctly. When you see snow and hear crackling, you know that both the audio and the video signals are bad. So you look for a problem in the source of these two signals. That makes you suspect either the radio-frequency amplifier in the tuner or one of the internal-frequency amplifier tubes. You start with the R-F amp, and you try replacing the tubes one at a time until you fix the problem.

David: That's right.

Discussion

Jim is the lead interviewer in this interview. Mary's role is secondary questioner. The interview in the first dialog would have been more productive if Mary had been a silent observer. When Mary found Jim's example unreasonable, she should have kept quiet rather than challenging his lead. Before saying anything, she should have waited to see how *David* reacted to the example. As it turned out, the example was realistic; it was a problem that David recognized easily. If David *had* encountered difficulties with the example, Mary could have asked, "Jim, do you think it would help if you changed the example so that only one thing was wrong—say, the sound?" This would have shown teamwork rather than divisiveness.

As secondary questioner, Mary's questions should follow the topics Jim chooses. Instead she appears to have her own agenda. When Mary asks what David would have done if the picture alone had been bad, she not only derails Jim's current line of questioning but she also leaves David frustrated at having to switch gears. Mary's next question about the similarity between the R-F and the audio amplifiers seems to have a single purpose: to return to *Mary's* line of questioning. The question is not relevant to anything David has said; it serves to disorient David once again.

Although Mary's behavior obstructed progress in the interview, Jim should have dealt with her interruptions more gracefully. By glaring at her triumphantly when his example succeeded, he fostered a feeling of competition. This may have encouraged Mary to continue to pursue her own agenda. When Mary side-tracked the discussion later in the dialog, Jim's nonverbal communication of glowering at Mary would have been inappropriate if Jim's expression were visible to David. Jim would have emphasized the conflict between the knowledge engineers. Although David could hardly have missed the problems, Jim should have done whatever he could to minimize the tension. If, on the other hand, David could not see Jim scowl at Mary, Jim might have succeeded in letting Mary know that her questions were inappropriate without emphasizing the problem to the expert.

The interview in the second dialog proceeds much more smoothly because of cooperation and good technique on the part of both knowledge engineers. Mary is a model secondary questioner. Her questions follow the current conversation, rather than changing the topic. When Jim needs time to write notes about David's answer to his question, Mary keeps the discussion moving by asking the next question. When David uses an unfamiliar term, she asks him to define it. When David has finished with his description, Mary carefully summarizes her understanding of David's answers and asks for confirmation that she has understood correctly.

Table 13.1 Interactions during Knowledge-Acquisition Interviews

Do	Don't
Consider the expert an important member of the project team.	Make the expert ill at ease.
Ask the expert to participate in scheduling and planning.	Exclude the expert by discussing implementation details.
Include the expert in discussions with project management.	Use knowledge-engineering or computer-science jargon.
Include the expert in project social activities.	Imply that you think the expert's job is easy.
Make sure the expert understands why you want to discuss each topic.	Challenge, belittle, compete with, or condescend to the expert.
Discuss only topics that need the expert's input or that interest the expert.	Lose your patience.
Use language the expert will understand.	Send the expert nonverbal signals that contradict your words.
Show you respect the expert's knowledge, skill, and experience.	Let the expert know (or think) you are bored, disinterested, angry, frustrated, or irritated.
Show you want to learn from the expert.	Interview in a team that is too large for the expert's comfort.
Learn the expert's individual style.	Set a pace that tires the expert.
Pay attention to the expert's nonverbal signals, and learn what they mean.	Appear to side with one expert over another when experts disagree.
Correct misunderstandings when the expert misinterprets your nonverbal signals.	Argue with other knowledge engineers during an interview.
Adapt to the expert's cultural expectations.	
Learn what different interaction styles work best with the different experts on the project.	
Remember personal differences when you switch from one expert to another.	
Act as moderator and interpreter among the experts in an interview.	
Work as a team with other knowledge engineers.	

13.4 Points to Remember

The success of a knowledge-acquisition interview depends on appropriate interactions among the participants. The knowledge engineers' overriding concern in an interview should be to keep the expert comfortable with the interview itself and with the project as a whole.

- Knowledge engineers should be sensitive to the individual styles, concerns, and preferences of the experts with whom they interact.

- When several knowledge engineers interview an expert, they should work together smoothly and cooperatively and should follow the direction set by the lead interviewer. They should be particularly careful that their number does not intimidate the expert or make the interview more tiring.

Table 13.1 contains guidelines for interactions among the participants in a knowledge-acquisition interview.

Chapter 14

Preparation for an Interview

Once Howard Hacker had become familiar with the different knowledge-acquisition roles, he understood how the participants in an interview should interact with one another. He was ready to start to develop his own interviewing skills. Howard asked Patricia Programmer, "Where do I begin? Is there anything I can learn outside the interviews?" Patricia responded that one key to a successful interview is careful preparation. Howard's next task was to learn how to prepare for an interview.

As Patricia Programmer indicated, a good way to ensure a productive interview is to prepare well beforehand. This chapter describes the process by which knowledge engineers can prepare for a knowledge-acquisition interview. In Chapter 3, we saw that thorough preparation is crucial for the first interview. Patricia planned the content of the interview and identified the materials she and Frank Fixit would need to bring to the meeting. She prepared Frank with an initial telephone call, a follow-up letter, and a confirmation telephone call. To prepare themselves, Patricia and Howard Hacker reviewed the project plan and tried to learn the basic terminology of toaster repair. Preparation for subsequent interviews may require less time, but it remains equally important. Frank is a typical expert: his time is at a premium. Patricia and Howard must make good use of their limited opportunities to interview Frank. Careful preparation for each meeting will help them accomplish their goals without wasting precious time.

Patricia uses a checklist (Figure 14.1) to guide her preparation for each knowledge-acquisition interview. As we look in more detail at the five items in this checklist, we shall illustrate how Patricia prepares for a typical interview in the detailed investigation stage of knowledge acquisition. This interview is one in a series of meetings to discuss

Figure 14.1 Checklist for knowledge-acquisition preparation. Careful preparation can help ensure the success of an interview. Identify *what* you will discuss. Decide *when* and *where* the interview will take place. Plan *how* you will obtain the information you need. Select the appropriate knowledge-acquisition activities, and identify the materials you will need to support these activities. When you know the what, when, where, and how of an interview, you can prepare all the participants: the expert, yourself, and the other knowledge engineers.

PREPARATION FOR AN INTERVIEW

☑ Plan content of the interview.

☑ Arrange the time and location.

☑ Identify the necessary materials.

☑ Prepare the expert.

☑ Prepare the knowledge engineers.

how Frank handles no-latch problems in toasters. The interview occurs after the team has covered no-latch problems with two-slice toasters in detail; they are now ready to move on to four-slice toasters.

14.1 Planning the Content

Your first step in planning an interview is to *identify the topics for discussion.* State as specifically as possible what you want to learn during the interview. Review the goals for the current stage of knowledge acquisition and identify which ones are relevant to this interview. Keep these knowledge-acquisition goals in mind as you plan the interview; be sure that your discussion topics address all the relevant goals. In early interviews, pay particular attention to team-building goals. In later interviews, concentrate on information-gathering goals.

Next *identify your own assumptions and prejudices* about the topics you plan to discuss. During the interview, you should be careful to avoid introducing your own opinions. If you identify the assumptions you bring to an interview, you can guard against bias. If your discussion topics imply assumptions, add new topics to learn whether your assumptions are correct.

> Patricia Programmer prepares a list of topics for her meeting with Frank Fixit. When she reviews these topics, Patricia recognizes a strong assumption that four-slice toasters are similar to two-slice toasters. She assumes that the knowledge about four-slice toasters will be slight extensions of, and modifications to, the knowledge she has already acquired about two-slice toasters. Patricia adds a new topic to her list (Figure 14.2); during the interview, she will ask Frank whether her assumption is well founded.

When you have decided what information you hope to obtain, *list activities that will be useful* in eliciting this information (Figure 14.3). Part 1 described knowledge-acquisition activities in detail. Some examples are:

- Ask the expert to give a brief overview of the new area to be addressed by the expert system.

- Discuss details of a particular case—that is, a particular situation in which the task was (or could be) performed.

- Present an intermediate representation of the information you acquired in previous interviews, and ask for comments.

- Give the expert a demonstration of the expert system, and ask for feedback.

Next, *create your agenda* from the list of activities you selected for the meeting (Figure 14.4). Estimate the amount of time each activity

Figure 14.2 Planned topics for an interview. Patricia Programmer prepares a list of topics to discuss with Frank Fixit. She divides the topics into *follow-up topics* that continue the discussion from the previous interview, *assumptions to confirm*, and *new topics*. Patricia organizes the new topics according to the three goals of detailed investigation. Because Patricia is already familiar with no-latch problems in two-slice toasters, she is able to list some fairly specific topics. For the first interview on any particular subject, she will only be able to list very general topics.

FOLLOW-UP TOPICS

How well does the system handle no-latch problems with two-slice toasters?

ASSUMPTIONS TO CONFIRM

No-latch problems in four-slice toasters are very similar to no-latch problems in two-slice toasters.

NEW TOPICS

Goal: Identify steps in performing the task.

What steps does Frank take in identifying and repairing no-latch problems with four-slice toasters?

How is this process different from Frank's process for finding and repairing no-latch problems in two-slice toasters?

Goal: Understand how the expert reasons.

How does Frank confirm the cause of a no-latch problem and decide on the repair?

Frank considers two possible causes for no-latch problems in two-slice toasters: defective carriage-latch spring and displaced release projectile. Does he consider any different or additional causes of no-latch problems in four-slice toasters.

Goal: Identify what information is needed.

How does the latch mechanism on a four-slice toaster differ from the latch mechanism on a two-slice toaster?

Do all models of four-slice toaster use the same latch mechanism?

Do four-slice toasters have one carriage-latch spring or two?

---

will take. The purpose of the agenda is to check that the content is reasonable given the available time. Working out the agenda will help you to avoid trying to squeeze in more than you have time to discuss. Your agenda will also reduce the possibility that you might schedule more time with the expert than is necessary.

Your agenda should be a flexible outline of your objectives, not a

Figure 14.3 Planned activities for an interview. Patricia Programmer lists the knowledge-acquisition activities that will help her obtain the necessary knowledge from Frank Fixit.

ACTIVITIES FOR THE INTERVIEW

- Show Frank a demonstration of the system. Use cases that illustrate no-latch problems in two-slice toasters.

- Discuss the demonstration with Frank. See what needs to be changed.

- Ask Frank to present an overview of no-latch problems in four-slice toasters that describes how these problems differ from no-latch problems in two-slice toasters.

- Discuss examples of no-latch problems in four-slice toasters. Go through as many cases as time permits.

rigid plan. Early in the project, your time estimates may not be accurate. Before you get to know your expert, you will not have a good sense of how much time to allow for various activities. Later in the project, you will be able to make more accurate estimates, but you should still be prepared to deviate from your plan if necessary.

As we shall discuss in Chapter 15, each interview should begin with a short introduction and end with brief closing remarks. When you develop your agenda, remember to leave time for these two activities. If the meeting is more than one or two hours long, leave time for breaks. As you work with your team members, learn how frequently your project team needs breaks. Initially, schedule a ten-minute break after each hour of discussion.

Figure 14.4 Interview agenda. Patricia Programmer uses her list of activities to prepare the agenda for her meeting with Frank Fixit.

AGENDA

9:00	Introduction
9:10	Demonstration
9:30	Discuss demonstration
10:00	Break
10:15	Overview of no-latch problems in four-slice toasters
10:30	Start discussion of first case
11:45	Closing

14.2 Arranging the Time and Location

Set a time and location for the interview that is convenient for all participants. If possible, at the end of one interview decide on the time for the next interview. As a project progresses, it is often possible to schedule standard meeting times (for example, interview every Wednesday afternoon from 1:00 until 5:00). Similarly, it may be possible to arrange to hold all interviews in the same room. The perfect arrangement is to meet in a room that is reserved for the project so common reference materials, project notebooks, and so on can be left in the project room.

> Early in the toaster-repair advisor project, Patricia Programmer, Howard Hacker, and Frank Fixit settled into a schedule of meeting each week on Tuesday morning. They have a standard meeting room, but occasionally corporate meetings are scheduled in this room so the project team must meet elsewhere. To arrange for her interview, Patricia simply has to check that the room is available at their regular meeting time.

14.2.1 Frequency of Interviews

The frequency and duration of interviews will vary during the project. A deciding factor may be the expert's schedule. How long an absence can the expert take from other obligations? Half a day at a time? A whole day? A week?

When you schedule an interview, be sure to give both the expert and the knowledge engineers adequate preparation time. For example, if Frank Fixit needs to identify five relevant cases and prepare case descriptions before an interview, Patricia Programmer should verify that he has enough time to prepare the case descriptions (in addition to his other commitments) between one interview and the next. Similarly if Patricia plans to demonstrate new functionality in the expert system, she needs to allow herself and Howard Hacker enough time to design and implement the enhancements before the next meeting.

14.2.2 Time of Day

The meeting time should be convenient to the entire project group. Ideally you should schedule meetings at times when you can have the expert's undivided attention. If your expert carries a beeper, for example, try to plan meetings at times when the expert can ask a colleague to answer beeper calls.

If you have any flexibility in choosing the time of day for a meeting, try to select a time that works best with the expert's personal clock.

For example, if the expert is a morning person who tires by late after-noon, try for early morning meetings.

Pay special attention to the time of day when working with an expert from a different location. For example, suppose that you and your colleagues are knowledge engineers who work for a consulting firm in Boston, and your expert works for a company in Seattle. Interviews are scheduled in blocks of three days at the beginning of each month. The expert flies to Boston for half of the meetings, and the knowledge engineers fly to Seattle for the other half. You should try to schedule meeting times with sensitivity to differences in time zones. Early morning meetings in Boston will be difficult for the expert; late afternoon meetings in Seattle will be difficult for the knowledge engineers.

14.2.3 Interview Location

Arrange to hold interviews in an enclosed room with a door to shut out distracting noises. The room should be large enough to accommodate the entire project team comfortably, with all participants seated at a table. This seating arrangement gives everyone a good writing surface, a clear view of display media, and easy access to shared materials such as manuals, models, and equipment. Although it is not necessary to demonstrate the expert system in the same location where the interviews are held, it is often convenient to do so. When you consider a meeting room, see whether you will be able to set up the necessary equipment for demonstrations in the room. Pick a location where you can work with the fewest disturbances.

> At the beginning of the toaster-repair advisor project, Patricia Programmer needed to choose between the conference room in the computation department and a meeting room in the service department. She initially decided to meet in the service department because that location was more convenient for Frank Fixit. Unfortunately, that location proved to be too disruptive. Frank receives frequent telephone calls, and other interruptions occur. The other members of the repair staff soon learned to look for Frank in the meeting room when he was not in his office. The switchboard operator soon learned to transfer Frank's calls to the meeting room. These continual interruptions made interviews difficult for Frank and frustrating for Patricia. Both agreed that it would be better to meet in the computation department where they could work undisturbed.

Although Frank was able to work undisturbed in Patricia's building, some experts must go farther from their work location to avoid interruptions. Some expert-system projects teams have found it necessary to meet off-site because their experts could be tracked down in any building on location.

14.3 Identifying the Necessary Materials

Review the planned agenda and *specify what materials you will need at the meeting*. Recording materials are standard for all interviews.[1] Display media are also important in all interviews. Include whiteboards or flip charts that are located conveniently for writing outlines and diagrams where the whole group can see and discuss them. As you consider what materials you will need, think about what you want to show the expert, what you want the expert to show you, and what reference material might be useful to your discussions. Table 14.1 lists materials useful for various knowledge-acquisition activities. Refer to this table when you prepare your interviews.

When you have identified the materials you will need, *decide who should be responsible for bringing each item to the meeting*. Make sure all team members know what they are expected to bring. Patricia Programmer's list of materials for her interview is shown in Figure 14.5.

Table 14.1 Auxiliary Materials for Interviews

Activity	Useful Materials

All	Recording materials
	    Project notebooks
	    Tape recorder and cassettes
	    Video camera–recorder and videotapes
	Display media
	    Flip chart
	    Whiteboard (especially electronic)
	Reference materials
	    Notes from previous interviews and design discussions (in project notebooks)
	    Descriptions of cases discussed in earlier sessions
	    Listing of knowledge base
	    Manuals, catalogs, or books the expert uses in performing the task
	Clock visible to entire group

Overview discussion	"Props" to help facilitate descriptions: relevant instruments, equipment, models, or parts Projector if expert would like to show slides or transparencies
Classification of cases	Index cards with summaries of inputs for each case Index cards with summaries of results for each case

---

1. Chapter 15 describes techniques for recording the content of an interview.

Table 14.1 (continued)

Activity	Useful Materials
Case discussion	Written description of the case, including input data, the sequence of problem-solving actions and decisions, and the output results Relevant instruments, equipment, models, or parts to illustrate what the expert does
Review of recorded case discussion	Written description of case Tape recorder and recording of case discussion
Comparison of a case with its hypothetical alternatives	Written description of case Tape recorder and recording of case discussion (if any)
Comparison of similar cases	Written description of cases Summary of differences between inputs to the cases, the expert's actions in the cases, and the expert's conclusions in the cases
Review of an intermediate representation	Written copy of the intermediate representation of information from recent interviews
Demonstration	Computer or terminal Input data for cases to be demonstrated Typescript of interaction with the expert system (for discussion following the demonstration)

If your list includes written materials to be discussed, arrange to have a copy for each person in the meeting. Written materials include the meeting agenda, case descriptions, typescripts of interactions with the expert system, and intermediate representations of information from earlier interviews. If possible, distribute copies of these materials to the team members before the meeting.[2]

14.4 Preparing the Expert

A productive interview requires that all participants be prepared. You should do all you can to *see that the expert comes to interviews prepared.* Be sure the expert knows the time and location of the meeting; give the expert a copy of the meeting agenda. If necessary, remind the expert what materials to bring. Check whether the expert has sufficient time

---

2. As we discussed in Chapter 10, you should *not* distribute an intermediate representation before the meeting unless the expert already knows how to interpret the representation.

Figure 14.5 Materials for an interview. Patricia Programmer reviews her agenda to identify the materials that will be needed for the interview. She organizes her list of materials to indicate which team member should bring each item to the meeting.

PATRICIA

Meeting agenda

Toaster-repair manual

Project notebook (with notes from interviews and design meetings) for recording today's meeting

HOWARD

Project notebook for recording today's meeting

Personal computer for demonstration

Listing of the knowledge base

Input data for cases with no-latch problems in two-slice toasters to use in demonstration

FRANK

Disassembled four-slice toaster

Case descriptions for four-slice toasters with no-latch problems

---

to collect or prepare all the materials before the meeting. If not, it may be best to reschedule the interview or to work out an alternative agenda. Ask whether you can help in any way. For example, you might arrange to have the expert's materials copied and distributed to the team members. Your main aim at this step is to remind the expert politely what you expect. Early in the project, you will need to provide more information and offer more help. When meetings are infrequent, your reminders to the expert will be more important. On the other hand, when you meet regularly, a quick, informal reminder will suffice.

Before Patricia Programmer's meeting, she prepares Frank Fixit with a quick telephone call.

Dialog 14.1 Preparing the Expert for an Interview

Dialog

The telephone rings; Frank picks it up.

Frank: Service department; Frank Fixit speaking.

Patricia: Hi Frank; it's Patricia. We're set for our meeting on Tuesday in the usual place.

Frank: Good. I got the agenda you sent over.

Patricia: Will you have time to prepare the case descriptions?

Frank: You bet! I've got three already, and I think I should be able to finish a couple more by Tuesday. Do you want me to send over copies for you and Howard like I did before?

Patricia: Yes, thanks. Just send us what you have ready by Monday. We'll probably only have time to discuss two or three cases in detail at the meeting.

Frank: I've been looking for a toaster to bring to the meeting. I think I can find a model that is particularly susceptible to no-latch problems.

Patricia: Good. See you on Tuesday.

Frank: See you then. Bye.

Discussion

Notice that Frank is now familiar with interviews. When he received Patricia's agenda, he knew what materials he needed to collect and to prepare for the meeting. Contrast this dialog with Dialog 3.2. Notice how much more explanation and guidance Patricia had to provide at the beginning of the project.

14.5 Preparing Yourself

Shortly before the meeting, review your agenda and your notes from earlier sessions so that the important issues relating to your planned discussion topics will be fresh in your mind. If you have copies of materials that will be discussed during the meeting, review these and prepare comments or questions for the discussion.

In preparation for her meeting, Patricia Programmer works with Howard Hacker to make the expert system ready for demonstration. She also reviews their conceptual model for diagnosing no-latch problems in two-slice toasters. During the interview, she will look for similarities and differences between the current model and Frank Fixit's approach to diagnosing no-latch problems in four-slice toasters. When Patricia receives her copies of the new case descriptions Frank prepares for this meeting, she reads through them and compares them to the examples of no-latch problems with two-slice toasters the group discussed in the past.

14.6 Points to Remember

Careful preparation can help to ensure the success of an interview. You will be able to make the most productive use of the available interview time if you plan the content of each meeting. Your plan should anticipate topics to discuss during the interview, materials to review before the interview, and materials to support the interview discussion (Table 14.2).

Although you will follow the same steps to prepare for all interviews, the nature of your preparations will change as the project progresses (Table 14.3).

Table 14.2 Preparing for an Interview

Step	Details
Plan the content.	Identify topics for discussion. Identify your own assumptions and prejudices about these topics. Plan new discussion topics to find out whether your assumptions are correct. List the knowledge-acquisition activities that will help you to obtain the information you seek. Create your agenda. Remember to include an introduction and a closing. Estimate times for the planned activities. If the meeting will last for more than an hour, include one or more breaks.
Arrange the time and location.	Select a time and a location convenient for all participants. Choose a location free from distractions. Schedule enough time between interviews to allow all participants to prepare adequately.
Identify necessary materials.	Decide what materials are needed to support the planned activities. Consider: 　Recording materials 　Display media 　Materials the expert should show you 　Materials you should show the expert 　Reference materials
Prepare the expert and other knowledge engineers.	Notify all team members of the time and location of the interview. Verify that each team member will have time to collect or prepare the necessary materials. Collect, copy, and distribute written materials to all team members before the meeting.
Prepare yourself.	Review written materials your teammates prepared before the meeting. Review relevant notes from earlier meetings.

Table 14.3 Changes in Preparation Through the Course of a Project

Step	Early in the Project	Later in the Project
Plan the content.	Focus on *team-building* goals. Identify topics in general terms.	Focus on *information-building* goals. Identify specific questions to ask and issues to resolve.
Arrange the time and location.	Make an effort to find a time and a location that will suit the expert. Experiment with different times and locations if necessary.	Follow a standard schedule; meet in a standard location. Confirm times and locations arranged in the previous interview.
Identify necessary materials.	Find out what relevant materials exist that might be helpful (for example, documents, models, instruments, or pieces of equipment).	Suggest materials that have proven helpful in earlier interviews.
Prepare the expert.	Explain carefully what preparation is required and why this preparation is necessary. Provide examples to illustrate what materials the expert should prepare. Remind the expert to bring the necessary materials. Offer to help the expert prepare materials.	State briefly materials the expert should bring. If necessary, refer to materials used in earlier discussions.
Prepare yourself.	Focus on the project. Review materials about the application subject area to become familiar with terminology and simple concepts.	Focus on the expert system. Review materials from earlier discussions.

Chapter 15

Transfer of Information during an Interview

When Howard Hacker had learned to prepare for an interview, he became impatient to take part in his first interview. Howard knew that he and Patricia Programmer had to learn about toaster repair from Frank Fixit during each interview, but he was uncertain *how* they would accomplish this aim. Patricia explained that there are two facets to learning from Frank. The first facet is the *verbal communication* of information. During the interview, Frank would tell them how he repairs toasters. The second facet is the *capture* of information in a permanent record. Patricia and Howard would have to preserve the information that Frank communicated so they could analyze this information and use it to develop an expert system. Patricia said they could facilitate communication by providing a structure to each interview. They could capture information by taking notes and using electronic recording devices.

The successful transfer of information during a knowledge-acquisition interview requires:

- Communication of information from the expert to the knowledge engineers (Section 15.1)

- Capture of the information by the knowledge engineers for later use (Section 15.2)

15.1 Verbal Communication

As we discussed in Chapter 12, much of the verbal communication in a knowledge-acquisition interview occurs through a series of questions and answers. The communication will be most productive if the questions present *a logical sequence of topics*. Although knowledge engineers generally set the direction of the discussion by asking questions, the expert must be able to understand and follow this direction. The expert should:

- Know the knowledge engineers' goals for an interview

- Understand what topic each question addresses

- Recognize when the discussion leaves one topic and proceeds to the next

- Understand how successive topics are related and why they are included in the same interview

- Know, at the end of an interview, what to expect in the future

Knowledge engineers should *structure* interviews to keep the expert at ease with the interview process and to keep the expert oriented to the current topic of discussion. Each interview should consist of three segments:

1. An *introduction* (Section 15.1.1)

2. A *body* (Section 15.1.2)

3. A *closing* (Section 15.1.3)

15.1.1 Introduction to an Interview

Start each interview with an informal introduction in which you exchange pleasantries and let the expert know what you have planned. In the first several meetings, you will also need to explain what you are trying to accomplish and what you expect of the expert. In later meetings, your introduction should include a quick summary of what you discussed in the previous meeting and what you have accomplished since then. In general, the introduction should take just a few minutes. Its purpose is to share your plan with the expert.

Patricia Programmer might introduce an interview as illustrated in Dialog 15.1.

Dialog 15.1 Introducing an Interview

Setting

Patricia Programmer, Howard Hacker, and Frank Fixit have recently discussed no-latch problems in two-slice toasters. Patricia wants to review the system's performance on these problems and then to begin the discussion of no-latch problems in four-slice toasters.

Dialog

Patricia: Hi, Frank! Good to see you again. Why don't we get some coffee before we start?

Patricia pauses as the team members pour their coffee, walk to the table, and sit down.

Last week we went over several toasters with faulty latch mechanisms. As I recall, you said that these cases covered the most common no-latch problems in two-slice toasters.

Frank nods.

We have another demo for you today. Howard and I have updated the system to handle those no-latch problems. We'd like to start this morning by showing you how the system handles the toasters we discussed last week. Then you can tell us how the system looks, what you like about it, what you don't like, and what changes we need.

Frank: Good. It always helps me understand how we're doing when I get to see how the system performs.

Patricia: If you find major problems with the demo, we'll probably spend the rest of this morning going over the changes we need to make. Otherwise I'd like to start working on no-latch problems in four-slice toasters.

Frank: That sounds fine to me.

Discussion

Patricia does not start the interview abruptly. She takes a little time to greet Frank as she would any colleague. Patricia has learned that Frank likes a cup of coffee at their morning meetings so she allows time for the team members to get coffee and to seat themselves before she starts the interview discussion. When she does begin the discussion, she first reviews what the group accomplished at the last interview, and she lets Frank know what to expect in the current interview.

15.1.2 Body of an Interview

During the body of an interview, the sequence of topics should flow smoothly. All participants should understand when the discussion leaves one topic and proceeds to the next. Adherence to the interview agenda will make the sequence of topics clear to the expert. Many interviews, however, deviate from the planned agenda. Some deviations are due to poor questioning technique (Chapter 16); others occur because the lead interviewer is unable to keep the interview on track (Chapter 17). And certain deviations are appropriate.

- The discussion of a planned topic may require more time than expected.

- The expert may not be prepared to discuss a planned topic.

- The knowledge engineers may discover that they cannot proceed with a planned topic until they obtain explanatory material they did not anticipate needing.

- The discussions of one topic may identify topics that should be covered during the current interview. This kind of deviation is common at the beginning of a project when the knowledge engineers do not know enough about the subject matter to plan exactly what topics they should discuss.

The lead interviewer is responsible for deciding when to alter the direction of an interview. Other questioners need to follow a change in direction by adjusting the focus of their questions. Often a change in direction will be obvious to the entire team. When such a change is more subtle, however, the lead interviewer should *state the change of direction explicitly*. For example, Patricia Programmer changes the direction of an interview in Dialog 15.2.

Dialog 15.2 Signaling a Change in Direction

Setting

The planned agenda for this interview[1] calls for Frank Fixit to present an overview of no-latch problems in four-slice toasters. After the overview, the team plans to discuss a few cases in detail.

Patricia Programmer, Frank Fixit, and Howard Hacker are seated at a table. A four-slice toaster is on the table in front of Frank. Frank is just concluding his overview.

Dialog

Frank: So that gives you the general picture of no-latch problems in four-slice toasters. Do you want me to start on the first case now?

---

1. Patricia Programmer's agenda for this interview appears in Figure 14.4.

Patricia: Let me ask one question first. You said that you use the normal operation of the latch mechanism to guide you as you track down the problems.

Frank nods.

Do all four-slice toasters use the same latch mechanism?

Frank: No—that's what I meant. I first check to see *what kind* of latch mechanism the toaster has. The normal operation for *that particular mechanism* is going to tell me how to look for the problem.

Patricia: Thanks. Are the various mechanisms very different from one another?

Frank: Oh, yes!

Frank points to the toaster in front of him.

I think you both could recognize the latch mechanism in this toaster. As you see, it has two separate latches that are just like the ones we saw in two-slice toasters. But other toasters use a more complicated mechanism that controls all four slots at once. Still other toasters have a mechanism that is activated by the weight of the bread. The bread racks in the slots that contain bread engage the carriage, but the racks in the other slots don't. There are a few other varieties, too. At any rate, I have to know which kind of latch mechanism the toaster has. Each kind works differently.

Patricia: So your approach is different, depending on the kind of latch mechanism?

Frank: Completely! What I'd do for this toaster wouldn't work for a toaster with a different mechanism.

Patricia: This is very interesting. Before we start the case discussion, maybe you should explain more about the different kinds of latch mechanisms and how they work. Do you think a discussion of latch mechanisms would help us to understand how you track down the problems?

Frank: Yes. Latch mechanisms would be the best thing to talk about next. I don't think you two will follow what I do until you understand how the different mechanisms work.

Patricia: OK. Let's start with the latch mechanism in this toaster.

Discussion

It is important to include the expert in a decision to change the focus of a discussion. Patricia is careful to ask Frank whether *he* believes that the change in topic would be worthwhile. Patricia continues with the discussion of latch mechanisms only after Frank has agreed *this topic is relevant* to the current discussion and that he is *prepared to discuss* latch mechanisms in the current interview.

Although it is up to the lead interviewer to decide when to change the focus of the discussion, another questioner can suggest that a change seems appropriate. The suggestion should be phrased as a question to the lead interviewer. For example, in the situation illustrated in Dialog 15.2, Howard Hacker might have suggested the change in topic (Dialog 15.3).

Dialog 15.3 Suggesting a Change in Direction

Dialog

> *Frank has just told Patricia and Howard about the different kinds of latch mechanisms.*

Patricia: So your approach is different, depending on the kind of latch mechanism?

Frank: Completely! What I'd do for this toaster wouldn't work for a toaster with a different mechanism.

Howard: I'm not sure I understand enough about the different kinds of latch mechanisms. Patricia, do you think we should spend some time discussing the latch mechanisms now?

Patricia: Yes, I think that might be a good idea. Frank, do you think such a discussion would be helpful?

Frank: Yes. Latch mechanisms would be the best thing to talk about next. I don't think you two will follow what I do until you understand how the different mechanisms work.

Discussion

> Patricia agreed with Howard's suggestion. Under other circumstances, she might have preferred to continue as planned. In a team interview, all the questioners should defer to the leader's decisions. If Patricia had elected to defer the discussion of latch mechanisms, Howard would have followed Patricia's lead without complaint.

15.1.3 Closing of an Interview

The closing of an interview is as important as is the introduction. The closing can ensure that all team members consider the discussion complete and that they all know what is expected of them before the next interview. To close an interview:

1. Give all participants an opportunity to make final remarks about the current discussion or to post topics for future interviews.

2. Summarize what the group has accomplished in the interview. Quickly identify agenda topics that were discussed completely, those that were partially discussed, those that were not discussed, and unplanned topics that were discussed.

3. Agree on a tentative list of discussion topics for the next interview.

4. Identify the preparation each participant will need before the next meeting.

5. Schedule the next meeting (tentatively if necessary).

Before you leave the meeting, be sure to thank the expert (and any nonproject attendees) for taking time to prepare for, and to participate in, the meeting.

Dialog 15.4 illustrates how Patricia Programmer ended an interview.

Dialog 15.4 Closing an Interview

Setting

The toaster-repair advisor team is discussing for the first time no-latch problems in four-slice toasters. They have just finished their second case discussion.

Dialog

Patricia: We're just about out of time. Frank, is there anything you'd like to add before we wind things up?

Frank: No. I think we've finished with this last case. But remember that these two toasters don't give you the whole picture. No-latch problems in four-slice toasters can be very tricky. You might want to look through the descriptions of the other three cases I sent you. They'll show you a completely different side of things.

Patricia: I understand. Well, we got quite a lot done this morning. I think Howard and I understand what we need to do to fix the current system.

Howard: Yes. I'm sure that I can put those changes in by the end of the week.

Patricia: Great. When you're done with the changes, why don't you make type-script files that record the system's interaction on the cases you used in today's demonstration. Then you can make hard copies of the type-scripts for us to review at the beginning of next week's meeting. The changes are so minor that I don't think we need to have another demo next week. So it looks like we're just about done with no-latch problems in two-slice toasters, and we've made a good start on no-latch problems in four-slice toasters.

Patricia turns to Frank.

Frank, Howard and I will go over our notes and see if we come up with any questions for you. Next time we can continue going through the cases you prepared. Do you think that the two toasters we talked about today and these three others cover all the major no-latch problems in four-slice toasters?

Frank: No. We'll need at least five additional cases. I'll start working on more case descriptions. I should have them ready by the time we finish our discussions of the first five cases.

Patricia: That would be perfect. Is this same time next week good for everybody?

Howard and Frank both nod.

Good. I'll try to arrange for the same room.

Patricia gathers up her copies of the case descriptions that Frank prepared for today's meeting.

For next week, we should each bring our copies of these five case descriptions. Frank, please bring the toaster again.

Frank: Will do.

Patricia: OK. That's it for today. Thanks again for your help, Frank. I'll give you a call to confirm where the meeting will be. See you next week.

15.2 Information Capture in a Permanent Record

In a successful interview, knowledge engineers obtain important information from the expert—information they must use to design and implement a knowledge system. They cannot rely on memory to record all this information; if they forget a relatively minor point, the expert system may not function correctly. If they have to repeat discussions with the expert, they waste valuable project time and undermine the expert's confidence in their abilities. Knowledge engineers can capture information by taking notes (Section 15.2.1), by using flip charts and whiteboards (Section 15.2.2), or by making audio (Section 15.2.3) or video (Section 15.2.4) recordings of the interview.

15.2.1 Note Taking

As we all know from our course experience in school, the most common way to record verbal communication is with handwritten notes. Each knowledge engineer should keep a project notebook. During an interview, the knowledge engineer can use this notebook to log important ideas, definitions of new terms, and questions for later discussion. Handwritten notes can capture more than what the expert says: They also can record the knowledge engineer's thoughts about:

- What information is especially important

- How a new piece of information fits into the current system design

- What topics should be discussed in the current interview

- What topics should be explored with the expert in future interviews

- What topics the knowledge engineers should discuss among themselves (without the expert) after the interview

Note taking is the most condensed and versatile way to capture information from an expert; there is no substitute for careful note taking during an interview.

Unfortunately, handwritten notes are not always the most reliable method for capturing the details of a discussion. The challenge for the knowledge engineers is to *keep pace with the discussion.* An expert may become bored with an interview or lose a train of thought while waiting for a knowledge engineer to write notes. In the remainder of this section, we outline techniques that can minimize this problem.

Develop a Shorthand Notation

As you take notes in interviews, try to develop a concise notation to capture ideas. Use abbreviations whenever possible. Invent your own shorthand, which may be specific to the particular project. You may also want to *devise special symbols* or signs to highlight your notes. For example:

- Circle unfamiliar words to remind yourself to ask for definitions.

- Underline particularly important items.

- Draw an arrow in front of topics you want to discuss later. Precede the arrow with an *E* if the discussion should include the expert and with *KE* if the topic concerns the knowledge engineers only.

- Put parentheses around your notes to yourself to distinguish them from information you learn from the expert.

You may also find it convenient to *use the location of notes* to categorize the kind of information they record. For example, you might write notes to yourself in the margins of your notebook and record additions to the current agenda on a separate sheet of paper rather than in your project notebook. If the expert has prepared written notes for an overview presentation or a written case description, you may be able to add simple annotations to these materials instead of taking more detailed notes. Another technique is to *use different colored pens* for different kinds of information. Similarly you could use colored see-through markers to highlight particularly important items or to categorize different kinds of information. The possible techniques are endless; we suggest you explore several different techniques to find the ones that work best for you. Refine your note-taking skills by practicing your chosen techniques in meetings other than knowledge-acquisition interviews.

Select a Designated Note Taker

In a team interview, it is often convenient to designate someone other than the lead interviewer to take notes. This person can focus on recording information as accurately and completely as possible while the lead interviewer concentrates on conducting the interview. After the interview, the note taker can prepare a summary of the meeting and distribute copies to all members of the team (including the expert of course).

Alternate Questioners

When no single knowledge engineer is responsible for taking notes, it is useful for the questioners to take turns asking a question and recording the answer. For example, when Howard Hacker is ready to be a secondary questioner, Patricia Programmer might ask the first question. While she is busy writing down the important points from Frank Fixit's answer, Howard can ask the next question. Then while Howard is writing, Patricia can ask another question.

Although this technique can prevent pauses in the discussion, it should be used with care. Try to keep changes of questioner to a minimum. A new questioner should ask a question only when the previous questioner needs extra time to record an answer or appears not to have another question to ask. As in any interview, it is crucial that all questioners follow the same line of questioning (see Section 13.3). Even with careful coordination among the knowledge engineers, some experts may become distracted by the back-and-forth nature of the questioning. If you find that the expert is uncomfortable with alternate questioners, stop using the technique.

15.2.2 Using Flip Charts and Whiteboards

Project teams often use large display media such as flip charts and whiteboards to stimulate discussion. One person can write ideas, important points, or diagrams on the medium for all team members to see. The team can work together to organize information into a coherent form or to develop an intermediate representation for the expert's knowledge. Many experts express themselves more easily when they can stand at a display medium and write notes or draw diagrams to illustrate the points they need to explain.

When projects use display media, they make information capture an active element of the interview. At the end of the interview, the knowledge engineers must ensure that the information is recorded in a *permanent* form so it can be used throughout the project.

Flip Charts

Flip charts provide a permanent record. Knowledge engineers can fold the pages and store them in a file folder along with other project-related materials. In many projects, the team will discuss certain diagrams repeatedly. If the diagram has been written on a flip-chart page, the team can post the page on a wall whenever they need to refer to the diagram. Some diagrams are so central to a task that the project team may choose to display the pages permanently in the project room.

Sometimes the information on flip-chart pages will be more accessible if it is included in a project notebook. After the interview, the knowledge engineers can copy the information into the notebook. Although the transcription process may be tedious, using a flip chart still has an advantage over note taking: This practice involves the *expert* in the decision of what information is important enough to be recorded.

Whiteboards

Whiteboards come in a variety of sizes. A large whiteboard can be used to display a long list or a large diagram that would not fit legibly on a single flip-chart sheet. Many experts (and knowledge engineers) prefer whiteboards over flip charts. The primary advantage of whiteboards is that they permit erasure and easy modification. Whiteboards, however, have two disadvantages with respect to flip charts.

1. Whiteboards generally are not portable but must be installed in the interview room. This fact limits a project's choice of meeting rooms.

2. Standard whiteboards do not provide a permanent record. Knowledge engineers must copy the information from the whiteboard before it is erased.

The simple, but time-consuming way to copy information from a whiteboard is of course to transcribe it by hand into a project notebook.

An alternative method that has been used with success in some projects is to *photograph* the board. No fancy equipment is required; an inexpensive camera that produces instant pictures is sufficient. Before you rely on photography to capture the contents of a whiteboard, we recommend you experiment with the particular board in the particular room.

- You may find that some areas of the board do not photograph well because of glare from overhead lights or light through windows.

- Test all the pens to see which colors appear most legible in the pictures; in general dark colors (black, brown, blue, and green) show up the best. Be careful to avoid using pens that are drying out; their marks may be too light to be photographed.

- Gauge how large you have to write and how big an area of the board you can capture in a single picture.

Electronic Whiteboards

Electronic whiteboards combine the best characteristics of flip charts and ordinary whiteboards. Like flip charts, these boards are portable (often they have wheels) so they can be moved into any available meeting room. In general they are larger than flip charts so a single "page" can contain more information than can a flip-chart page. The best feature, however, is that these devices can print the image of the whiteboard directly onto 8½ × 11 inch paper. This feature eliminates the need for tedious transcription or photography. Furthermore it produces a permanent record of standard page size rather than the large flip-chart sheets or the small instant pictures. The disadvantage with electronic whiteboards is their expense. These whiteboards are not yet standard equipment for most companies so they are not an option for all knowledge engineers.

If you have access to an electronic whiteboard, we suggest that you experiment with it before you rely on it in an interview.

- Test all the pens to see which colors are most legible. Different boards have trouble copying certain colors. Avoid pens that are drying out.

- Check how close to the edges of the board you can write. Some boards do not copy writing that is within an inch or two of their edges.

- Test writing with different sizes of letters; identify the size that will allow you to fit the most information on the board and still produce legible copies.

15.2.3 Audio Recording

Many knowledge engineers like to augment their notes with audio recordings of interviews. Recordings can be particularly useful when a team member cannot be present for an interview and would like to hear the interaction or when the interview involves a single knowledge engineer (who must conduct the interview as well as take notes). The basic guidelines for tape recording interviews are:

- Get the expert's permission before you record the interview. Some experts object to being recorded. Some experts will not talk as freely when they are being recorded.

- Abide by any restrictions the expert places on your use of the tape. Experts may divulge sensitive or controversial information that should not be heard by anyone outside the project team.

- Label each tape with the date, the participants, and the topics of discussion. It is often advisable to list the discussion topics *after* the interview, because interviews do not always follow the planned agenda.

- At the beginning of each tape, record a brief identification message that tells the date, participants, and planned topics. If a meeting is long enough to require more than one tape, include the tape number (tape one, tape two, and so on) in your identification message.

It can be extremely tiresome to listen to the entire recording of an interview. To overcome this problem, annotate your notebook to help you locate the corresponding dialog on the tape. Make a note to indicate when you change tapes in an interview. For example, write *Start Tape 2* in the margin of your notebook. If your tape recorder has a position counter, try to place the recorder where you can read the counter. When a new topic is introduced or an important issue is raised, read the current tape position, and write it in your notebook. For example, write *Tape Pos 001276* in the margin. If your tape recorder does not have a position counter, try to judge how much of the tape has been wound onto the second spool. For example, write *1/8 inch from beginning* when the thickness of the tape on the second spool appears to be about ⅛ inch.

15.2.4 Video Recording

If you have access to video recording equipment, you may want to videotape some or all of your interviews. For optimal capture of information, use a recording speed that allows stop-frame and stepping operations when the tape is played. Follow the same guidelines that apply to audio recordings.

- Obtain the expert's permission before you record the interviews.

- Abide by the expert's restrictions on who may see the tape.

- Label each tape.

- Record an identification message at the beginning of each tape.

- Annotate your notes to indicate which tape records the discussion of each topic and the approximate position on the tape at which the discussion can be found.

Some knowledge engineers prefer to videotape all interviews and to use transcripts of the videotapes to augment their own notes The authors prefer to use videotapes only as a means of observing and so of improving interviewing skills as we shall discuss in Chapter 16. We have found that audio tapes are satisfactory for recording the content of the interviews. Many people are distracted by video cameras; tape recorders are much less disruptive.

If you decide to make video recordings, set up the equipment to operate as unobtrusively as possible. The ideal facilities consist of an interview room with an adjoining observation room. If you have access to such facilities, make sure of course that the expert knows when an interview is being taped.

15.3 Points to Remember

The ultimate objective of any knowledge-acquisition interview is the transfer of information from the expert to the knowledge engineers. Successful information transfer requires both *the expert's verbal communication* of information and *the knowledge engineers' capture* of the information in a permanent record.

Knowledge engineers can facilitate verbal communication by providing a structure to each interview.

- An interview should begin with an *introduction* that orients the expert to the goals of the interview.

- In the *body* of the interview, the knowledge engineers should lead the discussion smoothly from one topic to the next; as they do so, they should make sure the expert follows the change in focus.

Table 15.1 Recording Knowledge-Acquisition Interviews

Method	Guidelines

Written notes	Write down:
	    Highlights of expert's explanations and answers
	    Indications of what information seems particularly important
	    Ideas about how new information might fit into the current system design
	    Topics to be added to the current agenda
	    Topics to be discussed with the expert in later meetings
	    Topics for the knowledge engineers to discuss after the interview
	Make your notes concise.
	Develop your own notation to allow your note taking to keep pace with the discussion.

Table 15.1 (continued)

Method	Guidelines
Display media	Write on flip charts and whiteboards to stimulate discussion. Encourage *the expert* to use the display media. Keep flip-chart pages in project files, or transcribe the contents into project notebooks. Photograph whiteboards with a camera that produces instant pictures, or transcribe the contents into project notebooks. Use electronic whiteboards if available. Print contents you would like to save.
Audio recording	Get the expert's permission to record interviews. Abide by any restrictions the expert places on your use of the recording. Label each tape with date, participants, and content. Record a brief identification message at the beginning of each tape. Keep notes that indicate *where* on the tapes of an interview you can find discussions of the various agenda topics. If the tape recorder distracts the expert, discontinue recording, and do not record future interviews.
Video recording	Get the expert's permission to record interviews. Abide by any restrictions the expert places on your use of the recording. Label each tape with date, participants, and content. Record a brief identification message at the beginning of each tape. Record at a speed that will allow stop-frame and stepping operations when you view the tape. Keep notes that indicate *where* on the tapes of an interview you can find discussions of the various agenda topics. Set up the recording equipment to provide as little distraction as possible. If the video equipment seems to interfere with the expert's concentration and with the productivity of interviews, discontinue recording, and do not record future interviews.

- An interview should end with a *closing* that presents a brief summary of the results of the interview. The closing should discuss plans for the immediate future so the expert knows what steps to take next.

Knowledge engineers can capture the information the expert communicates by taking notes, by writing on display media, and by making audio or video recordings of the interviews (Table 15.1).

Chapter 16

Interview Dialog

In the early interviews with Frank Fixit, Howard Hacker participated as a silent observer. He was eager to become a secondary questioner. As Howard observed interviews, he paid close attention to how Patricia Programmer asked questions and how she responded to Frank's answers.

This chapter presents the techniques for carrying on an interview dialog. As Figure 16 1 illustrates, interviewers perform a sequence of five activities during an interview. Sections 16.1 through 16.5 describe these activities in detail.

16.1 Introducing a Topic

In Chapter 15, we saw that the structure of an interview helps to keep the expert oriented to the goals of knowledge acquisition. Within an interview, the structure of the dialog serves the same purpose. The lead interviewer should *introduce each new topic of discussion*. The introduction serves two purposes. First, it keeps the expert and the other knowledge engineers aware of the current focus. Second, it establishes the relevance of the questions that will follow.

Your introduction should tell the expert *why* the chosen topic is

Figure 16.1 Sequence of activities in an interview. During an interview, Patricia performs a sequence of five activities. First she introduces a topic. Next she asks a question on the topic, listens to the expert's answer, and responds to the answer. She continues asking questions until she has gathered all the necessary information on the current topic. Then Patricia closes the topic and repeats the entire sequence of steps for a new topic.

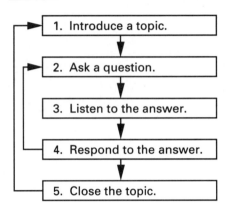

important. You may need to explain what you are trying to find out and why this information is important to your goal of building an expert system. For example, Patricia Programmer introduces a new topic of discussion in Dialog 16.1, which occurs during initial inquiry. As she changes her focus from classifying toaster problems to comparing the classifications, Patricia wants to be sure that Frank Fixit and Howard Hacker shift their focuses as well; she wants them both to understand how the new topic is pertinent to their goals.

Dialog 16.1 Introducing a New Topic

Setting

Patricia Programmer is trying to decide how to subdivide the functionality of the toaster-repair advisor for incremental development. Patricia has learned that Frank Fixit tends to group problems according to the customer's initial complaint (color problems, no-latch problems, and so on). Now Patricia wants to learn how Frank compares the different problems with one another.

Dialog

Patricia: Frank, you've told us that you classify a toaster problem according to the customer's initial complaint.

Frank: Yes, that's right.

Patricia: What I'd like to do now is compare the different problems to get a feel for which are the most common, which are the most difficult for you, and which are the most serious from the customer's perspective. These issues will help us decide which problems we should address first, which we can ignore initially, and so on. First, I'd like to discuss how often you see each kind of problem.

Frank: So for example, I only see a few toasters where the toast comes out too light. Does this mean the computer system won't help with these problems?

Patricia: That's the sort of decision we need to make. You and Margaret Major should discuss the alternatives and decide which problems to include in the initial version of the system and which to add later. Right now, I'd like to get the information you and Margaret will need to discuss when you evaluate the alternatives. Our job is to organize a summary of the frequency of the different problems, their severity, and their difficulty. Then we'll go over this information with Margaret and see which problems she thinks are most important to include in the first version of the system.

16.2 Asking a Question

After you have introduced a topic, proceed to ask questions on this topic. The act of asking a question can be broken down into four steps (Figure 16.2), which are described in Sections 16.2.1 through 16.2.4.

16.2.1 Identifying the Information to Request

The first step in formulating a question is to identify an objective: the item of information you want to learn from the expert.

During the course of the project Patricia will need to find out:

- How Frank repairs toasters
- What kinds of toaster problem Frank can fix
- Whether electrical problems are more difficult than mechanical ones
- What leads Frank to suspect a short in the toaster wiring
- Why Frank looks for failed components before he checks for wiring problems

Notice that these items range from very general information to very precise details that expand on information that Patricia obtained in

Figure 16.2 Asking a question. When Patricia Programmer asks a question, she performs three or four distinct steps. She first decides what information to request. Next she selects the words to use; then she utters the question for Frank Fixit to hear. At that point, Patricia must judge whether the question elicited an answer. If so, she proceeds to the next dialog activity—she listens to Frank's answer. If the question failed to elicit an answer, Patricia tries to understand why it failed. She then rephrases the question to try to correct the problems that caused failure.

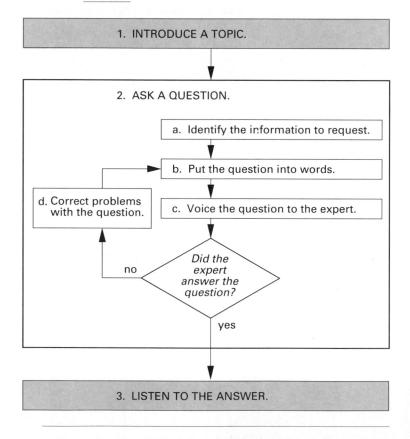

earlier interviews. At the beginning of the project, Patricia will be able to request the broad category of information she needs; she will not know enough to ask for the specific items within this category. Similarly, when the team starts to discuss a new area of coverage for the expert system, Patricia will need to begin by requesting general information.

During each interview, Patricia keeps a list of *information to obtain*.

To identify the objective of a question, she refers to this list; every question will address some particular item on the list. Patricia creates her list from the discussion topics she planned for the interview. (See Figure 14.2 for an example list of planned topics.) In the course of the interview, Patricia may modify the list of information she wants to obtain. For example, Frank's answer to a general question might tell Patricia what additional, more specific information she should request. Section 16.4.5 describes how Patricia adds an item to her list.

16.2.2 Putting the Question into Words

After you identify *what* to ask, decide *how* to ask the question. To put your request for information into words:

1. Select the appropriate type of question.

2. Phrase the question to request the information that you want.

Selecting the Appropriate Question Type

Questions can be classified on a spectrum from highly open to very closed. The knowledge engineer should select the appropriate openness for the situation.

> Patricia Programmer first decides how open ended to make her question. At one extreme, she could specify the topic to be covered and allow Frank Fixit a great deal of freedom in determining the amount and kind of information to provide. For example, she might ask the highly **open** question: *Tell me about your job as a toaster repairman.* At the opposite end of the spectrum, Patricia might limit Frank's possible answers by asking him to select from a specific set of options. For example, she might ask the very **closed** question: *Which do you look at first, the line switch or the heating element?*

Select the openness of a question based on three factors.

1. The generality of the information you want to obtain

2. The pattern of the dialog—that is, the sequence of questions you have asked in this interview

3. The expert's earlier reactions to your questions

Generality of Information

As a rule of thumb, *favor more open questions to request general information and more closed questions to ask for specific details.*

> At the beginning of the project, Patricia Programmer will use open questions frequently. These questions allow *Frank Fixit* to decide what information to supply; they provide an easy way for him to adjust to knowledge acquisition. Open questions let Frank talk while Patricia

listens and observes; they give Frank the opportunity to volunteer information that Patricia may not know enough to ask. Frank's answer can reveal what he thinks is important. Using open-ended questions in early interviews will keep Patricia from narrowing her focus and concentrating on a particular area before she knows enough about toaster repair to judge what is important.

After Patricia becomes familiar with Frank's vocabulary and has a general understanding of toaster repair, she will be able to use closed questions effectively. She will favor more closed questions for indepth discussions of particular toasters that Frank has repaired; she will use closed questions when she knows what specific information she needs. Closed questions make it clear to Frank exactly what Patricia wants him to tell her. As a consequence, it often takes less effort for Frank to compose an answer to a closed question; also, answers to closed questions are usually shorter than are answers to open questions.

In general, Patricia's closed questions will be *moderately* closed; they will ask Frank to volunteer specific information, for example: *What possible faults would you consider in this case?* She will *avoid very closed multiple-choice questions* unless she is sure she knows enough to specify alternatives. When Patricia's questions do include alternative answers, she will use only alternatives *that she has learned from Frank*. She will not suggest alternatives that she assumes or that she knows from her own experience with toasters.

Pattern of the Dialog

Pay attention to the pattern of the dialog in a particular interview. Often it will be most comfortable for the expert if you *use a mixture of open and closed questions*.

> Frank Fixit may get very tired of talking (and thinking) when he has to answer a long series of open questions. Patricia can intersperse a few closed questions to give Frank a little relief. On the other hand, because answers to closed questions are often shorter, less time elapses between one closed question and the next. A long series of rapid-fire closed questions can seem like an interrogation. Patricia can alleviate this problem by taking time to show interest after each answer and by mixing in a few open-ended questions such as requests for explanations.

Reactions of the Expert

Pay attention to *your expert's* reactions to questions. Some experts have difficulty answering very open-ended questions; other experts are threatened by very closed questions.

> As Patricia Programmer gets to know Frank Fixit, she will watch for his reactions to her questions. Frank might hesitate when asked very open questions, because he is not sure what Patricia wants to know. Some experts do not talk freely without direction. If this is the case with Frank, Patricia can use a moderately open question that includes some guidance, for example, *Tell me about the last toaster that you repaired.* Alternatively, Patricia might find that Frank seems threatened by questions that are too closed. This problem can occur when a knowledge engineer asks an expert for reasons. The question, *Why did you*

replace the carriage assembly? can sound like a challenge; the alternative, *Would you explain how you decided what repair to perform?* is much less threatening. Because Patricia is concerned with making knowledge acquisition a comfortable experience for Frank, she will modify the style of her questions to accommodate his individual preferences.

In addition to learning Frank's usual reactions to different question types, Patricia will be sensitive to his reactions *within each interview*. If he has difficulty answering an open question, she might try asking a series of more closed questions instead. If he seems bothered by a closed question, she might switch to a more open question.

Phrasing the Question

After you select the basic question type, put your question into words. Your primary concern should be to *make the question as clear as possible*.

1. Choose words from the vocabulary you share with your project expert.

2. Avoid words and phrases with ambiguous meanings.

3. Make your questions simple.

4. Avoid words with undesirable implications.

Choosing the Vocabulary

Selects words you know your expert will understand.

> When Patricia Programmer has to ask a question that refers to parts of a toaster, she tries to use the words that Frank Fixit would use. She incorporates a word from Frank's technical vocabulary into her question only when she is *sure* of its meaning. As the project progresses, Patricia uses terms from the project dictionary.

Selecting the appropriate vocabulary is particularly important for a knowledge engineer who works with an expert whose native language is not English (or whatever language is used during interviews). If you encounter this situation, be sure to use plain and common words; avoid slang and colloquial expressions. Be especially diligent to use simple sentence construction.

Avoiding Ambiguity

Try to phrase each question in such a way that it has a single interpretation.

- Avoid using the pronouns *this, that,* and *it;* their meaning may not be clear to the expert.

> Patricia Programmer would not say, *If you suspect that you have a wiring problem, but also think that a component might be bad, would this test confirm it?* Frank Fixit might think she means, *Would this test confirm*

a wiring problem? when she really intended to ask, *Would this test con-firm that a component is bad?*

- Choose words with unambiguous meanings.

> Patricia would prefer, *Do you perform a standard series of tests on each toaster?* rather than, *Do you perform a standard battery of tests on each toaster?* because the word *battery* has a different common interpretation in the context of electrical equipment.

- Consider how your question *sounds;* try to avoid phrasings that can be misconstrued.

> If Patricia were to start a sentence, *Wire problems, like these* . . . , Frank might hear, *Why are problems like these* . . . . Patricia can avoid this confusion by saying *wiring problems* or *problems with wires* instead of *wire problems.*

Maintaining Simplicity

Make each question short and simple, and avoid complicated intro-ductory clauses. If it is necessary to explain the context of a question, do so as clearly as you can *before* you ask the question itself. Always *ask a single question at a time*, rather than folding multiple queries into one question. Most people cannot remember all the components of a multipart question; they tend to answer only the last question. Mul-tipart questions can be unsettling to an expert especially early in knowledge acquisition.

Avoiding Undesirable Implications

In addition to the actual meanings of the words, think about their implications. Each question should have neutral or positive conno-tations for the expert. The only message a question should convey is that you are eager to learn from the expert. Phrase questions to ask for *the expert's* answer rather than to suggest your own answer.

> Patricia Programmer is careful not to introduce her ideas about how toasters are repaired or to suggest her biases about what facets of the task are most important. For example, to find out how Frank Fixit classifies toaster problems, Patricia would resist suggesting a possible classification. Instead of saying, *The toasters we have discussed illustrate two categories of problem, electrical and mechanical. Right?*, Patricia would say, *Think about the toasters we have discussed. I'd like you to try to group similar cases together so I can learn whether you classify problems in any way. How would you group those cases?*
>   Patricia also words her questions to avoid giving the impression that she considers one possible answer preferable in some way to other answers. For example, after the discussion of several toasters Frank repaired recently, Patricia gets the impression that Frank occasionally disregards the results of tests. She wants to confirm this impression. Instead of asking, *Do you sometimes ignore test results?*, she asks, *Are test results always reliable?* The first question is almost an accusation.

The word *ignore* has a negative connotation; using this word gives the impression that "no" is a preferable answer. A "yes" answer would seem to be an admission that Frank does not pay attention to things that are important. On the other hand, the second question suggests that *test results* themselves might be erroneous. Frank can answer "yes" or "no" without giving the impression that *he* does anything wrong.

16.2.3 Voicing the Question to the Expert

Once you have put your question into words, your next step is to utter the spoken words for the expert to hear. Be careful to keep your tone of voice and your inflection neutral. Speak clearly, and enunciate carefully. Make sure your rate of speech is not too fast for the expert to follow. This practice will increases the chances of your expert understanding you.

> When Patricia Programmer needs to ask Frank Fixit why he performed a particular step, she says:
>   Why did you do that?
> in her normal speaking tone, with equal stress on each word. This lets Frank know that she is interested in his reason, but conveys no other message. In contrast, if Patricia had said:
>   Why did you do *that?*
> in an incredulous tone of voice, her tone might imply that she suspects that Frank had made an error.

Be sensitive to your project expert's special needs when you speak. If your expert's native language is not the same as your own, speak slowly, and pronounce each word distinctly. After you ask a question, verify that the expert has understood you. Be particularly patient. Remember that knowledge acquisition can be difficult for an expert, and recognize that the difficulties are magnified when the expert has to communicate in a foreign language. If you work with an expert who is hard of hearing, be careful not to mumble. Speak slowly and clearly and in a loud voice. Keep in mind that the expert may need to read your lips; always face the expert when you speak.

16.2.4 Correcting Problems with the Question

A question that does not elicit an answer is said to *fail*.[1] To detect failure you must be able to judge how long you should wait for the expert to answer a question. Your sensitivity to the project expert will enable you to detect and correct failed questions. As we discussed in

---

1. As we shall see in Section 16.4.6, a question that elicits an answer is not always free of problems; some questions elicit *irrelevant* answers.

Chapter 13, different experts have different communication styles. As you work with an expert, you need to learn the pattern that constitutes that particular expert's normal style and how to interpret deviations from this pattern. The typical indications that a question has failed are silence or a blank stare from the expert. If the expert hems and haws in an attempt to answer the question, the question may have failed. Your aim should be to detect failure as soon as possible and to take immediate steps to correct it.

During early knowledge acquisition, it may be difficult to know when to assume that a question will not produce an answer. Be sure that you *give the expert enough time to answer the question.* If the expert is silent but seems to be concentrating, the question may not have failed. On the other hand, if the expert seems nervous, worried, or uncomfortable and gets more uncomfortable as time goes on, the question probably did fail. During your first several interviews, pay attention to how quickly your expert responds to your questions. Use this to gauge when to try to correct a problem.

> Patricia Programmer finds that Frank Fixit answers most questions after about three seconds. She allows twice this much time before deciding that a question has failed. It might take Frank four or five seconds to formulate the answer to a particularly difficult question. It would be very frustrating for him to have Patricia rephrase her question just when he is ready to answer.
>
> Occasionally when Patricia hears her own question, she realizes that it was not worded clearly. Rather than asking a rephrased question immediately, she waits for Frank to respond. If Frank does not answer after about six seconds, Patricia tries to correct her question. Although her question was confusing, it would have confused Frank more to hear two questions at once. He would have needed to listen to and try to remember both; he might or might not have realized that both questions requested the same information.
>
> Sometimes, while she is uttering a question, Patricia will detect a problem. She may realize that she cannot finish the question without making it too complicated for Frank to understand. When this happens, Patricia simply tells Frank that her question is not working and apologizes for the confusion. Then she starts over and tries to phrase the question more simply.

Questions can fail for many reasons. The most common reasons for failure are:

- The question is too general.
- The question is too specific.
- The expert does not understand the question.
- The expert does not see the relevance of the question.

- The expert does not want to answer the question.

- The expert is insulted by the question.

- The expert does not know the answer.

In the remainder of this section, we use dialogs between Patricia Programmer and Frank Fixit to illustrate how to correct these problems. Remember that your expert is an individual who may behave differently than Frank does. You may not be able to identify the cause of a problem in the same way Patricia does. When you first begin to work with an expert, you may find it difficult to decide what caused a question to fail. You may need to ask for the cause of the problem (for example, ask: *Did you understand my question?*). As time goes on, you should learn what to expect from your expert.

The Question Is Too General

Every open question has many possible answers. Sometimes, the expert gets bogged down trying to decide what the question means, what answer would be most interesting, or what answer the knowledge engineer really wants. Often an expert will hesitate to respond to such a question for fear of giving the "wrong" answer.

If your expert is not able to answer a very general question, try to make it more specific. Be careful as you narrow your questions, however; avoid setting a direction based on your own knowledge, assumptions, or prejudices. Try to give the expert guidance without excluding areas that may be important. Dialog 16.2 indicates how Patricia Programmer narrows a question that is too open for Frank Fixit.

Dialog 16.2 Correcting a Question That Is Too General

Dialog

Patricia: When do the other people in the repair staff need your help?

Frank: Well—I guess—Sometimes—Uh—

Patricia: Try to think of the last few times that people have come to you for advice. What did they ask you?

Frank: Let's see. Dick came in just yesterday. He's new in the department and a little unsure of himself. He thought he had found a problem in the carriage assembly, but he wanted to check it out with me first. He talked through the problem and asked if he was going about it correctly.

Sue came in later that afternoon. She's been with the department about a year. She had a toaster with an electrical problem she had never seen before. She had tried everything she knows and came up with a blank.

Discussion

Patricia's first question is so general that Frank is not sure what she wants to know. He thinks of one way to respond and starts to give an answer. As he does so, he thinks of an alternative answer that might be more interesting. He hesitates because he wants to provide the information Patricia needs, but he is not sure what information that is.

Frank's false starts at answering the question tell Patricia that her question was too general. She provides a little guidance by asking him to think of recent experience. Notice that the resulting question is still open; it leaves Frank the freedom to volunteer information that is important to him.

The Question Is Too Specific

Questions often fail when they are based on incorrect assumptions; such questions are too specific. For example, Frank Fixit might be hesitant to answer a question that limits him to an unacceptable range of answers. If the expert does not answer a very closed question, check whether it includes ungrounded assumptions. Try to avoid multiple-choice questions. Instead of suggesting possible answers, phrase the question to ask the expert to volunteer an answer. Dialog 16.3 illustrates how Patricia Programmer corrects a question that is too specific.

Dialog 16.3 Correcting a Question That Is Too Specific

Dialog

Patricia: Is it easy or difficult to repair a toaster in which the toast doesn't pop up?

(pause)

Frank: Well—

(pause)

Patricia: When other people in the department repair toasters with this problem, how often do they have to ask for your help?

Frank: I'd say that I see about three problems like that each week. And we probably get about six toasters with this problem in a week. So I need to help about half the time.

Discussion

Patricia's first question is very closed. This question implies two underlying assumptions: that there are only two alternatives and that they are poles apart. This malfunction is either "difficult" or "easy"; there is no in-between answer. Frank's problem with this question is that some of these problems can be fixed quickly whereas others take a long time. It depends on the toaster model. He cannot classify the malfunction itself as "easy" or "difficult." Even if he considers a single model, he is not sure how to answer. He views the difficulty of a problem as a continuum. He is not sure how easy a problem has to be before he should classify it as "easy." He does not know whether "easy" means easy *for him* to fix or easy for the other members of the repair staff.

Frank's long pauses give Patricia time to reflect on her question. She realizes it was too specific and poses it again in a way Frank can answer. Patricia tries to approximate the difficulty of the problem based on how frequently Frank has to assist with the repair of these problems.

The Expert Does Not Understand the Question

Sometimes this problem is easy to detect: the expert may say, *I don't understand*. More often, however, the expert will try to figure out what you mean or to answer the question without really knowing what to say. When you note that a question has failed, look for signs of confusion. Also look for anxiety. Some experts will act worried or concerned because they view a failure to understand as *their* failure.

While you wait for the expert to answer, review the question mentally to see if you can detect ambiguities. If so, try to rephrase the question more clearly. If the question seems perfectly clear to you, try to explain in a different way what you are trying to find out. Remember your goal of keeping the expert comfortable. Be patient; do not give the impression that failure to understand is the expert's fault. Take the blame yourself, even if you do not think you deserve it. Apologize for not being clear.

In Dialog 16.4, Patricia Programmer realizes that Frank Fixit did not understand her question.

Dialog 16.4 Correcting a Question That Was Not Understood

Setting

Frank Fixit has just identified the various parts of a toaster and has described how a toaster works.

Dialog

Patricia: What is the relationship between the main spring and the lock spring?

Frank scowls slightly, tips his head to the right, bites his lower lip, and looks intently at the toaster on the table in front of him. After about six seconds, Frank still has not answered. In that time, his scowl has deepened.

I'm sorry. That wasn't very clear. I'm not sure that I understand the difference in the function between the main spring and the lock spring. Could you please explain what each spring does?

Frank: Sure. Basically, the lock spring holds the carriage *down* while the bread is being toasted, and the main spring pulls the carriage back *up* when the toast is ready. Let me show you how it works.

Discussion

Frank's initial reaction to the question is similar to his reaction when he understands a question and is thinking about an answer. On average, however, he starts to answer the question after about three seconds. The longer pause, and Frank's deepening scowl, indicate that he does not understand the question.

During his silence, Frank tries to decide what kind of "relationship" Patricia is interested in. To him, the two springs are not *related*. He considers their spatial relationship, but cannot think what to say about it. The exact placement of the two springs differ from toaster to toaster.

While waiting for Frank's answer, Patricia realizes that her question was not clear. She apologizes for the confusion and restates the question.

The Expert Does Not See the Relevance of the Question

An expert who does not understand the relevance of the knowledge engineer's questions may become reluctant to cooperate or to communicate freely. Although you may *think* you have explained why a question is important, the expert may have missed your point. The connection between your introduction to a topic and your questions may not be clear. Be particularly wary of this problem in your early interviews. Do not let the expert think you are wasting time with irrelevant questions.

When you ask a question and the expert reacts as though you had changed the topic abruptly, you may need to explain how your question is relevant. If the expert appears not to see the pertinence of a question, take time to explain what you are trying to accomplish and why. Then reask the question. Dialog 16.5 shows how Patricia Programmer clarified her purpose in asking a question.

Dialog 16.5 Explaining the Relevance of a Question

Setting

The following dialog takes place during initial inquiry. Patricia Programmer is trying to understand how the full coverage of the system can be subdivided for incremental development.

Dialog

Patricia: Now I'd like to consider how we should plan the development of the system. As quickly as we can, Howard and I will implement a simple version of the toaster-repair advisor that can help the repair staff in limited circumstances. Gradually we'll add more knowledge to the system so it can help with about 80 percent of the toasters that come into the service department. What kind of toaster malfunction is most common?

Frank stares blankly at Patricia for several seconds.

One of the ways that we might limit the system is to have it help with some problems but not others. If we chose that approach, we might start first with a very common problem. Then members of the repair staff could try out the system on real toasters when they see this kind of problem. What particular malfunctions do you see most frequently?

Frank: We see a lot of toasters where the toast is too dark or too light. We also see . . . .

Discussion

Patricia explains that she wants to investigate how to plan for the incremental development of the toaster-repair advisor. This provides the motivation for her question. To her, it is obvious that she should consider limiting the system to certain malfunctions and that she should find out which malfunctions are most common. This approach is standard knowledge-engineering methodology. Frank, however, has no idea what Patricia's question has to do with what she said she was trying to accomplish. Rather than answer the question, he stares at her blankly as he tries to follow her train of thought. Patricia realizes that her question seemed like a non sequitur to Frank. She explains more clearly its relevance to her current goal.

The Expert Does Not Want to Answer the Question

Occasionally a question will make the expert uncomfortable; the expert will try to evade giving an answer. This often indicates that you have hit a controversial topic or one that is politically sensitive within the expert's work group. The expert may have engaged in a long, heated, and frustrating debate on the topic with colleagues and management and may not want to discuss the matter further. For example, management may have dictated that a certain procedure should be followed while the expert feels strongly that a different approach is preferable.

When an expert wants to avoid a question, you should either drop the topic and return to it later or express your concern about the expert's reaction to the question. In the early stages of knowledge acquisition, it is often best to postpone the topic. Once the expert knows you and feels comfortable with you, you may be able to uncover the cause of concern. Dialog 16.6 illustrates how Patricia Programmer reacted to Frank Fixit's reluctance to answer a question.

Dialog 16.6 Investigating the Expert's Reluctance to Answer

Setting

> The dialog takes place after Patricia Programmer, Howard Hacker, and Frank Fixit have been working together for three months.

Dialog

Patricia: When we listed the different toaster malfunctions, you mentioned a situation in which the operating lever won't go down so the bread remains sticking out of the toaster. That's the only problem we haven't discussed yet. What do you do in cases like that.

> *Frank grits his teeth, suppresses an angry look, then snorts out his reaction.*

Frank: Hmmph!

> *After a very slight pause, Frank continues. He speaks more quickly than usual.*

I don't know—I'll have to think about it.

> *Patricia leans forward slightly and looks concerned.*

Patricia: You sound a little unhappy with this question. Is this a sore subject with you?

> *(slight pause)*

Frank: Yes. What we do and what we *should* do are two different things.

> *(angrily)*

I have told the repair staff again and again that it isn't necessary to replace the entire carriage assembly whenever the operating lever won't go down. Sometimes the carriage hangs up because there's a little rust on the vertical shaft—or a burr. All you have to do is file it smooth. The trouble is that most of the staff just won't take the time to check the vertical shaft. They immediately replace the whole assembly without even looking to see what the problem is.

    And now, Margaret Major says she *wants* us to replace the carriage assemblies! It turns out that a number of customers had to bring their toasters back right after we had fixed this problem. The guys who fixed those toasters *said* they had filed rust off the vertical shaft. I know what happened—they just quickly filed off a little rust and said they were done. You need to file all around the shaft to be sure you clean off all the rust. It doesn't take any longer than it does to replace the carriage assembly, and it's a lot less expensive for the customer.

Patricia *(sympathetically):* This must be very frustrating for you.

Frank: It sure is! A few of the repairmen were too lazy to learn the right way to fix the problem, and now they're all being taught the wrong approach.

Patricia (*still with a sympathetic tone*): I'm not sure what we'll end up doing in the system, but I'd like to understand how *you* think a stuck operating lever should be handled.

Discussion

Patricia notices Frank's initial angry response to her question. She knows him well enough to realize that he does not say, *I don't know,* when he does not know the answer to a question. He thinks about it and starts to give a tentative answer. This fact, plus Frank's rapid speech, indicate that he wants to dismiss the question rather than answer it.

Patricia and Frank know each other well enough that Frank is willing to explain why he is upset. This disclosure requires a high degree of trust. At the beginning of the project, Frank would not have been willing to air the service department's dirty laundry in front of an outsider or to let Patricia know that he disagrees with one of Margaret's decisions. If Patricia had encountered the same reaction at the beginning of the project, she would have dropped the question and gone on to a different topic.

The Expert Is Insulted by the Question

A question may fail because something about the question itself or the way it was asked, makes the expert upset, angry, or insulted. If you find that a question has insulted the expert, try to figure out what you did or said to evoke this reaction. Check that your wording does not include negative implications. For example, *When was the last time you ignored a test result?* implies that you think the expert ignores test results. Check also whether your inflection or other nonverbal behavior might have sent negative messages. If you find a problem in your words or manner, apologize and reask the question, correcting the problem.

Occasionally, a knowledge engineer will find absolutely no problem with the question or the way in which it was asked. This situation is more likely to occur when the expert and knowledge engineer are from different geographic regions. It usually indicates that the expert has misinterpreted the knowledge engineer's nonverbal signals because of cultural differences. In this situation, the best approach is to realize that there *is* a problem even though you do not know what the problem is. With your words, *overcompensate* for your inadvertent negative signals. If this problem occurs frequently with a particular expert, you may need to adopt a regular questioning style that is excessively deferential.

Patricia Programmer never encounters this particular problem in her interactions with Frank Fixit. Dialog 16.7 illustrates what can happen and shows how to correct the situation.

Dialog 16.7 Overcompensating for Inadvertent Negative Signals

Setting

William is a knowledge engineer who has lived all his life in the northeastern United States. He is working as a consultant to a company in Texas, leading a project to develop an expert system. Lou is the project expert; he has lived all his life in Texas. William's rate of speech and the loudness of his voice are about average in his home region; however, he speaks more quickly and more loudly than the average Texan. William is outgoing, confident, and exuberant. He is very direct; he says what he means and asks what he needs to know without beating around the bush. Like many Texans, Lou speaks slowly and carefully; he is softspoken. Although equally confident about his abilities, Lou's style is more subdued than William's. When Lou talks to people less knowledgeable than himself, he tries to downplay the difficulty of his job; his manner is almost self-effacing.

In their first several interviews, Lou appeared a little put off by many of William's questions. William was always polite and respectful. He was very careful to avoid unwanted implications in his questions. He kept his tone of voice neutral and avoided doing anything that would send negative signals. William tried to adapt his interaction style to be closer to Lou's style. He made a conscious effort to speak more slowly and more softly than is his custom. Despite all William's efforts, however, Lou still reacted negatively. The problem was particularly pronounced when William asked for the rationale behind Lou's actions or decisions.

We join this conversation after Lou has explained how he identified a recent problem in his plant. Lou and William are seated at a table. A large sheet of paper with a schematic of the plant is on the table in front of them. In his description, Lou has emphasized that he checked the steam valve first.

Dialog

William *(enthusiastically, politely, and with even intonation):* Would you please explain why you checked the steam valve first?

Lou *(angrily):* What is the problem with that?

William *(apologetically):* I'm sorry; please bear with me. This is all new to me. I don't have your years of experience working with this kind of equipment, so it takes me a while to follow the complexity of what you do. I'd like you to help me to understand exactly what is important so the expert system will behave the way you'd like.

You said that it's important to check the steam valve first. I'm afraid that I don't know enough about the equipment to understand why you would look at the steam valve first. Can you please explain this to me.

Lou *(appeased):* Sure. This diagram should make it clear why the steam valve is so important.

Lou points to schematic of the plant.

You can see that the main pipe from the boiler goes right to the steam valve . . . .

Discussion

William would have had no problems whatsoever working with an expert from the northeastern United States. Lou reacted to an *unfamiliar communication style*, rather than to William himself or to anything William did. There is nothing incorrect or offensive in William's slightly loud voice, his rapid speech, or his energetic and direct style. To Lou, however, these characteristics make William appear brash, pushy, and disrespectful. Even though William is careful to speak more slowly and more softly than usual, Lou still finds a large difference between William's style and the style that is considered polite in Texas.

During Lou's description of the recent problem in the plant, William had noticed Lou's emphasis on the steam valve: Lou had seemed to indicate that the steam valve was particularly important. In the dialog, William is anxious to find out more about the steam valve so he asks why Lou looked there first. Lou misreads William's eagerness in asking the question. He assumes that William thinks that the steam valve was the *wrong* place to start. From Lou's frame of reference, William seems gleeful in pointing out this error; William seems to gloat that he was able to detect Lou's mistake.

William does not know what provoked Lou's defensive response. Nevertheless he realizes that Lou thinks William has challenged his expertise. To correct the problem, when William reasks his question, he emphasizes Lou's expertise and his own lack of knowledge.

The Expert Does Not Know the Answer

Although you rely on your project expert to provide you with the knowledge you need, remember that an expert is not a walking encyclopedia.

When Patricia Programmer and Frank Fixit discuss problems that occur infrequently, Frank may need to refer to manuals or to notes that he wrote in the distant past; he may not have all the facts at his fingertips. When Patricia raises questions that Frank has never before contemplated, he may need to think about the issues awhile or to discuss them with colleagues before he commits himself to an answer.

Often, you will be able to detect this problem because the expert seems to want to answer the question, but is reluctant to do so. Be sure not to put the expert on the spot. Avoid giving the impression that you *need* an answer sooner than the expert can comfortably provide one. Let the expert know that you can defer the discussion to a later interview. In Dialog 16.8, Frank Fixit is unable to answer Patricia Programmer's question off the top of his head.

Dialog 16.8 Deferring a Question That the Expert Cannot Answer

Patricia: You said that problems in which the toast doesn't pop up are a little different in toasters that hang under a cabinet. What do you do for those toasters?

Frank: Yes the toast comes out horizontally instead of vertically.

Frank sighs.

Let's see—I worked with one of those about four months ago. As I recall . . .

Frank looks across the room, staring at the empty whiteboard as if he is trying to make out what is written there but is not quite able to read it.
Patricia starts to speak about fifteen seconds after Frank said "Let's see."

Patricia: I don't need to get an answer today. Would you prefer to save this topic for next time?

Frank: Yes. I'd like to go over my notes and check the service bulletins to be sure I don't leave anything out. I don't see many under-cabinet toasters.

Patricia: Will you have enough time by next week, or should we schedule it for another time?

Frank: Next week will be fine.

The Same Question Fails Repeatedly

To close our review of common problems, we consider questions that fail repeatedly. An unsuccessful question can increase both your and the expert's frustration. It can make the expert anxious, thereby undermining the productivity of an interview. To keep the expert comfortable with knowledge acquisition, you must be willing to give up a particular question that does not work.

If you have tried to ask the same question in two or three different ways without success, drop it and go on to something different. Record the question for discussion in the future. After the interview, think about this part of the dialog. If you made an audio or video recording of the interview, play the tape and try to discern the problem with the question. If you did not record the interview, talk through the entire interchange with a colleague. As you review what happened, you may identify problems that were not apparent during the interview.

16.3 Listening to the Expert's Answer

After you ask a question *pay attention to the expert's answer*. Remember that you cannot obtain information unless you listen to what the expert has to say. Be careful to avoid common problems that interfere with a knowledge engineer's focus on the expert's answer.

- Often inexperienced knowledge engineers are anxious about their ability to keep the discussion moving. As soon as they have asked one question, they start to formulate the next one; they concentrate on their own questions instead of listening to the expert's answers. This approach may succeed in keeping the dialog going, but it misses the point of the interview. It is better to have pauses in the dialog than to repeat the same discussion in a later interview.

- Knowledge engineers sometimes become distracted by sights and sounds outside of the interview. For example, if the interview room has a window, a knowledge engineer may become fascinated by activities that occur outside. If an intercom or paging system is audible in the interview room, the knowledge engineer may listen to the details of a message on the intercom and ignore the expert.

- Late in a long meeting, knowledge engineers may become too tired to concentrate on the interview, their thoughts may wander while the expert speaks.

- Sometimes knowledge engineers' personal problems disturb their ability to focus on the interview.

- Certain experts provide so much information so quickly that the knowledge engineers cannot fully comprehend. Rather than interrupt to slow the expert down,[2] an inexperienced knowledge engineer often panics and stops listening.

When the expert answers a question, *listen for comprehension.* It is important to understand what the expert means, not just to hear and record what the expert says. Taking notes can help you to judge the completeness of your understanding. If you are not sure what to write down or if your notes do not tell you everything you need to know, you will need to ask follow-up questions to get additional information. Be watchful, however, that your note taking does not interfere with your listening. The skillful note taker is able to write and listen at the same time. Concentrate on the *content* of the notes, not the *form.* Do not get distracted trying to keep your notebook neat and your notes grammatical.

Notice what the expert emphasizes and mentions multiple times. Emphasis and repetition may indicate what the expert considers important. Listen for the expert's opinions or feeling about various aspects of the task. Pay particular attention to statements that start with phrases such as:

---

2. Chapter 17 describes situations in which it is necessary for a knowledge engineer to interrupt the expert and explains how to interrupt.

In my opinion . . .

My hunch is that . . .

My instinct would be to . . .

These phrases indicate how the expert actually approaches a problem
or situation. The expert's approach may differ from standard practice,
and this difference may be the reason the expert can perform the task
better than nonexperts can.

Before you start to respond be sure you *identify every aspect of the
answer that requires a response.* Analyze the completeness and clarity
of the answer and the completeness of your understanding. Check
whether the answer fits with your current perception or seems to contradict what you learned in earlier interviews. Pay attention to the
expert's nonverbal messages; they are an important component of what
the expert means. Look for new words in the expert's vocabulary; be
sure that you understand their meanings. See whether the expert's
answer suggests additional topics to be discussed or raises questions
you had not considered.

16.4 Responding to an Answer

Always respond to the expert's answer before you ask your next question. The process of listening to the expert's answer to identify situations that require responses and then responding appropriately is called
active listening. This process not only improves your understanding
but also shows the expert you are paying attention. Table 16.1 describes
the active listening techniques that can be used to ensure that you get
a clear and complete understanding of the expert's answer to your
questions. These techniques can also be used to encourage the expert
to continue or to expand on a topic.

These techniques can be grouped into five kinds of response.

1. If you do not think you have a complete answer, you should *ask
   follow-up questions.*

2. When you think you have a complete answer, you should paraphrase
   the answer and ask the expert to *confirm your understanding.* If the
   expert's answer concludes a topic, summarize the important points
   for this topic before you ask for confirmation.

3. If the answer appears inconsistent with your current understanding,
   you should *resolve the contradictions.*

Table 16.1 Active Listening Techniques

Technique	Purpose	Example Responses
Verbal nudge	Prompt the expert to continue with the previous answer.	I see. And then? Tell me more.
Verbal probe	Request more details.	Tell me more about. . . . What happened after. . . ? You said. . . . Would you please explain that further?
Clarification	Ask the expert to clarify your understanding of an answer.	I'm not sure I understand your point. What did you mean when you said. . . ?
Paraphrasing	Explain your understanding to the expert.	As I understand it. . . . On the basis of what you've told me, it seems that. . . .
Summarization	Tie together a number of points that were mentioned over several minutes of conversation. Explain your understanding to the expert	First, you. . . . Second, you. . . . Third, you. . . . The important points seem to be. . . .
Confirmation	Ask the expert to confirm or to correct your understanding.	Is this correct? Did I understand you correctly? How would you modify my description? What am I missing?
Term definition	Ask the expert to explain the meaning of a word.	What is a. . . ? What does . . . mean? I'm not sure I know what you mean by. . . . Please define . . . for me.
Topic scheduling	Note a topic for inclusion in this interview.	*Add this topic to your list of topics to discuss in the current interview.*
Topic deferral	Note a topic for discussion at a later time.	*Write a note to remind yourself to include this topic in a later interview.*

4. When you hear an unfamiliar term, you should *learn how the expert uses this word.*

5. When the answer suggests additional topics and questions, you should *update your agenda.*

Sections 16.4.1 through 16.4.5 describe these five kinds of response in more detail.

16.4.1 Asking Follow-up Questions

Keep the objective of the question in mind as you respond to the expert's answer. Try to judge whether you have acquired the information you requested. You will need to ask follow-up questions if the answer seems incomplete, superficial, inexact, or vague. In Dialog 16.9, Patricia Programmer verbally **nudges** Frank Fixit to complete his answer.

Dialog 16.9 Verbally Nudging an Expert to Complete an Answer

Patricia: Would you please describe how you replace a heating element?

Frank: First I remove the rear panel and pull the case out.

Patricia: And then?

Frank: Then I cut the terminals of the defective element from the busbars.

Dialog 16.10 shows how Patricia Programmer **probes** for more details when an answer seems superficial.

Dialog 16.10 Probing for More Details

Setting

> Patricia Programmer, Howard Hacker, and Frank Fixit are seated at a table. A toaster is on the table in front of them.

Dialog

Patricia: What do you do when the toaster just doesn't work at all—you push the lever down, and nothing happens?

Frank: Well if nothing happens at all, the electricity isn't reaching the element. I suspect a problem with the line switch actuator.

Patricia: Tell me more about the line switch actuator.

> *Frank positions the toaster so that Patricia can see how the mechanism works.*

Frank: You see how the end of the bread rack sticks through the back wall? When the lever is lowered, the bread rack goes down and hits the line switch actuator, like so.

Frank pushes down the lever and points to the line switch actuator.

That closes the contacts on the line switch and starts the current.

If the answer contains generalities, you should ask for **clarifications** as Patricia Programmer does in Dialog 16.11.

Dialog 16.11 Clarifying a Vague Answer

Patricia: You said that electrical problems are more difficult to fix than are mechanical ones. What makes electrical problems so difficult.

Frank: There are so many kinds of toasters, and each one is different.

Patricia: What do you mean by *many kinds of toasters?*

Frank: Well, there are two-slice, four-slice, and under-cabinet toasters and toaster-ovens. I guess those are the main kinds.

Follow-up questions can also identify misunderstandings. Sometimes misunderstandings occur because the knowledge engineer confuses similar sounding words or misinterprets the meaning of a word. The latter situation occurs frequently when the expert uses a special technical meaning of a common word.

Patricia Programmer did not encounter that sort of confusion with the vocabulary of toaster repair. Dialog 16.12 illustrates how a follow-up question can clear up a misunderstanding and teach the knowledge engineer a word in the expert's technical vocabulary.

Dialog 16.12 Discovering a Technical Meaning for a Common Word

Setting

Bill is a knowledge engineer. George is an expert who supplies telephone equipment to companies. Bill and George are working on an expert system to help select the appropriate telephone equipment to address a company's needs.

This dialog occurs while George is giving an overview of how he selects telephone equipment for his clients.

Dialog

George: Finally, after I've selected the kind of telephone-exchange system for the company, I look at each station in the exchange. Generally a station is a private office or a desk within a shared office. I find out what usage is expected at each station; then I select the kind of instrument for the station.

Bill: What sorts of things do you measure with the different kinds of instrument?

George: What do you mean? I don't really *measure* anything. I ask questions about who works in the office, what they do, and how much they need to use the phone. That tells me what kind of instrument to choose.

Bill: I guess I don't have a clear idea what you do when you select an instrument for a station. Can you give me some examples of different instruments you might use?

George: Well there's a standard single-line instrument or one with many lines. There are several different multiline options. First is the number of lines. Typically you might have between 4 and 20. Then there are special features like call forwarding and call waiting. Some instruments have additional buttons the user can program. For example, you might set one button to dial a number you call frequently.

Bill *(laughing):* I see! You're talking about *telephones*. Sorry for the confusion. When you said *instrument*, I thought you meant some kind of measuring device; I couldn't figure out what you needed to measure.

George chuckles.

So you refer to the telephones themselves as *instruments?*

George: Right. That's the word we generally use.

Discussion

Initially Bill is not aware that the word *instrument* has a special meaning in George's technical vocabulary; Bill bases his follow-up question on the common interpretation of the word. (If Bill had realized that *instrument* was a technical word, he would have asked for a definition as we shall discuss in Section 16.4.4.) George's reaction to Bill's follow-up question makes it clear that there has been a misunderstanding. When Bill tries to clear up this misunderstanding, he learns the special meaning of *instrument*.

16.4.2 Confirming Your Understanding

When you believe that you understand an explanation, repeat it to the expert in your own words, emphasizing what appears to be important. This gives the expert the opportunity to correct any misconception you may have and to elaborate on important points you may have missed.

In Dialog 16.13, Patricia Programmer paraphrases Frank Fixit's explanation and asks for confirmation that she has understood.

Dialog 16.13 Confirming Your Understanding

Setting

Patricia Programmer, Howard Hacker, and Frank Fixit are discussing how Frank repaired a toaster that burned the toast.

Patricia, Howard, and Frank are seated at a table; each has a copy of a case description that Frank prepared for the meeting.

Dialog

Frank: After I replaced the thermostat, I toasted a slice of bread on medium. It came out too dark, so I knew that the thermostat was not calibrated correctly.

Patricia: You tested the toaster to see whether you had fixed the problem. You found that the new thermostat *did* fix the problem but that the thermostat required calibration.

Frank nods.

What did you do next?

Frank: The toast was too dark so I needed to shorten the toasting time. That means I had to turn the adjustment screw clockwise. The question is— how much to turn it? I had to do some timing tests to get the calibration right. I checked the thermometer and measured the line voltage to the toaster.

Frank glances at his case description.

Here it is—the room was at 70°, and I measured 120 volts. Those two numbers told me that the toasting time should be between 65 and 70 seconds. I set the toaster on medium, started it up, and timed how long it took to pop up. It took 75 seconds—too long. I made a small adjustment and repeated the timing. This time it took 68 seconds, which is within the acceptable range. If my time had still been too long or if I had turned the screw too far so the time was *less* than 65 seconds, I would have had to repeat the timing and correction until I got a time in the correct range. I can usually get the timing right in one or two tries. Some of the new people take five or six times because they turn the screw *way* too much.

Patricia: Let me see if I've got this right. You measure the temperature in the room and the voltage to the toaster. You use those two numbers to decide what toasting times are acceptable. You set the toaster on medium and measure the actual toasting time. If the time is too long, you shorten the toasting time by turning the adjustment screw clockwise. You would lengthen the time by turning counterclockwise. If necessary, you repeat the timing and adjustment until the toasting time is in the right range. Is that it?

Frank: Yes. Also, if the toasting time is far out of range, I have to turn the screw more than if it's close to the acceptable range. In general, I make *very* small corrections. A small turn of the screw can make a *big* difference in the toasting time.

Discussion

> When Patricia first speaks in this dialog, she *paraphrases* Frank's description of his actions; Frank nods to confirm that Patricia's understanding is correct. At the end of the dialog, Patricia provides a *summary* of Frank's process. A summary involves more judgment than a paraphrase because it requires *selection* of the points that seem the most important. Patricia follows her summary with a question that asks Frank to confirm her understanding. Frank's answer shows that Patricia missed one point Frank feels is important.

16.4.3 Resolving Contradictions

In addition to making sure you understand the answer, make sure it seems consistent with everything else you have learned. If the answer seems incompatible with something you learned earlier, you need to resolve the apparent contradiction. Inconsistencies are fairly common during knowledge acquisition; they generally do not indicate serious problems. You may have misunderstood the expert in the past, or you may have misunderstood the current answer. The expert may have given a simplified explanation before and a detailed answer now. The expert may have overlooked some important facts in earlier discussions and remembered them today.

In many applications, the expert's own understanding evolves as a side effect of the knowledge-acquisition process. You should expect the expert's increasing insight and suppress your frustration if the expert gives you a different answer each time a particular question comes up. When you try to clarify contradictions, *never challenge the expert*. You should assume that *you* have misunderstood, not that the *expert* has made a mistake. Instead of raising the topic with an accusation, simply indicate that you are not sure which option is correct or the conditions under which each alternative is appropriate. For example, instead of saying:

That seems wrong.

You told us just the opposite last week.

I think you made a mistake, don't you mean. . . .

you should say:

I apparently don't understand something you have told us, I thought. . . .

I am surprised by what you just said. I would have expected X instead of Y. Can you explain why you chose Y and when you would choose X instead?

Dialog 16.14 illustrates how Patricia Programmer cleared up an apparent contradiction.

Dialog 16.14 Resolving an Apparent Contradiction

Setting

Patricia Programmer, Howard Hacker, and Frank Fixit are seated at a table. Patricia's project notebook is in front of her on the table. Frank is describing how he repaired a toaster by adjusting its thermostat.

Dialog

Frank: The bread was too dark so I tried to adjust the thermostat. To make the toast lighter, I turned the adjusting screw counterclockwise.

Patricia: I think I've got that. You toast a slice of bread on medium; if the color isn't right, you turn the adjusting screw. Counterclockwise will make the toast lighter.

Frank: Right.

Patricia *(scowling slightly)*: Let me just check something before we go on.

Patricia flips back through her project notebook until she finds what she's looking for. Then she reads her notes silently.

Hmmm. Frank, I think I'm confused about the adjusting screw. I'd like to tell you my understanding, and then you can tell me what I'm missing.

Frank: Fine.

Patricia: A couple of weeks ago, we discussed a toaster with a bad thermostat.[3] It kept burning the toast, and you had to replace the thermostat. You described how you calibrated the new thermostat to shorten the toasting time.

Frank: Yes, I remember.

Patricia: For the toaster we discussed last week, you shortened the toasting time by rotating the adjusting screw *clockwise*. I assume that shortening the toasting time means the toast comes out lighter.

Frank: That's right.

Patricia: Well, when you adjusted the thermostat in the toaster we've been discussing, you said you turn the screw *counterclockwise* to get lighter toast. I would have expected you to turn it *clockwise*. Can you tell me what's different between these two cases?

Frank *(laughing)*: You know, this drives all our new repair people crazy! One new guy came to me last week. He had adjusted the thermostats on a couple of toasters before and had this toaster he couldn't adjust. He was doing exactly what he had done before, but he just couldn't get

---

3. Patricia is referring to the toaster discussed in Dialog 16.13.

the toast right. The problem was that he was turning the screw the wrong way!

The toaster we talked about before was made by *General Appliance;* this one is a *Toasts-Best* toaster. For some reason, the different manufacturers do things differently. That's why it's important to keep in mind both the make and the model of the toaster you're fixing. With General Appliance, a clockwise turn shortens the toasting time. With Toast-Best, a clockwise turn *lengthens* the time.

16.4.4 Learning the Expert's Terms

As you listen to the expert's answer, you should make a note of any unfamiliar word you hear. You will need to ask the expert to define what the word means. Your note can be as simple as a circle around the word, or you may prefer to keep a separate vocabulary list. If you are fairly sure you have a general understanding of the word and you need to ask follow-up questions, wait until you are finished with the follow-up questions before asking for the definition. On the other hand, if you are not able to understand the expert's answer because you do not understand the word, you should ask for a definition immediately. Keep track of all the words whose definitions you need to know, and be sure you ask for definitions before you close the current topic. Even if you *think* you know what a word means, verify your understanding with the expert to be sure.

In Dialog 16.15, Patricia Programmer recognizes that Frank Fixit has introduced a new technical term.

Dialog 16.15 Noting a Word to Be Defined Later

Setting

Patricia Programmer, Howard Hacker, and Frank Fixit are seated at a table. In front of Patricia is her project notebook. In front of Frank is a partly disassembled toaster.

Dialog

Patricia: Would you please give us an overview of how the toaster functions?

Frank: When you push down on the operating lever, this action lowers the carriage. The lock spring snaps into place to hold the carriage down.

As Patricia writes down what Frank says, she circles the word carriage.

Patricia: I see.

Frank: This stretches out the main spring; the trigger keeps the main spring stretched.

.
.
.

[Frank has just finished his overview.]

Patricia: I think I've got all that, but I want to be sure I understand your terminology. You used the word *carriage* several times. I assume that the carriage is the part of the toaster that holds the bread and moves up and down. Is that correct?

Frank: That's close. The carriage is this whole mechanism that moves up and down on the vertical shaft and pulls the main spring.

Frank points to the toaster carriage.

The *bread rack* is what actually holds the bread. It's connected to the carriage so the carriage moves the bread rack up and down.

Discussion

From the context of Frank's description, Patricia can get a general understanding of the word *carriage*. This general understanding is sufficient for her to follow Frank's explanation so she lets him continue. If she had asked for an explanation, she would have interrupted Frank's train of thought. Before she moves on to the next topic, however, Patricia makes sure she has understood the word correctly.

Compare Dialog 16.15 to Dialog 16.16.

Dialog 16.16 Asking for the Definition of an Unfamiliar Word

Setting

Patricia Programmer, Howard Hacker, and Frank Fixit are seated at a table. In front of Frank is a partly disassembled toaster. On the wall facing Patricia and Frank is a whiteboard. Frank is describing how a toaster works.

Dialog

Frank: As long as the trigger is held down, the main spring will stay stretched out, and the toast will stay down. When the trigger is released, the main spring pulls the carriage back up, and the toast pops up.

Frank lowers the carriage on the toaster and points to the trigger.

You can see this little wire sticking through the toaster frame above the trigger. This is the trip wire—it's what holds the trigger down. The trip wire is connected to the bimetal. As the toaster heats, the bimetal pulls the trip wire backward. When the wire is pulled all the way back, the trigger is released, and the toast pops up.

Patricia: Frank, before you go on with your description, would you please explain what *by-meddle* means? I don't understand what causes the wire to be pulled back.

Frank goes to whiteboard and draws as he talks.

Frank: The bimetal is a strip composed of two different metals sandwiched together. It sticks up from the thermostat not quite perpendicular. It's inclined toward the front of the toaster, maybe about two degrees. You know that metal expands when it's heated?

Patricia nods.

Well, different metals expand at different rates; this is the principle behind a bimetal. The side closer to the front of the toaster expands faster than the rear side. Because the two metals are bonded together, the uneven expansion bends the bimetal backward. This pulls the trip wire back, releasing the trigger.

Patricia: OK. I understand now. Thank you.
To get back to your description, you had just told us that the trigger releases the main spring, so the carriage comes back up.

Frank: That's right. When the trigger is released. . . .

Discussion

This time, Patricia cannot understand Frank's explanation without knowing what *bimetal* means, so she asks for a definition immediately. After Frank has explained the term, Patricia reminds him what they had been discussing before she asked for the definition.

16.4.5 Adding Items to the Agenda

The expert's answer to one question often raises additional questions or suggests topics that need to be discussed. As you listen to the expert's answer, be alert for such topics and questions. When an answer suggests another question, be careful not to interfere with the expert's train of thought. Write the questions down so you will remember to pursue them at the appropriate time; do not interject tangential questions into the middle of the expert's explanation.

You can respond to items suggested by the expert's answer in one of two ways. You can defer the topic to a later discussion, or you can add the topic to the current agenda—that is, you can update your list of information to obtain in the current interview. To decide whether to pursue a topic in this interview or later, ask yourself:

- Does the topic contribute to the goals of *this* interview?

- Is the topic *necessary* to my understanding of the topics I had planned to discuss in this interview?

If the topic is pertinent to the goals of the current interview, add it to your agenda for the current interview. If not, defer this topic. Dialog 16.17 indicates how Patricia Programmer handles questions raised by one of Frank Fixit's explanations.

Dialog 16.17 Identifying Topics to Discuss Later

Setting

Patricia Programmer, Howard Hacker, and Frank Fixit are in the development phase of the toaster-repair advisor project. The current cycle of development focuses on heating-element problems in standard two-slice toasters. The main topic for this interview is the repair of toasters that toast only one side of the bread.

As we join the interview, Frank is describing a toaster he fixed recently.

Dialog

Frank: When a customer says only one side of the bread gets toasted, we always ask two questions:

Which side gets toasted?

Does this happen in both slots, or just one?

Usually, they don't know the answers, but we ask anyway. In this case, the customer didn't know so I toasted two slices to see what happened.

Patricia: When you see which sides of the two slices get toasted, what does that tell you?

Frank: We're just talking about simple two-slice toasters, Right?

Patricia nods.

In these toasters, the problem has *got* to be that an element isn't heating up. There are a number of other problems on models with a bakery switch.

Patricia writes in her notebook:

Topic for future discussion: What other problems can occur in a toaster with a bakery switch?

At any rate, I want to know which of the three elements is the problem. If the inner side of both slices remains white while the outer sides are toasted, I look at the middle element. If the outer side of only one slice remains white, I know it's that outside element.

Patricia writes in her notebook:

What about other possibilities such as outer side of both slices remain white or inner sides are both toasted?

Now in this case, it turned out to be the middle element. I first checked to see that both busbars were attached to the element. I found that the bottom busbar was loose. So the element wasn't getting any electricity. I used a little silver solder to reattach the loose busbar. After that, the toaster worked fine.

Patricia writes in her notebook:

What if the busbars are both attached?

Patricia: Let me know if I understand correctly. You toast two slices to see which element is bad. . . .

Discussion

Patricia identifies three questions to ask in the future:

1. What additional problems can cause a toaster with a bakery switch to toast one side only?

2. What element(s) does Frank suspect when he sees different combinations of toasted and untoasted sides on the two slices?

3. If the busbars are attached to the element, what other possible causes of the problem does Frank consider?

The first question is outside the scope of the current cycle of development; Patricia saves this question for a later cycle when they discuss two-slice toasters with bakery switches. The other two topics are relevant to today's discussion; Patricia adds them to her list of information to obtain in the interview. She will raise these two questions after she and Frank complete their case discussion.

16.4.6 Responding to an Uninformative Answer

Occasionally, you may find that the expert's answer is irrelevant to the question you asked. If this happens, you will need to reask the question. Analyze the expert's answer to try to identify the problem. Consider all of the reasons a question can fail to elicit an answer (see Section 16.2.4). These same problems can elicit a meaningless answer; the same solutions apply. For example, if the expert's answer does not provide the information you thought you were requesting, you may not have been specific enough. Try making the question less open. If the answer does not provide as much information as you wanted, you may have asked too focused a question. Try making it more open.

16.5 Closing a Topic

After you have asked all the questions that you need on a topic, close the topic. Your closing will signal the expert that you are finished with the current topic and ready to move on to a new one. Remember to ask for definitions of any new terms you heard. Summarize the important points, and tie together all the ideas you discussed. Before you leave a topic, check with the expert to be sure you have obtained all important, available information on the topic. For example, you might ask:

Have we covered all important aspects of this topic?

Would you like to add anything before we go on?

Can you think of anything important that we haven't discussed yet?

Patricia Programmer closes a topic in Dialog 16.18.

Dialog 16.18 Closing a Topic

Setting

Patricia Programmer, Howard Hacker, and Frank Fixit are seated at a table. A partly disassembled two-slice toaster is on the table in front of them. Patricia has been questioning Frank about the procedure for replacing a faulty heating element. Frank has answered all the relevant questions so Patricia closes the topic.

Dialog

Patricia: Frank, you told us you check the solder before replacing an element. By *solder* do you mean this little silver blob that joins the busbar to the element terminal?

Patricia points to a busbar solder.

Frank: Yes. A touch of silver solder is used to connect the busbars to the element.

Patricia: Thanks. I think that wraps up our discussion of how to replace an element. In general, only one element goes bad at a time, but occasionally it is necessary to replace two elements or all three.

Frank nods.

The procedure is the same whether you replace one element or more than one. You have to cut the terminal from the busbars to disconnect the element. Then you remove the bread-guard wire next to the defective element, lift the element out, and put the new one in. We've gone through the procedure in a fair amount of detail. Can you think of anything important that we haven't discussed?

Frank: The only thing I'd add is that the center element is a little different because you have to remove *two* bread-guard wires, and one of these includes the trip wire. Before you can remove this bread-guard wire, you have to pull the trip wire back to release it from the front of the toaster.

Patricia: Thanks. Is there anything else?

Frank shakes his head.

All right. Next we need to discuss the procedure for replacing the thermostat. Why don't we take a break before we move on.

16.6 Dialog Examples

We have discussed a number of techniques for asking questions and responding to the expert's answer. The examples in this section illustrate some of these techniques in the context of ongoing dialogs.[4] You

---

4. Dialogs 16.19 and 16.20 contains adaptations of dialogs that appear on the "Knowledge Acquisition Problems and Solutions" videotape used in the *Knowledge Acquisition Workshop* at Cimflex Teknowledge Corporation.

will notice that the knowledge engineers are able to accomplish the various functions we have discussed without being verbose. For example, a single utterance of one or two short sentences may serve as a paraphrase, a request for confirmation, and a closing. As you read the dialogs, try to identify introductions and closings. Analyze the questions. Identify which active listening techniques are illustrated.

Dialog 16.19 illustrates that the phrasing of questions can make a big difference in the productivity of an interview. Read the example critically. Try to identify good and bad questions. Try to reword bad questions.

Dialog 16.19 Asking Questions

Setting

Laura is an expert who helps people to configure personal computers to meet their needs. Richard is a knowledge engineer assessing an application to help the sales staff in Laura's company. Richard is considering an expert system that would help a sales person to recommend the personal computer configuration that best addresses a customer's needs.

This is the first meeting between knowledge engineer and expert, and Laura is a little apprehensive. Richard is trying to get an overview of the task of configuring personal computers.

Dialog with Problems

After introductions, Richard proceeds to the main topic of the interview.

Richard: When someone comes into your store interested in buying a complete computer system, there are undoubtedly a lot of things you have to take into account: price versus performance, upward compatibility with any software they already have, what kind of peripherals they need, new software they may need. What order do you think about the components in? Do you consider the CPU first then the monitor or the monitor then the CPU? How do you take all of these factors into account?

Laura: Uhhh—well, let's see—I probably think of the peripherals first.
Usually I start by asking what the customer wants to do with the machine. Someone who wants a computer for word processing just needs a minimal system. On the other hand, someone who plans to develop a complicated software program will need a larger system.

Richard: So the first thing you ask is whether the customer is going to do word processing or software development. Right?

Laura: Not exactly. Those are two extreme applications. There are many other things people might use the system for. Generally I want to let *them* tell me how they want to use the system.

Richard: Let's take a hypothetical example. I'm a customer. I come into your store and I want a system for home use.

Laura: Could you be more specific? Do you know what you'll use the computer for?

Richard: Yes. I want a system I can use for word processing, and I want to be able to draw graphics for business.

Laura: I see. That reminds me of a customer who came into the store recently and told me that she wanted a system for home use. She wanted to develop presentation materials like overhead slides. This implied to me that she wanted to work with graphics and to be able to mix text with graphics.

Richard: Ah! So then one of your first concerns was picking the best graphics card, right?

Laura: Er—The best graphics card out now in a medium price range is the VGA card. Another one that comes close is the EGA card. If you get the right program, you can choose between these two. I'd generally recommend the EGA card because it's cheaper—unless the customer needs to use a specific program that requires the VGA card. In this case, the SuperGraph software turned out to be suitable for this application, and I recommended that plus the EGA card.

Richard: I have heard a lot about WonderDraw. If your customer had wanted to use WonderDraw, would that have required an EGA card too or a VGA card?

Laura: Well, neither. For WonderDraw, she would have needed a workstation running X-Windows, and she probably would have required a big processor like an 80386 or a 68000. I wouldn't recommend WonderDraw for a moderately priced system. It's really not suited for a personal computer. So it really never came to mind in this case.

> Before you read further, think about the preceding dialog.
>   Look at each question. Is it open or closed? Is the question type appropriate in this context? Is the question well phrased?
>   What problems can you identify with this dialog? What would you have done differently?

Dialog without Problems

After introductions, Richard proceeds to the main topic of the interview.

Richard: Laura, this afternoon I'd like to discuss how you go about selecting a computer system. When someone comes to you for advice about purchasing an entire computer system, where do you start?

Laura: I usually ask what the customer plans to use the system for. That tells me a lot about what to recommend. It's also helpful to know what their budget is and how much experience they have with computers. Usually, if I know those three things, I can come up with the right system—if there *is* a system that can do what they want in the right price range.

Richard: Could you tell us about a recent example where you gave advice to someone who was interested in buying a system?

Laura: Let me think.

Laura pauses for a while, staring at ceiling in the corner of the room.

Yes, last week I spoke to a customer who wanted to develop a variety of materials for presentation purposes—things like overhead slides. She said that she works in her home a lot and would be using the system at home.

Richard: Does the fact that the customer works at home suggest something to you?

Laura: Now that I think about it, yes. I assumed that she wanted a *moderately priced* system. I asked her if that was the case, and she said it was.

Richard: In general then, if the computer is for home use, this suggests a moderately priced system. Do you always confirm this with the customer?

Laura: Yes.

Richard: Was there other information her requirements suggested to you?

Laura: The fact that she wanted to prepare presentation material told me that she would need some fairly sophisticated graphics and that she'd want to mix text with graphics. She'd probably want different sizes of text, too. This brought to mind a package I like to recommend because it's performance is very good for a moderate price—SuperGraph.

Richard: If you select a package like SuperGraph, does that impose additional requirements on the system you're putting together?

Laura: Yes. In order to support that program, you need the EGA or VGA card, because you'll need higher-resolution graphics. I usually recommend the EGA card for a moderately priced system because it costs less.

Richard: You mentioned that the SuperGraph package requires a graphics card and that you would recommend the EGA card due to its capabilities and price. Did the fact that the customer would be working at home and using the SuperGraph package to prepare presentation materials suggest other requirements for her computer system?

Laura: Oh yes. For example, she would need a mouse in order to operate the graphics part of the program; she would need a good color monitor, a good quality laser printer so that she could get the high quality output for her slides. She would also need at least 640K of memory.

Richard: Let me see if I've got all of that: a mouse, a color monitor, a laser printer, and at least 640K of memory.

Richard looks to Laura for confirmation. Laura nods.

I'd like to go over each of these items and hear what you recommended, let's start with the mouse. What mouse did you suggest?

Discussion

In the first dialog, Richard starts the interview with a little speech about what *he* assumes Laura does. This is completely inappropriate.

He is conducting an interview to learn *from Laura;* he should ask her questions, not tell her what she does. When Richard does get around to asking Laura for information, he asks three questions before giving her a chance to answer. By the time Richard finishes his minioration, Laura cannot remember all the questions he asked; she is not entirely sure what information he wants. Before the interview, Laura was uneasy. She had only a vague understanding of what was expected of her and was a little worried that she would not measure up as an "expert." Imagine how her anxiety increases and her confidence diminishes, when Richard's initial question is a verbal barrage she cannot answer!

The result would not have been much better if Richard had asked his questions one at a time. He uses closed questions that imply that Laura considers the different components in a fixed order and that she bases her decisions on the factors that he lists. Richard does not know enough at this point to ask such specific questions. He should have used much more open questions that would have allowed him to learn *from Laura* what factors she considers or how she goes about selecting components. Richard's questions imply that *he* is the expert, not the student. He does not use his familiarity with personal computers to facilitate communication; on the contrary, he uses it to try to impress Laura with the breadth of his understanding of the field.

Throughout the interview, Richard continues to use questions that are too closed; he interjects his own suggestions, rather than asking Laura what she does. When Laura mentions that her customer wanted to work with graphics, Richard proposes (incorrectly) what Laura would do next. The result is a change in the topic of discussion, adding to Laura's discomfort and confusion.

Richard fares much better in the second dialog. He eases Laura into knowledge acquisition with an introduction that explains the purpose of the discussion. Richard's first question is open-ended; it asks Laura what *she* does rather than suggesting alternatives. After he asks one simple question, Richard waits for Laura's reply. Laura can answer this question easily; this question is just what she needs to allay her apprehensions about the interview. Before the interview Laura was not sure what to expect, but now she is more confident of her ability to answer Richard's questions.

Richard lets the expert talk; he listens to her responses. He allows Laura to continue with one train of thought. The second interview is much more comfortable for Laura than the first and much more productive for Richard.

In Dialog 16.20, the knowledge engineer is very familiar with the subject matter of the application. Problems arise when this knowledge engineer is guided by her own ideas of how the task is performed rather than listening to the expert to discover how she performs the task. As you read the dialog, decide how you would have responded to each of the expert's answers.

Dialog 16.20 Listening to the Expert

Setting

Rachel has three years of experience as a product-support representative for an expert-system shell called Expert-Wise. Andrea is a knowledge engineer; she is also an experienced Expert-Wise user, having built several expert systems with this shell over the last four years. Rachel and Andrea are working on a project to develop a "help desk" application that would provide customer support to the Expert-Wise users.

The dialog takes place during initial inquiry. Andrea is trying to get a clear understanding of what the expert system will do.

Dialog with Problems

After introductions, Andrea proceeds to the main topic of the interview.

Andrea: I understand that, as a product-support representative, you tell people how to use Expert-Wise. Isn't that right?

Rachel: Not really. I don't *tell* them how to use Expert-Wise so much as *help them* through the problems they have.

Andrea: So you must break their problems down into categories like recursion and iteration and then tell them how to accomplish those things.

Rachel: Not exactly. The real task is to get them past their current problems. Later, if I can educate them about some of those categories, I will. But I don't really start thinking in terms of those categories.

Andrea *(breaking in aggressively):* Well when *I* solve a problem in Expert-Wise, I look at what I'm trying to do—whether I need recursion or iteration. Then I look at the constructs I can use in Expert-Wise to accomplish this.

Rachel: Well, that's OK for writing Expert-Wise code, but this is a different situation entirely. I try to help customers get their code straightened out. My main aim is to give customers a feeling that our product-support group will give them the help that they need when they encounter problems.

Andrea *(a little frustrated):* Maybe you can give me an example of solving a problem—nested loops, for example. I've had a few problems with nested loops.

Rachel: OK. Say a guy calls in with a problem. The first thing I do is to try to get an idea of what he's trying to do. I have him read me some code, to get an idea of how well he understands the tool. If he seems well versed in Expert-Wise, I might ask if he's tried using the Count-and-Repeat feature.

Andrea *(sounding exasperated):* Well it sounds like you *are* breaking it into categories like recursion and iteration!

Rachel *(calmly):* Well, *eventually*. But if I did that up front, I'd really confuse the issue. I'm not *writing code*, but helping a person through some trouble. I tend to think about the person's ability and background more than the type of Expert-Wise problem he's having. My goal in these situations is to educate the caller so he doesn't need to call back again.

Andrea *(frustrated):* Lets try another example. One time, I was working on a problem in Expert-Wise. It was a nested loop problem, which is why I brought this up—those problems are a bit complicated. I used an iterative technique rather than a recursive technique because it was more efficient. But there are so many different ways that I could have solved the problem. I could have used pattern-matching variables, multivalued expressions, or Count-and-Repeat.

   If you don't teach people all these alternatives, won't they just keep calling back?

Rachel: True, but I wouldn't want to overwhelm someone immediately on a call. My tactic is to solve the caller's problem. Then maybe I can go back and explain, "This is looping. . . ."

Before you read further, think about the preceding dialog.
   Look at Andrea's questions. Are they phrased well?
   Look at Andrea's responses to Rachel's answers. Does each new question indicate that Andrea has understood the answer to the previous question?
   What problems can you identify? What would you have done differently?

Dialog without Problems

After introductions, Andrea proceeds to the main topic of the interview.

Andrea: I'd like to learn more about your job as a product-support representative. What do you do when someone calls you?

Rachel: The first thing is to put the person at ease. Then I ask for a general description of the problem. Some people are better at that than others. As quickly as possible, I'll figure out what kind of problem they have. Is it difficult technically? Is it something I can answer right away? Do I need to start with some basic education?

Andrea: It sounds as though you categorize problems into three groups. Can you tell me a little more about these categories?

Rachel: Yes, I guess you could think of them as different categories. If the call is about a problem that is technically difficult, I'll handle it differently from a simple call. The simple calls fall into two camps: ones I can answer immediately because the person has the background to understand and ones where the person needs some education before they'll understand the fix to their problem.

Andrea: OK. So from their general description you do two things. You classify the problem according to technical difficulty, and you classify the person according to degree of familiarity with Expert-Wise.

Rachel: Yes, that's right. I look for familiarity with Expert-Wise in particular and knowledge of programming in general.

Andrea: So from the technical difficulty of the problem and the person's background you select one of three approaches to handling the call?

Rachel nods.

Let's start with the educational calls. Do you have an example of a recent call that required a little education?

Rachel: Yes. Someone called in last week with a question that's pretty common. I get a lot of calls concerning looping in Expert-Wise. This guy was confused about the concept of iteration first, and then he was confused about how to write loops with Expert-Wise.

I had him start by describing the problem. This was his first system—he sounded really confused, especially whenever he tried to tell me how he was using pattern-matching variables. From the words he used and the difficulty he had explaining, I could tell he needed a little bit of nomenclature and education about looping as a general programming method.

Then we got into the syntax of Expert-Wise. I spent about an hour and a half going over how variables work in Expert-Wise. Then, once he understood that, I could say "Just use the Count-and-Repeat feature. It is on page such and such in the Reference Manual and works like so."

Andrea: How do you decide how deep to go with these explanations?

Rachel: Well, it depends. I try to attack misunderstandings immediately so concepts fall into place. The key is when they say, "Aha, I understand!"

Discussion

In the first dialog, Andrea commits the cardinal sin of knowledge acquisition. She tries to impose her own assumptions and organization on Rachel, rather than listening to find out how Rachel thinks about the task. Every time Andrea speaks, she talks about what *she* thinks, how *she* solves problems, and how *she* categorizes problems. Andrea seems to ignore what Rachel has to say. Andrea practically argues with Rachel in an effort to convince herself that Rachel really does things the way Andrea suggested from the start.

By not listening to the expert, Andrea wastes the knowledge-acquisition session. She knows no more at the end of this interview than she did at the beginning. To make matters worse, this approach is no way to encourage an expert to collaborate in developing a system. Rachel has been asked to supply her expertise. Why should she bother, when the knowledge engineer does not listen to what Rachel has to say? Why should Rachel be willing to work with a knowledge engineer who thinks she knows more about performing the task than Rachel does?

In the second dialog, Andrea listens to Rachel. Rachel's description tells Andrea that Rachel categorizes the phone calls. Andrea pursues this topic to get a clearer definition of the categories. She also identifies the factors that Rachel uses in categorizing the calls. Andrea never suggests her own categorization. In fact, nothing in the entire second dialog gives a hint that Andrea herself is a very experienced Expert-Wise user.

Notice how Andrea paraphrases and asks for confirmation of her understanding of each answer before asking the next question. Notice how Andrea probes for additional information when Rachel's answers suggest that she has not told Andrea all pertinent details.

The tone of the second interaction is much more cooperative. Instead of competing with the expert, Andrea learns from her. Rachel will be much more inclined to participate in the project after this interaction than after the one depicted in the first dialog.

16.7 Becoming Proficient

We have illustrated several considerations that go into asking questions and responding to answers; now, we need to review the process in the context of an ongoing interview. Patricia Programmer clearly does not have enough time to ponder what exact degree of openness is appropriate for each question, to weigh alternative wordings, and to review potential questions for clarity and neutrality. She cannot delay the dialog as she contemplates possible responses to Frank Fixit's answers. She must keep the dialog moving smoothly. As Patricia formulates questions, she keeps in mind the general principles that make questions understandable; she lets these principles guide her choice of words. She selects words quickly, without taking time to deliberate over specific alternatives. Because Patricia is an experienced interviewer, she is able to pose well-worded questions promptly; while she listens to Frank, she can immediately identify situations that require responses. Patricia has had a great deal of practice; her skills have improved over time.

To become proficient at asking questions, you should *practice formulating questions* then take the time to *analyze the questions you formulate.*

> As a silent observer to knowledge acquisition, Howard Hacker tries to formulate questions during interviews. He writes down questions as they occur to him. He compares his questions with the ones Patricia Programmer asks, and he tries to discover whether hers were preferable. After an interview, Patricia and Howard review each of Howard's questions to check whether he chose an appropriate degree of openness for the question, phrased it simply, and avoided interjecting his own ideas. When Howard has time to think about the phrasing of his questions, he usually can recognize questions that he phrased poorly. The exercise of reviewing his questions and recognizing his mistakes makes it easier for Howard to avoid the same mistakes in the future. With practice, Howard is able to write well-phrased questions immediately.
>
> Howard also practices formulating questions *before* an interview. He reviews Patricia's list of topics to discuss and writes down the questions that he would ask. He tries to pose at least the first question on each topic. When Howard is ready to serve as acting interviewer, he includes this step in his preparation for an interview: After listing the topics to discuss, he composes and reviews as many questions for Frank as possible.
>
> Howard practices responding to Frank's answers in a similar manner.

He makes a list in his notebook of situations that require responses.[5] As he listens to each of Frank's answers, Howard checks off the situations that he identifies and notes the appropriate response. He compares the responses he chose with Patricia's responses. After an interview, he and Patricia discuss any discrepancies between Howard's approach and Patricia's. With practice, Howard is able to pose appropriate responses without referring to his list of situations that require responses.

Howard Hacker has the luxury of learning to ask questions while a more experienced knowledge engineer takes responsibility for leading the interviews. If you are not so fortunate, you can practice using many of the same techniques Howard uses. Practice as much as your schedule permits *before* you interview the expert. Try to find colleagues or friends who are willing to play the role of expert for you. Interview a variety of "practice experts," and notice how you need to adapt your style to their individual differences. Interview your practice experts about their jobs, their hobbies, or other subjects on which they are knowledgeable. If you have a colleague who is also learning to interview, take turns observing each other conduct interviews. The observer can take notes that indicate what the interviewer did well and poorly. After each interview, the two of you should review the observer's notes and discuss how the interview could have been improved.

Videotapes can serve as valuable aids to the development of your interviewing skills. If you have access to video equipment, record your practice interview sessions. Review the videotapes critically and pay particular attention to your nonverbal signals and the interviewee's reactions to them. Also look for the interviewee's nonverbal signals, and check whether you noticed these signals during the interview and responded appropriately. If video equipment is not available, make audio recordings. As you listen to audio or video recordings, check whether your inflection and intonation are appropriate.

If the majority of your early interviewing practice must take place while you are interviewing your project expert, be sure to formulate questions as part of your preparation for each interview. Write down all the questions you think you may need to ask. Review the wording carefully. If possible, have another person read the questions and tell you whether they are clear.

If you tape record interviews, review your tapes after each interview. If video equipment is available to you, ask whether the expert is willing to have the interviews recorded on videotape. If you are unable to record the interview, include observations about the interview itself in your notes, or enlist a colleague to observe the interview and write down interesting elements of the dialog.

---

5. Such a list of situations that require responses can be found in Table 16.5.

As you review the notes or recording of an interview (practice or real):

- *Analyze each question.* Is the question open or closed? Was the choice of openness appropriate? Is the question phrased simply and clearly? Is the question free from your own bias?

- *Check for questions that did not elicit relevant answers.* Did you realize during the interview that a problem had occurred? Did you correctly identify the cause of the problem?[6] Were you able to correct the problem? If not, how should you have responded to it? How do you think you could have prevented the problem?

- *Review each of the expert's answers, and identify all aspects of the answer that require a response.*[7] During the interview, did you correctly identify all the responses that were needed? Did you respond appropriately? If not, how should you have responded?

16.8 Points to Remember

To keep the expert oriented to your goals during an interview, introduce each topic of discussion by explaining what you need to find out and why this topic is important. When you ask questions on the topic, pay attention to both the words you use in your question and the way in which you ask it. Table 16.2 summarizes how to ask questions during an interview. Before you go on to the next topic, close the current topic with a summary of what you have learned, and ask whether the expert has anything to add.

After asking a question, see whether it successfully elicits a relevant answer from the expert. If not, determine what went wrong, and correct problems with your original question. You will need to learn your expert's individual communication style in order to judge how long to wait for a response before deciding that a question will not produce an answer. Similarly, you will need to learn how your expert reacts to different problems so you can rephrase your question to avoid the problem. Table 16.3 lists common problems with questions and the corresponding solutions.

After you ask a successful question, listen carefully to the expert's answer so you will be able to respond appropriately (Table 16.4).

As you listen to the expert's answer, try to identify every aspect of

---

6. Refer to Table 16.3 for a list of common problems with questions and their solutions.
7. Refer to Table 16.5 for a list of situations that require responses.

Table 16.2 Guidelines for Asking Questions

Do	Don't
Ask for the *expert's* answer.	Suggest answers based on *your* knowledge or assumptions.
Use open questions to request general information.	Ask closed questions *until you have learned enough from the expert to ask for specific details.*
Use closed questions to ask for specific details.	
Use a mixture of open and closed questions.	Tire the expert with too many consecutive open questions.
Learn what kind of question your expert prefers.	"Grill" the expert with too many consecutive closed questions.
Make questions simple and clear.	Ask more than one question at a time.
Use words the expert will understand.	Use words whose meaning or sound is ambiguous.
Use words with neutral or positive connotations.	Use knowledge-engineering or computer-science jargon.
Speak clearly and enunciate carefully.	Imply that one possible answer is preferable.
	Convey negative messages in your vocal inflection.

Table 16.3 Correcting Questions that Fail

Problem	Solution
The question is too general.	Provide more direction; use a less open question.
The question is too specific.	Rephrase the question to be more open. Be sure not to suggest alternatives unless you have learned these alternatives *from the expert.*
The expert does not understand the question.	Apologize; correct any impression that failure to understand is the expert's fault. Restate the question more clearly, or explain in a different way what you want to know.
The expert does not see the relevance of the question.	Explain the point of the question in more detail (or more clearly). Then reask the question. (Rephrase the question if necessary.)

Table 16.3 (continued)

Problem	Solution
The expert does not know the answer.	Suggest postponing the discussion until the expert has had time to think about the question, to look up information, or to confer with colleagues.
The expert does not want to answer the question.	Before you know the expert well, just defer the question to a later date. If you have been working with the expert long enough to have a good relationship, express concern. Try to find the reason for the expert's reluctance.
The expert is insulted by the question.	Make sure that neither your words nor your actions convey negative messages. If you are unable to detect the reason for the expert's reaction, overcompensate in your words for inadvertent nonverbal signals.
The same question fails repeatedly.	Defer the question to a later interview. In the interim, try to identify problems with your question. Try to think of different ways to request the information.

Table 16.4 Guidelines for Listening to the Expert's Answers

Do	Don't
Listen carefully to the expert; try to comprehend the expert's meaning.	Try to formulate your next question while the expert is answering your last question.
Listen for indications of what the expert thinks is important.	Get distracted by activities, sounds, or problems outside the interview.
Write down what you understand.	Continue the interview when you are too tired or distracted to listen.
Identify every aspect of the answer that needs a response.	Let the expert provide more information than you can comprehend.
	Write down the expert's words verbatim without regard for their intent.
	Respond too quickly.

Table 16.5 Situations That Require Responses

Situation	Response
The expert pauses or stops talking, but the answer does not seem complete.	Verbally nudge the expert to finish.
The expert's answer seems vague.	Ask the expert to clarify.
You do not understand the expert's answer.	Ask the expert to clarify.
The expert's words and nonverbal messages are inconsistent with each other.	Ask the expert to clarify.
The expert's answer seems to contradict information from an earlier interview.	Ask the expert to clarify.
The expert's answer seems superficial.	Probe for more details.
The answer seems complete, and you think you understand it.	Paraphrase the answer. Ask the expert to confirm your understanding.
You hear a term that you do not understand.	Ask the expert to define the term.
The expert's answer suggests a topic pertinent to the goals of this interview.	Schedule the topic into the current agenda.
The expert's answer suggests a topic not closely related to the goals of this interview.	Defer discussion of this new topic to a later interview.

the answer that requires a response. Then respond to each item you identified. Table 16.5 summarizes situations that require responses and the appropriate active listening techniques with which you can respond.

Chapter 17

Keeping an Interview Productive

In time, Howard Hacker mastered the techniques for asking questions and making sure that he understood the answers. Howard could then serve as secondary questioner in interviews with Frank Fixit. Howard had to acquire one additional skill before he could assume the responsibilities of acting interviewer. To lead an interview, Howard would need to keep the discussion focused. He would have to ensure that each interview provided information he and Patricia required for the development of the toaster-repair advisor.

This chapter presents interviewing techniques that help to keep a discussion productive. In Section 17.1, we discuss how knowledge engineers can balance the control of an interview between themselves and the expert. In Section 17.2, we describe common problems that can derail an interview from its intended focus, and we present techniques for getting the discussion back on track.

17.1 Balance of Control in an Interview

In an interview, **control** is the interviewer's or the interviewee's capacity to influence both the nature of the interview process and the outcome of the interview. Control is an element of every interview; what varies is the *amount* of control each participant possesses. A productive knowledge-acquisition interview requires a careful balance of control between the expert and the lead interviewer. Knowledge engineers use the distribution of control to further two objectives.

1. To keep the expert at ease with the interview process

2. To obtain the information necessary for the development of an expert system

Knowledge engineers must give up as much control as is necessary for the expert's comfort. At the same time, they must retain sufficient control to ensure that they acquire the necessary information. Early in a project, when knowledge engineers concentrate on establishing a good working relationship with the expert, the first objective often overrides the second. In early interviews, many experts are unsettled by uncertainties about their roles. At the beginning of a project therefore, an interview that puts the expert at ease with the knowledge-acquisition process is a productive interview. The knowledge engineer may let the expert set the direction of discussion even if that direction does not provide much useful information. Later, after a good relationship has been established, the second objective becomes the more significant one. At that stage, an interview is productive only if it furnishes the knowledge engineers with new, useable information.

> Frank Fixit is the senior member of the service staff. In meetings and informal discussions with his co-workers, Frank generally takes charge. Patricia Programmer realizes that Frank is most comfortable with a leadership position so she tries to give him as much control in interviews as he wants. Early in the project, Frank did not have a clear understanding of the role he was to play; he was happy to let Patricia guide discussions. As the project progressed, Frank became comfortable with his role; he came to think of interviews as opportunities for him to instruct Patricia and Howard in toaster repair. As time passed, Frank very naturally started to assume more control in interviews. After the project had been underway for several months, Frank was able to direct many interview discussions with little guidance from Patricia.
>
> Although Frank is most comfortable taking the lead in interviews, Patricia cannot relinquish *all* control to Frank. She is responsible for the development of the toaster-repair advisor. If Frank inadvertently leads discussions in directions that do not contribute to the development of the system, the project may fail, and the failure would be Patricia's, not Frank's.

Knowledge engineers can influence the balance of control in two ways. First they can select questions that give control to the expert or that restrict the expert's control. Second they can exert control when necessary by interrupting the expert. As we discussed in Chapter 16, different questions give the expert varying degrees of latitude in the choice of an answer. A highly open question gives the expert the most control; it leaves the expert free to decide the direction the discussion will take. A very closed question gives the expert no control; it specifies a set of answers from which the expert must choose. A knowledge engineer can often keep an interview productive simply through judicious choice of the degree of openness of questions.

Unfortunately, the judicious selection of the appropriate question type is not always sufficient. The knowledge engineer must have a natural opportunity to ask the question—that is, the expert must agree it is the knowledge engineer's turn to speak. Sometimes the knowledge engineer will recognize the need to redirect a discussion but will not have a turn to speak. At those times, the knowledge engineer must interrupt the expert.

Interrupting is a fine art. To interrupt skillfully, you must interrupt without giving offense and without seeming rude. The guiding principle is to *interrupt only when you need to do so.* Interrupt only when you are reasonably confident that the expert's current direction will not lead you to useful information. Never interrupt the expert with a question that will derail a productive line of thought; record questions, and ask them at a more appropriate time. Do not interrupt to tell anecdotes unless you feel that the expert has become bogged down and that the story would relieve tension.

Always interrupt politely and respectfully. In general, you should apologize when you interrupt. Above all, *interrupt at the right time.* Wait until you detect a shift in topic so you do not break the expert's line of thought. If possible, wait for a break in the expert's speech, such as a pause between sentences. If the expert speaks without pauses, you may need to start to speak while the expert is still speaking. You should start to speak *as soon as you hear the end of a sentence.* Start to talk just as the expert begins the next sentence; do not wait until the middle of a sentence to interrupt. When you have interrupted, give a summary of the important points that the expert made before the digression, and ask a question that will set the discussion back into a productive direction. The example dialogs in Section 17.2.2 will illustrate the correct way to interrupt.

17.2 Problems that Impede Interview Productivity

17.2.1 Problems Caused by Knowledge Engineers

As we have seen in earlier chapters, good interviewing practices are crucial to the productivity of an interview. The knowledge engineers must work constructively with the expert and with one another. They must select their questions thoughtfully and ask them carefully. When the expert answers a question, the knowledge engineers must listen for comprehension and ensure that they have understood correctly. In Chapters 13 through 16 we discussed helpful interviewing activities and the difficulties that can arise from poor technique. In summary, the most common errors through which knowledge engineers diminish the productivity of an interview are that they:

- Are insensitive to the needs of the expert and so fail to establish a good working relationship with the expert (Dialog 13.2)

- Do not work together cooperatively in a team interview (Dialog 13.3)

- Ask questions inappropriately or ask inappropriate questions (Dialog 16.19)

- Fail to listen attentively to the expert or to verify their understanding (Dialog 16.20)

17.2.2 Problems Caused by Experts

Even the most skilled knowledge engineer cannot always keep an interview on course. When the discussion diverges to the point that the interview is not productive, the knowledge engineer must lead the discussion back to a constructive topic. In this section, we show how to correct problems that commonly side-track interviews.

- The expert consciously takes control of the interview and inadvertently hinders the achievement of current project goals.

- The expert digresses from the current topic of conversation and ceases to provide useful information.

- The expert leads the discussion away from the current topic and provides useful information but not the information the knowledge engineers need at the moment.

- The expert provides information more quickly than the knowledge engineers can fully comprehend.

- In an interview with multiple experts, the experts argue among themselves.

The Expert Sets an Inappropriate Direction

Perhaps the most difficult problem in keeping an interview on track occurs when the expert consciously sets the direction of the discussion and chooses a topic that does not contribute to the achievement of project goals. It is important to encourage an expert who wants to play such an active part in the project. The knowledge engineer must steer the discussion to a more productive topic without discouraging the expert's future participation, without appearing to challenge the expert's lead, and without instigating a struggle for control of the interview. The best way to prevent this problem is to involve the expert in project planning and interview agenda planning and to make sure that the expert understands the requirements imposed by the project goals and schedule.

In an interview, if the expert introduces a topic you did not antic- ipate, encourage the expert's suggestion with enthusiasm. Be as flexible as the project plan permits, and accommodate the expert's preference if you can. If the expert's topic is outside the scope of your current development increment, however, you will need to change the topic. When you need to redirect the expert, explain what you need to ac- complish, why you need to discuss the topic you prefer, and when you will get to the topic the expert proposed. Try to encourage the expert to work with you to achieve the project goals.

Dialog 17.1 illustrates how a knowledge engineer can redirect an expert who proposes an inappropriate topic.

Dialog 17.1 Redirecting an Expert

Setting

>Catherine is an expert horticulturist. Nancy is a knowledge engineer working with Catherine to develop an expert system for a chain of plant nurseries. Customers in the nurseries will be able to obtain expert gardening advice from this system. The project plan calls for initial fielding of a system whose scope is limited to flowering plants. Later the system will be extended to cover garden vegetables, then fruit trees, and finally ornamental trees and shrubs.
>
>The project is currently in its first cycle of development, with a focus on flowering plants. At the end of the last interview, Catherine and Nancy set the agenda for today's interview. They agreed that they would discuss pruning (of flowering plants), and then would start to discuss common pests (in flowering plants).

Dialog with Problems

>*Catherine has just finished her discussion of pruning.*

Catherine: That about covers pruning. Do you have any questions?

Nancy: No I don't; your description was very clear. Let me just make sure I've got all the important points. First, you need to know the kind of plant being pruned and the reason for pruning—to shape, to thin, to increase flower production, and so on. You also take into account the time of year. On the basis of this information, you can recommend the appro- priate tools and the best pruning techniques. We discussed some general principles as well as guidelines specific to roses or other particular kinds of plants.

Catherine: Good. Now while we're on the subject of pruning, I want to discuss pruning fruit trees. You'll see some similarities with flowering plants but also some important differences.

Nancy *(surprised):* Catherine, we were supposed to talk about pests next.

Catherine *(enthusiastically):* Yes, I know; but when I was preparing my notes on pruning, I decided that it would be best to cover *all* the various kinds of pruning at one time.

> *Catherine points to the stack of paper on the table in front of her.*

As you can see, I've prepared quite a lot of material on pruning fruit trees.

Nancy *(scowling):* I'm sorry that you spent your time with that preparation, because we really need to talk about pests today.

Catherine *(impatiently):* Well, I'm not *prepared* to talk about pests.

Nancy *(a little angrily):* Well you *should* be prepared. We agreed last time that we would start on that topic today. I really thought I could depend on you to stick to the agenda. Just start on pests, and tell me as much as you can.

Catherine *(a little angrily):* No. I'm not organized to start talking about pests.

> *Nancy sighs and looks disgruntled.*

Nancy: OK. Go ahead and tell me about pruning fruit trees.

Catherine *(with a smug grin):* Good. A common reason to prune fruit trees is to encourage fruit production.

> Before you read further, think about the preceding dialog.
>   What problems does Nancy encounter? Which of these problems are her own fault? What would you have done differently?

Dialog without Problems

> *[Catherine has finished her discussion of pruning. Nancy has just summarized the discussion and has confirmed that she understands correctly.]*

Catherine: Now while we're on the subject of pruning, I want to discuss pruning fruit trees. You'll see some similarities with flowering plants but also some important differences.

Nancy *(calmly and evenly):* Catherine, we had planned to talk about pests next.

Catherine *(enthusiastically):* Yes, I know; but when I was preparing my notes on pruning, I decided that it would be best to cover *all* the various kinds of pruning at one time.

> *Catherine points to the stack of paper on the table in front of her.*

As you can see, I've prepared quite a lot of material on pruning fruit trees.

Nancy: That's great! Thank you for taking the extra time to prepare that material. We'll need to discuss it in detail when we add fruit trees to the system so your work now will save us a lot of time then.

　　As you know, the first system we deliver will be limited to flowering plants. I need to be sure we can meet our schedule for delivery so I'm afraid we will have to limit our discussions to flowering plants for now. I'm sorry to have to switch gears on you, but could we talk about pest instead?

Catherine *(disappointed):* Well, I'm not prepared to talk about pests.

Nancy *(sympathetically):* I understand. If you feel comfortable giving me an overview off the top of your head, we can start that way. Then we can fill in the details after you've had a chance to prepare. If you would prefer not to start this new topic, that's fine, too. We can end the meeting early, and I can get a head start on adding pruning advice to the knowledge base. How would you prefer to proceed?

Catherine: Well, I guess I can start talking about pests, but I might not be very organized.

Nancy: Thanks. Don't worry about being organized, we can sort things out later if necessary.

Catherine: OK. I guess we need to think about two major groups of pests. First are animals that might eat the plants. Deer and rabbits are a problem in rural areas. Gophers and moles often attack bulbs and roots. Birds can be a nuisance too, especially to newly planted (or transplanted) seedlings. Second we must consider smaller pests like insects and snails.

Discussion

Notice how these two dialogs differ from the dialogs we have seen before. Instead of the knowledge engineer announcing the close of a topic and asking whether the expert has anything to add, the *expert* in this example closes the topic and asks whether the *knowledge engineer* has questions. The expert clearly is directing the interview. This in itself is not a problem. Many projects go through stages in which the expert sets the direction of interviews.

　　In the first dialog, Nancy's initial problem is that Catherine is eager to discuss a topic outside the scope of the current development increment, but Nancy does not have enough leeway in the project schedule to include this topic now. Nancy herself exacerbates the problem, however, by her reaction to Catherine's proposed agenda. Catherine has put a great deal of effort into her preparation for the wrong topic. Instead of acknowledging this work as a valuable contribution to the project, Nancy acts as though Catherine's work was a waste of time. Nancy insists on keeping to the original agenda and criticizes Catherine for suggesting an alternative. Nancy herself introduces conflict into the interview; her behavior encourages Catherine to be uncooperative so Catherine will not even consider discussing pests. Too late, Nancy realizes that she has alienated Catherine; to appease Catherine, Nancy agrees to discuss pruning fruit trees. Although this discussion may placate Catherine, it is a waste of Nancy's time. Nancy should use the time on activities that will help her to achieve her current project goal— to deliver a system that gives advice about flowering plants. In all likelihood, the discussion is a waste of Catherine's time as well. Nancy is so irritated at having to discuss this topic that she probably will not pay close attention; she will not learn all the details she would have requested if she were interested in the topic. Nancy will probably need to ask Catherine to repeat the discussion later in the project when the focus is on fruit trees.

In the second dialog, Nancy reacts calmly to Catherine's proposed change of agenda. Nancy thanks Catherine for all the time she has put into her preparation and assures her that the time has not been wasted. Nancy reminds Catherine of the project goals and apologizes for not being able to take the time to discuss Catherine's topic. Note that Nancy herself does not demand they adhere to their original agenda—the *project schedule* necessitates that they do so. Nancy does not reprimand Catherine for being unprepared to discuss pests. Nancy acknowledges that Catherine *did* prepare adequately for the interview (even if some of her preparation was misguided). Nancy suggests two options, both of which would make good use of her time and Catherine's: they can continue with the planned agenda or they can end the meeting. Nancy lets Catherine choose how to proceed; by doing so, Nancy lets Catherine continue to control the interview. Everything in Nancy's behavior has fostered a feeling of cooperation. In response, Catherine cooperates and elects to begin the discussion of pests.

The Expert Digresses

The most common reason why an interview diverges from its planned topic is that the expert unintentionally wanders away from the topic under discussion. Diversions of this kind can take two forms. First the expert may digress completely from all subjects relevant to the expert system. Second the expert may move to a new, relevant topic before the knowledge engineer has learned enough about the current topic. This section discusses the first of these two situations; the next section discusses the second situation.

If an expert digresses from the current topic and ceases to provide useful information, the knowledge engineer's obvious course of action is to interrupt politely and return the expert to the topic at hand. The problem for the knowledge engineer is to detect when the expert has started to ramble. An expert who finds it difficult to formulate or articulate an important idea may appear to digress. The start of an anecdote could signal a digression; on the other hand, the anecdote might serve as an easy way for the expert to recall a specific case or problem relevant to the discussion.

Expert digressions are especially difficult to recognize in the first several interviews of a project, when the knowledge engineer is not familiar with either the application subject area or the expert. The knowledge engineer lacks the background knowledge to judge what information is relevant. Similarly the knowledge engineer has not had enough time to learn whether the expert has a penchant for story telling or whether the expert gives long-winded explanations that eventually reach important points. Until you are familiar enough with the subject matter and the project expert to recognize digressions, you should follow two guidelines.

1. If the expert has talked for more than five minutes and you have been unable to discern any connection with the current topic, the expert has probably digressed. Interrupt and ask the expert to explain how the recent discussion is relevant to the topic.

2. If your expert has told several stories that have had little relevance to the discussion, interrupt the next story as soon as it begins.

Dialog 17.2[1] illustrates how to bring an expert back to the topic when he or she digresses.

Dialog 17.2 Interviewing a Rambling Expert

Setting

Joyce is a senior member of the sales staff in a company that sells software products and services. Evelyn is a knowledge engineer. Evelyn and Joyce are working on a project to develop an expert system that will help junior sales representatives. The project has been in the development phase for several months. This is the first knowledge-acquisition session in four weeks.

Dialog with Problems

Evelyn: Hi, Joyce! It's good to see you again. Did you get the copy of the agenda I mailed you?

Joyce nods.

Good. As you saw from the agenda, today's topic is skeptical sales prospects. What do you recommend when a sales rep is on the phone with a prospect who is skeptical about your software?

Joyce *(enthusiastically):* Well skepticism is a real problem when you're selling a product that has so many capabilities and is better than anything else on the market. First of all we need to have a good understanding of the customer's needs—find out what the customer wants, what kind of business the company is in, how they're going to use the package, and whether they have used any similar software before. After we've figured out the customer's needs, we put together a package of software and services for that customer.

We sometimes find that customers are skeptical that we can really

---

1. Dialogs 17.2 through 17.5 contain adaptations of dialogs that appear on the "Knowledge Acquisition Problems and Solutions" videotape used in the *Knowledge Acquisition Workshop* from Cimflex Teknowledge Corporation.

deliver what they want. You can handle a skeptical prospect in many ways. For example, we have one rep who has a lot of problems overcoming skepticism. One of the things he does is to tell stories He starts every conversation by telling this story about a professor who is building a superintelligent robot. When the professor gets the robot to the stage where it's ready for field testing, he gives it to a friend to test over the weekend. The professor says the robot can do incredible things, but the friend is skeptical. Anyway, the guy wakes up Saturday morning, and the robot is sitting there waiting for him. It says,

(in a monotone, imitating synthesized speech)

"Ready for work."

(in a regular voice)

The guy says, "Well, start by mowing the lawn. When you finish that, do all the laundry; then you can paint the porch." The robot says,

(in a monotone)

"Will do."

(in a regular voice)

The robot trundles off. About four hours later, it comes back; the guy is lying in bed reading the newspaper. The robot says,

(in a monotone)

"Lawn is mowed; grass is trimmed to three centimeters. Laundry is washed, folded, sorted by color, and stacked in closet. Porsche is painted—you made error this morning: Porsche is really BMW."

Before you read further, stop and think about the preceding dialog.

At what point did you detect that Joyce had digressed. Should Evelyn have interrupted Joyce? If so, when?

Dialog without Problems

Evelyn: Hi, Joyce! It's good to see you again. Did you get the copy of the agenda I mailed you?

Joyce nods.

Good. As you saw from the agenda, today's topic is skeptical sales prospects. What do you recommend when a sales rep has a prospect on the phone who is skeptical about your software?

Joyce *(enthusiastically):* Well, skepticism is a real problem when you're selling a product that has so many capabilities and is better than anything else on the market. First of all, we need to have a good understanding of the customer's needs—find out what the customer wants, what kind of business the company is in, how they're going to use the package, and whether they have used any similar software before. After we've figured out the customer's needs, we put together a package of software and services for that customer.

We sometimes find that customers are skeptical that we can really deliver what they want. You can handle a skeptical prospect in many ways. For example, we have one rep who has a lot of problems overcoming skepticism. One of the things he does is to tell stories. He starts every conversation by telling this story about a professor—

Evelyn *(interrupting tactfully):* Excuse me, Joyce. Let me see if I understand what you've told me. When you have a skeptical customer, the first thing you do is to understand the customer's needs and capabilities. Is that right?

Joyce: Well, you have to do that anyway, in order to put together the package. But if you do a good job of understanding the customer, and you design the right package for their needs, then you can often sidestep the whole problem of skepticism.

Evelyn: I see. You also mentioned story telling. I wasn't sure whether you meant that story telling tends to *generate* skepticism or whether the rep that you mentioned told stories to *overcome* skepticism.

Joyce: I don't know if it generates skepticism. I think story telling and humor can be good, but you have to pick the right time to use them.

Evelyn: If you have put together a good package and the customer still seems doubtful, what would you recommend?

Joyce: We have a brochure that contains successful case histories that show how customers have used our packages in the past. As soon as I detect skepticism, I mention this brochure and offer to send a copy to the prospect.

After I've sent the brochure, I search our sales database to find a customer in the same (or a similar) business who has had experiences and problems like the ones the skeptical prospect described. If I find a current customer that fits the bill, I see whether that customer would be willing to act as a reference.

Discussion

Evelyn starts the first dialog well with a friendly greeting and a quick orientation to today's topic. After that, Joyce assumes control of the interaction. She starts out by answering Evelyn's question, but she soon digresses, rambling on and wasting valuable interview time. If a similar dialog had taken place at the beginning of the project, Evelyn would have been correct to let Joyce ramble. At that stage, it is most important to put the expert at ease with the knowledge-acquisition process. Many experts relieve their initial anxiety by meandering into story telling. Knowledge engineers should indulge a certain amount of digression in the interest of making the expert feel secure. Remember, however, that Joyce and Evelyn have been working together for a long time. By now, Joyce is quite comfortable with the knowledge-acquisition process. She is not rambling to ease apprehensions. She just likes to talk.

In the second dialog, Evelyn correctly interrupts when Joyce starts to wander; Evelyn eases Joyce back to the topic under discussion. As soon as Evelyn hears, ". . . this story about a professor," she knows Joyce has stopped talking about the sales representative who tells a story and has started to recount the story herself. This is Evelyn's signal to redirect the discussion. In this dialog, Evelyn learns how to avoid and respond to skepticism; in the first dialog, all she learns is a new joke.

The Expert Goes Off on a Tangent

When an expert wanders from the topic under discussion but continues to provide useful information, the knowledge engineer must judge whether to follow the expert or to return to the current topic. If the expert's detour occurs at a convenient breaking-point, there may be no harm in letting the expert continue. In fact, a discussion that follows the expert's train of thought may provide valuable insight into how the expert thinks about the problem. On the other hand, if the expert leaves a topic unfinished, a diversion may mean that the knowledge engineer does not obtain a sufficiently detailed understanding of that topic.

When it is necessary to return the expert to an unfinished topic, be sure to acknowledge that the expert has introduced important topics for discussion later. Explain why you need to focus on the topic at hand.

Dialog 17.3 illustrates how to prevent an expert from going off on a tangent.

Dialog 17.3 Keeping an Expert Focused

Setting

Al is an automotive diagnostic expert, and Sharon is a knowledge engineer. They are developing an expert system to help novice mechanics diagnose problems with cars. Al and Sharon have been working together for six months; the project is well into the development phase. The current development increment focuses on problems in the fuel-injection system. Today's discussion deals with cars whose engines will crank when the key is turned but will not start.

Dialog with Problems

Sharon: Last time we had just started to talk about the symptom *cranks but won't start*. Let's go through some recent cases.

Al: OK. That's an easy symptom to deal with because the engine just isn't running at all. Anything with the fuel-injection system could cause this problem or no fuel getting to the injector—also problems with the injector wiring.

Sharon: OK, let's start with the first situation: No fuel is getting to the injector. Do you remember a car with that problem?

Al: Yes, I saw a car like that just a couple days ago. There was a lean trouble code so I checked out the oxygen-sensor system. We've talked about that before haven't we?

Sharon nods.

I didn't find a problem there. The next thing I did was to take a look at the fuel-injection system. I had my assistant, Bob, crank the car—turn the key to see if the engine would start—but it didn't. While Bob cranked the car, I checked for fuel spraying from the injector. Nothing was coming out. So then we pulled off the fuel filter, and there was rust all over the place. It was completely clogged; so that was the problem.

But these things are really tricky. Another car came in a couple months ago, and it seemed like exactly the same thing. I was expecting a fuel filter problem or maybe a clogged filter in the tank. But when we finally got around to dropping the tank, there was just no gas, and the customer had a broken fuel gauge! You just can't tell.

Sometimes it's the injector wiring. We had another car that looked about the same, but when I looked at the fuel injector, I realized that the injector wasn't pulsing. Now that's something different because, when the injector isn't pulsing, it means that the electrical signal isn't getting in from the ECM. What we finally found in that case was an open in the wire from the ECM.

Sharon: OK. Can we talk about the tests you do to isolate the cause of the problem?

Al: Where do you want to start?

Sharon: Well we've got quite a few cases here, how about if we start. . . .

> Before you read further, think about the previous dialog.
>   What problems do you see? What would you have done differently?

Dialog without Problems

Sharon: Last time we had just started to talk about the symptom *cranks but won't start*. Let's go through some recent cases.

Al: OK. That's an easy symptom to deal with because the engine isn't running at all. Anything with the fuel-injection system could cause this problem or no fuel getting to the injector—also problems with the injector wiring.

Sharon: OK, let's start with the first situation: No fuel is getting to the injector. Do you remember a car with that problem?

Al: Yes, just a couple days ago, a car came in with a lean trouble code. I checked out the oxygen-sensor system. That wasn't a problem so the next thing to check was the fuel injector. We cranked the car and took a look at the injector, and there was just nothing coming out. So we opened up the fuel lines and checked the fuel filter because that's an easy thing to check. It was clogged solid with rust. There was no way for the fuel to get through. So that was the problem.

But these things are really tricky. Another car came in a couple months ago. . . .

Sharon (*interrupting politely*): Pardon me—I hate to interrupt. I do want to hear about this other case, but before I do, I need to focus on the first case to be sure that I understand. Let me just review. First of all, the car wouldn't start, so you checked the codes and saw there was a lean trouble code. Then you checked the oxygen sensor, and that was OK. The third step was to check the fuel injector to see whether any fuel was coming out. You did that, and nothing was coming out. So then you checked the fuel filter and found the problem.

Al: Well actually, before we checked the fuel filter there was another step I forgot because it was OK. After you crank it and look at the injector, the next thing you do is to turn the key on—not cranking, just on—and you listen. What you want to hear is the fuel pump running. You can hear the hum—it's an electric pump. If you *don't* hear the pump, then you know it's a pump problem.

Sharon: So in this case, you did listen for the fuel pump after you checked the fuel injector, and you heard the pump?

Al: Yes. Then the next step was to look at the fuel filter because it's the easiest part of the fuel lines to take apart, and it's also a common location of problems.

Sharon: And that's where you found the problem in this case?

Al nods.

Is there anything else you would consider in cases where the fuel filter looks OK?

Al: Well, from there on things get hard to do. It takes a while to pull out the fuel lines and check them, but that's the next thing to do. If you find that the fuel lines themselves are clear, then you have to drop the fuel tank. It's pretty inconvenient to do that, but if you're not getting fuel, that's what you'd have to do.

Sharon: It sounds like those two tests are very time consuming. Is that why you leave them till last?

Al: Right. And in this case we didn't have to do them because we found a problem in the filter.

Discussion

Al and Sharon have been working together for six months. Notice that they have developed a vocabulary that both understand. Al is comfortable describing the car in terms of *symptoms*. Sharon recognizes *ECM* as the electronic control monitor, and she understands the function of this part. Al and Sharon have already made up a short name for the symptom under discussion, *cranks but won't start*.

During the first dialog, Al remains focused on this symptom. When Sharon asks for cases in which a car's engine cranks but will not start, Al gives her exactly those cases. All the information Al provides is relevant to the discussion. Although Sharon gets an overview of various problems that can cause this symptom, she does not get a clear picture of the *process* by which Al considers alternative causes and by which he decides what is causing the problem. In the detailed investigation stage of knowledge acquisition, case discussions should concentrate on

Al's problem-solving strategies—that is, the process by which he performs the task.

In the second dialog, when Al says, ". . . another car came in a couple months ago," Sharon recognizes that he is about to leave the current case and tell her about a different one. She immediately interrupts him and explains that she needs to focus on the first case. Notice the words Sharon uses when she interrupts. From Al's point of view, he has not diverged from discussion of the current symptom. Sharon is sensitive to Al's perception and is careful not to discourage him from thinking about different cases. These cases are important to her, and she will need to return to them later. Sharon's interruption is more apologetic than would have been necessary if Al had digressed to talk about a different symptom or to relate an anecdote about the case. Al has participated in this project long enough to understand what is expected of him, and he always tries to provide Sharon with the information she requests. Sharon is very careful not to act as though Al had digressed from the topic when he does not believe that he has.

After she interrupts, Sharon tries to confirm her understanding with a review of Al's diagnostic process. When Al hears Sharon's summary, he remembers an additional step. Al had overlooked this step initially because he tried to recall the important events of the case—a simple check that did not help him solve the problem was not significant enough to remember. Sharon's focus on Al's problem-solving process enables her to learn about the missing step. Furthermore, this approach allows her to discover the rationale behind the ordering of steps: Al does the quick and easy checks first and leaves the more time-consuming checks for last.

The Expert Provides Too Much Information

In addition to monitoring the content of interviews, the knowledge engineer must moderate the pace. The pace of an interview must be slow enough to enable the knowledge engineer to understand the expert. In Chapter 16, we discussed active listening techniques that a knowledge engineer can use to obtain a thorough understanding of the expert's knowledge. In some interviews, the knowledge engineer must interrupt the expert in order to use these techniques. Dialog 17.4 illustrates how to deal with one of the nicest problems a knowledge engineer can encounter—getting too much information too quickly from the expert.

Dialog 17.4 Managing Information Overload

Setting

Marjorie is in charge of writing all the software licensing agreements for a company that sells expert-system shells. Steve is a knowledge engineer who is working with Marjorie to develop an expert system that will help a clerk generate simple software licensing agreements.

The system will also advise the clerk when to refer an agreement to the company's legal department. Steve and Marjorie have been working together for a few months and are just starting a new cycle of development.

Dialog with Problems

Steve turns on the tape recorder as he has done in each interview on this project. He speaks into the microphone.

Steve: It's May 16, 1990. Steve and Marjorie are meeting to discuss clients who have multiple licenses.

(to Marjorie)

Now that our system can handle a customer's first license, I'd like to learn what is involved when a customer wants additional licenses. Let's talk about a customer who already has one Expert-Wise license and who wants another license—for a different machine.

Marjorie pulls her chair next to Steve's and opens a binder on the table in front of them.

Marjorie: Oh, that's easy! I brought along this binder of agreements so you can see exactly what we do.

Marjorie speaks quickly and enthusiastically with no pauses. As she speaks, she flips through the binder and points to examples. Steve continually tries to look at Marjorie's examples before she flips to a new page; he is only occasionally successful. When Steve is not looking at the binder, he takes notes frantically. As the dialog progresses, he looks more and more bewildered.

Here's a copy of the *General Terms and Conditions*, and here's *Paragraph A*. When a customer wants a new license, we find their agreement in the file, and we look at the *General Terms and Conditions*. If there are changes to it, we know we'll have a problem. But if there *aren't* any changes, all we have to do is to go to *Paragraph A* and fill it out again with the site-license type, what product they have, and what machine it's on. And that's easy—they just sign two copies of it, send them back to me, then I sign and execute them, and we're all set. That refers back to the *General Terms and Conditions* they originally signed with us.

Now if they *have* made any changes, we're talking about something completely different. I have to look through the agreement and check each of the sections. And some of them are more important than others. The kinds of things that I'm looking for are *Maintenance and Support* or the *Termination Rights*—and *Warranty* is a big one, too. People often want to change the type of warranty to lifetime whereas we only provide a 90-day warranty. There's *Limits of Liability;* mostly I ask the attorney for guidance on that because it's a very complex area. But the questions we look at most often are: What are the limitations? How high can we go with responsibility for this contract as opposed to the amount the contract is worth? So you have to balance out those factors.

Now another problem is export. A lot of people don't realize that the U.S. Department of Commerce has put *significant* restrictions on the export of AI software. So we spend a lot of time explaining to people what they *should* know in their own contracting department. And finally there are people who want to . . .

Before you read further, think about the previous dialog.
Does Steve obtain the information he needs? Should he
have interrupted Marjorie? If so, when?

Dialog without Problems

Steve turns on the tape recorder as he has done in each interview on this project. He speaks into the microphone.

Steve: It's May 16, 1990. Steve and Marjorie are meeting to discuss clients who have multiple licenses.

(to Marjorie)

Now that our system can handle a customer's first license, I'd like to learn what is involved when a customer wants additional licenses. Let's talk about a customer who already has one Expert-Wise license and who wants another license—for a different machine.

Marjorie pulls her chair next to Steve's and opens a binder on the table in front of them.

Marjorie: Oh, that's easy! I brought along this binder of agreements so you can see exactly what we do.

Marjorie speaks quickly and enthusiastically with no pauses; as she speaks, she flips through the binder and points to examples.

Here's a copy of the *General Terms and Conditions*, and here's *Paragraph A*. When a customer wants a new license, we find their agreement in their file, and we look at the *General Terms and Conditions*. If there are changes to it, we know we'll have a problem. But if there *aren't* any changes, all we have to do is to go to *Paragraph A* and fill it out again with the site-license type, what product they have, and what machine it's on. And that's easy—they just sign two copies of it, send them back to me, then I sign and execute them, and we're all set. That refers back to. . . .

Steve *(interrupting):* Marjorie, do the *General Terms and Conditions* plus *Paragraph A* compose the whole license agreement?

Marjorie: Right. Everyone signs the *General Terms and Conditions* and *Paragraph A* at the very beginning. And then. . . .

Steve *(interrupting):* So there are two signatures?

Marjorie: Right, one on the *General Terms and Conditions* and one on *Paragraph A*, and there is this reference number at the top.

Marjorie points to top of current page in the binder. She continues speaking quickly and enthusiastically without pauses.

So the next time they want to license a copy of the software, they just reference the *General Terms and Conditions* by using that number, then all they have to do is sign *Paragraph A*. But, if there *are* changes, that's a different situation entirely. Then I have to go through the agreement, read every section, and see if I can find anything in there that is objectionable, that we don't want to include the second time they buy the software. So if there are changes, I can't just send them *Paragraph*

A, there's a lot of extra work to be done. The kinds of things that I'm looking for are the *Maintenance and Support* or *Termination Rights*. Then there's the *Warranty* section—that's *very* important. We generally provide 90-day warranties, and sometimes people want the warranty period to be longer. Then there's *Limits of Liability*. . . .

Steve *(interrupting):* Hold on a sec. Why would they want a longer warranty period?

Marjorie: Well, it's not a matter of the warranty period not being long enough. They just want some assurance that the product is going to operate in the way that they expect, that it matches the user documentation, and so on. So when we provide software updates, that's really not part of the *warranty*, that's part of the maintenance and support.

Steve: I see.

Discussion

Marjorie provides a wealth of information in the first dialog. Unfortunately Steve probably will not be able to make use of it. Steve himself has no experience working with software licensing agreements. Consequently he is not able to comprehend everything he hears from Marjorie. With the tape recorder catching the entire interview, Steve does not worry about understanding Marjorie completely; he plans to slow her down when he listens to the tape. The problem with Steve's plan is that, although the tape recorder captures the *text* of Marjorie's descriptions, it does not captured her *meaning*. After the interview, Steve will be able to review his notes and to use the tape recording to fill in parts of the discussion that he missed. When he does so, he will have a number of questions. Marjorie gave a broad overview. Because they are in the detailed investigation stage of knowledge acquisition, Steve needs more depth and more specific details. He has lost his first opportunity to obtain those details and will have to wait until the next meeting. By not slowing Marjorie down, Steve has wasted his time and hers.

In the second dialog, Steve listens for comprehension. When he hears Marjorie say, "we're all set," he knows that she has finished her overview of agreements in which no changes are made to the *General Terms and Conditions*. He realizes that he doesn't quite have a complete and coherent picture of the process so he interrupts and asks for clarification.

Note that Steve never interrupts Marjorie's chain of thought. He waits until he hears her finish one topic and start the next, then he interrupts *immediately*, before she has a chance to get into the second topic. Throughout the interview, Steve lets Marjorie proceed to a new subject only when he has all the information he needs on the current subject.

Experts Argue among Themselves

An interview with multiple experts is subject to all the problems we have discussed before plus an additional problem: The interview may cease to be productive because the experts argue among themselves and do not provide useful information. The knowledge engineer needs to distinguish fruitless arguments from productive debates in which experts air their opinions and work together toward a solution. When an argument occurs, the knowledge engineer should try to defuse the argument, being careful not to take sides.

Arguments among experts are most common when the experts share the same area of expertise and are accustomed to performing the task individually rather than in teams (option 2b in Figure 2.6). When you ask a question, you may get different answers because the experts follow different hypotheses or because they have had different experiences. If arguments arise, try to understand the *source* of the disagreements so you can focus (in this interview or in a later one) on the resolution of these disagreements. Organize the interview to allow each expert to express opinions without interruption from the other experts. For example, ask the experts to role-play so only one of them acts as expert at a given time. Dialog 17.5 illustrates problems that can arise in an interview with two experts who share the same area of expertise.

Dialog 17.5 Managing Disagreements between Experts

Setting

Alan is a knowledge engineer who is working on an expert system to help in the identification and correction of problems that occur in the manufacture of glass. Miriam and Jon are both experts in manufacturing glass. Miriam has 15 years of experience in this field. Jon works at a different site and is also a recognized expert. He is more recently out of school and has much less on-the-job experience than Miriam has.

This interview takes place early in the development of the expert system. Alan's current understanding can be summarized as follows. Sand and other raw materials are delivered to the plant and are stored in bins. The correct amounts of the various raw materials are weighed and mixed together into batches. The batches of raw materials are fed into large furnaces where they are melted. The molten glass is released to harden into the finished product. Contamination of a raw material with another substance is common; often the contaminant is a different raw material.

Dialog with Problems

Alan: Let's talk about this recent problem in Plant 1.

Alan hands out copies of a problem report that describes the recent situation.

The manager from Plant 1 called about a viscosity problem. He said there was a 50-degree drop in viscosity this morning at 9 A.M. Production had dropped off at 7 P.M. last night. The under-glass temperatures had dropped at 3 A.M. this morning. Samples showed an efficiency of 61 percent at 3 A.M., down from 85 percent. What is the best way to approach this problem?

Miriam *(to Alan):* It's clear they need to stop mixing batches immediately. I would ask for a number of tests right away. I'd ask for the results of the preshipment sample test. I'd ask them to review the unloading records for errors, check samples from top and bottom of the bins for contamination, and look for possible leakage in the system. In addition, I'd want them to do the scale, the mixed-batch, and the glass-chemistry tests. I'd want to know about any recent batch changes.

Jon *(scowling slightly and addressing Alan):* Well, I agree that we need to find out about any recent batch changes and that they should stop mixing batches right away.

(turning to Miriam)

But I think you're asking for too many tests. You only really need to ask for three tests. I agree that you would need to request the mixed-batch test. I'd have them check for contamination too, but only on samples from the *bottom* of the bins. And I'd ask for the X-ray fluorescence test. That should be enough. It's important to concentrate on only a few tests.

Miriam *(to Jon):* In my experience, that won't work very well. When I ask the plant managers to run tests, they usually only do about half of the tests I request. In addition, I almost never ask for the X-ray fluorescence test. It's too expensive, and the technicians don't like to do it. I generally ask for the cheap and easy tests so the technicians are more likely to do them.

Jon *(to Miriam):* But the X-ray fluorescence test tells you everything you need to know! It is very reliable. I asked for exactly those three tests from Plant 5 last week, and they came back quickly and reliably.

Alan *(interrupting politely):* These tests are interesting. We will want to come back and discuss them in more depth, but let's try to continue with the case.

Let's say that the plant manager calls back and says that the raw-material contamination tests from the bins came up clean, the mixed-batch test shows no problems, and a new type of clay is being used in one of the bins. What do you do next?

Miriam *(to Alan):* This is Plant 1 right?

Alan nods.

Then I want them to check for contamination again. I also want to know *who* checked those bins and how they checked them.

Jon *(interrupting Miriam):* Check for contamination again? Why, they just did that! You shouldn't have to ask for that information again. Don't you believe them?

Miriam *(to Alan):* You wouldn't believe those jokers at Plant 1! They are the laziest bunch of technicians I have ever seen. They often say they have checked for contamination without ever even glancing into the bin. We need to do that test over and then sit this one out.

Jon *(to Alan):* Well I think it's important to get the detailed technical tests back and possibly do an as-received test on that clay.

Alan *(interrupting again):* OK, OK, let's hold on for a second.

> Before you read further, think about the previous dialog.
>   Does Alan control this interview effectively? Does Alan obtain the information he needs?
>   What would you have done differently?

Dialog without Problems

Alan: Let's talk about this recent problem in Plant 1.

Alan hands out copies of a problem report that describes the recent situation.

The manager from Plant 1 called about a viscosity problem. He said there was a 50-degree drop in viscosity this morning at 9 A.M. Production had dropped off at 7 P.M. last night. The under-glass temperatures had dropped at 3 A.M. this morning. Samples showed an efficiency of 61 percent at 3 A.M., down from 85 percent. What is the best way to approach this problem?

Miriam *(to Alan):* It's clear they need to stop mixing batches immediately. I would ask for a number of tests right away. I'd ask for the results of the preshipment sample test. I'd ask them to review the unloading records for errors, check samples from top and bottom of the bins for contamination, and look for possible leakage in the system. In addition, I'd want them to do the scale, the mixed-batch, and the glass-chemistry tests. I'd want to know about any recent batch changes.

Jon *(scowling slightly and addressing Alan):* Well, I agree that we need to find out about any recent batch changes and that they should stop mixing batches right away.

(turning to Miriam)

But I think you're asking for too many tests. You only really need to ask for three tests. I agree that you would need to request the mixed-batch test. I'd have them check for contamination too, but only on samples from the *bottom* of the bins. And I'd ask for the X-ray fluorescence test. That should be enough. It's important to concentrate on only a few tests.

Miriam *(to Jon):* In my experience, that won't work very well. When I ask the plant managers to run tests, they usually only do about half of the tests I request. In addition, I almost never ask for the X-ray fluorescence test. It's too expensive, and the technicians don't like to do it. I generally ask for the cheap and easy tests so the technicians are more likely to do them.

Jon *(to Miriam):* But the X-ray fluorescence test tells you everything you need to know! It is very reliable. I asked for exactly those three tests from Plant 5 last week, and they came back quickly and reliably.

Alan *(interrupting politely):* This is interesting. It sounds as though the two of you have quite different strategies for finding the problem. I'd like to get full details on both techniques, but I find it too confusing to talk about them in parallel.

   Let's try a different approach. I want to hear each of you simulate solving the problem as if you were actually talking to the plant manager on the phone. To do this I'd like to have one of you play the role of the plant manager. The other will ask for test results from the manager. Does this sound reasonable?

Miriam: You mean, if I am playing the plant manager, I provide the answers like the manager would give in a phone call to me?

Alan: That's right. Jon, how does this sound to you?

Jon: OK. Let's try it.

Alan: I'd like to go back to the beginning of this case we've been discussing and start over with Jon playing the plant manager, calling Miriam for advice. When we finish, you two can switch roles, and we'll go through the case again. So Jon you start.

Jon: OK. Let's see. I'm the plant manager.

(to Miriam)

We have a problem here at Plant 1. Here's what's going on. There was a 50-degree drop in viscosity at 9 o'clock this morning. Production dropped off at 7 last night. At 3 in the morning, the under-glass temperatures dropped. Samples taken at that time showed a conversion efficiency of 61 percent, down from 85. What should we do?

Miriam: You should stop mixing batches right away. Then I need you to do some tests for me. I'd like you to look at the results of the shipment-sample test, review the unloading records, check the top and bottom of the bins for contamination, and look for possible leakage in the system. I'd also like you to do the scale, the mixed-batch, and the glass-chemistry tests. In addition, could you tell me if you have changed the batch recently?

Jon flips through his copy of the problem report.

Jon: Yes, there has been a change in the batch.

Miriam: In that case, I want you to check the unloading records around the time when the change occurred. I want a summary of the new materials, which bins they went into, and the tests done on them on receipt.

Jon: OK, I'll get right on it.

Jon turns to Alan.

That would be the end of this phone call.

Alan *(to Miriam):* Can you explain why you asked for those particular tests?

Miriam: When I ask the plant managers to run tests, they usually do about half of the tests I request. I generally ask for the cheap and easy tests so the technicians are more likely to do them. I asked for the glass-chemistry test just to be safe—results won't come back for a week. If it turns out that we *still* have a problem a week from now, the results of the glass-chemistry test will be *very* helpful.

In this case, there was a large drop in conversion efficiency so we may have a major problem. It's particularly important to get as many tests results as I can to cover all bases. Some of these tests may be shots in the dark, but they are easily done, and they may give us *just* the information we need.

Alan: OK. Let's go on to when the plant manager calls back with the results.

Jon scans the problem report. Then he puts his hand to his ear as if holding a telephone receiver and looks at Miriam.

Jon: I've got the test results. The raw-material contamination tests from the bins came up clean. The mixed-batch test shows no problems. We did find that a new type of clay is being used in one of the bins. The batch change involved switching to Georgia kaolin clay in Bin 3; that bin used to have borax in it.

Miriam *(to Jon):* Oh really? In that case, I'd like you to recheck Bin 3 for contamination. I also want to know *who* checked those bins and how they checked them. Call me back as soon as you get the results.

Alan *(to Miriam):* Is that all you'd ask for?

Miriam nods.

Can you explain your line of reasoning to me?

Miriam: The contamination tests aren't always accurate. I don't know whether to believe the results or not. With Plant 1, I'm particularly suspicious. The bins are old and very difficult to inspect. It's quite likely that contamination in Bin 3 is the problem. If borax had been substituted for the kaolin, it would have produced exactly the conditions we saw. Also the manager said that the material in Bin 3 had been changed. I suspect that the bin wasn't cleaned properly. This happens often.

If I'm right about contamination, the mixed-batch test indicates that all the contaminating material has already passed into the furnace so we just have to wait until it comes out.

Alan: Good. Thanks, Miriam. Now let's try reversing the roles. I want to see how Jon would have approached the problem. Miriam, you get to play the plant manager this time. Why don't you start.

Miriam: Same case?

Alan nods.

OK.

Miriam puts her hand to her ear, as if holding a telephone receiver and looks at Jon.

We've got a problem at Plant 1. This morning, we had a 50-degree drop in viscosity at 9 o'clock. Production dropped off at 7 last night. At 3 A.M., the under-glass temperatures dropped, and the samples showed an efficiency of 61 percent. What should I do?

Jon: Well, I want any information you can get about recent batch changes. You need to stop mixing batches right away, and you should do three tests. First do the mixed-batch test. Check for contamination in samples from the bottom of the bins. And do the X-ray fluorescence test. That should tell us enough for us to figure out what the problem is.

Miriam: OK, I'll send out for the tests.

Miriam turns to Alan.

Alan *(to Jon):* What is your strategy in asking for this set of tests?

Jon: I like to ask for only a few tests so the plant people can concentrate on those. The X-ray fluorescence test will tell me everything I need to know. It is very reliable. The results from this test will indicate very quickly *exactly* which materials and what amounts of these materials have contaminated the furnace. This sounds very much like a contamination problem, and this combination of three tests should help me narrow down the possibilities.

Alan: Good. Let's keep going.

Miriam: The raw-material contamination tests from the bins came up clean. The mixed-batch test shows no problems. A new type of clay, a kaolin clay, is being stored in a bin that used to contain borax.

Jon: Thanks. Is that kaolin clay being used in other furnaces?

Miriam checks her copy of the problem report.

Miriam: No.

Jon: And this is the only furnace at the plant with a problem?

Miriam flips through the problem report again.

Miriam: That's right.

Jon: We really need to concentrate on getting the detailed technical tests back. In the mean time, Why don't you do an as-received test on that clay?

Miriam: OK. I'll call you back when I get more test results.

Jon *(to Alan):* Since no contaminants were found, it's possible that a complete shipment of raw material was bad. That new clay is very suspect. Any time a raw material is changed at a plant, the odds are that the problem lies there. I would immediately check the as-received sample of that clay. I'm also suspicious of that clay because it's only being used in this one furnace, and no other furnaces have problems. When we get the results of the X-ray fluorescence test, we'll have exactly the information we need to get to the heart of this problem instead of waiting for it to pass.

Discussion

Early in the first dialog, it is apparent that the two experts would handle the case differently. In spite of strong disagreement between the experts, Alan tries to proceed with a step-by-step discussion of the problem. At each step, the experts argue between themselves about the best approach. Consequently Alan does not get a coherent picture of how either expert would handle the problem, much less how the expert system should handle it. Furthermore, the experts' arguments do not give Alan a clear understanding of the source of their disagreement.

In the second dialog, Alan manages the discussion more effectively; he lets each expert step through the entire case without interruptions from the other expert. This procedure gives Alan a precise picture of the approach each expert takes, and allows him to ask for the reasons behind each action and decision. Alan not only gets a clearer understanding of the process, but he also identifies the factors the experts consider in selecting tests. These factors can provide the common ground for later discussions between the experts.

Although the two experts would not handle this case in the same way, they both suspect contamination. They each order tests that will confirm contamination as the cause of the problem. In this interview, Alan learns some of the factors the experts consider when they evaluate whether to order a test: the cost of the test, the time it takes to get the results back, the accuracy of the test, the amount of information the test provides, and the likelihood that the technicians will perform the test. Neither expert argued when the other mentioned advantages and disadvantages of particular tests. Alan suspects that they agree on the advantages and disadvantages, but they differ on how much *weight* each gives to the different advantages and disadvantages. In a later interview, the team can itemize the pros and cons of particular tests and can discuss the circumstances under which each test is appropriate. Through such discussions, Alan and the two experts can work together to derive an acceptable scheme by which the expert system can choose the tests to recommend. They may find that the expert system should take account of the differences in equipment, in operating practices, or in personnel at different plants. For example, Miriam's approach may work best at Plant 1, whereas Jon's approach may work best at Plant 5.

17.3 Points to Remember

The lead interviewer must ensure that an interview is productive: Either the interview must serve to make the expert more comfortable with the knowledge-acquisition process or it must provide information necessary for the development of an expert system. Interview productivity depends on the manner in which the knowledge engineers interact with the expert, ask questions, and listen and respond to the expert's answers.

Another contributing factor to the productivity of an interview is the appropriate balance of control between the expert and the knowledge engineers. The expert may need more control to feel at ease in the interview; on the other hand, the knowledge engineers may need to maintain control to keep the discussion focused on relevant topics. Knowledge engineers can vary the balance of control through their use of open and closed questions. More open questions give the expert more control; more closed questions give the knowledge engineers more control and can prevent the expert from digressing. In some interviews, however, the expert will digress, and the lead interviewer will need to interrupt to bring the discussion back to a productive topic (Table 17.1).

Table 17.1 Guidelines for Interrupting the Expert

Do	Don't
Interrupt politely and respectfully.	Appear to admonish the expert for making an interruption necessary.
Apologize for interrupting.	
Interrupt *as soon as* you detect a shift in topic.	Interrupt at a time that would break the expert's line of thought *even if that line of thought appears unproductive.*
Interrupt to ease tension if the expert gets bogged down.	Interrupt with a question that will derail a productive line of thought.
Interrupt when you cannot follow the expert's meaning.	Interrupt to tell an anecdote.
Interrupt when the expert stops providing the information you need.	
Summarize the important points the expert made before the digression and redirect the expert with a question.	

Table 17.2 Common Problems in Keeping an Interview on Track

Problem	Solution
Expert takes control and proposes an unproductive topic.	Try to prevent the problem: Involve the expert in project planning, and make sure that the expert understands the goals and the schedule for the project.
	Let the expert know that the proposed topic *is* important.
	Explain what you need to accomplish in the current interview, how your topic will address your objective, and when you will return to the expert's topic.
Expert digresses and does not provide useful information.	Allow more digression in early interviews to help the expert adjust to the knowledge-acquisition process.
	Interrupt as soon as you detect a digression.
	Ask a question that will lead the expert back to the relevant topic.
	Do not call attention to the fact that you are redirecting the discussion; the expert may not have digressed intentionally.
Expert goes off on a tangent to a new topic before the knowledge engineer is finished with the current topic.	Apologize for interrupting.
	Let the expert know that you want to return to the new topic at an appropriate time.
	Explain why you need to continue with the current topic.

Table 17.2 (continued)

Problem	Solution
Expert provides information more rapidly than the knowledge engineer can understand.	Interrupt as soon as you get behind. If you wait, you probably will have to make the expert repeat long descriptions.
	Use active listening techniques (Chapter 16) to ensure that you understand completely before you let the expert move on.
Experts disagree and argue among themselves.	Stop arguments as soon as they occur.
	Do not side with one expert against a second expert.
	Structure the interview so each expert can speak without interruptions from the other experts.
	Try to identify the source of the disagreements so you can schedule a separate discussion to resolve them.

Knowledge engineers frequently encounter problems in keeping the interview focused on productive topics. Table 17.2 lists these problems and the techniques that can be used to restore the dialog to a fruitful topic.

Part 3

Review

Chapter 18

Knowledge-Acquisition Challenges

The toaster-repair advisor project has come to an end. Patricia Programmer and Howard Hacker have installed the system in the service department. Members of the repair staff use the system frequently. They call the system "little Frank," and they frequently joke, "I'll see if I can get little Frank to help me with this toaster." Now that "little Frank" is available to assist the staff, Frank Fixit is able to devote much more of his time to toaster problems that challenge him. He now has time to help Barbara Burnt as she prepares to take over as the senior member of the repair staff. Frank is looking forward to retirement. He tells Barbara, "I feel good about going because I'm leaving the staff with everything I have learned through my years of working here. That's how I see little Frank. I don't have to worry how the department will manage without me. In a way, I'll still be here."

As Howard looks back on the project, he reflects on all he has learned. He is now an accomplished interviewer. He knows what information he must obtain from an expert, and he has learned the techniques that will help him obtain this information. He has learned how to analyze the information he acquires to produce a conceptual model and how to organize the information to produce a project dictionary, a design document, and a case library. Howard understands the issues he must consider when he selects an expert-system shell to meet the requirements of an application. He has learned the basic principles of knowledge-base design, and he has become a proficient user of one expert-system shell. Howard tells Patricia, "There is a lot more to knowledge acquisition than I thought at the beginning of the project. Do you think I've learned all the techniques I'll need in future projects?" Patricia responds that Howard has demonstrated a good grasp of the basis knowledge-acquisition techniques. With each new project, however, he can expect to learn new techniques and to acquire new skills. Knowledge acquisition, she explains, will vary from expert to expert and from project to project.

As we have seen in Parts 1 and 2, knowledge acquisition is a multifaceted process. The new knowledge engineer must learn many different skills and techniques; mastery of knowledge acquisition requires a great deal of practice and experience. Although this book could not provide the reader with the experience that taught Howard Hacker so much, we hope that our examples have furnished insight into expert-system projects. We close our discussion of knowledge acquisition by reviewing:

- The challenges that pose difficulties for new knowledge engineers (Section 18.1)

- The techniques and skills to overcome these challenges (Section 18.2)

- The importance of good knowledge-acquisition skills to the success of an expert system project (Section 18.3)

18.1 Understanding the Challenges

Novices often overlook the fact that knowledge acquisition is an ever-changing activity. A knowledge engineer who conducts a successful interview may presume to have discovered the recipe for success: a manner of interaction that yields a productive interview and a set of techniques that elicit important information. Unfortunately there is no single recipe for a successful interview. Knowledge acquisition is inextricably intertwined with the other activities required to build an expert system. As a result, *the character of knowledge acquisition changes throughout the course of an expert-system project.* The kind of information a knowledge engineer must obtain changes as the project progresses (Table 18.1). Different styles of interaction and different techniques are appropriate for obtaining different kinds of information.

As a project progresses, the effectiveness of communication increases. Much of this improvement is due to changes in the *expert*, not in the knowledge engineer. The expert begins to understand what kinds of information the knowledge engineer needs. In many applications, the expert also develops a clearer understanding of the problem-solving

Table 18.1 Information Needed for Development of an Expert System

Step	Questions to Be Answered
Identification	What task will the system perform? How is this task performed currently?
Assessment	What are the potential benefits of a computer system that performs this task? Whom will the system benefit? Can the potential benefits be quantified? Do the benefits justify the cost of developing the system? Are knowledge and expertise important for good performance of the task? Are human experts rare? Is it difficult for a new practitioner to become expert at performing the task? Is the information a practitioner needs to perform the task already codified in some form? Is it difficult or time consuming for a practitioner to obtain the information needed to perform the task? Is a human expert available to participate in the development of the system? Are data available from cases in which the task has been performed? Complete case data consist of inputs to the problem-solving process, the sequence in which the data were needed, and the results of performing the task. If the system is developed, will it be used?
Familiarization	What general kinds of information are needed to perform the task? How and from where can this information be obtained? What is the result of, or "output" from, performance of the task? How and by whom will the system be used? How will the system fit into current normal operations at the location where it will be used? Along what dimensions do cases vary? Which classes of cases are most common? Most difficult? Most important?
Conceptual design	What steps does the expert take in performing the task? In what order and under what conditions are the individual steps performed? What lines of reasoning are relevant to each step? What specific information is needed to perform each step? How and from where can each piece of information be obtained?

Table 18.1 (continued)

Step	Questions to Be Answered
Implementation design	Did the conceptual design step yield all the specific details needed for implementation?
Implementation	What additional details are necessary?
Evaluation	Which test cases were handled incorrectly?
	What would the expert have done differently in these cases and why?
	Does the system meet the users' needs?

process he or she follows in performing the task. This clearer under-standing enables the expert to answer the knowledge engineer's ques-tions more readily.

Of course, the knowledge engineer's improving knowledge-acqui-sition skills also contribute to the effectiveness of communication as the project progresses. Some knowledge engineers, however, assume that their skills are the *only* contributing factor; they interpret easy of interaction with the expert as evidence that they have mastered knowl-edge acquisition. These knowledge engineers may encounter rude awakenings at the start of their subsequent projects because *the char-acter of knowledge acquisition changes from project to project*. For ap-plications of different types, knowledge engineers will have to obtain different types of information and to learn different kinds of problem-solving behavior. Different experts respond differently to various knowledge-acquisition styles and techniques. Knowledge engineers must adapt their interaction styles and their choice of techniques to accommodate the current project situation.

Knowledge acquisition must be viewed within the larger context of expert-system development. Novices may forget that a knowledge en-gineer's goal is not to learn as much as possible about the application subject area but rather to develop an expert system. Invariably knowl-edge engineers obtain more information from the expert than they need to implement the expert system. Some of this information pro-vides a useful background that enables the knowledge engineers to understand the expert. Some information initially appears relevant to the system's task but later proves unnecessary. Skilled knowledge engineers are able to obtain the information they need with a minimum of additional unnecessary information. Inexperienced knowledge en-gineers, on the other hand, may view knowledge acquisition as an isolated activity that forms a single step in the process of developing an expert system. In an attempt to be thorough, they may devote interviews to topics irrelevant to the expert system. They may invest a great deal of time and care to design representations for knowledge that the expert system will never use.

18.2 Applying Knowledge-Acquisition Techniques

In this book, we have presented a wide range of techniques that knowledge engineers can use to overcome the difficulties we outlined in Section 18.1. The real challenge for the novice is to know when to apply these techniques. We sum up the lessons of this book in three guidelines.

1. *Be flexible* (Section 18.2.1).

2. *Use cases throughout the project* (Section 18.2.2).

3. *Review your understanding frequently* (Section 18.2.3).

18.2.1 Be Flexible

A successful knowledge engineer must be flexible and creative to keep the expert at ease with the knowledge-acquisition process. No single technique is a rigid procedure; each technique can be adapted to the particular expert and the particular application. Use the techniques described in this book as starting points; extend and tailor these techniques to the needs of your project and to the preferences of your expert. Bear in mind that this book presents *the authors'* approach to expert-system development; it illustrates this approach primarily with reference to a single expert system. Our approach is by no means the *only* approach. Different knowledge engineers would recommend different approaches for the toaster-repair advisor; we would recommend somewhat different approaches for different applications.

Although this book has presented each technique in conjunction with a particular knowledge-acquisition goal (defining the expert system, dividing its functionality, and so on), the techniques are not limited to specific goals. Techniques do not have to be applied in any fixed order during a project. Each expert-system project is different and requires a different set of techniques. Instead of learning the *sequence* of techniques, you should understand *what each technique will help to accomplish* so you can apply the technique at the appropriate times. For example, we described case discussions as a means for obtaining a general understanding of the task, *after* the expert system has been defined. In many applications, however, case discussions provide the means by which the expert and knowledge engineers define the task the expert system will perform.

18.2.2 Use Cases throughout the Project

The use of cases as a focus for knowledge-acquisition activities enables knowledge engineers to identify the unique aspects of an application. Through case discussions, knowledge engineers come to share *the expert's* perspective on the task the expert system will perform. Thus the use of cases can prevent knowledge engineers from assuming that the task will fit into the familiar mold of an earlier project. Cases can be used in a variety of ways throughout the development of an expert system (Table 18.2). The use of cases throughout the project can keep the members of the project team focused on the *expert system's task* and can prevent them from being sidetracked by knowledge the system does not need.

18.2.3 Review your Understanding Frequently

Skilled knowledge engineers do not presume that they understand everything the expert tells them. They *review* their understanding with

Table 18.2 Using Cases in the Development of an Expert System

Use	Description
Obtain an overview of the task the expert system will perform.	Ask the expert to discuss at a general level the process of performing the task for a particular case. Focus on the expert's *process*. Do not delve into unnecessary details. Record questions to pursue during detailed investigation.
Identify ways to classify the situations in which the expert system might perform its task.	Put a brief description of each case on a separate index card. (Describe either major input data or major results.) Ask the expert to arrange the cards into groups that share similar characteristics. Ask the expert what characteristics of the case distinguish the different groups.
Elucidate the procedure or method by which the expert performs the task.	Discuss in detail the actions the expert would take to perform the task for a specific case. Do not interrupt the expert's train of thought; avoid questions about the expert's reasoning process or about alternative situations.
Delineate the reasoning process that allows the expert to infer facts and hypotheses about a case.	Review a case discussion. Identify parts of the discussion in which the expert appeared to have made a conclusion. Ask *why* the expert made each conclusion.

Table 18.2 (continued)

Use	Description
Identify special circumstances that necessitate modifications to the expert's general strategy or reasoning process.	Compare similar cases or explore hypothetical alternatives to a case. Find out *why* the expert's procedure varied in similar cases. Find out *why* the expert would make different decisions in similar cases.
Identify the data the expert uses.	Ask a professional in the expert's field to prepare a case description. Ask the expert to describe how to perform the task for this case. Ask the expert to request information about the case from the person who prepared the case description.
Test an evolving expert system to ensure that extensions do not introduce problems in the system's behavior.	Collect a suite of test cases. Record the input data and the correct results for each test case. After each major extension, test the system on the entire collection of test cases. Compare new results with saved "correct" results. Fix problems uncovered by the test procedure, then retest the system before you continue with further system development.

the expert and verify that they have understood correctly. Successful knowledge acquisition is a cycle of three activities.

1. Knowledge engineers *obtain* information from the expert.

2. They *analyze* and *organize* the information to illustrate their understanding of the information and its importance to the task of the expert system.

3. The knowledge engineers *review* their understanding with the expert. They may ask the expert for comments either on the intermediate representations of their conceptual model or on the behavior of the expert system itself.

Each review that identifies misunderstandings gives rise to additional knowledge-acquisition sessions, which in turn lead to additional reviews. With each cycle of acquisition, analysis, and review, the knowledge engineers refine their understanding of the knowledge that will enable the expert system to perform its task.

18.3 Avoiding Project Failure

Many expert-system projects encounter problems that doom the projects to failure; by the time these problems are manifest, it is often too late to correct them. The majority of these problems, however, could have been prevented by the adroit application of knowledge-acquisition techniques. If you follow the guidelines presented in this book, you can avoid some of the common pitfalls that await novice knowledge engineers.

Problem: After working with the expert for a short while, the knowledge engineers realize they need to redefine the system's task.

Prevention: As soon as the project begins, define the expert system carefully and completely.

Learn enough about the task *as part of the definition process* to enable you to specify with confidence what the system should do.

Problem: The expert never becomes a champion of the project and is not interested in working with the knowledge engineers.

Prevention: At the beginning of the project, place more emphasis on *team-building* goals than on information-gathering goals.

Be flexible. Adapt your knowledge-acquisition techniques to the expert's preferences.

Never insist on pursuing an activity the expert views as pointless.

As early as possible in the project, show your expert a demonstration of the expert system. Demonstrate your first prototype; do not wait until you have perfected the system.

Include the expert in project-planning discussions.

Show the expert that you are making progress on the project. Give the expert copies of your project documents, progress reports you prepare for your management, and so on.

Problem: Early in development, the expert becomes unwilling or unable to answer the knowledge engineers' questions or to provide the information the knowledge engineers need.

Prevention: Base your conceptual model on the organization *you have learned from the expert.*

Work with the expert to adapt your intermediate representations into frameworks congruent with *the expert's* way of thinking about the information.

Never design a framework for organizing knowledge *before* interviewing the expert. If you choose an inappropriate framework, the expert may be unable to work within it.

Problem:	The project team wastes time or reaches a stalemate trying to resolve irreconcilable differences among experts.
Prevention:	As soon as the project begins, define the expert system carefully and completely.

Anticipate the possibility of disputes among experts. When you define the system, decide on a final arbiter to resolve any disputes that may arise.

As soon as you realize that the experts will not reach agreement, take the issue to the final arbiter. |
| Problem: | Members of the project team get bogged down because they are overwhelmed by the complexity of the task. |
| Prevention: | Before you start the development phase, identify manageable units of functionality. Focus on a single unit of functionality in each cycle of development.

If you realize that the current development increment is too complex, repeat the process for identifying divisions of functionality. Learn how the current development increment can be subdivided. Replace this one cycle of development with a number of cycles of smaller scope. |
Problem:	After months of knowledge acquisition and no tangible evidence of progress on the project, the expert loses interest in the project and becomes reluctant to devote time to it.
Prevention:	Define the scope of the first cycle of development to be small enough that you can demonstrate a prototype system early in the development stage.
Problem:	The expert system does not implement the expert's knowledge.
Prevention:	Never *assume* you understand the expert. Avoid misunderstandings by asking the expert for confirmation. Review your conceptual model with the expert and verify that it is accurate *before* you start implementation.

Problem:	The expert system performs its task well, but it cannot function within the intended operating environment.
Prevention:	As soon as the project begins, define the expert system carefully and completely.
	Specify the operating environment as part of the definition process. Make sure that it is possible to integrate the expert system into the necessary data-processing environment.
	Start a software-engineering effort in parallel with the knowledge-engineering effort. Keep the two efforts closely coordinated throughout the project.
Problem:	The project produces an expert system that does not accomplish management objectives.
Prevention:	As soon as the project begins, define the expert system carefully and completely.
	Get agreement from management on the project objectives *before* you make a final decision about the definition of the system's task.
	Make sure that the definition of the task addresses the project objectives.
Problem:	The project produces an expert system no one will use.
Prevention:	As soon as the project begins, define the expert system carefully and completely.
	If the expert system is interactive, obtain requirements for a user interface as part of the definition process.
	Be sure to learn and to plan for the needs and preferences of the users.
	If necessary, obtain management assistance to ensure that the use of the system will fit naturally into someone's job (even if this requires the definition and the creation of new jobs).
	If the expert system is interactive, get frequent user evaluation during interface development. Accommodate user preferences and suggestions as much as possible.
Problem:	It becomes difficult to extend the expert system.
Prevention:	In each cycle of development (starting with the first), understand the function of each piece of knowledge you acquire.

Develop a conceptual model *before* you decide how to implement the knowledge for the chosen expert-system shell.

If the use of a particular knowledge-base entry is not obvious (for example, you rely upon side-effects that occur when the inference engine uses the entry) document carefully the function of the knowledge-base entry.

When the time comes to modify the knowledge base, do not make quick local changes until you consider the context within which the change is made. Look at global interactions to see whether your change will have undesirable repercussions.

18.4 Beyond the Basic Techniques

When you have mastered the techniques presented in this book, you will be a proficient interviewer. You will know how to avoid problems that plague inexperienced knowledge engineers, and you will be well prepared to solve any knowledge-acquisition problems that arise. You will understand what information you must obtain from an expert at the various steps in the development of an expert system, and you will be familiar with a variety of techniques that facilitate the acquisition of this knowledge.

In this book, we have focused on *general* knowledge-acquisition techniques—that is, techniques that will be useful in the majority of expert-system applications. As you participate in the development of a variety of expert systems and as you read more about knowledge acquisition, you will discover additional techniques that are applicable in special circumstances.

- Certain techniques are appropriate for particular types of application. For example, the knowledge-acquisition activities most useful for a scheduling application may be unimportant for a diagnosis or configuration application.

- Some types of expert reasoning pose particular challenges for knowledge acquisition; one example is spatial reasoning. Special-purpose knowledge-acquisition techniques allow knowledge engineers to learn about these more complicated or more specialized reasoning processes.

This book should provide you with a solid foundation for further exploration of knowledge acquisition.

Glossary

**acting
interviewer**

An interview participant who is practicing to become the lead interviewer. Under the supervision of the lead interviewer, this person plans the interview, asks most of the questions, and keeps the discussion focused on productive topics.

**active
listening**

The process by which a knowledge engineer analyzes the expert's answer to a question and responds to the answer. Active listening techniques ensure that the knowledge engineer acquires a clear and thorough understanding of the expert's answer.

**analysis
phase**

The initial phase in the development of an expert system. In this phase, interested parties explore the possibility of developing an expert system.

**ancestor of
a node in a
tree**

For any node N in a tree, an ancestor of N is another node that is above node N and connected to node N by a path of arcs. If the tree is drawn from left to right instead of from top to bottom, an ancestor is a node that is to the left of node N.

**annotated
interaction
log**

Part of a case report; an annotated interaction log is a complete description of an expert system's performance for a particular case. The log illustrates how the system will interact with its environment; annotations explain any of the system's reasoning steps that are not apparent from a record of the system's interactions. An annotated interaction log uses terminology the system's intended users can understand, not special project terminology. See also *performance outline*.

arc in a graph A line or an arrow that joins two nodes in a graph. Each arc in a graph represents the existence of a particular relationship between the two nodes that it joins.

assessment step The second step in the analysis phase of expert-system development. In this step, the project team assesses the suitability of knowledge-engineering technology for the proposed application.

basis characteristic A characteristic of a case that serves as the basis for a particular inference. The condition of the inference tests facts and hypotheses about the basis characteristic.

body of an interview The second and longest part of an interview. The body is the major portion of the interview during which the participants conduct a dialog to exchange information.

brainstorming A technique for stimulating a group discussion. Group members are encouraged to suggest ideas on a topic and are restricted from criticizing each other's suggestions.

case A particular situation in which a task can be performed as defined by the complete set of input data that describes the situation. Either a human or an expert system may perform the task for the case (that is, may respond to the input data).

case description A written description of the complete set of data for a situation, or *case*, in which a task is performed. The data include:

- Information that could be provided by a human (for example, by a person speaking to a human expert or by a user of an interactive expert system)

- Information available in databases

- Information that can be read from sensors, computer files, and other such on-line sources

In addition to input data, the case description should specify the major conclusions that should be made, the actions that should be taken in the performance of the task, and the chronological sequence in which these conclusions and actions should occur.

case discussion A discussion of the process by which the expert would perform the task for a specific case. See also *initial case discussion* and *review of a case discussion*.

case library An organized collection of case reports with a table of contents that provides a quick summary of the cases in the library. A case library is a convenient tool that enables knowledge engineers to decide which cases are relevant to particular design discussions or testing activities.

case report A written description of the expert system's intended performance for a particular case. A case report consists of a cover sheet with a summary of the case and a complete description of system performance. The latter description can take the form of an *annotated interaction log* or a *performance outline.*

case-independent fact A fact that specifies the value of a characteristic of an object or that specifies a relationship among objects. The fact is relevant to any case for which the expert system's task is performed. For example, the fact *the price of part number R71995 is $1.25* is case independent. This fact will be valid in all toaster-repair cases (though it may not be needed in all cases).

case-specific fact A fact that specifies the value of a characteristic *for a particular case*. For example, the fact *the toaster model for the toaster to be repaired is TB10445* is valid for a particular case but would be invalid for other cases.

category of functionality A subdivision of the full intended functionality of an expert system. In many expert-system projects, a category of functionality will be:

- A *subtask* that was identified by limiting the functions the expert system can perform

- An *input category* that was identified by limiting the inputs to which the system can respond

- A *result category* that was identified by limiting the results the system can produce

causal relationship An association among states or actions that indicates how certain states or actions induce other states or actions.

certain conclusion See *definite conclusion.*

characteristic of a case Some particular type of information about a case that an expert system will use when it performs its task. For example, some characteristics of a toaster-repair case are the *toaster model* and the *customer complaints.*

chronological relationship An association among events that indicates the temporal order in which the events occur.

clarification An active listening technique in which the expert is asked to clarify an answer that the knowledge engineer did not understand completely.

classification of functionality The process of dividing the full intended functionality of an expert system; the classification process identifies categories of functionality that can be used as the focus for separate cycles of development. In many expert systems, the functionality is classified by functions the system can perform, by the inputs to which the system can respond, or by the results the system can produce.

closed question
A question that limits the possible answers, for example, by supplying a list of choices.

closing of an interview
The final part of an interview. In the closing, the knowledge engineer ends the discussion with a quick review of the progress made during the interview. If the interview is one of a series of discussions, the closing may include a discussion of plans for the next interview.

conceptual-design step
A step in the development phase of an expert-system project. In this step, knowledge engineers learn how the expert performs the task and develop a conceptual model of the expert system.

conceptual model
A coherent description of the sequence of steps the expert system will take in order to accomplish its task, the reasoning it will perform, and the information it will use. The conceptual model is described through a collection of intermediate representations of the knowledge needed for performance of the task. A conceptual model consists of:

- A framework that is created in the first cycle of development and that changes only slightly through the remainder of the development phase

- Details that are filled into the framework in each subsequent cycle of development

conclusion characteristic
A characteristic of a case about which a particular inference provides new information. The conclusion of the inference specifies facts or hypotheses about the conclusion characteristic that can be asserted when the condition of the inference is true.

conclusion of an inference
A description of facts or hypotheses that can be inferred when the condition of the inference is true.

condition of an inference
A logical requirement that must be satisfied before an inference can be made. The condition of an inference tests facts and hypotheses about the basis characteristics of the inference.

control in an expert system
The process by which an inference engine causes actions to be performed. Actions typically consist of steps in which the expert system accepts input, reasons about the case, or produces output.

control in an interview
The capacity of a participant in an interview to influence the nature of the interview process and the outcome of the interview.

control mechanism
A means of ordering the actions of an expert system; when an expert system performs its task, its inference engine's control

mechanisms direct the system to use an entry in its knowledge base at a particular time. For example, many expert system shells support two basic control mechanisms.

1. Goal-directed backward chaining of rules—rules are used when the expert system's goal is to determine a value for the conclusion characteristic

2. Data-directed forward chaining of rules—rules are used when the expert system learns the value of a basis (trigger) characteristic

coverage   See *scope*.

current case   An actual situation in which the expert performs the task. In a case discussion of a current case, knowledge engineers watch the expert perform the task.

cycle of development   A single iteration of the steps that form the development phase of an expert-system project: conceptual design, implementation design, implementation, and evaluation. During a cycle of development, the project team focuses on a limited scope of functionality for the system called a *development increment*.

data-processing environment   The collection of hardware and software relevant to the operation of an expert system. The data-processing environment includes the machine on which the expert system executes, network connections the system uses, and other software with which the system interacts.

decision table   A two-dimensional matrix that indicates how values of a conclusion characteristic can be concluded based on different combinations of values for a number of basis characteristics. Two two forms of decision table are the *general decision table*, which can specify any number of basis characteristics, and the *two-basis decision table*, which can specify exactly two basis characteristics.

decision tree   A tree structure that specifies how to make a particular decision. The nodes in the tree correspond to questions that must be asked in the process of making the decision. The arcs from a node are the possible answers to the question. Each leaf node in the tree corresponds to a possible outcome of the decision-making process. Decision trees can be used to illustrate the process of inferring a particular conclusion characteristic. The nodes in such a tree correspond to the relevant basis characteristics, and the arcs from each node correspond to different possible values for the characteristic. The leaf nodes correspond to the different values for the conclusion characteristic.

declarative form of representation   A representation that states what is known but does not specify how to use this knowledge. For example, a database is a declarative representation. It specifies facts and relationships among entities, but it does not specify how this information should be used. See also *procedural form of representation*.

definite conclusion An unequivocal conclusion. The conclusion of an inference is definite if the basis characteristics of the inference *provide definitive evidence* for the conclusion characteristics.

definition A kind of judgmental knowledge; a definition specifies a definite conclusion that can be made on the basis of well-established relationships among objects, processes, or concepts.

demonstration review A review of expert-system performance in which the evaluator observes the system's performance of its task.

deployment phase The final phase in the development of an expert system. In this phase, the system is installed and made available for routine use.

descendant of a node in a tree A node that is below the current node and connected to the current node by a path of arcs. (If the tree is drawn from left to right instead of from top to bottom, a descendant is a node that is to the right of the current node.)

design document An organized collection of the definitions and diagrams that compose the conceptual model of an expert system. A design document illustrates *how* the expert system will use its knowledge to perform its task.

detailed investigation The stage of knowledge acquisition that coincides with the development phase of the project. In this stage, knowledge engineers obtain a comprehensive understanding of the process by which the expert performs the task so they can duplicate this same process in an expert system.

development increment The unit of functionality that is the focus of a single cycle of development in a expert-system project.

development phase The third and primary phase in an expert-system project. In this phase, knowledge engineers acquire the majority of the knowledge, and they design, implement, and test the expert system. The development phase is characterized by a cycle of activities through which the system is gradually extended in scope until it reaches its full intended functionality.

development team See *project team.*

difficulty of a category of functionality A measure of the complexity of the reasoning process and of the strategies that the expert employs in the performance of a task within the limits of the category of functionality.

environment See *data-processing environment.*

evaluation step The final step in a cycle of development for an expert system. In this step, the project team tests the system to verify that it performs correctly. In early cycles of development, the evaluation step may test the functionality that was added to the system in that cycle. In a cycle that precedes deployment, the evaluation may be a formal validation of system performance.

evaluator	A person who assesses the expert system's performance of its task. In many reviews, the evaluator is the project expert; in other reviews, the evaluator may be a manager, a potential user of the expert system, or an expert who is not associated with the project.
expert	A person whose knowledge and experience in some particular field exceed the average and whose performance of tasks related to this field is above average.
expert system	A computer program that consists of a knowledge base and an inference engine. The knowledge base encodes expert-level knowledge about a particular task; the inference engine interprets this knowledge to perform the task significantly better than the average person. See also *knowledge system*.
expert-system shell	A software system that provides a framework on which expert systems can be developed. A shell contains an inference engine and supports representation formalisms in which a knowledge base can be encoded.
fact table	A two-dimensional matrix containing a collection of case-independent facts about objects of a certain type. Each row in the matrix corresponds to an object; each column in the matrix corresponds to a characteristic. The cells in a row of the matrix contain the values of the characteristics for a particular object.
factual knowledge	Facts and hypotheses that indicate *what is true* (or believed) about the world or about a particular case.
familiariza-tion step	The single step in the specification phase of an expert-system project. In this step, the knowledge engineers start to interview the expert to become familiar with the task the expert system will perform.
fielding step	The first step in the deployment phase of an expert-system project. In this step, the system is put into regular use.
final authority	The person or persons who will judge whether the expert system's behavior is correct and settle disputes that may arise among the experts who participate in the the development of the system.
flow chart	A diagram that illustrates how to perform a sequence of actions. The diagram consists of a graph with three kinds of nodes.

1. A circular node represents a starting or stopping point.

2. A rectangular node represents an action.

3. A diamond-shaped node represents a decision point.

The arcs in the graph are arrows that indicate the order in which the actions should be performed. The arcs from a decision point are labeled with possible outcomes of the decision.

formula A kind of judgmental knowledge; a formula specifies how to calculate a particular numerical characteristic of a case from the values of other numerical characteristics.

framework of a conceptual model The components of the conceptual model that specify at a high level the structure of the knowledge and how it will be used. The framework consists of:

- A flow chart of the expert system's task and possibly flow-charts of some substeps

- A functional decomposition tree that identifies substeps in the task

- A classification of the characteristics of a case according to the type of object, process, or concept they describe.

full intended functionality The complete scope of the expert system at the end of its development. The development of an expert system is usually an iterative process that consists of a number of cycles of development. The full functionality of the expert system is divided into separate *development increments*, each of which is added to the system in a different cycle of development. The scope of the system is extended with each cycle until it reaches its full intended functionality.

functional relationship An association among actions or states that indicates the conditions under which particular actions can occur, and the reactions and the consequences that can result from those actions.

functional-decomposition tree A tree structure that indicates how the task of an expert system can be broken into increasingly smaller modular substeps. The root of the tree represents the entire task. Each additional node represents a step in the task; the descendents of a node represent the substeps that compose that step.

funders The people or the organization that pays for the development of an expert system. Funders often participate in identification of a potential application, definition of the expert system, project planning, and evaluation of the expert system.

general characteristic See *characteristic of a case.*

general decision table A decision table that specifies any number of basis characteristics. The columns of the table correspond to characteristics. The rightmost column corresponds to the conclusion characteristic, and the remaining columns correspond to the basis characteristics. Each row in the table specifies an inference. The cells in the row contain values of the basis characteristics, and a value that can be concluded for the conclusion characteristic when the basis characteristics have the indicated values.

graph A diagram that consists of boxes called *nodes* and lines or arrows called *arcs*. Each arc joins two nodes. In general, the nodes are labeled; the arcs may also be labeled. Graphs are a convenient method for illustrating a relationship among objects. The nodes represent the objects, and the arcs indicate which objects are related to which other objects.

heuristic A kind of judgmental knowledge; a heuristic specifies a rule of thumb that can guide decisions. Heuristics are not based on hard, scientific evidence but instead express relationships learned by experience and true most of the time.

hierarchy See *tree*.

historical case A situation in which the task was performed in the past (by the expert or by some other person). In a case discussion of an historical case, the expert explains the actions and the decisions that were performed.

hypothetical case A description of a situation that might occur in which an expert system's task could be performed. In a discussion of an hypothetical case, the expert explains the actions and decisions that would be necessary if the task were performed in that hypothetical situation.

identification step The first step in the analysis phase of an expert-system project. In this step, some group or individual identifies a potential expert-system application.

implementa-tion design A plan for implementation of an expert system that specifies how its task can be accomplished with the chosen expert-system shell. The implementation design indicates how various pieces of knowledge should be encoded in the knowledge base to produce an expert system with the desired behavior.

implementa-tion-design step A step in the development phase of an expert-system project. In this step, the knowledge engineers consolidate the requirements of their conceptual model of the expert system with the constraints of the system's intended data-processing environment. They map their conceptual model onto the representation formalisms and the inference and control mechanisms provided by the expert-system shell.

implementa-tion step A step in the development phase of an expert-system project. In this step, the knowledge engineers follow their implementation design to build a knowledge base and to integrate the expert system into its data-processing environment.

importance of a category of functionality A measure of the significance of a category of functionality to the objectives of the expert-system project. For example, the most important categories might address problems that occur most frequently or problems with which users need the most help.

inexact conclusion A conclusion about which some doubt remains. The conclusion of an inference is inexact if the basis characteristics *suggest* values for the conclusion characteristic but do not provide enough evidence for a definite conclusion.

inference	A decision or a deduction that uses known (or believed) information to conclude (or to hypothesize) additional information about a particular situation. An inference consists of a *condition* and a *conclusion* that can be made when this condition is true.
inference engine	The program part of an expert system. The inference engine employs inference mechanisms and control mechanisms that allow it to interpret the knowledge base thereby causing the expert system to perform a task.
inference mechanism	A means of using facts, hypotheses, and judgmental knowledge to infer additional facts or hypotheses. Most expert system shells support an inference mechanism called *modus ponens*. This rule of logic states that, if you know *P* and you know that *P implies Q*, then you can infer *Q*. In the context of an expert system, *P* is a condition on basis characteristics, *Q* is a conclusion about a conclusion characteristic, and *P implies Q* is an inference (often represented in the knowledge base as a *rule*).
inference network	A graph that indicates the structure of inferences within an expert system. The nodes in the graph are characteristics. The arcs in the graph are arrows that point from a basis characteristic to a conclusion characteristic. All arrows *from* a node show the characteristics that can be concluded on the basis of the characteristic in the node. All arrows *into* a node show the characteristics that can be used to conclude the characteristic in the node.
inference process	The process by which an expert system uses information that is already known to make deductions that add to the body of information known about a particular situation. See also *reasoning process*.
initial case discussion	The first discussion of a case, in which the knowledge engineers concentrate on the process by which the expert performs the task. During an initial case discussion, knowledge engineers should not disturb the expert's train of thought by asking about:

- Reasons behind the expert's actions

- Ways in which the expert's actions would have varied in different situations

See also *review of a case discussion*.

initial inquiry	The stage of knowledge acquisition that coincides with the analysis and specification phases of expert-system development. In this stage, knowledge engineers obtain a general overview of the task that the expert system will perform.
input category	A particular category of functionality for an expert system. An input category is one option within a classification of the inputs

to which the system might respond. For example, the *toaster style* might be used to classify the inputs to which a toaster-repair expert system might respond. One input category within this classification might be *simple two-slice toasters*.

input data The collection of all information that an expert system receives from external sources, such as a human user, a calling program, a database, an on-line file, or a sensor.

integration The process of connecting an expert system (or other piece of software) with the other components of its data-processing environment.

intermediate conclusions Information that an expert system deduces on the basis of its input data and that it uses to deduce its output results.

intermediate representa-tion A description or diagram that expresses the function that certain knowledge is to serve within an expert system. The collection of all intermediate representations forms a conceptual model of the expert system.

interview A person-to-person interaction between two parties, in which one party obtains information from the second by asking questions. A well-structured interview consists of three parts: an *introduction*, a *body*, and a *closing*. In a knowledge-acquisition interview, a knowledge engineer interviews a project expert.

introduction to an interview The first part of an interview. In the introduction, the knowledge engineer orients the expert to the purpose of the interview and to the topics the knowledge engineer would like to discuss.

introductory overview A presentation that describes the situation or problem the expert system will address. An introductory overview establishes the context for a series of discussions about the definition of the expert system. In most projects, a manager, an expert, or a user presents this overview.

iterative development The repetition of a sequence of steps during the development phase of an expert-system project. In each iteration, or *cycle of development*, the knowledge engineers focus on some limited functionality for the system. Each cycle of development, therefore, extends the scope of the system.

judgmental knowledge Guidelines that specify how to deduce new facts and hypotheses from facts and hypotheses already known (or believed). The guidelines may take the form of definitions, formulas, or heuristics (rules of thumb).

knowledge acquisition The process of obtaining all the information needed for the development of an expert system. The aim of knowledge acquisition is to achieve a coherent understanding of the process by which another person carries out some activity.

knowledge base The knowledge used by an expert system in declarative form, generally encoded according to a small number of representation formalisms.

knowledge engineer	A developer of an expert system. The knowledge engineers on a project must be able to obtain the necessary knowledge from an expert (or other source), and they must be able to identify the representation, inference, and control needs of the expert system.
knowledge engineering	A collection of activities through which expert systems are developed. These activities include:

- Knowledge acquisition

- Development of a conceptual model from the knowledge acquired

- Analysis of the conceptual model to determine requirements for an expert-system shell

- Selection or development of an expert-system shell that satisfies these requirements

- Design and development of a knowledge base that implements the conceptual model

knowledge system	A computer program that consists of a knowledge base and an inference engine. The knowledge base encodes knowledge about a particular task; the inference engine interprets this knowledge to perform the task. The knowledge about the task is not based on the experience of an expert; rather it is accessible to the average professional in forms such as training programs, manuals, or catalogs. See also *expert system*.
lead interviewer	The person who conducts an interview. This person has the responsibility to plan the interview, to ask most of the questions, and to keep the interview focused on productive topics.
leaf node	A node in a tree structure that does not have any descendant nodes.
maintenance step	The final step in the deployment phase of an expert-system project. In this step, bugs may be fixed and the software or the knowledge base updated. For many expert systems, the maintenance step periodically gives rise to a return to the development phase so current knowledge can be obtained and added to the knowledge base.
mixed signals	Spoken words coupled with contradictory nonverbal communication.
node in a graph	A box in a graph usually labeled with a concept or object the node represents.
nonverbal communication	The exchange of information through facial expressions, vocal inflections, speaking rate, pauses, hand gestures, body movements, and posture.
nudge	See *verbal nudge*.

object	A physical object, a process, or a concept relevant to the task of an expert system. An object is relevant to the task if the system needs to obtain or use information about the object.
object type used to classify characteristics	A type of object about which the expert system must gather information. The characteristics of a case can be classified according to the type of object they describe. For example, the characteristic *toaster model* describes objects of type *toaster* while the characteristic *part number* describes objects of type *toaster part*.
objectives of an expert-system project	The organizational goals for an expert system. The objectives specify the benefits that the organization expects will result from the introduction of the expert system.
open question	A question that specifies the topic of discussion but places minimal restrictions on the expected answer.
operating environment	See *data-processing environment*.
original case discussion	See *initial case discussion*.
output results	The product of the execution of an expert system. Output results include all conclusions, proposals, advice, and assessments that the system produces and delivers to a human user, another program, or an output device.
overview discussion	A dialog that follows (or replaces) an overview presentation (such as an introductory or a task overview). In this discussion, the knowledge engineers ensure that they have obtained and understood all the information they sought to learn from the overview presentation.
paraphrasing	An active listening technique in which the knowledge engineer explains his or her understanding of the expert's answers to recent questions.
performance outline	Part of a case report; a performance outline presents a concise description (using project terminology) of the sequence of actions and decisions an expert system should execute when it performs its task for a particular case. See also *annotated interaction log*.
probe	See *verbal probe*.
procedural form of representation	A representation that specifies a sequence of actions that should be taken to apply the knowledge. For example, a computer language is a procedural representation: statements in the language specify actions the computer should take. See also *declarative form of representation*.

procedural knowledge	See *strategic knowledge*.
procedure for performing a task	The sequence of steps a human or an expert system must take in order to perform the task. An expert system's procedure can be viewed as a sequence of input, reasoning, and output steps; a human expert's procedure is generally more complicated because it involves physical activities and sensory perceptions that the expert system cannot perform.
project dictionary	An alphabetized list of the terms in the vocabulary of an expert-system project. The dictionary should indicate which terms are part of the standard project vocabulary and which are not; it should define any term whose meaning is not obvious.
project expert	An expert who becomes a part of the team that develops an expert system. The project expert works directly with the knowledge engineers through interviews. Note that projects may obtain information from experts other than the project expert.

- The project expert may obtain information from a colleague and relay this information to the knowledge engineers.

- The project expert may invite a colleague to join an interview as a "guest lecturer."

project team	The group of people who work together to develop an expert system. A project team is made up of one or more experts and one or more knowledge engineers.
propagation of uncertainty	The use of the degree of certainty of beliefs about the basis characteristics of an inference to moderate the degree of certainty with which the conclusion of the inference is made. For example, if the values of the basis characteristics are known with certainty, the conclusion might be made with certainty, but if the values for the basis characteristics are believed with moderate probability, the conclusion might be made with moderate probability.
pseudorule	An intermediate representation of an inference. A pseudorule is a statement of the form *If condition then conclusion*. A pseudorule can be written in any combination of English (or other natural language) and special project terminology. The condition of a pseudorule can include any combination of logical operators *(and, or, not, for all, there exists)*; the conclusion can specify a degree of certainty.
question type	The classification of a question according to the degree to which it restricts the expected answer. Basic question types are *open* and *closed*. These basic types represent a continuum from highly open questions to very closed questions.
reasoning process	The process by which a person uses information already known to make deductions that add to the body of information he

or she knows about a particular situation. See also *inference process.*

refinement and extension

The process of starting another cycle of development for an expert system in order to make the system's knowledge more accurate *(refinement)* or to broaden the system's scope *(extension).*

representation

The process of encoding knowledge in a declarative form that can be used by an inference engine.

representation formalism

A format or structure that has syntax and semantics and that can be used to encode knowledge for use by an expert-system shell.

result category

A particular category of functionality for an expert system. A result category is one option within a classification of the results that the system might produce. For example, the results of a toaster-repair expert system might be classified according to the *type of problem the system is able to identify.* One result category within this classification might be *mechanical problems.*

results produced

See *output results.*

review of a case discussion

A discussion about a case that has been discussed before. A knowledge engineer may review a case discussion to find out:

- Why the expert took the actions he or she described in the initial case discussion

- What different actions the expert would have taken if the case had been slightly different

- What different conclusions the expert would have drawn if the case had been slightly different

- What different inputs the expert might have received

See also *initial case discussion.*

review of an expert system

A evaluation of the expert system's performance of its task. A review may take two forms: a *demonstration review* or a *typescript review.* Independent of the form, the review can focus on one or both of two aspects of the system's performance: the *results* the system produces and the *manner in which it interacts* with its user.

review of interaction

A review that assesses whether the user interface of an interactive expert system provides effective communication between the system and its user. The evaluator should answer the following questions.

- Does the system perform the appropriate sequence of input–output activities? Are questions asked in a logical order? Are instructions provided when they are needed?

- Are questions, explanations, instructions, and recommendations phrased clearly? Do they provide the appropriate level of detail?

- Are graphs, diagrams, and other illustrations clearly drawn and labeled so users can understand them? Would additional illustrations be helpful?

- Are text and diagrams arranged on the screen in a layout understandable and helpful to the user?

- Is interaction with the system self-explanatory? Is on-line help adequate?

In at least some reviews of interaction, the evaluator should be a user or an intended user of the system.

review of results   A review that assesses whether the expert system performs its task correctly. The evaluator should answer the following questions.

- Does the system perform the correct sequence of actions?

- Does the system make correct decisions?

- Does the system gather appropriate data?

- Does the system produce the correct output results?

- Are all the system's actions and decisions *necessary* to its task?

root of a tree   The single node that has no ancestors in the tree.

scope   Coverage of functionality; the extent of an expert system's full task that the system is able to perform at a given stage in its development and the range of situations in which it can perform this task.

secondary questioner   An interview participant who asks occasional follow-up questions on the topics selected by the lead interviewer.

shell   See *expert-system shell*.

silent observer   An interview participant who watches, listens, and writes notes but who rarely takes part in discussions.

size of a category of functionality   A measure of the amount of information that the knowledge engineers need to acquire before they can implement the indicated functionality for an expert system.

software engineering   A collection of activities through which software systems, including expert systems, are developed. The following software-engineering activities are relevant to expert-system development.

- Design and development of a user interface
- Integration of the system with its data-processing environment
- Determination of the acceptance criteria the system must meet and evaluation of the system against these criteria
- Fielding and maintenance of the system

specific example See *value for a characteristic.*

specification phase The second phase in the development of an expert system. In this phase, members of the project team lay the groundwork for system development by specifying what the system will do and by planning its development.

strategic knowledge Guidelines that indicate *what to do.* The strategic knowledge for an expert system specifies the steps the system should take when it performs its task, the order in which it should take the steps, and the conditions under which it should take each step.

structural relationship An association among the parts of an object or a system; this association indicates how the object or system can be decomposed into parts or subsystems.

subtask A particular category of functionality for an expert system. A subtask is one independent function the expert system will perform.

summarization An active listening technique in which the knowledge engineer ties together a number of points mentioned over several minutes of conversation. Summarization, like paraphrasing, is a means by which the knowledge engineer explains his or her understanding of the expert's answers to questions; summarization, however, involves more judgment than paraphrasing because it requires selection of the points that seem the most important.

task A major function that can be performed by a human or an expert system.

task overview A presentation that describes in very general terms the process of performing a specific task. During initial inquiry, the expert presents a task overview that focuses on the full task an expert system will perform. At the beginning of each cycle of development, the expert may present a task overview that focuses on the functionality of the current development increment.

taxonomic relationship An association among objects or concepts of the same general type that specifies how the most general description of these objects or concepts can be classified into increasingly more specific descriptions.

test suite A collection of cases that can be used to test an expert system. Generally, a test suite will contain on-line files that can be used to automate periodic testing of the expert system. For example, the test suite may contain two files for each case.

- An *input file* from which the system can read all input data for the case
- A *baseline typescript file* that illustrates the system's correct behavior for the case

topological relationship An association among physical objects that describes their spatial arrangement and the interconnections among them.

tree A special type of graph used to illustrate a hierarchical relationship—that is, a more general/more specific relationship in which each node has a single ancestor (but may have any number of descendants). By convention, a tree is drawn with its root node at the top. The root node is the single node in the tree that has no ancestor. The descendants of a node are drawn below the node and are connected to the node with arcs. Nodes with no descendants are called leaf nodes. (Trees are some times drawn with the root at the left and descendants of a node to the right of that node.)

trigger characteristic In an inference, a basis characteristic that triggers the use of the inference. In other words, when information is received about the trigger characteristic, the inference is used to deduce the consequences of this new piece of information.

two-basis decision table A decision table that specifies exactly two basis characteristics. The columns of the table correspond to values of one basis characteristic; the rows of the table correspond to values of the second basis characteristic. Each cell in the table contains a value for the conclusion characteristic. A cell represents an inference: When the basis characteristics have the values specified in the headings of the row and the column, the value in the cell can be concluded for the conclusion characteristic.

typescript A written record of an expert system's performance of its task for a particular case. A typescript should show:

- All input data to the expert system
- The source of each input
- All output the system produced
- The destination of each output
- The time sequence in which the input and output actions occurred

Typescripts can be used in a review of the system's performance. For some reviews, typescripts should also show important conclusions the system made that are not apparent from the input and output alone.

typescript review A review of expert-system performance in which the evaluator assesses performance as illustrated in written records of the system's performance.

uncertain conclusion See *inexact conclusion*.

user A person who supplies input to an expert system or who receives and uses the output results of an expert system.

value for a characteristic A specific example of a particular type of information about a case. A characteristic can be thought of as a variable that describes the case; the value of the characteristic provides specific information about the variable. For example, if *toaster model* is a characteristic, the value of this characteristic for a particular case might be *TB10445*.

verbal nudge An active listening technique in which the knowledge engineer prompts the expert to continue with the previous answer. The nudge generally consists of a few quick words, such as:

I see.

And then?

Tell me more.

verbal probc An active listening technique in which the knowledge engineer requests more details to the expert's previous answer.

working prototype An early implementation of the expert system; the prototype's functionality may be severely limited with respect to the full intended functionality of the system, but it should be sufficient to give an impression of what the completed system would do or how it could be used. The demonstration of a working prototype to the project expert *early in the development process* is often critical the the success of a project.

Additional Reading

In this book, we have looked at various aspects of knowledge acquisition, and we have mentioned other activities that go into the development of an expert system. If you would like to explore any of these topics further, we suggest the following references as the starting point for your investigation.

Assessment of Potential Expert-System Applications

Prerau, D. "Selection of an appropriate domain." *The AI Magazine*, 6(2):26, 1985. This short paper discusses how to select an appropriate domain for an expert system in a corporate environment. The paper presents a set of characteristics that can be used to assess the domain. These characteristics help the reader evaluate the domain based on the domain's suitability for expert-systems technology, the availability and nature of expertise, the amount of knowledge required, and the need for a solution to an organizational problem.

Slagle, J., and Wick, M. "A method for evaluating candidate expert system applications." *The AI Magazine*, 9(4):45, 1988. This paper describes a method that can be used to select expert-system applications based on the likelihood that they can be implemented and fielded successfully. The method examines such features as technology requirements, the need for a solution within the organization, and the characteristics of the expertise. The paper provides a set of forms to aid with the evaluation process.

Automated Knowledge Acquisition

Boose, J. "A survey of knowledge acquisition techniques and tools." *Knowledge Acquisition,* 1(1):3, 1988. This paper provides a framework for the analysis and comparison of automated knowledge-acquisition tools, techniques, and research strategies. Boose evaluates several knowledge-acquisition tools based on this framework.

Boose, J., and Gaines, B. (eds.), *Knowledge Acquisition Tools for Expert Systems.* London: Academic Press, 1988. This book is a collection of papers written by researchers in the field of automated knowledge acquisition. The papers range from discussions of the issues associated with automated knowledge acquisition to descriptions of automated knowledge-acquisition tools.

Gruber, T. *The Acquisition of Strategic Knowledge.* San Diego, Calif.: Academic Press, 1989. This book focuses on the acquisition of strategic knowledge from experts and the automation of that process. Part of the book discusses ASK, a system Gruber developed to automate the collection of strategic knowledge.

Development of Expert Systems

Giarratano, J., and Riley, G. *Expert Systems: Principles and Programming.* Boston, Mass.: PWS-Kent Publishing, 1989. This book discusses the implementation techniques associated with expert-system development. Significant sections of this book cover the topics of representation, inference, control, pattern matching, uncertain reasoning, and expert-system design.

Kline, P. J., and Polins, S. B. *Designing Expert Systems: A Guide to Selecting Implementation Techniques.* New York: John Wiley and Sons, 1989. This book presents guidelines for selection of different artificial-intelligence programming techniques based on the features of the application. The guidelines fall into the following categories: connection of the data to the conclusions, how and when data arrive, the fielding environment, knowledge-representation requirements, and special-case issues.

Prerau, D. *Developing and Managing Expert Systems.* Reading, Mass.: Addison-Wesley, 1990. Prerau covers many important topics about expert systems including: the basic concepts, planning and management, team formation, domain selection, shell and hardware selection, representation of knowledge, testing, evaluation, and system deployment.

Walters, J. R., and Nielson, N. R. *Crafting Knowledge-Based Systems: Expert Systems Made Realistic.* New York: John Wiley and Sons, 1988. This book is a how-to guide for running an expert-system project. It covers the basics of starting, assessing, and planning a project. It also discusses designing and building an application. The last section of the book focuses on the use of several different representation formalisms including *rules* and *frames*.

Evaluation of Expert Systems

Buchanan, B., and Shortliffe, E. (eds.), "Part 10: Evaluating Performance" in *Rule-Based Expert Systems.* Reading, Mass.: Addison-Wesley, 1986. *Rule-Based Expert Systems* covers many aspects of the development of expert systems. Part 10 focuses on the evaluation of these systems. In particular, Part 10 discusses the different approaches to evaluation taken for the MYCIN system.

Hayes-Roth, F., Waterman, D., and Lenat, D. (eds.), "Chapter 8: Evaluation of Expert Systems: Issues and Case Studies" in *Building Expert Systems.* Reading, Mass.: Addison-Wesley, 1983. *Building Expert Systems* covers many topics about the development of expert systems. Chapter 8 focuses on the evaluation of an expert system. This chapter discusses why evaluations are important, when to evaluate expert systems, common pitfalls of evaluation programs, and different approaches evaluation programs can take.

Examples of Successful Expert Systems

Feigenbaum, E., McCorduck, P., and Nii, P. *The Rise of the Expert Company.* New York: Random House, 1989. The authors discuss several case studies of how expert-system technology has affected the business practices of major companies including DEC, IBM, FMC, Westinghouse, Toyota, Canon, and American Express.

Rauch-Hinden, W. B. *Artificial Intelligence in Business, Science, and Industry, Volume II: Applications.* Englewood Cliffs, N.J.: Prentice-Hall, 1985. The author discusses expert systems in the areas of industry, business and finance, science, medicine, and engineering. The book presents the major issues associated with each area and explains how different groups have tackled those issues. The book also describes successfully fielded applications and identifies specific application areas with excellent potential for expert-system development.

Schorr, H., and Rappaport, A. (eds.), *Innovative Applications of Artificial Intelligence*. Menlo Park, Calif.: The AAAI Press, 1989. This books is a collection of papers presented at the first annual conference on Innovative Applications of Artificial Intelligence. The papers describe applications that have been deployed successfully in a wide range of industries: aerospace, banking and finance, media and music, military, operations management, personnel management, and retail packaging.

Explanations in Expert Systems

Buchanan, B., and Shortliffe, E. (eds.), "Chapter 18: Methods for Generating Explanations" in *Rule-Based Expert Systems*. Reading, Mass.: Addison-Wesley, 1986. In Chapter 18, the authors describe the importance of having explanations; they also identify the different kinds of explanation expert systems can produce. The chapter focuses on the kind of knowledge and information the system must have in order to give useful and complete explanations to the user. The MYCIN system is used as an example.

Ellis, C. (ed.), *Expert Knowledge and Explanation*. Chichester, Eng.: Ellis Horwood Limited, 1989. This book is a collection of papers about experts and explanations. Specific topics include explanation in intelligent systems, the benefit of employing user models to generate explanations, and automated advice and explanation.

Group Discussions

Auger, B. *How to Run Better Business Meetings*. St. Paul, Minn.: 3M Company, 1979. This book is a reference guide that explains how to run meetings. It discusses when to have a meeting, who should attend, how the room should be arranged, and how to present ideas most effectively. The book also discusses the role of leadership in meetings and how to maintain control of a discussion.

Gouran, Dennis G. *The Process of Group Decision-Making*. New York: Harper & Row, 1974. This book provides the reader with a good understanding of the dynamics of decision-making discussions. The book is useful for anyone who anticipates being involved in group decision making. It discusses how to be a more efficient participant, how to make meetings more productive, how to create good discussion questions, and how to use different discussion procedures. It also presents several common obstacles that occur in group meetings.

Shaw, M. E. *Group Dynamics: The Psychology of Small Group Behavior.* New York: McGraw-Hill, 1981. This book looks at group dynamics and behavior from many different perspectives. It covers topics like group formation and development, effects of group size on group behavior, effects of characteristics of the individuals of the group on group behavior, group tasks and goals, and the role of group structure. It also presents several issues and problems associated with group discussions.

Intermediate Representations as Design Aids

Martin, J., and McClure, C. *Diagramming Techniques for Analysts and Programmers.* Englewood Cliffs, N.J.: Prentice-Hall, 1985. This book describes itself as a tutorial for the diagramming of complex structures and logic. It discusses why the use of diagramming techniques in analysis and design is important. It covers over 19 different diagramming techniques in detail, describes the strengths and weaknesses of each technique, and gives examples of the use of the techniques.

Yourdon, E. *Modern Structural Analysis.* Englewood Cliffs, N.J.: Prentice Hall, 1989. This is an excellent book on the principles and techniques of systems analysis. For each modeling tool, the book describes its usage, applicability, and how it fits into the process of systems analysis.

Interviewing Techniques

Burley-Allen, M. *Listening: The Forgotten Skill.* New York: John Wiley & Sons, 1982. This book focuses on active listening skills. It is designed to help you to improve your ability to handle conflict, to increase your self-confidence, and to avoid problems with miscommunication. Burley-Allen covers important topics such as biased listening, the effects of emotions on listening, and only hearing what you want to hear. She also provides ways to improve your listening skills and your ability to communicate ideas to other people.

Gordon, R. *Interviewing Strategies, Techniques, and Tactics*. Homewood, Ill.: The Dorsey Press, 1969. This book presents a wide assortment of general interviewing tools. The book discusses topics including the use of silence as a technique, the details of question formation, and how the attitudes of the interviewer affect the outcome of the interview. Gordon also presents tactical information about interviews such as how to arrange the topics in an interview, to set the objectives for an interview, to prepare for an interview, and to deal with resistance from the respondent.

Kahn, R., and Cannell, C. *The Dynamics of Interviewing*. New York: John Wiley & Sons, 1982. In this book, Kahn and Cannell cover interviewing skills appropriate for nearly any field. They discuss the importance of setting objectives for the interview, formulating questions, and motivating the respondent. This book provides commentary on several transcripts of interviews from a variety of situations including a medical interview, a job interview, and an interview between a supervisor and a supervisee.

Stewart, C., and Cash, W. *Interviewing Principles and Practices*. Dubuque, Ia.: William C. Brown Publishers, 1985. This book identifies the elements of an interview and describes different types of interview. Of particular interest to knowledge engineers are the book's discussions of the relationship between interviewer and interviewee, communication interactions, the structure of an interview, and the appropriate use questions of different types.

Multiple Experts

McGraw, K., and Seale, M. "Knowledge elicitation with multiple experts: Considerations and techniques." *Artificial Intelligence Review*, 2(1):31, 1988. This article looks at several aspects of the issue of multiple sources of expertise. It describes why multiple experts might be needed for a project and what knowledge-acquisition techniques are useful for multiple experts. In particular, McGraw and Seale discuss how to reach consensus, the nominal group technique, and various debriefing techniques.

Nature of Expertise

Chi, M., Glaser, R., and Farr, M. *The Nature of Expertise*. Hillsdale, N.J.: Lawrence Erlbaum Associates, 1988. This book is a collection of papers about expertise from a conference held at the Learning Research and Development Center at the University of Pittsburgh in

1988. The introduction of the book describes what experts are and how they acquire their skills. The following sections focus on different fields of expertise including practical skills, programming skills, medical diagnosis, and ill-defined problems.

LaFrance, M. "The quality of expertise: Understanding the differences between experts and novices." *Knowledge Acquisition, SIGART Newsletter*, No. 108:6, 1989. This paper focuses on the qualitative difference between the knowledge of novices and that of experts and how that difference should influence the conduct of an interview. The article proposes seven ways in which an expert's knowledge can be distinguished from the knowledge of a less qualified problem-solver and how those differences indicate the most effective activities for knowledge acquisition.

Newell, A., and Simon, H. *Human Problem Solving*. Englewood Cliffs, N.J.: Prentice Hall, 1972. This book is an old standby written by two of the founders of the field of artificial intelligence. The book's goal is to advance the understanding of human reasoning. The book introduces the information-processing theory, gives examples of problem solving, and explains how the examples relate to the theory. The examples are taken from three problem-solving areas: chess, crypt arithmetic problems, and logical statement transformations.

Project Planning and Management

Brooks, F. *The Mythical Man-Month*. Reading, Mass.: Addison-Wesley, 1982. This book is a collection of essays about planning and management problems that occur with large software-development projects. Brooks recounts his experiences with poor project planning and ineffective division of labor while he was a project manager for IBM's Operating System/360 and other large projects.

DeMarco, T. *Controlling Software Projects*. Englewood Cliffs, N.J.: Prentice-Hall, 1982. This book provides several techniques for estimating the cost of software projects and tracking a project's progress with respect to the estimates. It describes the general issues associated with the cost of software development and how to address those issues. It provides a variety of cost models to fit a project's situation.

DeSalvo, E., and Bievowitz, J. (eds.), *Managing Artificial Intelligence and Expert Systems*. Englewood Cliffs, N.J.: Prentice-Hall, 1990. This book is written by a collection of practicing professionals in the fields of artificial intelligence and expert systems. They represent both research laboratories and business groups. The book covers issues such as staffing, technology transfer, the expert-system marketplace, justifying the cost of expert systems, managing the introduction of new technology into an environment, and managing the development of expert-system products.

Keider, S. "Why projects fail." *Datamation*, 20(12):53, 1974. This short article is about common mistakes that result in the failure of data-processing projects. The article discusses five stages of a project (preinitiation, initiation, duration, termination, and posttermination), focusing on the importance of each stage, the common mistakes made at each stage, and ways to keep the project successful.

Selection of Expert-System Shells

Harmon, P., Maus, R., and Morrissey, W. *Expert Systems: Tools & Applications*. New York: John Wiley & Sons, 1988. This book focuses on the different expert-system shells available on the market. It discusses the different categories of shell, how to select among them, and how to evaluate them. The book also includes sections on expert-system applications and the development of expert systems.

Uncertainty in Expert-System Reasoning

Buchanan, B., and Shortliffe, E. (eds.), "Part 4: Reasoning Under Uncertainty" in *Rule-Based Expert Systems*. Reading, Mass.: Addison-Wesley, 1986. Part 4 of this book focuses on how the MYCIN project dealt with uncertain reasoning. It not only discusses the evolution of certainty factors as they were used in MYCIN but also describes how the experts' problem-solving approaches led to that particular solution.

Shafer, G., and Pearl, J. (eds.), *Readings in Uncertain Reasoning*. Menlo Park, Calif.: Morgan Kaufmann Publishers, 1990. This book is a collection of papers on the subject of uncertain reasoning. The papers cover uncertain reasoning from both the perspective of human problem solving and of how best to reproduce the reasoning in a computer program. Sections most relevant to knowledge acquisition are: the meaning of probability, decision making, and numerical uncertainty in expert systems.

Index

Figures